# Cases
# In Production
# And Operations
# Management

# Cases
# In Production
# And Operations
# Management

Robert C. Meier
*Western Washington University*

Richard A. Johnson
*University of Washington*

William T. Newell
*University of Washington*

Albert N. Schrieber
*University of Washington*

*Prentice-Hall, Inc., Englewood Cliffs, N.J. 07632*

*Library of Congress Cataloging in Publication Data*
MAIN ENTRY UNDER TITLE:
Cases in production and operations management.

    1.  Production management—Case studies.
    I.  Meier, Robert C.
TS155.C316       658.5       81-4532
ISBN 0-13-118950-6      AACR2

*Editorial/production supervision and*
   *Interior design by Richard C. Laveglia*
*Cover design by Wanda Lubelska*
*Manufacturing buyer: Ed O'Dougherty*

Printed in the United States of America

10   9   8   7   6

Prentice-Hall International, Inc., *London*
Prentice-Hall of Australia Pty. Limited, *Sydney*
Prentice-Hall of Canada, Ltd., *Toronto*
Prentice-Hall of India Private Limited, *New Delhi*
Prentice-Hall of Japan, Inc., *Tokyo*
Prentice-Hall of Southeast Asia Pte. Ltd., *Singapore*
Whitehall Books Limited, *Wellington, New Zealand*

# Contents

PREFACE

xiii

AERODYNE, INCORPORATED

1

*Planned Tooling Program    1*
*Schedule Delay    5*
*Employment Constraints    5*
*Other Proposals    6*
*Discussion Questions    6*

AMERICAN CERAMIC AND GLASS PRODUCTS
CORPORATION

8

*Thomas Calligan    9*
*James King    9*
*Role of Inspection and Quality Control    10*
*Discussion Questions    11*

AUTOMATED PARKING SYSTEMS,
INCORPORATED

13

*Parking System    13*
*Operation of the System    15*
*Costs    17*
*Competitive Advantages    17*
*Discussion Questions    18*

# BAYERISCHE MASCHINEN WERKE GmbH 19

*Company History 19*
*Bid for a Kellering Contract 21*
*Kellering Contract 27*
*Quality Control Procedures and Problems 32*
*Follow-on Contract 48*
*Discussion Questions 50*

# BELNAP COMPANY 51

*Motivation Theories 52*
*Improvement Strategy 52*
*"Pride in Excellence" Program 58*
*Administration of the Program 61*
*Discussion Questions 64*

# BRISTOL SOUND SHIPBUILDING 65

*Present Solid Waste Disposal Method 65*
*Compaction Alternative 68*
*Incineration Alternative 68*
*Energy Recovery 71*
*Discussion Questions 72*
*Appendix 72*

# DELAWARE BAY SHIP AND FABRICATION COMPANY 83

*Overhead Budget 83*
*General Superintendent's Office 86*
*Industrial Engineering Unit 88*
*Production Control Unit 90*
*Production Engineering and Services 90*
*Discussion Questions 92*

# ENTERPRISE FIBERGLASS COMPANY 93

*Purchase of the Business 93*
*Search for the Product Line 94*
*Marketing and Distribution 97*
*Internal Operation 99*
*Production Costs 100*
*Financial Control 102*
*Discussion Questions 103*

# FIBERTEX PLASTICS CORPORATION 104

*Product Line   104*
*Marketing   105*
*Manufacturing Costs   106*
*Distribution Costs   107*
*Discussion Questions   108*

# HORIZON INDUSTRIES, INCORPORATED 109

*Lumber Department   110*
*Lumber Mill   111*
*Department Operations   114*
*Internal Control   117*
*Order Processing   118*
*Discussion Questions   120*

# ICELANDIC FREEZING PLANTS CORPORATION 121

*Role of the Cooperative   121*
*Organization Structure   122*
*Processing   123*
*Control System   124*
*Need for System Improvement   127*
*Discussion Questions   129*
*Appendix: Illustration of Sales Allocation by Plant   129*

# JOHN STARK 133

*Discussion Questions   137*

# LABEL-IT, INCORPORATED 138

*Products and Growth   138*
*Quality Control Problems   140*
*Statistical Control Charts   141*
*Discussion Questions   144*

# MAYNARD FARMS 145

*Grower Operations   146*
*Cherry Processing   149*
*Discussion Questions   151*

# MIDCENTRAL FOODS, INCORPORATED 152

*Canadian Plant Operations 152*
*Scheduling and Inventory Control 154*
*Problems at London Plant 156*
*Discussion Questions 162*


# NORTHUMBERLAND MACHINERY WORKS LTD. 163

*Inventory Problems 164*
*Order Release System 165*
*Computer Systems and Simulation 167*
*Control in the Production Gear Shop 169*
*Slope Programme 171*
*Discussion Questions 182*


# OHIO EQUIPMENT COMPANY 184

*Reorganization of the Company 185*
*Factory Operations 187*
*Quality Complaints 191*
*Discussion Questions 192*


# O-NUT, INCORPORATED 193

*"O" Nut Industry 193*
*"O" Nut Culture 195*
*Nut Harvesting 196*
*Processing 197*
*Market 198*
*Orchard Operations and Costs 199*
*Discussion Questions 199*


# OSBURN MANUFACTURING COMPANY 200

*Major Projects 200*
*Scheduling System 202*
*Addition of Project C to Schedule 203*
*Discussion Questions 207*

# OTHELLO PRODUCTS, INCORPORATED 208

*Variable Speed Gear Reducer  209*
*Assembly Method  211*
*Design of Assembly Line  211*
*Discussion Questions  212*

# PETERSON GENERAL CONTRACTORS 213

*Television Tower Bid  213*
*Preparation of Cost Estimates  214*
*Discussion Questions  218*

# QUICK-LUBE 219

*The Lubrication System  219*
*Sequence of Operations  220*
*Costs and Revenues  221*
*Discussion Questions  224*

# REGIONAL INFANT CARE CENTERS 225

*Regional Care Concept  225*
*Analysis of Level II Needs  226*
*Level II Costs  229*
*Discussion Questions  231*

# SOUTHERN HYDRAULIC SUPPLIES COMPANY 232

*Inventory Replenishment Procedures  232*
*Discussion Questions  234*

# SUPERIOR STEAMSHIP COMPANY 236

*Iron Ore Transport on Great Lakes  236*
*Changes in Vessel Design  240*
*Additional Capacity Requirements  241*
*Discussion Questions  250*

# SURFLINER BOATS 251

*New Cruiser Design 251*
*Production Plan 252*
*Discussion Questions 254*


# TEEM AIRCRAFT CORPORATION 255

*Potential Suppliers 256*
*Bid Evaluation Procedure 257*
*Evaluation of Bids 261*
*Selection Board 263*
*Discussion Questions 266*


# TORSION TRACTOR COMPANY 267

*Planning for New Tractor 267*
*Axle Procurement 269*
*Supplier Strike 271*
*Solutions to Strike Problem 273*
*Discussion Questions 275*


# TRANSCONTINENTAL AIRCRAFT COMPANY 276

*Stretch Press Request 276*
*Replacement Press 279*
*Cost Data 280*
*Capital Budget Request 287*
*Discussion Questions 292*


# U.S. FABRICATION COMPANY 293

*Estimating Costs 294*
*Alternative Prices 295*
*Discussion Questions 296*


# VERNON MEDICAL CLINIC 297

*Discussion Questions 303*

# YORK CONTAINER COMPANY

*Employment Fluctuations 304*
*Plant Operations 305*
*Production Planning 306*
*Discussion Questions 308*

# APPENDIX

*Table A: Improvement Curves: Unit Values 310*
*Table B: Improvement Curves: Cumulative Values 312*
*Table C: Present Value of a Single Payment 314*
*Table D: Present Value of an Annuity 316*
*Table E: Uniformly Distributed Random Numbers 318*

# Preface

The activities of an organization can be classified into three basic functions. The first basic function involves the management of relationships with customers or clients. In a business organization this is called the marketing function. The second basic function is the transformation of inputs into outputs. The inputs may involve materials, a work force, buildings and machinery, systems and procedures, and technical skills. The outputs are the products or services that are produced to satisfy customers or clients. This second basic function is called *production or operations management.* The third basic function is the management of resources, primarily money, to support the other two basic functions of marketing management and production–operations management. The third basic function, called *finance,* involves the gathering, recording, controlling, and disbursing of funds.

This case book is primarily concerned with the second basic function, that of production–operations management (POM). Almost all the cases involve important strategic decisions in POM. Such strategic decisions inevitably interact with the marketing and finance functions; hence many of the cases presented here include the tasks of coordinating the three basic functions. Because such issues involve the basic policies of an organization, they are presented from the view point of managers at the upper levels of the organizational hierarchy.

Although many of the basic concepts originally arose in manufacturing or production organizations, these ideas have now been extended to all types of organizations including banks, department stores, hospitals, universities, governmental agencies, and even religious organizations. Thus, the function of POM is a universal one, whether the organization operates in the public or private sector, engages in profit or nonprofit activities, and represents a manufacturing, financial, distribution, or service organization.

This book may be used in a number of different educational situations. It assumes, however, that the students have had work experience or have taken at least a first course in production–operations management. Thus, the book may be most useful in a second course in POM designed to integrate the techniques, philosophy, and descriptive material that the students may have obtained in a beginning course or from work experience in an organization. In addition to being used in a regular university curriculum, the cases have also been used successfully in advanced management seminars for executives actively working in various types of organizations. The cases provide sufficient descriptive and quantitative material to be useful at different levels of analysis, that is, for undergraduate, graduate, or industrial training programs.

Each case focuses on some specific problem that existed in the company that was studied. The focal point of the analysis should be on the facts of the case, with reference to the specific issues involved and the decisions that need to be made. In many of the cases, opinions of personalities in the situation need to be considered as do the facts and environmental conditions. In some cases the apparent problems or issues may in turn lead to examination of other problems or issues that were not originally stated in the case. Thus, the student is challenged to look beyond the immediate overt factors and to seek out subtle or latent problems that must be considered in our complex world.

During a class discussion of a case, several alternative solutions may be presented. The challenge of these conflicting ideas will help to develop the analytical capabilities of the participants. Although it may be possible to clearly distinguish between nonworkable solutions and possible workable solutions, it may be far more difficult to select a single optimum solution.

For students who have not had exposure to the case method of study, a few suggestions may be helpful. A typical approach is to read each case three times. The first reading should be done rapidly to gain a general overall impression of the situation. The second reading should be a careful analytical study of each detailed fact, clarifying the problems or issues, analyzing the variables that are significant, identifying alternative courses of action, and finally proposing a program that appears to be the optimum workable decision. This second reading will inevitably involve note-taking, some calculating and careful weighing of the importance of each fact, and evaluating each alternative recommendation. The third reading should again be a rapid one to get in proper perspective the overall view of the situation and to check that the final recommendation makes sense in terms of the total environment and variables that had to be considered.

Inevitably, there will be a desire on the part of the student for more facts than are presented in the case, or the student may find that some of the data given in the case are superfluous or irrelevant to the particular problem involved. This is typical of complex organizational problems in which the real test of an effective manager is the ability to select pertinent data from large quantities of information, much of which may not be relevant, and the ability to make plausible assumptions about other factors that are relevant but are unavailable or unknown.

The professional manager of today must have many skills. These skills not only involve the analytical ability to deal with facts and figures in a narrow functional area; they also involve the ability to deal with and respect the activities of other functional areas. Finally, care must be taken to consider the human aspects of each situation, and recognition must be given to the culture and habit pattern of persons in the situation that may have important influence on selecting a workable recommendation.

The authors are most grateful to the many organizations that kindly permitted us to collect the information about their activities that resulted in the cases in this book. To protect confidences, however, almost all of the names of the cases and personalities have been altered. In addition, geographical locations may have been changed, and selected data and facts have been disguised. Care has been taken, however, that such changes or disguises have not altered the original basic, authentic relationships or the facts as presented.

The situations described in the cases have not been selected as examples of typical or recommended practices. Rather, the cases are intended to serve primarily as a pedagogical device for developing analytical abilities covering a wide variety of POM problems. Students should not expect to find themselves involved in exactly the same types of situations as those described in the cases. The experience, however, gained from studying these cases should prove valuable in understanding and analyzing other situations that may be faced in the future.

In conclusion, we wish to extend special thanks to Dr. Louis R. Concordia and Dr. John S. Moore, both of Western Washington University, and to Mr. Henry C. Fischer of Washington State University, all of whom contributed materials to this casebook. The authors are also most appreciative of the support of their respective institutions during the writing and production of this book.

# Aerodyne, Incorporated

Aerodyne, Incorporated was a large, well-financed firm in the airframe industry. Its primary aircraft manufacturing facility was located in southern California. Aerodyne, Incorporated had developed a new commercial jet, the Aerodyne-4, which it was preparing to put into production. The company had letters of intent from two airlines to purchase 60 of the new planes on the condition that the company could deliver planes meeting promised fuel efficiency and capacity specifications on a firm delivery schedule. Although the price of the Aerodyne-4 was somewhat higher than that announced by its chief competitor, Aerodyne won these orders because of the slightly better performance characteristics of its proposed plane and a delivery promise that was six to nine months ahead of its competitor's.

## PLANNED TOOLING PROGRAM

Conditions that made this delivery commitment feasible were an early start on the design of the new airplane and the rapidly declining tooling labor requirements for current business that permitted a smooth time-phased relationship with tooling requirements of the Aerodyne-4 program. At the end of 1979, projected tooling labor requirements and costs for existing business by quarters to early 1984 were as shown in Table 1. Tooling for existing company programs was expected to be completed by the second quarter of 1982, at which time the 2,900 workers in tooling would be reduced to a permanent base of 500.

It was estimated that tooling for the Aerodyne-4 program would require approximately 6,050,000 labor-hours, or 13,000 labor-quarters dis-

TABLE 1

Projected Tooling Employment and Cost for Existing Business

| Year | Quarter | Labor-Quarters Required for Existing Business | Work Force | Labor-Quarters Scheduled Regular | Overtime |
|------|---------|-----------------------------------------------|------------|----------------------------------|----------|
| 1980 | 1 | 2,900 | 2,900 | 2,900 | 0 |
|      | 2 | 2,800 | 2,800 | 2,800 | 0 |
|      | 3 | 2,500 | 2,500 | 2,500 | 0 |
|      | 4 | 1,900 | 1,900 | 1,900 | 0 |
| 1981 | 1 | 1,250 | 1,250 | 1,250 | 0 |
|      | 2 | 900 | 900 | 900 | 0 |
|      | 3 | 700 | 700 | 700 | 0 |
|      | 4 | 600 | 600 | 600 | 0 |
| 1982 | 1 | 550 | 550 | 550 | 0 |
|      | 2 | 500 | 500 | 500 | 0 |
|      | 3 | 500 | 500 | 500 | 0 |
|      | 4 | 500 | 500 | 500 | 0 |
| 1983 | 1 | 500 | 500 | 500 | 0 |
|      | 2 | 500 | 500 | 500 | 0 |
|      | 3 | 500 | 500 | 500 | 0 |
|      | 4 | 500 | 500 | 500 | 0 |
| 1984 | 1 | 500 | 500 | 500 | 0 |
| Total |  | 18,100 | 18,100 | 18,100 | 0 |

Cost summary

| Work force, | (18,100 labor-quarters) | $120,365,000 |
|-------------|-------------------------|--------------|
| Hires, | (0 workers) | 0 |
| Terminations, | (2,400 workers) | 2,400,000 |
| Overtime, | (0 labor-quarters) | 0 |
| Total |  | $122,765,000 |

tributed over a 13-quarter period as shown in Table 2. The number of tooling employees required for the schedule beginning in April 1980 would offset the declining number required for existing business. This would permit total employment to remain approximately stable in 1980 and 1981. Tooling labor requirements and costs through the first quarter of 1984 for existing business plus the Aerodyne-4 program are given in Table 3. The difference in cost of $89,375,000 between Tables 1 and 3 was the expected cost of the Aerodyne-4 tooling program.

Costs in Tables 1 and 3 were computed as follows. The company's average regular hourly direct tooling labor cost was $14.30. Labor cost per quarter was $6,650 ($14.30 per hour multiplied by 465 hours per quarter). The average working month was 155 hours, comprised of 21 days, or 168 hours, minus 13 hours (8 percent) of allowance for absenteeism and vaca-

TABLE 2

Projected Tooling Labor
Requirements for Aerodyne-4 Program

| Year | Quarter | Labor Required (labor-quarters) |
|---|---|---|
| 1980 | 2 | 50 |
| | 3 | 200 |
| | 4 | 900 |
| 1981 | 1 | 1,700 |
| | 2 | 2,200 |
| | 3 | 2,500 |
| | 4 | 2,300 |
| 1982 | 1 | 1,600 |
| | 2 | 800 |
| | 3 | 400 |
| | 4 | 200 |
| 1983 | 1 | 100 |
| | 2 | 50 |
| Total | | 13,000 |

tions. Cost of terminating an employee from the company was estimated to be $1,000. The estimated rehiring cost for an experienced employee was $2,100 and for an inexperienced employee $3,500. In the cost computations in Table 3, it was assumed that all the people added after the slight slump in total tooling requirements would be experienced persons.

Straight-time capacity in the company's tooling operations was about 3,000 labor-quarters, or 1,395,000 labor-hours per quarter. Requirements over this amount could be met by overtime work up to about 15 percent of the available straight-time hours. Thus, if tooling employment was up to the maximum of 3,000 workers, the company could handle up to 3,450 labor-quarters in its own shop. Any requirements over this would have to be provided by subcontracting work out to the company's other divisions or to outside firms.

The cost of work obtained through overtime was about double the cost of straight-time work. This was based on an estimated extra cost of one third for each hour obtained through overtime because of a 25 percent loss of efficiency after 40 hours of work per week. This extra one third was compounded by the 50 percent premium paid for each overtime hour to arrive at the overtime labor cost estimate. Thus, obtaining on an overtime basis the equivalent output of 6 hours of normal tooling work would require 8 extra overtime hours to be incurred (6 × 1.333) for which 12 hours at the straight-time wage rate would have to be paid (8 × 1.50). Cost of subcontract work was estimated to be $14,000 per quarter, or about $30.00 per hour.

## TABLE 3

### Projected Tooling Employment and Cost for Existing Business Plus AD-4

| Year | Quarter | Labor-Quarters Required for Existing Business Plus AD-4 | Work Force | Labor-Quarters Scheduled Regular | Overtime |
|---|---|---|---|---|---|
| 1980 | 1 | 2,900 | 2,900 | 2,900 | 0 |
|  | 2 | 2,850 | 2,850 | 2,850 | 0 |
|  | 3 | 2,700 | 2,700 | 2,700 | 0 |
|  | 4 | 2,800 | 2,800 | 2,800 | 0 |
| 1981 | 1 | 2,950 | 2,950 | 2,950 | 0 |
|  | 2 | 3,100 | 3,000 | 3,000 | 100 |
|  | 3 | 3,200 | 3,000 | 3,000 | 200 |
|  | 4 | 2,900 | 2,900 | 2,900 | 0 |
| 1982 | 1 | 2,150 | 2,150 | 2,150 | 0 |
|  | 2 | 1,300 | 1,300 | 1,300 | 0 |
|  | 3 | 900 | 900 | 900 | 0 |
|  | 4 | 700 | 700 | 700 | 0 |
| 1983 | 1 | 600 | 600 | 600 | 0 |
|  | 2 | 550 | 550 | 550 | 0 |
|  | 3 | 500 | 500 | 500 | 0 |
|  | 4 | 500 | 500 | 500 | 0 |
| 1984 | 1 | 500 | 500 | 500 | 0 |
| Total |  | 31,100 | 30,800 | 30,800 | 300 |

### Cost summary

| | | |
|---|---|---|
| Work force, | (30,800 labor-quarters) | $204,820,000 |
| Hires, | (300 workers) | 630,000 |
| Terminations, | (2,700 workers) | 2,700,000 |
| Overtime, | (300 labor-quarters) | 3,990,000 |
| Total | | $212,140,000 |

## SCHEDULE DELAY

In February 1980 two events occurred that required management to consider a possible delay in the planned April 1980 start-up date. The design engineers had not been able to work out all the detailed specifications for the new airplane and release the necessary drawings. Also, although the sales department had letters of intent from two major airlines for 60 airplanes, Aerodyne's top management felt that this was too few for the company to start construction of the new craft. Management believed that firm commitments for at least 100 airplanes should be in hand before undertaking this expensive venture. Because the airlines were suffering from a slowdown in growth of passenger traffic and difficulty in obtaining financing for new equipment, it was questionable as to when additional orders would be obtained.

Consequently, it was proposed to move the start-up date back to July 1981. Potentially this could result in failure to meet the delivery promise made to the first two customers. For such a delay, the tooling–production–testing cycle would have to be compressed if the delivery promises were to be kept. The program planning group determined that part of the compression would have to come in the tooling phase, which would be compressed by three quarters, as indicated in Table 4, to a total time period of ten quarters. Because of a decrease in the expected efficiency of labor utilization under the compressed program, total requirements for the revised program would be increased by 695,000 hours to 6,745,000 hours or 14,500 labor-quarters.

## EMPLOYMENT CONSTRAINTS

In addition to the projected increase in hours, other difficulties were anticipated to arise from the revised tooling program. One problem was the fact that a large number of tooling workers would be laid off by the company and then rehired after a year or so. Company experience suggested that not over 40 percent of the original workers could be rehired after such a long time as they would find jobs elsewhere and, in many cases, leave the area. In addition, from past experience the company had determined that its maximum recruiting and training ability limited it to no more than doubling employment in one year. Consequently, it appeared impossible to build up tooling labor at the rate required by the revised schedule. For example, if the tooling employment level at the start of the program in the third quarter of 1981 were the 700 workers required by existing business plus 50 workers required by the Aerodyne-4 program, then maximum employment after a year would be only 1,500 workers. This would be far below the number

TABLE 4

Projected Tooling Labor Requirements
for Aerodyne-4 Program, Revised Schedule

| Year | Quarter | Labor Required (labor-quarters) |
|---|---|---|
| 1981 | 3 | 50 |
|  | 4 | 300 |
| 1982 | 1 | 1,150 |
|  | 2 | 2,100 |
|  | 3 | 2,600 |
|  | 4 | 2,900 |
| 1983 | 1 | 2,900 |
|  | 2 | 1,900 |
|  | 3 | 500 |
|  | 4 | 100 |
| Total |  | 14,500 |

required in the third quarter of 1982. The inevitable consequence of the delay appeared to be a substantial increase in the cost for the tooling program.

## OTHER PROPOSALS

Another proposal was to start work on the Aerodyne-4 in the second quarter of 1981 so as to hold total tooling employment for all work at 1250 during 1981 and then to continue on a schedule that would complete the program by the fourth quarter of 1983. It was estimated this plan would require 13,750 work-quarters in cost.

Still another proposal was that the work should proceed on the original schedule of Table 2. Some executives of the company felt that currently much of the design was stabilized and many drawings could be released for the tooling work to begin. It was estimated that future design changes might require some rework but it was unlikely that the rework would exceed 10% of the tooling work to be completed prior to July, 1981. There still remained the possibility that insufficient orders would be received by July 1981, and that the Aerodyne-4 program would then be canceled.

## DISCUSSION QUESTIONS

1. Determine the cost to Aerodyne of the proposed revision in the schedule for the tooling program. (Assume that tooling labor is reduced as existing

business declines and is increased as fast as possible as the Aerodyne-4 program expands.)

2. Is there any merit to the idea of retaining some tooling workers over the slack period when they are not really needed?

3. Prepare a decision tree with two decision points; one as of February 1980, and the other as of July 1981. On February 1980, the three alternatives were as follows:

      Plan A — Adhere to the original schedule starting in the 2nd quarter 1980 and completing the program in the 2nd quarter 1983.

      Plan B — Reduce the time schedule to begin in early 1981 and complete in the 4th quarter 1983, with level total employment of 1250 maintained in 1981.

      Plan C — Further reduce the schedule to start in the 3rd quarter 1981 and complete in the 4th quarter 1983.

On July 1981 assume the two alternatives to be as follows:

      Plan D — Continue the program as established in February 1980.

      Plan E — Cancel the program.

As of July 1, 1981, what will be the incremental costs of completing Plans B and C as compared to completing Plan A? What will be the cost of each plan if the Aerodyne-4 program is cancelled on July 1, 1981?

4. What plan would you recommend as of February 1980 if the estimated chance at that time of a cancellation of the Aerodyne-4 program on July 1, 1981 was 20%? 50%? 95%? How do you justify your conclusion?

5. How should the time value of money influence the decision? Note that the investments in tooling for plans B and C are made later than for Plan A. The tooling program is followed by the production phase of the Aerodyne-4, then the flight tests, certification, and finally delivery. At delivery, payment is made by the customer, part of which is for the recovery of the tooling investment. The first delivery was estimated to take place on July 1, 1985.

# American Ceramic and Glass Products Corporation

The American Ceramic and Glass Products Corporation employed a total of approximately 13,000 people, each of its three plants employing between 4,000 and 5,000 of this total. About three quarters of its sales volume came from standard glass containers produced on highly automatic equipment; the balance of the company's sales were of specialized ceramic and glass items produced in batches on much less automated equipment. John Parr, production manager for American Ceramic and Glass Products, had just completed a trip that covered eight states, seven universities, and three major industrial centers. The purpose of his trip was to recruit personnel for American's three plants. He felt that his trip had been extremely successful and that he had made contacts that would, he hoped, result in his firm's acquiring some useful and needed personnel.

Parr was anxious to secure a capable person to head up the inspection and quality control department of the largest of American's plants located in Denver, Colorado. The position of chief of inspection and quality control had just been vacated by George Downs, who had taken an indefinite leave of absence due to a serious illness. There was little possibility that Downs would be capable of resuming any work duties within a year and a substantial probability that he would never be capable of working on a full-time basis. During the ten years that Downs held the position of chief of inspection and quality control, he had completely modernized the firm's inspection facilities and had developed a training program in the use of the most modern inspection equipment and techniques. The physical facilities of Downs's inspection department were a major attraction for visitors to the plant.

## THOMAS CALLIGAN

During his trip, Parr interviewed two men whom he felt were qualified to fill Downs's position. Although each appeared more than qualified, Parr felt that a wrong choice could easily be made. Thomas Calligan, the first of the two men, was a graduate of a reputable trade school and had eight years of experience in the inspection department of a moderately large manufacturing firm (approximately 800 employees). He began working as a production inspector and was promoted to group leader within two years and chief inspector two years later. His work record as a production inspector, as a group leader, and as chief inspector was extremely good. His reason for wishing to leave the firm was "to seek better opportunities." He felt that in his present firm he could not expect further promotions in the near future. His firm was known for its stability, low employee turnover, and slow but assured advancement opportunities. His superior, the head of quality control, was recently promoted to this position and was doing a more than satisfactory job. Further, he was a young man, only 32 years old.

## JAMES KING

James King, the second of the two men being considered by Parr, was a graduate of a major southwestern university and had approximately five years of experience. King was currently employed as head of inspection and quality control in a small manufacturing firm employing approximately 300 people. His abilities exceeded the requirements of his job, and he had made arrangements with his employer to do a limited amount of consulting work for noncompeting firms. His major reason for wanting to secure a different position was a continuing conflict of interests between himself and his employer. King did not wish to make consulting his sole source of income, but he felt that his current position was equally unsatisfactory. He believed that by working for a large firm he would be able to fully utilize his talents within that firm and thus resolve conflict occurring between his professional interests and the interests of his employer.

King's work record appeared to be good. This was evidenced by the fact that he had recently been granted a sizable pay increase. King, like Calligan, began his career as a bench inspector and was rapidly promoted to his current supervisory position. Unlike Calligan, King viewed his initial position of bench inspector primarily as a means of financing his education and not as the beginning of his lifetime career. King was 31 years old.

## ROLE OF INSPECTION AND QUALITY CONTROL

Major differences between these individuals centered on their philosophies regarding the role of inspection and quality control in a manufacturing organization. Calligan's philosophy was:

> Quality is an essential part of every product. . . . It is the product development engineer's function to specify what constitutes quality and the function of quality control to see that the manufacturing departments maintain these specifications. . . . Accurate and vigilant inspection is the key to controlled quality.

When asked how important process control was in the manufacture of quality products, he stated,

> Process control is achieved primarily through the worker's attitude. If a firm pays high wages and provides good working conditions, they should be able to acquire highly capable workers. . . . A well-executed and efficient inspection program will, as it has done in my firm, impress the importance of quality on the employees and motivate high-quality production. In the few cases when quality lapses do occur, an efficient inspection program prevents defective products from leaving the plant. . . . Any valid quality control program must hold quality equal in importance to quantity. . . . Quality records must be maintained for each employee and be made known to both the employee and his immediate superiors. Superior quality should be a major consideration in recommending individuals for promotion or merit pay increases.

King's philosophy paralleled that of Calligan only to the extent that "quality was an essential part of every product." King made the following comments regarding his philosophy toward inspection and quality control:

> If quality is properly controlled, inspection becomes a minor function. The more effective a quality control system becomes, the less inspection is required. . . . The key to quality control is process control, and inspection serves only as a check to assure that the process controls are being properly administered. . . . An effective inspection scheme should locate and pinpoint the cause of defects rather than place the blame on an often innocent individual. A good rejection report will include the seeds from which a solution to future rejections can be developed. . . . One sign of an unsatisfactory quality control system is a large, impressive inspection program.

King was asked what steps he would take to develop such a program if he were to be offered and accept the job of chief of inspection and quality control in the Denver plant. He answered,

> I would design and install a completely automatic inspection and process control system throughout the plant. By automatic I do not mean a mechanical

or computer-directed system, but rather a completely standardized procedure for making all decisions concerning inspection and process control. The procedures would be based on a theoretically sound statistical foundation translated into laymen's terminology. The core of the program would be a detailed inspection and quality control manual.

When asked how long this might take King continued,

> I constructed a similar manual for my present employer in a period of less than twelve months and had the whole process operating smoothly within eighteen months after beginning work on the task. Since your firm is somewhat larger, and accounting for my added experience, I would estimate it to take no longer than two years and hopefully significantly less time. . . . As previously stated, I would place major emphasis on process control and would minimize inspection by applying appropriate sampling procedures wherever possible. . . . Employee quality performance should be rated on the basis of process control charts rather than on the basis of final inspection reports. The employee should be trained and encouraged to use these charts as his chief tool toward achieving quality output.

King further stated that one of the reasons for his desire to find a new employer was that he had developed the quality control program in his present firm to the point where it was no longer offering him any challenge. He further stated that he felt this situation would recur at American Ceramic and Glass Products but that, because of the size of the firm, he could direct his attention to bigger and more interesting problems rather than be required to seek outside consulting work to satisfy his need for professional growth.

When asked what his real interests were, King stated, "Application of statistical concepts to the nonroutine activities of a manufacturing organization." He cited worker training, supplier performance, and trouble shooting as areas of interest. King submitted several reports that summarized projects that he had successfully completed in these or related areas.

This was the extent of information that Parr had on each of the two individuals he felt might best fill the position vacated by Downs, the retiring chief of the inspection and quality control department.

## DISCUSSION QUESTIONS

1. What is quality, who determines it, how is it described, and how is it attained?
2. What should be the role of the chief of inspection and quality control?
3. What was Calligan's philosophy toward quality control?
4. What was King's philosophy toward quality control?

5. Under what conditions would you expect Calligan and King, respectively, to be most effective?
6. Excluding the differences in philosophies between King and Calligan, what other factors relative to each require consideration?
7. Which of the two candidates, if either, should be selected for the position of chief of the inspection and quality control department?
8. Where could each man be utilized outside of the area of inspection and quality control?

# Automated Parking Systems, Incorporated

Automated Parking Systems was formed for the purpose of building automated parking structures. Principal stockholders in the company were a mechanical engineer and a building contractor who had jointly developed what they felt was a unique and technologically advanced parking concept. The plan of Automated Parking Systems was to construct standardized, modular structures for organizations needing concentrated parking facilities such as banks, hospitals, department stores, hotels, restaurants, and parking lot operators. Automated Parking would build the structures for their clients, who would then own and operate the facilities.

## PARKING SYSTEM

As shown in Figure 1, the structures were of circular, concrete design, 20 levels high, and approximately 70 feet in diameter. Each level had provision for ten vehicles and was serviced by a computer control system, vertical hoist, turntable, and transfer mechanism capable of automatically parking or retrieving one vehicle each minute.

Each level, except for support columns and exterior wall panels, was open space. Floors sloped toward an exterior drain trough to accommodate dripping water or melting snow carried in on vehicles. A stairway, used only for maintenance and emergencies, serviced each level; a lock and access alarm at ground level limited entrance to authorized persons.

Safety barriers were used at the ground level together with remote TV surveillance by a cashier-operator to minimize the possibility of accidents to customers. Ingress and egress ramps could be designed to be compatible with any site configuration and traffic flow pattern. The cashier's office and control room occupied the space of a ground-level parking stall or could be

## FIGURE 1
### Automated Parking Structure

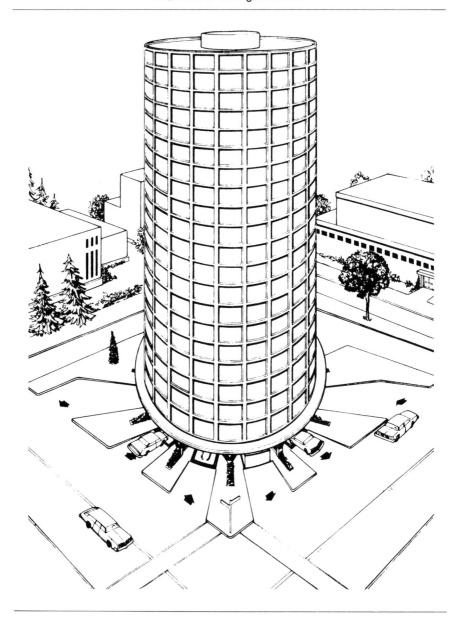

in a separate building. It was contemplated that a single cashier-operator could handle the complete operation, exclusive of maintenance, of from one to three 200-car structures.

The vehicle hoist was an open-frame platform capable of vertical travel at speeds of up to 400 feet per minute. The hoist shaft was 26 feet in diameter with guide rails to assure platform stability and alignment. Hoist drive was a 75-hp DC motor that operated through a speed-reducing mechanism. Power was provided by a 50-Kw motor generator set operated from the incoming AC line power. The hoist drive motor provided dynamic braking. Also, the hoist drive assembly was equipped with an electromechanical brake.

A rotary turntable as shown in Figure 2 was mounted on the hoist platform to position the vehicle transfer device to any of ten positions. The transfer device, which was mounted on the platform, was approximately 24 feet long. The transfer device raised the vehicle, moved it onto the hoist, and moved it off of the hoist into the parking stall.

## OPERATION OF THE SYSTEM

Control of all vehicle parking was provided by a small computer system. Normal system operation was completely automatic, although the cashier-operator could elect semiautomatic operation and control each operating step through the computer console. A complete manual control station located on the hoist platform could bypass the computer system in an emergency or service situation.

The computer system stored all information relative to any vehicle parked within the facility. Vehicle identification code and entry time were contained on the customer's parking ticket. When the ticket was read by a system ticket reader, the computer initiated vehicle retrieval and calculated parking charges. These were displayed for the cashier-operator and recorded on tape for later use in preparing management and accounting reports. The operator console had provision to manually program vehicle retrieval in case of a lost or mutilated parking ticket.

In a typical case, a customer would enter an ingress stall, park, lock, and leave the vehicle. The customer would then activate a ticket dispenser at departure. This would start the computer park cycle and code the time on a claim check. Prominent signs would provide instructions and remind the customer to take the claim check from the dispenser. The vehicle would then be automatically parked in the nearest available stall. The vehicle would not be moved until the ingress stall was clear and a protective barrier was in place.

When the customer returned, he or she would present the claim check to the cashier. The claim check would be inserted in a reader that would transmit the information to permit the computer to compute the parking fee and retrieve the vehicle. The customer would be directed to an egress stall while the vehicle was being retrieved. A barrier would protect the customer while the vehicle was being delivered to the egress stall.

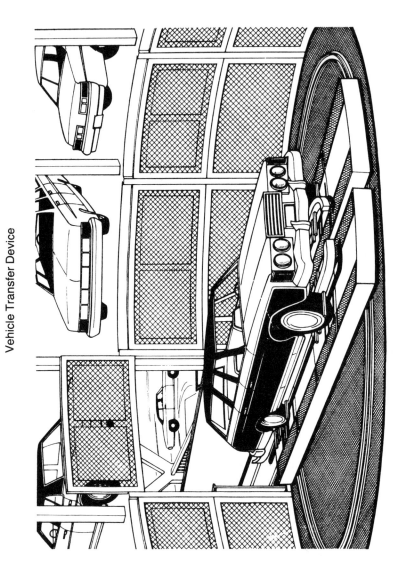

FIGURE 2

Vehicle Transfer Device

16

## COSTS

Major costs of operating the system were salaries and fringe benefits for the cashier-operators and costs of maintenance, utilities, taxes, and insurance. These costs would, of course, vary depending on the city and specific site on which a structure was located. However, the developers estimated that the single cashier-operator would cost approximately $9.25 per hour, including fringe benefits, and that maintenance, utilities, taxes, and insurance might run about $475 per stall per year.

## COMPETITIVE ADVANTAGES

The developers of the automated parking structure believed that the following were the most important features in terms of competing with other parking systems:

1. *Speed of operation.* Automated parking structures could pick up one car or deliver one car in an average time of 60 seconds and could provide multiple entrances and exits for every 200 cars parked.
2. *Productivity.* An automated parking structure could provide a land use–productivity ratio of 10:1 on average with substantial savings in land and related costs. Twenty-two automobiles parked on the ground required roughly 6,500 square feet whereas an automated parking structure could park 200 automobiles in the same area.
3. *Price.* Estimates showed that an automated parking structure could be sold for the same price per stall as any competing indoor parking system.
4. *Operating economics.* Estimated operating costs were less than those for other parking systems due to fewer operating personnel and a smaller area to be cleared, lighted, and controlled for security.
5. *Computerized operations.* Traffic counts and tabulation of revenues were handled automatically by the computer, which was impervious to tampering by employees. The computer could provide centralized accounting records and reports via telephone interface, if desired.
6. *Adaptable.* The client could use one structure or as many as needed to meet any parking requirements.
7. *Protection.* A structure could be closed in to afford protection from the elements, thieves, and muggers. Cars would be protected from dents, scratches, and pilferage, as no person other than the customer would drive the car.
8. *Air pollution.* No carbon monoxide or nitrogen oxide would be generated in a structure because the motor on a car would be turned off on entry and not started again until after the customer entered the car to drive it away.

Small scale models and prototypes of portions of the automated parking structure and equipment had been built by the developers, but no complete system had been built or tested. However, the developers were confident that the design concept was sound and that the systems were sufficiently simple so that little difficulty would be encountered in actually building a structure. In addition, detailed specification and engineering drawings had been prepared for the concrete structure and equipment.

Using engineering drawings, architectural sketches, and other promotional literature, representatives of Automated Parking Systems engaged in a sales campaign in San Francisco and in several cities in Nevada. After six months of effort, ten prospects had indicated interest in their proposals, and negotiations were in progress to obtain contracts for building a total of 33 structures with an estimated cost of $34,308,000. Details of the proposed projects are shown in Table 1.

TABLE 1

Automated Parking Systems Projects in Contract Negotiation

| Project | No. of Structures | No. of Spaces | Approximate In-Place Cost[1] |
|---|---|---|---|
| San Francisco | | | |
| 1. Bay Medical Center | 1 | 200 | $ 1,045,000 |
| 2. Golden State Bank | 1 | 200 | 1,188,000 |
| 3. Main police station | 3 | 600 | 3,000,000 |
| 4. Toyota dealer | 3 | 600 | 3,000,000 |
| 5. Chang property | 4 | 800 | 4,000,000 |
| Nevada | | | |
| 6. Casino A | 5 | 1,000 | 4,875,000 |
| 7. Casino B | 3 | 600 | 3,000,000 |
| 8. Casino C | 6 | 1,200 | 7,200,000 |
| 9. Casino D | 4 | 800 | 4,000,000 |
| 10. Casino E | 3 | 600 | 3,000,000 |
| | | | $34,308,000 |

[1]Cost of structure alone; does *not* include land.

## DISCUSSION QUESTIONS

**1.** Is the automated parking structure a technically sound concept?
**2.** Is the automated parking structure operationally feasible?
**3.** Is the automated parking structure financially feasible?
**4.** Select a potential customer for an automated parking structure in your vicinity and evaluate the feasibility of such a structure for filling that organization's parking needs.

# Bayerische Maschinen Werke GmbH

The first few observer seats and control stands had just been shipped by the Bayerische Maschinen Werke GmbH[1] (BMW) from Anderbach, Germany to the Kellering Airplane Company (KAC) on the West Coast of the United States. Mr. Hans von Halle, sales manager of the aircraft division of BMW, planned to review the condition of the DM 9,000,000 contract and evaluate the difficulties and problems experienced to date on this program for 150 seats, 100 control stands, and related tooling. He faced the necessity of recommending a future policy for his company regarding the expansion or the elimination of sales effort directed toward prime contractors in the U.S. aerospace industry.

## COMPANY HISTORY

Bayerische Maschinen Werke GmbH was the surviving entity of a 1955 merger between BMW and Allgemeine Flugzeug Werke (AFW). BMW itself, before the merger, had a history dating back to the early 1920s when it had been founded as a machine shop in Anderbach, a small town not far from Nuremberg. Throughout the pre–World War II years the machine shop had grown in size until it was converted, during the war, into an ammunition factory that suffered complete destruction as a result of military actions. After the war the plant was reconstructed as a repair yard for railroad cars and later eventually expanded as a railroad car, hydraulic press, and truck trailer manufacturing facility.

---

[1]GmbH is the abbreviation for *Gesellschaft mit beschrankter Haftung*. This is a "closed corporation" form of business organization having limited liability and stock that is privately held.

The AFW half of the present company had been founded in 1910 in Potsdam and was one of the pioneers in aircraft manufacturing. The company had been a major contributor of military aircraft during World War I and had gone on, between the two wars, to create an excellent reputation for itself in civilian aircraft by establishing several world speed, altitude, and endurance records. Immediately prior to World War II the company again began producing military aircraft and continued to do so, despite severe destruction, during the war. The partition of Germany at the war's end resulted in its manufacturing facilities being located in the Eastern Zone, and these were dismantled and taken to the Soviet Union. All land, buildings, and equipment was expropriated by the Soviet occupation government. Most of the company's management and engineering personnel, however, managed to escape to the West, and the company was reestablished in Nuremberg. Here the AFW staff, forbidden by the Allied Powers from building airplanes, was only able to do limited design work on modern airframes and related projects.

In 1955, airspace sovereignty was returned to the Federal Republic of Germany (FRG), and AFW found itself with technical knowledge about aircraft but with no manufacturing facilities. It was under these circumstances that the BMW–AFW merger was arranged, with BMW supplying capital, facilities, and manufacturing know-how and AFW supplying aircraft technology and a small organization that believed it could undertake new product design and development work. At the completion of the merger the old AFW offices were moved from Nuremberg to the BMW plant at Anderbach, and the company was reorganized into a railroad division (that included truck trailers and hydraulic presses) and an aircraft division.

By the early 1960s the aircraft division of the company had established itself as a reliable supplier on several NATO subcontracts, on parts contracts awarded by the newly reconstituted Luftwaffe, and on subcontracts from several German commercial airplane companies. The designs were supplied by the buyers, and BMW's work consisted of the manufacture and assembly of such items as wings, wing sections, tail assemblies, fuel tanks, compartment bulkheads, airducts, doors, helicopter rotor blades, cockpit canopies, and radomes. Many of these items required extensive development effort in such fields as plastics, metal bonding, and other new techniques. As a result of this effort, BMW gained a reputation for a high level of competency.

In addition to its subcontract work, the company produced and marketed several small civilian aircraft, including both piston and jet designs. One sports plane was of a prewar design, and another was built under a license from the foreign designer. Concurrently, the railroad division had rapidly expanded its own domestic and foreign sales volume as a designer and manufacturer of original equipment. During the past five years, the combined company operations tripled in turnover (sales) from DM 61,000,000 to DM 185,000,000.

BMW's entire facilities were located in the small town of Anderbach, situated on South Germany's rail and highway network, with direct connections to the major rail and air centers of Nuremberg and Munich. Thus, it had excellent transportation arrangements to the whole of Western Europe.

Although Anderbach was too far from Nuremberg for daily commutation, BMW had relatively little trouble — by German standards — in encouraging employees to work for the company. The town could be classified as a typically quaint Bavarian town and was well liked by Germans as a place to live and work. The surroundings were pleasant and housing was adequate.

Most of the BMW workers lived in the adjacent countryside and many drove to work by auto. As a result, the company faced the necessity of expanding its 400-car parking lot. This was in contrast to the prewar situation when only the managing director and a few other executives came to work in private autos.

BMW, with 2,500 workers, was the largest employer in the town that had a total population of 11,000. Located on an adjoining property was a major farm implement manufacturer that employed 800 people. The other businesses were the typical supporting service activities for such a community.

Despite its generally favorable location, however, BMW did have some problems in finding enough skilled employees to fulfill all its operating requirements. For any skilled worker who might temporarily be out of a job, there were usually several job openings in his home location. This made it difficult to get workers to move to Anderbach.

As a result BMW found it necessary to recruit and transport to Anderbach approximately 100 Turkish workers who were employed on a two-year contract basis. These foreign employees were hired by the production manager who periodically visited Turkey and made the necessary arrangements through a Turkish government agency. The Turkish workers spoke little or no German, but one of their group had a good command of the German language and did the necessary translating so that there were few communication problems. Although some of the workers developed skills such as welding, most of them were assigned unskilled manual tasks. After saving up a "nest egg" during their two-year contract, most of the Turkish workers returned to their native land. Some, however, preferred to stay as long as possible.

## BID FOR A KELLERING CONTRACT

When Kellering Airplane Company invited BMW to submit a bid, top management was delighted as it had long desired to do subcontract work for a U.S. firm. BMW felt that such work would give it entry to the U.S. aerospace industry and access to its technology. The company saw in the United

States some of the world's largest airplane makers and the most scientifically advanced aerospace organizations. If BMW were able to establish a direct link with U.S. firms, it could open for the firm a large and profitable market and permit BMW to participate in a rich technical information pool.

Kellering was also interested in establishing relationships with overseas suppliers. The firm's own facilities were operating at full capacity, and the company had a growing order backlog. Although it was expanding its facilities rapidly, the company still found it imperative to maintain and even enlarge its broadly based network of suppliers in the United States and Canada. Kellering felt that foreign suppliers had the advantage of low labor costs, created relationships that could provide a potential base for stronger sales entry by Kellering into foreign markets, and offered Kellering the opportunity for making technical contacts with other foreign aerospace companies. In any case, Kellering felt it needed some direct experience with a major overseas supplier before Kellering could determine its own long-range policy regarding foreign procurement.

Kellering had previously been involved in an engineering agreement on a consulting basis with a South German aircraft company for the joint design and development of military hardware for NATO. It was through this activity that Kellering first heard of BMW. On a trip to Germany regarding the NATO project, several of the Kellering executives visited BMW to inspect the plant. During this visit they informally questioned the management as to the firm's willingness to bid on a U.S. subcontract. BMW management indicated that it would like to submit a bid on anything it could handle. BMW also carefully pointed out its long experience in the airframe business, its previous subcontract performance (some of which involved U.S. designs), and its competence and familiarity with such management techniques used in the aircraft industry as network analysis and improvement curves.

Shortly after this visit BMW was invited to bid on a contract for observer seats and control stands to be used on a large commercial jet airplane that Kellering was building. The observer seats were installed on such aircraft immediately behind the pilot and co-pilot for use by government inspectors, instructors, trainees, and visitors. The seat was a mechanical device constructed of welded steel tubing with upholstered cushions and with a lever system to adjust its position. The control stand, located between the pilot and co-pilot, was an electromechanical–electronic device with levers, switches, and cable connections to actuate devices for moving the aerodynamic control surfaces of the airplane. By moving these surfaces the pilot could trim the vertical and horizontal position of the airplane and control the flaps and airbrakes in the wings for landing. Because of its importance to the flight characteristics and to the safety of the airplane, the specifications for the control stands were comprehensive and had precise requirements for performance and tolerances.

With the invitation to bid in hand, BMW set about to prepare its bid price. It knew that several U.S. companies along with BMW had been invited to bid, and it realized that, despite Kellering's interest in placing an overseas subcontract, BMW would have to submit the lowest bid to win the award. BMW's competitive advantage was a labor rate that it knew was currently lower than those in the United States. The trend of labor wage rates and the effect of exchange rates, however, was eroding the labor cost advantage. This fact was evident from data obtained from the latest issues of the *Yearbook of Labor Statistics,* published by the International Labor Office; Business International, a private advisory service; *International Financial Statistics,* published monthly by the International Monetary Fund; *Survey of Current Business,* published monthly by the U.S. Department of Commerce; and *Wirtschaft und Statistik,* published by Statistiches Bundesamt Wiesbaden. Wage trends and exchange rates were reported as follows:

| Hourly Wage Rates for Production Employees | 1970 | 1980 |
|---|---|---|
| Federal Republic of Germany (DM) | | |
| All manufacturing | 6.45 | 13.55 |
| Aircraft industry | 6.26 | 13.68 |
| Bayerische Maschinen | 4.70 | 11.50 |
| Fringe benefits as % of | | |
| labor wage rates | 52% | 69% |
| United States ($) | | |
| All manufacturing | 3.36 | 7.01 |
| Transportation equipment | 4.05 | 8.90 |
| Fringe benefits as % of | | |
| labor wage rates | 34% | 42% |
| Exchange rates | | |
| DM per $US | 3.648 | 1.732 |

The BMW wage rates were lower than average German rates because the company was located in a rural rather than in an industrial area and it employed a significant number of foreign workers for unskilled jobs.

Although BMW was unable to compare its productivity with that of competitive U.S. companies, BMW noted the following from available ILO reports:

### Indexes of Productivity in Manufacturing

| | 1970 | 1971 | 1972 | 1973 | 1974 | 1975 | 1976 |
|---|---|---|---|---|---|---|---|
| Germany[1] | 100 | 105 | 112 | 120 | 124 | 128 | 138 |
| United States[2] | 100 | 106 | 111 | 114 | 110 | 110 | 117 |

[1]Based on net production (value added) per labor-hour.
[2]Based on gross production (sales or turnover) per labor-hour.

BMW's handicaps were in its limited familiarity with U.S. procedures, especially those of Kellering, and its geographical remoteness from Kellering, which would add to shipping costs and the costs of communication. Communication costs could be high, not only from the standpoint of transmission, but also from the standpoint of translation and interpretation. Transmission costs could be controlled by the careful use of inexpensive communication channels, but the cost of translation and comprehension of the many documents involved remained an imponderable.

A set of drawings and specifications for bidding purposes was provided BMW by Kellering. These were studied by the engineers and estimators who developed a tentative manufacturing plan and determined the bid price in the normal BMW manner, as shown in Figure 1.

The direct labor component of Figure 1 was derived by estimating the required labor-hours and multiplying by the standard labor rate. This was primarily a task of estimating productivity, as 80 percent of the jobs at BMW were on a piece-rate basis using a 100 percent incentive plan — either by group or by individual. The remaining 20 percent of the jobs were on a time–wage basis for such operations as chemical processing. Piece rates were established by time studies using a stopwatch method in accordance with the REFA system — a standard time study procedure used throughout Germany. This system provided standards for such things as personal allowances, cycles to be timed, and leveling procedures. The motion and time study engineers applying the REFA system were required to have a certificate indicating that they had completed a special course of study in the technique and had passed a standardized examination. Labor unions generally accepted without question the piece rates established by persons who had the REFA certificate. The normalized time was set at 100 percent. Piece rates were established by applying a base labor rate to the time required on an 80 percent speed basis. If an actual operation resulted in workers' operating at 30 percent above the normal speed, then the planning department rechecked the study.

Production overhead was derived from direct labor costs broken down by cost centers. Each cost center had its own overhead rate that ranged from 150 percent (carpenters, upholsterers, etc.) to as high as 2,000 percent (for the chemical processing department). An overall average labor overhead rate normally amounted to about 250 percent of direct labor cost.

To the estimated total material requirements per unit was applied an associated overhead and some supervision. The technical overhead was allocated at fixed rates on direct labor-hours for technical work.

Categories for general and administrative expenses included allowances for sales expense, taxes, contingencies, and profit. The long-term cost trend for general and administrative expenditure (excluding contingencies, taxes, and profits) had averaged about 10 percent of total manufacturing costs.

FIGURE 1

Estimating Sheet:
Observer Seat — 150 Shipsets

|  | Hours | Rate | Total | |
|---|---|---|---|---|
| Direct expenses | | | | |
| Direct labor-hours | 126 | | | |
| Sustaining labor-hours | 13 | | | |
| Total labor-hours | 139 | | | |
| Direct labor rate | | DM 9.75 | DM | 1,355 |
| Engineering and sustaining | | | | |
| tooling | | | | 135 |
| Total labor cost | | | | 1,490 |
| Material cost | | | | 495 |
| Total direct expense | | | | 1,985 |
| Overhead expense | | | | |
| Production | | 250% | | 3,387 |
| Engineering and tooling | | 300% | | 405 |
| Material | | 25% | | 123 |
| Total overhead expense | | | | 3,915 |
| Factory cost | | | | 5,900 |
| General and administrative | | | | |
| expense, contingencies, | | | | |
| taxes, and profit | | 20% | | 1,180 |
| Total | | | | 7,080 |
| Packaging | | | | 144 |
| Sales price per shipset | | | DM | 7,224 |
| Total contract price, 150 shipsets | | | | 1,083,600 |
| Total tooling costs | | | | 54,000 |
| Total program costs | | | | DM 1,137,600 |

Control Stand — 100 Shipsets

|  | Hours | Rate | Total | |
|---|---|---|---|---|
| Direct expense | | | | |
| Direct labor-hours | 660 | | | |
| Sustaining labor-hours | 132 | | | |
| Total labor-hours | 792 | | | |
| Direct labor rate | | DM14.55 | DM | 11,524 |
| Engineering and sustaining | | | | |
| tooling | | | | 1,725 |
| Total labor cost | | | | 13,249 |
| Material cost | | | | 10,425 |
| Total direct expense | | | | 23,674 |

FIGURE 1 (continued)

Control Stand — 100 Shipsets

| | Hours | Rate | Total |
|---|---|---|---|
| Overhead expense | | | |
|   Production | | 250% | 28,810 |
|   Engineering and tooling | | 300% | 5,175 |
|   Material | | 25% | 2,606 |
|     Total overhead expense | | | 36,591 |
| Factory cost | | | 60,265 |
| General and administrative | | | |
|   expense, contingencies, taxes, | | | |
|   and profit | | 20% | 12,053 |
|     Total | | | 72,318 |
| Customer variation | | | 1,155 |
|   Total | | | 73,473 |
| Packaging | | | 1,050 |
|   Sales price per shipset | | | DM    74,523 |
| Total contract price, 100 shipsets | | | 7,452,300 |
| Total tooling costs | | | 384,000 |
|   Total program costs | | | DM  7,836,300 |

Turnover taxes required special attention. There was a value added tax of 13 percent (recent range, 4–15 percent) on items manufactured for domestic consumption. There was, however, no value added tax on items manufactured for export. In the past manufacturers of exported items received an ad valorem tax rebate to encourage export shipment, but this was no longer available.

Normally BMW included in its contracts an escalation clause for changes in the cost of materials and wages. During recent years the cost increases subject to the escalation clause had averaged about 6 percent per year. Kellering would not accept such an escalation clause; hence BMW made an estimate of future cost increases and included this in its estimate for contingencies. Thus it carried the full risk for such cost changes.

Tooling costs were estimated in a similar manner but were treated in a separate formal contract. BMW had investigated prices and costs in the United States. When BMW management reviewed its final bid, it felt confident that it was not only competitive but probably the low bidder.

As it turned out BMW had, in fact, submitted the low bid. After sending a small team of Kellering engineers from the NATO project to briefly inspect BMW's facilities, Kellering accepted the bid and awarded BMW the observer seat and control stand contract. Usually the Kellering buyer went to great lengths to help new suppliers become acquainted with Kellering methods and procedures. But, after receiving the favorable report of the visit by the senior executives, Tim Lester, the Kellering buyer, felt that BMW could be treated in the same fashion as any experienced U.S. supplier and that special assistance to BMW was not necessary. He was also aware of the distance and language barriers.

## KELLERING CONTRACT

Shortly after the contract was awarded, Hans von Halle, sales manager of BMW, came to the United States to review the details of the contract at the home office of Kellering. Mr. von Halle had an engineering degree from a university in Germany and a variety of experience in commercial activities, including one year in the United States when he worked as a sales engineer for a major pump company. He was about 35 years old, an enthusiastic sales representative, and the son of the managing director of BMW.

The final contract agreed to by both companies was typical of the form used by Kellering, but it had several features that were new to BMW. One such new aspect was the provision for value engineering, which provided for a 50:50 sharing between Kellering and BMW of all savings accruing from the application of value engineering principles to the work under the contract.

The delivery requirements were clearly and explicitly established by the contract. Delivery of the seats was to begin in 9 months at a limited rate. The first stands were due in 13 months. The delivery rate was to accelerate to a maximum of 12 seats and 8 control stands per month and then taper off until the contract was completed.

The contract also contained procedures for progress reporting. This was to be done monthly with Gantt-type charts identifying "milestones," such as the receipt of drawings, procurement of material, completion of manufacture, and shipments. These charts showed both the actual and planned performances — side by side — and were forwarded to both the Kellering U.S. headquarters and to the Kellering NATO project team in Germany who might be able to provide assistance if difficulties were encountered by BMW.

A vital section of the contract covered the quality control policies that were to be implemented by detailed procedures. These were to be developed by BMW into a QC manual, subject to approval by Kellering. The QC procedures used by BMW on previous work had been reviewed by the Kellering inspection team, and their apparent similarity to the requirements of the contract had convinced Kellering that BMW could perform satisfactorily. The contract did not provide for source inspection (final inspection at the supplier's plant, subject to guarantees), instead the final inspection and acceptance were to be conducted at the home plant of Kellering.

Related to quality control and inspection was the requirement for approval by the U.S. Federal Aviation Agency. The FAA had to pass on all equipment that went into U.S.-made planes. This approval consisted of two distinct steps: (1) approval of the design and (2) approval of the manufacturer. Although the FAA had an office in Brussels and could perform its inspections and grant its approval without too much difficulty, BMW would have preferred to deal with PFL, the German counterpart of the FAA. BMW had heard that this had been done in other situations, and it felt that PFL could at least have been asked to certify the manufacture of the seats and stands because the FAA had already certified the design.

In submitting its bid, BMW had been required to submit a breakdown of its price as shown in Figure 1. The contract included a clause regarding the cost control and accounting procedures. These procedures at BMW had also been checked by the Kellering review team before the contract was awarded, and it appeared that they followed the generally accepted U.S. concepts about accounting methods, although there were certain differences reflecting European practice. To ensure that Kellering could obtain experience in German accounting methods, Kellering had included a clause in the contract giving it the right to audit BMW's books where they pertained to the contract. Commenting on the bid requirements for a cost breakdown and for the audit, Mr. von Halle said, "We would not have accepted such clauses from anyone but Kellering. We have great respect for them and we were anxious to do business with them." Although BMW had been audited frequently in the past by FRG, such audits were always associated with "cost-plus" contracts. Mr. von Halle did not think such an audit was either necessary or justified on a fixed price contract.

As soon as the contract went into effect, BMW began to receive the necessary drawings, specifications, manuals, and documentation from Kellering. Although BMW had had previous experience on its NATO contracts in dealing with United States firms, the adaptation phase still had its difficulties. Mr. von Halle said, "Any changeover, even from one United States manufacturer to another, is difficult. This is especially true if the changeover involves differences in language and measuring system."

The translation aspects were particularly difficult for BMW. Since only about 20 persons in the company spoke English (some very limited), it was desirable that all documents be translated into German. In Anderbach, BMW did not have ready access to outside translation facilities that were available in larger cities. Furthermore the type of translation involved did not appear to justify permanent "expert" translators who could command substantially more in salary than a technician with merely a knowledge of English. Some 1,500 pages of text were to be translated at a rate of about 2 to 4 pages per hour. This work was greatly reduced, however, by published translations that were available, such as those covering many United States military specifications. In addition the Kellering engineers in Germany were available to assist with the translating of special technical terms. More important than the *cost* of translation was the *time lag* involved. If a particular piece of information was immediately needed and if that information had never been translated, it might take several hours to make the translation and get the information to production personnel. This lost time could delay the schedule by as much as a full day.

Drawings were received from Kellering in the form of a transparency for each plan. BMW entered the German translation directly onto the transparency, side by side with the original English wording, including the metric equivalents for the imperial units of measure. Thus, below a dimension shown in inches would be the equivlent dimension in centimeters. The transparency was then used to reproduce the necessary blueprints or black-and-white prints for shop use.

The problem of translating dimensions from the imperial system to metric system and vice versa was generally a minor one. BMW had, from its previous work, a large supply of gauges and tools based on the decimal inch, and the company's workers were largely familiar with this system. Although all dimensions on the drawings were given in both centimeters and decimal inches, BMW did most of its work in decimal inches.

Another problem was the cross-referencing of the various parts on a drawing. In many cases BMW engineers found the Kellering system of cross-referencing complex and confusing. Furthermore, after tracing a particular part number back through the system to its original drawing, BMW engineers on several occasions found that Kellering had not sent the required detailed drawings. Communicating this back to the United States and getting the required drawings could consume several weeks. The engineering staff of BMW felt that all cross-referenced detail drawings pertaining to the contract should have been assembled in the United States and sent, as a complete set, to Germany. They felt that the delay in receiving some drawings had a serious effect on the production schedule.

Besides having to identify cross-references BMW also had to deal with changes and modifications. Internal procedures for dealing with changes had been established for the various NATO contracts on which they had worked previously. There were new problems, however, with *modifications.* Unlike changes, these did not alter the basic drawing but introduced a minor modification for only a few units to suit one particular customer of Kellering. BMW was still receiving modifications eight weeks beyond the promised cut off date for units that were to be delivered in four months, and this created serious production problems.

Another problem area involved approved sources of supply for purchased parts and materials. During the final negotiations it was clear to BMW that all purchasing would have to be done in strict conformity to the specifications required by Kellering. BMW understood, however, that it could use any supplier who could certify that its material was in accordance with the required specifications. On the basis of this understanding, BMW purchased some special control cable from a well-known French company that supplied the European aircraft industry.

This order suggested new sales possibilities to the French company. It had its U.S. representative contact the buyer at Kellering headquarters on the basis that, if it could provide parts for Kellering through BMW, it should also be able to sell directly to Kellering for other purposes. The Kellering buyer who discussed the matter with the French representative immediately checked the Kellering-approved list of suppliers and was surprised to find that the French company was not on the list. The buyer then sent a telegram to BMW advising that the French cable could not be used on the Kellering contract. From this incident BMW learned that it could only purchase from suppliers who were previously approved by Kellering. The only suppliers that were approved were located in the United States. The French company requested Kellering to add it to Kellering's approved list of suppliers. The Kellering buyers responded that it already had two suppliers in the United States that it felt were sufficient because the special cable was purchased in small quantities. To send an inspection team to France to certify the French company could not be economically justified.

BMW felt that some of its purchasing problems could be avoided if Kellering would remove its restriction requiring the use of specified U.S. sources and would permit the use of European suppliers and the corresponding European specifications. Many equivalent parts were available in almost identical form from competent European sources. BMW felt that it did not yet have enough business in the United States to establish a permanent U.S. representative for its U.S. purchases. Most U.S. suppliers were not export oriented and increased their prices to overseas customers. The customers also had to bear the extra cost of shipment, duties, and insurance. Even at the higher prices many U.S. firms were still not interested in overseas customers because of the unfamiliar procedures that were encountered. Thus BMW was forced in many cases to depend on its freight forwarders to handle many administrative details that suppliers might refuse to do. Mr. von Halle, underlining the importance of the freight forwarder, asserted that a skillful and cooperative freight forwarder was a necessity to purchase from and ship to U.S. firms.

An example of a purchasing problem that arose was that of obtaining special tubing of an odd shape that was required by the FAA specification. This tubing was available only in the United States from a single supplier. BMW had great difficulty locating and contacting the supplier, which it did without help from Kellering. Even then, the tubing did not exactly meet the precise specifications, though further investigation revealed that it was acceptable to Kellering. Later BMW learned that the Kellering buyer would have been glad to assist if he had been notified of BMW's problem. Mr. von Halle's response was "Kellering didn't clearly advise us at the beginning that they would help us, and anyway we had to show them that we were capable of independently doing our own job."

BMW management was very concerned about the problems of drawing interpretation and sources of supply because of the effect on delivery. If additional Kellering subcontracts were to be obtained, management believed that it had to perform well on the present one. If necessary, BMW was prepared to reduce the six to eight weeks' delivery required by ocean and rail transport and to ship the finished units to the United States by air at its expense.

BMW management felt that its relationship with Kellering was generally satisfactory, but it would have preferred a greater degree of mutuality. Mr. von Halle recognized the reasons for using English exclusively in BMW's dealings with Kellering, but he would have appreciated some use of German in informal discussions. With most other foreign customers, correspondence was carried on in the language of the customer, but usually some German was used in personal negotiations. With French customers it was normal practice for all correspondence to be sent and received in both German and French. Although it was obvious to the Kellering people that the contract was being performed by a German firm, there was almost no one at Kellering who could or would use German.

This was reflected in Kellering's communications with BMW. Almost all communications were written in English that required about four days' transit time by air mail and three weeks' time by surface mail. Kellering had a sales office in Paris with a direct telex connection to its United States headquarters. On a few occasions BMW sent telexes through the Paris office for important matters that necessitated immediate response. Except for one or two occasions the telephone was not used, even for pressing problems when the expense could have been justified.

Immediately after Mr. von Halle's trip to the United States after the contract was awarded, there was little face-to-face contact between the two firms except for occasional visits from the Kellering engineers in Germany.

As the contract progressed Mr. von Halle was concerned that his views and his problems were not completely understood by Kellering management. Finally, three months after the contract award, BMW sent one of its engineers to the Kellering headquarters to review technical problems on the drawings and to clarify some matters that were very difficult to translate. Six months after the contract award, Tim Lester, the Kellering buyer responsible for the BMW contract, visited Anderbach for a general review of the situation. One month later he was followed by Carl Gothel who came as the resident inspector. In the following month, two executives from BMW stopped off at the Kellering headquarters while on other business to the United States and were able to clarify some technical questions and special problems.

## QUALITY CONTROL PROCEDURES AND PROBLEMS

The quality control department at Kellering was completely independent of other functional departments and, through its own line organization, reported directly to the president. It was the policy of this department to provide a resident inspector at the plant of those suppliers who had large and complicated contracts that required inspection during the manufacturing process. In this way the department was able to catch many errors during manufacture and thus to save the cost and time of shipping parts back to the supplier if they were not satisfactory. In addition to handling quality control matters, the resident inspector was to assist the subcontractor with other activities such as materials, engineering, production planning, manufacturing processes, and so on. He was not, however, involved in contract negotiations as such, although he was aware of the general terms of the contract.

The department had always planned to send a representative to BMW at the proper time. Gothel arrived at BMW as the resident inspector six weeks prior to the scheduled first shipment. Gothel's arrival, however, was unexpected by most of the BMW executives, and for several weeks he was merely greeted courteously but largely ignored by the plant personnel. But after he made it known that he planned to reject the first units because of defects, the local BMW quality control department members complained and resisted for the following reasons:

1. Gothel's interpretation of the specifications was only one point of view, and there was no need for BMW to comply with his interpretation when it could read the same specification and arrive at a different interpretation.
2. His recommendations were contrary to BMW's previous procedures.
3. He required records to be kept that were unnecessary.
4. His recommendations and requests involved additional costs that were not provided for in the original estimate.
5. The additional record keeping and inspection procedures that were re-

quested required a larger work force, and the quality control department did not have sufficient people with the ability needed to comply with Gothel's recommendations.

6. None of the other customers of BMW required such quality control procedures, and Gothel's request involved unnecessary special favors for only Kellering's benefit.

Gothel based his activities on a document entitled "Quality Control Requirements for Kellering Suppliers," which established basic policies and was incorporated as a part of the contract with BMW. Figure 2 contains excerpts from this document. He also had a supplementary document, "Operating Instructions Manual for Resident QC Inspectors," of 27 pages, which was largely concerned with the manner of making a survey of the subcontractors' QC procedures to properly qualify the supplier in compliance with the contract.

## FIGURE 2

### Excerpts from Quality Control Requirements for Kellering Suppliers

Section 1: General

1.1 Policy

The contractual obligations of the Kellering Company, and the highly competitive and technical nature of the industry, cause quality control requirements to assume a most vital role. The proportion of the Kellering product fabricated by suppliers, the greater complexity of many of such components, and the essentially high level of reliability make it impractical or impossible to adequately assure product quality by inspections and controls at Kellering plants alone.

To assure product quality, appropriate inspections must be made, controls initiated, and/or data gathered for each phase of the life cycle of the product, from the refining and compounding of raw materials to customer service.

Therefore, because Kellering is obligated to assure the overall quality of the end product, including its service reliability, Kellering must verify that each supplier of material going into the end product is aware of, is enforcing, and is recording accomplishment of adequate quality controls.

This requires that all work performed pursuant to a Kellering purchase order shall be subject to inspection, surveillance, and test and quality control audit by Kellering at all reasonable times, including the period of performance, and at all places, including the plant or plants of the supplier or any of its suppliers engaged in the performance of work to fulfill the Kellering purchase order.

. . .

FIGURE 2 (continued)

Section 2: Publication of Requirements

2.1 Procedures
    The supplier shall establish and maintain written procedures defining the supplier's quality control system. These procedures shall be subject to the right of disapproval by Kellering.
    A. Management responsibility for the quality control function will be set forth on the supplier's organization chart. The responsibility for the quality control function will be so placed that schedules and cost will not compromise quality.

. . .

Section 3: Records and Stamps

3.1 Records
    Adequate records of inspection and tests performed under the responsibility of the supplier shall be maintained.

. . .

Section 4: Facilities

4.1 Measurement and Test Equipment
    All test and measurement equipment used to check product components and systems, to check materials that are used in a product, or to check control of the processing of a product shall be checked against a standard that has greater accuracy. The required accuracy of shop test and measurement equipment is the accuracy required to evaluate the most precise tolerances of any item required to be checked by the equipment. The standards against which test and measurement equipment is periodically checked shall have their accuracy verified directly by or through a precise comparison with legal standards traceable to the National Bureau of Standards.

. . .

Section 5: Procurement Control

5.1 Procurement by the Supplier
    The supplier shall assume the responsibility for the quality of all purchased materials, articles, and services. This responsibility includes:
    A. Selection of qualified procurement sources.

. . .

Section 6: Process Control

. . .

Section 7: Product Control

. . .

Section 8: Functional Tests

. . .

FIGURE 2 (continued)

Section 9: Special Procedures

9.1 Discrepancy Controls
The quality control procedures will assure that nonconforming materials, tools, or test equipment will be identified as discrepant and segregated and reviewed for disposition.
9.1.2 Reliability
9.2 Single Standard Quality Control
9.3 Statistical Quality Control
9.4 Training
9.5 Quality Control Audit Program
The supplier shall audit the adequacy of quality program procedures, inspections, tests, process controls, and certifications performed in each area on a timely basis. The audit shall be performed by an impartial team familiar with written procedures and standards applicable to the areas being audited, but not having specific line responsibilities in those areas.

The audit shall include examination of all quality operations and documentation, comparison with established requirements, notification of required corrective action, and follow-up to assess results of corrective action. An example of an examination of an inspection operation would include, but not be limited to:

A. A reinspection of work accepted by the inspectors in the areas.
B. An investigation of the availability of all required documents.
C. A determination of the familiarity of personnel concerned with required documents.
D. A review of failure analysis and corrective action taken.
E. An evaluation of the adequacy of acceptance and rejection documents.

Gothel commented on his observations and problems at BMW.

"I have had a hard time trying to find direct answers to who does what. They have an organization chart, alright (see Figure 3), but several people seem to be doing the same job; on the other hand, for some problems I can find no one who accepts responsibility. Many times my questions merely get a shrug of the shoulder answer.

"The production manager is a very capable man but he has five major programs under his jurisdiction, only one of which is the Kellering project, and he cannot give it sufficient attention. I feel there is a serious 'management gap' at the middle level. Part of the trouble is that too many decisions must be made at the top level. Lower-level people have a great deal of trouble getting prompt decisions about their problems — many of which could have been delegated to a lower level. There is not enough information filtering down from the top management regarding basic policy, terms of the

## FIGURE 3

### Bayerische Maschinen Werke Organization Chart

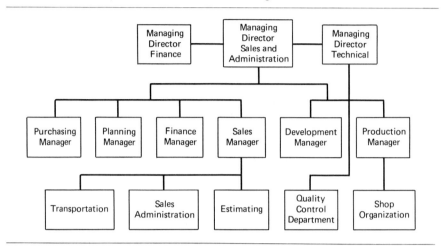

contract, relationships with customers, and other types of information that would help coordinate the job. At the same time, they don't give the shop much information on how to do a job — they just throw the blueprints into the shop and let the workers figure out what to do. If some materials or parts are missing the workers are just hung up because no special group is assigned to expedite deliveries.

"It's also very difficult for lower-level people to get their problems passed up the line. For example, the most trivial kind of capital expenditure has to be approved at top levels, and usually it is not accepted if it was not entered in the capital budget that may have been made a long time ago. As a result, new problems turn up that require minor tools or equipment, but these cannot be quickly purchased. This causes serious production delays, or the shop finds a way to get around the problem by an expensive method that does not require the tools or equipment.

"We had a mix-up because of this and because of language misunderstanding. The throttle handles and reversing levers on the control stand have to be tested for the torque required to move them. The test specifications call for the use of a precision scale. At home this means the use of a measuring device that has been certified as to its accuracy. Here they understood 'precision scale' to mean a simple spring scale, and I found them using a scale for weighing fish to run the test. Obviously this was unsatisfactory. I insisted they get a proper device. Then the question was raised when they could buy it because it was not allowed for in the budget, and getting approval for this 'capital expenditure' would involve a substantial delay. After a lot of pressure on my part they finally borrowed a satisfactory precision scale that was certified for accuracy from another aircraft company.

"I have to keep pushing them to use some imagination when they run into an unexpected problem. Let me give you an example. On one of the seat drawings the length specified for a few screws was too short. It was an engineering oversight. At home the mechanic would go to an open bin and get longer screws that would have enough threads to properly hold the nuts. Here they did not have the extra-length screws and work on the job stopped because no one knew what to do. Finally they requested the purchasing department to buy longer screws. Because of the specifications, these screws had to be purchased in the United States, and it would take at least six weeks to get delivery. That's the way they left it. When I heard about it I blew my top because this meant that the first deliveries would be delayed another six weeks beyond the current schedule, which was already late. I insisted that they get the screws right now, somehow! Finally, at my suggestion, they contacted Lufthansa and found that they could get the few screws that were needed from the airline's maintenance stores.

"One of my biggest problems is to get them to put things down in writing. For example, when a part is rejected by their inspector, it is usually done on a verbal basis and the part is thrown in the junk pile. Once in a while it even gets pulled out of the junk pile and slipped back into production. Our quality control policy manual requires them to tag every rejection with a full explanation so that we can retrace problems and get the correction made at the proper place. This sometimes means changing shop procedure or even going all the way back to get a change in the drawing. In order to control these rejected parts they are supposed to have a locked rejection cage to provide secure segregation of bad parts. This cage requirement is in the policy manual and everyone here says they are going to set it up, but so far there is no cage.

"The inspectors here seem to have great faith in what other people say is okay. They have to learn to check everything. For example, on a special control knob for the stand the inspectors assumed that the dimensions were okay because the vendor stated the part was made in accordance with the specifications. They didn't even make a first part inspection, let alone check all of the shipment. Later I found that the part did not fit properly and had to reject it.

"Although the shop people here have had a great deal of experience in working on pre-jet aircraft parts, they have not quite grasped the jet-age situation. For example, a minor gouge on a forging is okay for planes flying at 200 miles an hour. But in a 600-mile-per-hour plane minor scratches and gouges can cause concentrated stresses that may result in failure. This concept has not yet been fully recognized here. They also leave too much to the worker to decide on how to make this part. They need a great many more detailed process specifications to explain to the worker exactly how each operation should be done. These fellows complain badly when I insist on this because they say they are expert mechanics. I agree, but they don't understand the new situation.

"Let me explain what I want to avoid. On my previous job I checked a landing gear part that was a forging and failed in service, causing a great deal of havoc. After much investigation, we traced the error to a worker who had drilled a hole in the forging. He used a dull drill and exceeded the feed speed stated in the process specifications. Because of the dull drill, the inside of the hole had minor scratches, and the fast speed caused the part to overheat around the hole during drilling. In use, under great stress, vibration and severe weather conditions, the scratches in the hole allowed some corrosion to begin, and the extra heat from the drilling had changed the crystalline structure so that the corrosion cracks rapidly developed through the part, like a hot knife going through butter. This minor mistake on the part of the mechanic could have jeopardized a $25-million airplane and the lives of more than 200 people.

"The buyer at Kellering has to start at the negotiating table to stress the need for quality and precise adherence to process specifications. Most buyers don't fully understand this and do an inadequate job of conditioning the vendor. The buyer tells the vendor he has to provide good quality in accordance with the specifications. The vendor says yes, but nobody really understands what this means. It is bad enough in the States, but over here the problem is really fierce.

"They have very good people here. Most of their mechanics have been through a long apprentice program. They are better trained and can do a larger variety of jobs than most of the mechanics back home. As a result they do not place so much importance on inspection because they depend on the mechanic to do the job right in the first place. The inspectors and quality control people are paid less than the mechanics; hence they get less effective people to do this work than they should have. Also, because the inspectors are paid less than the mechanics, they hesitate to reject parts or complain about quality. With these old habit patterns in quality control, the inspectors cannot understand why I insist on so many details, and this forms a mental handicap that prevents improvement. I have many fights here with the people, but now they are beginning to understand what I want and why, and they are starting to comply with the requirements in the policy manual.

"This problem of poor communications up the line of command is partially due to too much respect for authority and social position. For example, one of the top executives here was going back to the Kellering headquarters for a meeting. BMW needed a small part very badly that was readily available at Kellering spares pool stores. The local shop people here refused to ask him to get the items and bring it back in his pocket because they felt he was too high an executive to help them.

"I suppose the problems here are the same as with any new subcontractor in the United States who is not completely familiar with our requirements and system. Here, of course, we have the additional problem of language translation. Why didn't buyers at Kellering expect and prepare for these problems?"

Gothel was about 35 years of age. He was selected for the BMW job because of his experience, personality, and German background. As a child he had learned German from his parents, although he had not used it during his adult life to any extent. Upon graduating from high school he joined the U.S. Air Force. After receiving his basic training, he advanced to flight engineer and had extensive experience as a flight crew member. Later he became an instructor in maintenance and emergency procedures. After five years in the Air Force, he joined the Kellering Company and was assigned to the pre-flight quality control department. Here he was involved with final inspection procedures of completed airplanes prior to their first test flight. After one year in this assignment, he was moved to the material review department where he investigated material failures and the processing of material that did not conform to specifications. As a result of the care he displayed in this job, after two years he was advanced to work in the customer service department where he remained for the next seven years prior to his assignment at BMW. In the customer service department he processed complaints from customers under contract warranties and became very much aware of how minor and trivial errors in the manufacture and maintenance of airplanes could create serious problems. For example, he was involved in a situation in which scratches on highly stressed parts had caused serious failures. He was also aware of a service mechanic's having connected the control surface cables backward, which caused a plane crash with a serious loss of life.

After accepting his new assignment to BMW, Gothel received what was considered to be an adequate amount of indoctrination regarding his new job, was given an airplane ticket and a letter of introduction, and was sent off to Anderbach.

Upon his arrival at the Nuremberg airport, he discovered that his language facility was more limited than he had realized. Because of an unfortunate mix-up he was not met at the airport by the local representative of Kellering who had been assigned to meet him. After some trouble with the local telephone and with making himself understood by a taxi driver, he managed to get to the railroad station and took a train to Anderbach where he arranged to stay at a hotel.

Two weeks later his wife and eight-year-old daughter arrived from the United States. They did not speak German. Since there was no English-speaking school in Anderbach for his daughter, the family decided to move to Endigen where such a school was available because of several large U.S. military bases located in the vicinity. This required Gothel to commute each day by railroad between Endigen and Anderbach, a trip of approximately 45 minutes each way. Endigen was an old community with a population of about 125,000, but it had modern facilities and many shops for English-speaking customers.

Mrs. Gothel had great trouble learning German and, for a time, stopped taking lessons. At first she only traded at those shops and stores where the sales people spoke English. Gothel commented that "as a result, we always paid the highest prices." Their language limitation also restricted social contacts with local people, but it caused the family to be closely drawn together. They did find a comfortable apartment from a "For Rent" listing at the local U.S. army base. They paid, however, a substantially higher rental than would have been charged to a native German. This appeared to be the only reason that local landlords rented apartments to Americans. Fortunately, their landlord spoke English, and they developed a very pleasant relationship with him and his wife. After several months in their new location, Mrs. Gothel's ability to speak German improved, and she became comfortable with shopkeepers and neighbors.

The quality control problem at BMW was repeatedly called to the attention of the Kellering management by means of weekly reports that Gothel sent back. Figures 4 and 6 are excerpts from some of these reports. As a result, the Kellering management decided to make an independent check and sent Jan Parker from the Kellering NATO team to check on the "Gothel" problem. The report of his short visit is included as Figure 5. He also commented that he could understand why BMW had troubles with the drawings. For example, Kellering's drawings had a large number of "flag" notes that were uncommon with many other companies. In addition, the drawings for electrical cables had a special complex system for designating wires, which was completely new to BMW. Most of the important drawings got to BMW on time, but a few dribbled in late. These late drawings, however, caused a great deal of trouble because they were difficult to identify and to determine if they were really needed.

## FIGURE 4

Activity Report: Observations and Thoughts Arising During QC Survey[1]

---

Observations and thoughts that occur during the QC survey.

During disucssions with the managing director, the impression is conveyed that there is a great interest in obtaining and holding Kellering Company business. This establishes the fact that the intent to attempt to comply with our policy manual exists, however, at this point the

---

[1]Written by Gothel three months after his arrival at BMW.

FIGURE 4 (continued)

intent to comply seems to end in the form of the resistance or non-development of the Quality Control department. The thought seems to be "let's operate on a shoestring," which connotes to me that the Quality Control department does not have the stature that it has in the USA.

The Quality Control inspectors are not paid as high as the work force so there is a continual problem in obtaining good QC people. It would appear at this point desirable to strengthen the QC department by an increase in wages which would attract more people, and then a selection of the best candidates could be made. This kind of an action is apparently not in the picture because the one QC man who is the real spark plug for the stand production has not been advanced in wages. Whether this situation is a company policy or QC department policy I have not determined.

Another disturbing thought is the fact that aircraft production is under a railroad man and not under an aircraft man. The thought of an aircraft QC man reporting to a railroad man suggests the possibility of diluted standards and of course the lack of aircraft guidance at that level.

Another disturbing line of reasoning put forth by some people in the QC organization is that "Kellering must consider that BMW has other contracts also and that Kellering cannot expect special attention," which is quite a distorted line of reasoning. It has to be recalled that we expect only what is required by the basic purchase agreement, part of which of course is an adequate QC organization. An adequate QC organization cannot be construed as "special attention" in any form.

It is my personal opinion that the QC organization can be termed as being of the 'old school' that is not readily receptive to the jet age requirements. To date there has been very little QC response to organizing along the lines of our policies.

The argument that BMW did not receive the Kellering QC policy manual until two months ago, rather than during the initial contract

FIGURE 4 (continued)

negotiation, has in all probability some merit, however, it appears to
be an excuse of convenience. Aircraft production in general, regardless
of who it is for, has certain basic guides to work to. These guides,
of course, are the drawings and all the related specifications that are
called for by the drawings. Additional requirements for a QC department
are adequate records of the work accomplished through the medium of inspection operating procedures and rejection and rework systems, all of
which can be termed as 'standard QC tools'. These standard QC tools
have not existed.

The proposed solution to the entire problem is for high level
management to direct the BMW QC organization to begin compliance with
our policy manual.

Gothel

# FIGURE 5
## Report by Parker on BMW visit[1]

William Morrissey
International Office
Kellering Headquarters

Subject:  Your TWX re: Gothel Problem

Bill:

At your request, I drove up to Anderbach yesterday to

a) Familiarize myself with the facility as a potentially
   continuing Kellering subcontractor and

b) to investigate the "Gothel problem".

I had considerable discussion with Gothel and a German who is part of
the Q.C. organization and is assigned to work with Gothel, sort of as
his opposite number.  I also toured the plant with them and finally,
had about a half hour disucssion with von Halle.

I came away with the following findings and conclusions:

1.  Findings

a)  BMW had to start production of the seats and flight control
    stands in question before it had access to any translations of

[1]This memorandum was written six months after Gothel arrived at BMW.

42

FIGURE 5 (continued)

Kellering manufacturing and inspection process standards.

b) The job of translating these standards is now being accomplished at a rapid pace.

c) BMW had to start work on the flight control stands working
from Kellering detailed final assembly and part drawings which
are so different from comparable German blueprints, that the
average German production worker has to have quite a lot of
exposure before he can really "read" them.

d) The Germans do not traditionally keep Q.C. records that are
remotely comparable, quality- and quanitywise, to ours.

e) Inspection processes employed routinely at BMW for production of aeroplane seat category hardware are generally not
yet comparable to what we would require of a vendor in the
U.S.

f) The inspection processes identified above are improving
quickly as Gothel continues to identify the necessary requirements for improvement.

g) The first seat category hardware presented to Gothel for
"buy-off" was definitely characterized by deficiencies that
would have caused rejection at Kellering shops.
Examples:

    1) Nuts on bolts without washers.

    2) Faulty rivets.

    3) Faulty machining, etc.

h) BMW is doing repair work on FRG Luftwaffe airframe structures
that would compare favorable with similar work done in the U.S.

i) Gothel has, per copies of memos to the BMW workforce managers,
demonstrated considerable understanding of their problems and
has stretched application of our standards as far as any Q.C.
supervisor in Kellering would ever back him up.

j) BMW people felt at first that Gothel was nitpicking and over-
doing the Q.C. bit.

k) Gothel felt at first that BMW was so far behind us, Q.C.-wise,
that they would just never be able to "hack it".

FIGURE 5 (continued)

1) BMW no longer feels that Gothel is exaggerating the Q.C. bit.

m) Gothel is convinced now that BMW is making good progress and will soon be capable of passing the "Source Certification Inspection" that they have not yet been subjected to but will ,ultimately have to pass to be able to continue on as a supplier to Kellering.

II. Conclusions

a) The "Gothel Problem" stemmed essentially from:

1) Inadequate time for proper BMW preparation and indoctrination before initiation of production.

2) Basic initial differences between Kellering and BMW approach to Q.C.

3) BMW standards for production of something like "seat" hardware being initially admittedly lower than minimum Kellering quality requirements.

4) Naturally, the language problem.

b) The "Gothel Problem" has essentially gone away because:

1) Gothel has been able to get across to BMW that there are certain minimum standards that he has to enforce without hopelessly alienating them.

2) BMW wants more Kellering business and has realized now that part of getting it is learning to live with a "Gothel".

3) The overall situation is improving very rapidly.

4) To have to go through a "Gothel Problem" cycle in breaking in a new foreign vendor source is to be expected.

5) BMW was probably "lucky" in drawing a Q.C. inspector who has been as "understanding" as Gothel has apparently been.

III. Actions

a) I think I was able to help ease the situation further by:

1) Commending Gothel for demonstrating the 'understanding' that he has to date and encouraging him to continue in that vein.

FIGURE 5 (continued)

He now feels that he is not quite so isolated and he
is more confident in being on his own.

2) Explaining better to the BMW people that Gothel is only
the first stage in a screening operation that goes on
until Kellering has, in fact, delivered the assembled
aeroplane to a customer, .....that Gothel could do them
more harm in the long run by backing off from standards
to a degree that he knows would not be 'bought' than
by insisting that they meet his interpretation of Kellering standards.

Finally I received a call from Gothel a few minutes ago to tell
me that the managing director for production came to his office yesterday afternoon after I left and made a very impressive speech to him to
the effect that BMW is in complete sympathy with Kellering Q.C. standards and intends to do anything and everything Gothel requires to be
able to routinely meet those standards.

Sincerely,

Jan Parker

(Note: This memorandum was written six
months after Gothel arrived
at BMW.)

---

# FIGURE 6

## Activity Report[1]

Control Stands

The first control stand has been completed and things were really
humming this week. Every member of the BMW organization, from the
Director on down felt that they had to be on the scene, and I am not
sure whether they became part of the problem or part of the solution.

---

[1]Written by Gothel eight months after his arrival at BMW.

FIGURE 6 (continued)

At the last minute, the BMW QC department decided that they could not come up with a satisfactory inspection package, so I had to make up one. Now that a sample one exists, it can serve as a pattern for the future ones.

The first stand appeared to be a pretty good item, considering everything. The proof of the thing, of course, will be the acceptance by Kellering Receiving Inspection and the actual installation into the airplane. I'd appreciate any and all comments on the thing in order to initiate any correction that would be required. I keep wondering what I have overlooked. There are times when a person cannot see the forest for the trees when you are very close to a thing.

Planning

The response to my request for a more complete planning package has been most gratifying. The planning package that is emerging is quite complete and in detail. The planning portion of the survey will receive a 'satisfactory' classification.

The department is absorbing the Kellering way very readily.

Quality Control

I am of the opinion that as the result of meetings between the QC people and myself, I am on the verge of a break-through. It appears that I have finally gotten their attention and there are indications that compliance with our policies is forthcoming. I realize that 100% compliance with it is not a reality, however, I'm going to shoot for the moon. The possibility of some new QC people who will be more effective than the present ones appears to be in the formation process.

Lufthansa three seat combination

I have learned Lufthansa has contacted an Engineering organization to produce a three seat combination for use in their new airplanes. The seat will weigh about 10 to 12 pounds less than the seat that Kellering uses, and its reclining feature is based on a sliding sitting platform rather than the conventional tilting back

**46**

FIGURE 6 (continued)

type. The prototype seat has a fairly clean look about it. I
have no idea as to who will manufacture it, to what specifications,
and where it will be installed.

Failures of NATO Fighter Plane

The failures that have plagued the NATO fighter airplanes produced
on a joint basis by several companies in Europe, appear to have ended.
I believe the last one has been taken out of active service and that,
according to the newspaper, is the predicted end of the thing. Many
implications are flying back and forth between the military and poli-
ticians.  One of the accusations by the military is that they were forced
to buy the airplane under political pressure and some of the material
purchased was defective.  It is not possible to ferret out just what
was defective, although steel strengths are being discussed.  There
existed an interchangeability problem also.  The military selected a
number of airplanes at random and proceeded to remove and attempt to
interchange the more major components.  The test revealed that interchangeability between components manufactured in different countries
was not controlled very well.

The above situation alerts me to watch for anything and everything in European production.

Gothel

Parker stated that "I feel one of the real problems here is that they have an organization that is mixed up in too many different kinds of work. I don't like aircraft work being done with railroad work and truck trailer work, even if they are in physically separate facilities. Each type of work requires the mechanics to have a certain mental approach to the production methods, and I think that it is easy for the workers to get confused when they are switched back and forth between rough railroad car work and precise aircraft work.

"It is also possible that the QC requirements were overstressed. Rather than pursue a practical and responsible approach, it is easy to reject a part in case of doubt."

Hans Dobrin, the financial officer for BMW, commented on the problem. "I'm not a technical person myself, but I think I know a little bit about the problem. The top management here is very anxious to follow all of the Kellering requirements, but the problem is with the lower-level people. You must appreciate that our mechanics all have a long apprentice background and they feel that they know how to do things without detailed process specifications. In fact, they are insulted when you tell them how to do their job.

"The Kellering drawings had many errors, even though they were minor ones. The layout is relatively poor compared to the beautiful draftmanship on most German drawings, and many drawings were late. As a result, some of the plant people lost confidence in the precise requirements and felt that it was not absolutely necessary to follow what, to them, seemed to be unnecessary detail in the specifications.

"Also many of the people don't fully understand what Gothel is driving at. They feel he is going in opposite directions at the same time. On one hand he claims that the shop people don't show enough initiative and imagination in solving their problems, as illustrated by the difficulty with the short screws and the fish scale. On the other hand, he claims they are too independent because they won't precisely follow detailed specifications that they believe are unnecessarily restrictive. You Americans have to make up your mind what you are really complaining about and what you want us to do. Why doesn't Kellering just tell us what it wants and leave us alone to do the job?"

The first shipment of observer seats was ready to ship eight weeks late, and the first control stand was ready six weeks late. The responsibility for late delivery clearly belonged to BMW, according to Tim Lester, the buyer at Kellering; nevertheless, the items were urgently needed, and BMW was authorized to make these first shipments by air to save the time that surface transportation would require. Kellering agreed to pay for the extra air-freight charges. The observer seats were accepted by the Kellering quality control department.

## FOLLOW-ON CONTRACT

Just after the shipment of the first control stand was made, but before the unit had passed final inspection at the Kellering plant, Mr. von Halle received an inquiry from Kellering inviting him to negotiate for a follow-on order for additional control stands and observer seats. He now faced the necessity to make an effective assessment of past costs and future expectations.

Cost accounting details were generally available about 45 days after the end of a month. When available, the data were reasonably accurate regarding direct labor costs for the assembly of each unit that was completed and the lot costs of parts that were fabricated awaiting assembly. The total accumulated project labor-hours at the end of the monthly accounting period was also known, but there was no formal method of determining the percentage of completion of work in progress.

Because Mr. von Halle was familiar with improvement curve theory, he expected the cost per unit to be quite high at the beginning of the contract but to rapidly decrease as work progressed. The problem was how to interpret the high cost of the first few units that were delivered and how to project future costs using the improvement curve.

Mr. von Halle's latest cost data included most of the information regarding the first shipment of seats, but it contained only partial information about the stands. After carefully reviewing the limited accounting figures that he had available and discussing the project with various supervisors and other executives, Mr. von Halle came to the tentative conclusion that the observer seat project was progressing satisfactorily from a cost point of view but that the control stand project costs appeared to be running substantially above expectations. He now felt that, at the time of preparing the bids, BMW did not have enough drawings and specifications to fully understand the project. In addition, some of the documents that were on hand had not been translated and thus were not considered at the time of bidding. The firm also underestimated the cost of obtaining parts from the United States and the airfreight charges for expediting delivery to BMW.

From the limited data he had available, Mr. von Halle had to decide what to do about his present contract and how to react to the invitation to negotiate for additional quantities of seats and stands.

The Kellering buyer had also requested firm fixed costs for transportation and insurance and had requested that the BMW bid include allowances for the following clauses that were to be part of the contract. The final contract was written up in U.S. dollars.

*Observer Seat Engineering Change Allowance*

The prices include the total cost effect of all future engineering (planning and scheduling, production, rework, tooling, and termination and obsolescence costs created by engineering changes) that may exceed the statement of work hereunder, the total price of which is less than $100 per change per shipset or less than $8,000 per change for the entire contract, whichever is first exceeded.

*Control Stand Engineering Change Allowance*

The price shall include all engineering, planning and scheduling, production, rework, tooling, and termination and obsolescence costs created by engineering changes, that may exceed the statement of work hereunder, the total price of which is less than $450 per change per shipset or less than $30,000 per change for the entire contract, whichever is first exceeded.

The preceding dollar figures are applicable to price increases only. Changes exceeding the limitation cited will be negotiated separately by the parties.

## DISCUSSION QUESTIONS

1. From BMW's point of view, what kind of policy should Hans von Halle recommend regarding future U.S. aerospace subcontracts?
2. Why should Kellering seek overseas suppliers?
3. What do you think of the bid preparation shown as Figure 1? Should escalation be allowed?
4. Did BMW need special treatment from the Kellering procurement department? If so, what kind?
5. Should BMW have accepted the cost audit on their fixed price contract?
6. How much of the "language problem" should Kellering have assumed?
7. What factors need to be considered regarding
   a. drawing cross-references
   b. design changes
   c. modifications
   d. late information
   e. parts procurement and certification of U.S. versus European suppliers
8. How do you view Gothel's relationship with BMW?
9. How could Gothel's indoctrination have been improved?
10. How serious is the fact that BMW works on railroad cars, truck bodies, and presses in addition to aircraft?
11. Parker suggests that QC requirements were overstressed. What do you think?
12. Dobrin says "leave us alone." Would this be desirable?
13. How do you interpret the data on comparative Germany and U.S. wages, exchange rates, and productivity?
14. How should von Halle proceed to evaluate production performance for adequate monitoring of the contract on an ongoing basis?

# Belnap Company

With an upturn in economic outlook, new orders received or anticipated by the marketing department of the Belnap Company had resulted in a tentative manufacturing schedule that could require a doubling of employees during the next year. Donald Cadin, director of manufacturing, was attempting to anticipate and respond to the pressure for expanded production. He wondered whether the significant improvement in performance over the past several years, during which employment levels had been reduced substantially, could continue in a period of rapidly increasing employment levels and expansion of production.

Three years ago Donald Cadin was made director of manufacturing with two main factory units under his direction. The fabrication unit manufactured parts and minor subassemblies. The assembly unit contained subassembly areas, final assembly, testing, and delivery. Approximately 6,000 workers were employed in the two factories. These were directly supported by engineering design, tooling, industrial engineering, manufacturing engineering, production control, industrial relations, finance (cost control), quality control, facilities, and purchasing.

Donald Cadin was a long-time employee. Due to lack of funds he had dropped out of the university in his third year and was employed as a shop employee with Belnap. His pleasant personality and excellent performance had permitted him to move rapidly up the managerial ranks. He was aware that the success of his present position depended on his making significant improvements in the performance of the organizational units under his jurisdiction.

# MOTIVATION THEORIES

Several years ago Cadin had attended a three-week executive management seminar and became aware of the "X" and "Y" theories of motivation. He was aware that in the past theory X had primarily been the approach to motivation used by upper management. This theory was based on the following assumptions regarding workers, particularly in large organizations:

1. Most people do not like to work.
2. Most people desire to avoid responsibility, are not ambitious, and are more comfortable when they are carefully directed.
3. Most workers are unable to be creative or to contribute to correcting problems.
4. Most workers are primarily motivated by money, physical comforts, and provisions for their safety.
5. As a result of these factors, close supervision and frequent coercion of most workers is necessary to obtain effective results.

These assumptions led to the conclusion that problems were caused by line workers and lower-level managers who needed to be pushed to become interested and effective in their jobs.

Cadin, however, set out to restructure his organization to apply theory Y, which was based on a different set of assumptions:

1. Work can be as exciting and interesting as any recreational activity if the environmental conditions are favorable.
2. Organizational and personal goals can be reconciled so that workers strive to achieve both.
3. The ability to solve problems and be creative is a potential characteristic of all workers.
4. Workers can be strongly motivated when attention is given to their social needs, self-esteem, and personal goals.
5. When properly motivated, workers can be self-directed to plan and contribute to solutions for organizational problems.

# IMPROVEMENT STRATEGY

Cadin decided to develop an operational strategy that would focus on theory Y. He felt that the overall company climate was favorable to such a strategy. The president of the company had repeatedly expressed the view that "people are our most important asset."

Cadin felt that improvement in performance could come about as a result of three categories of change: (1) technical factors, (2) worker-controlled factors, and (3) environmental factors beyond worker control.

Technical factors included engineering design changes and equipment or process improvements. In the past some of the following led to reduced cost:

1. Relaxing dimensional tolerances that were not required for safety or performance.
2. Simplifying engineering designs.
3. Increasing machine speeds and torque by use of larger motors on equipment that could accommodate increased loads.
4. Use of numerically controlled machines to reduce setup time and decrease skill required in machining complicated parts.

To achieve these types of improvements, it was necessary that the engineering design group, the industrial engineering office, and shop floor personnel cooperate with each other to maintain technical performance and safety requirements and at the same time reduce production costs.

Improvements from worker-controlled factors depended on individual skills, intelligence, training, mental attitude, and motivation. Cadin hoped that his new program would be particularly effective on the last two items: mental attitude and motivation.

The environmental factors of the organization included all those items that influenced production costs and were outside the control of the "direct labor" factory worker but did not involve design changes. This included availability and quality of tools, availability of parts and supplies, adequacy of instructions and communications, job sequence, job size, ease of accessibility of parts, timeliness of quality inspection, proper scheduling of work, correct shop loading, and other factors that represented "support" for the worker. These environmental factors were not only influenced by the skill with which management dealt with factory operations, but they were influenced by performance of other departments such as production control, store keeping, purchasing, and industrial relations.

Cadin wondered how important each of the three factors was in the production performance. He investigated a number of situations that had involved difficulties and delays and came to his personal conclusion that normal production performance (including expected improvements) was influenced by each factor to the following degree:

| | |
|---|---|
| Technical factors | 25% |
| Worker-controlled factors | 15% |
| Environmental factors | 60% |

These percentages were based on the typical situation in a shop and assumed that workers were expected to and did perform according to theory X.

There were several other factors that Cadin felt were important to the success of his production strategy. One important element was the need for "discipline" on the part of top management not to expect impossible results. In the past there had been occasions when the company was "hungry" for business and had accepted orders that were unreasonable, if not impossible, to be met by the production organization. Whenever unrealistic estimates of cost and time were made, they resulted in serious problems in production that later appeared as incidents of poor performance. In reality the failure could be traced to the poor estimates and improper demands that were made upon the manufacturing organization.

Another important idea was that the first-line supervisor was the key person on whom the support organization had to focus its efforts. The first-line supervisor typically had charge of 15 to 20 workers who performed the productive work. The first-line supervisor was often treated as the "person in the middle" who was under pressure from employees demanding their "rights" and who was also under pressure from higher-level management demanding improved performance and output. First-line supervisors were unable or did not know how to resist such pressure and found themselves continually squeezed between pressure from workers and from higher levels of management. In fact, common knowledge about the difficulties of these and other supervisors had resulted in many workers refusing promotions to these ranks. It was often stated that the extra money and prestige to be a supervisor was not worth the headaches and sleepless nights that the job entailed.

Because Cadin felt that first-line supervisors represented the most important managerial level in the entire organization, he set about to ensure that they were given full support to do their jobs effectively. He carefully reviewed and improved procedures, paperwork, and channels of communication. He modified the organizational structure and clarified the authority and responsibilities of each manager. This corrected several situations of overlapping jurisdiction that had previously created conflicts and also identified several gaps in the organization that had previously resulted in omissions and oversights.

Cadin also worked with organizational units outside his jurisdiction to improve availability of materials when needed, to obtain adequate and timely cost control data for evaluation purposes, and to improve ways of communicating to the factory departments the design information, schedules, and process instructions.

Of particular importance was the selection and training of supervisors to assure that they understood and believed in the new management philosophy. Existing supervisors, as well as new supervisors, were exposed to three to six short management training programs that involved procedures and systems, budgeting, cost control, forecasting, and human relations. Although persons promoted from the worker rank to the first supervisory level were expected to be competent mechanics, particular attention was paid to their potential leadership qualities that would result in effective direction of others.

With improvements under way in the technical and environmental factors that affected production, Cadin then gave careful attention to improving worker attitudes and motivation. He believed in theory Y, not just to get employees to work harder but also to encourage them to be creative in identifying problems, suggesting improvements, and implementing changes to reach better performance. Just working harder could probably increase productive output by as much as 25%, but making improvements through creative changes had the potential of improving output by 100 percent, 200 percent, or even more.

To communicate to workers and first-line supervisors his feelings about their importance, Cadin first improved the plant facilities serving personal needs. All the toilets were modernized, repainted, and kept spotless so that they were equivalent to similar facilities at the headquarter's office. In each production area space was set aside for attractive tables and chairs to be used exclusively during lunch and rest periods. These areas were brightly painted, and the tables were provided with attractive tablecloths. Soon after these dining areas were established, Cadin noticed that workers often brought flowers for the tables. The new dining environment was in sharp contrast to the previous practice of workers usually eating their brown-bag lunches in their own working areas. Shop areas were made brighter and more attractive. Lighting was improved to increase illumination levels in every area. Walls, ceilings, piping, machinery, fixtures, and other equipment were painted in attractive, bright, and contrasting colors. Lines and areas on floors were carefully painted to identify walkways, storage areas, and working areas.

Another environmental factor considered important was effective communication of information important to employees. A weekly newspaper distributed to all employees contained general news about the company's overall programs. It also reported personal news, such as the meetings of clubs and athletic teams, awards to individuals, and announcements of promotions, weddings, births, retirements, and hobbies. Each work unit also had a large bulletin board on which was posted current announcements about rules, procedures, safety hints, recommendations for improving traffic and parking, and other announcements. Throughout all work areas a speaker system permitted announcements about special events, news items, and other information. These announcements were generally made during the lunch period.

It was also believed to be important to inform workers clearly and promptly about their performance. In each work area a very large bulletin board contained charts, posted daily, showing progress for various activities of the work unit. One chart listed each employee and his or her attendance record. Other charts showed progress of the unit: work hours compared with a predetermined standard, scheduled vs actual performance, amount of overtime work, quality rating, safety record, cost improvements and savings, and work that had been rejected. In some cases data or charts were broken down by crews within the work unit when such team work was applicable. In other situations performance records were posted for individual workers.

The typical chart had a time scale along the horizontal axis, usually for about a month. Each month a new chart would be displayed for the next period. The vertical scale related to the activity being measured. The data for the charts could be entered as bars or lines or in numerical form. In every case, standards (budget, target, or goal) were positively identified. These standards or goals were established jointly between the workers and their supervisor. Actual progress was then compared with the standards on a daily, weekly, biweekly, or monthly basis, as appropriate.

In each work unit a clerk spent a small amount of time each day collecting necessary information and posting it on to the charts. Although the company had a very sophisticated computer system for preparing records of elapsed time, work hours, output, inventory, and so on, it was found that the computer system could not generate needed reports fast enough to provide the necessary data in a timely way. The manual system permitted the charts to be posted each morning to record progress of the previous day. If there were multiple shifts, there were separate charts for each shift.

Performance and progress charts in each work unit were a focal point for the workers, who examined them with great interest. Common data among various work units were grouped together into summary charts resulting in a series of charts for all factory operations. Charts for the individual shops and summary charts were also displayed and analyzed at biweekly meetings for review of costs and schedules by the general supervisors. Each general supervisor presented the situation under his or her jurisdiction and identified problem areas. A general discussion would then seek solutions to these exposed problems.

The director of manufacturing also had a daily control using "special status control" charts. These were very simple charts based on the "management by exception" principle. A single control line represented satisfactory performance. If actual results were below the control line, an explanation was required and in some cases a "recovery" plan was established. Status control charts were maintained in each shop, and each chart, down to the smallest work unit, was duplicated each morning and assembled into a packet approximately an inch and a half thick containing about 300 pages that was on the desk of the director of manufacturing, Donald Cadin, each morning by 9:00 A.M. He considered the daily review of these charts to be one of his most important tasks. Review normally only took about ten minutes since he thumbed through the charts to compare progress with the expected standard. Where there were significant deviations or unfavorable trends, he would take note and make a point to visit the supervisor whose charts indicated a difficult or undesirable situation. Normally there were few surprises and the director of manufacturing needed only to check with a few supervisors each day. The knowledge was widespread among the supervisors, however, that the director of manufacturing did review each shop's daily progress carefully and that he took immediate action to obtain improvements or corrections.

Cadin used several techniques to overcome problems and difficulties, improve productivity, establish common goals among the various work units, and reflect the contribution by support organizations to factory performance. These techniques involved team studies, stand-up meetings, and producibility studies.

Team studies involved establishment of a temporary committee that might consist of both supervisors and workers to study a specific problem and make recommendations. Usually these team studies were devoted to a problem within an individual work unit.

The first-line supervisors had an open invitation to request a stand-up meeting to discuss those problems that were beyond the supervisor's scope of responsibility. Such meetings were also requested by higher levels of management. Stand-up meetings consisted of calling all first-, second-, and third-level supervisors to a meeting held on the shop floor at the site of the difficulties. Usually 15 or 20 supervisors would attend such a meeting. Each supervisor in turn would be called upon to report his or her involvement in the problem and what he or she could do or suggest to overcome the difficulties. The objective was to expose problems; only then could solutions be found. The emphasis was on the problems and the solutions, not on whom to blame.

At one stand-up meeting, for example, over 80 problem areas were identified that had influence on the performance of shop workers and the responsible first-line supervisor. Some of the problems could be resolved within the shop, but the majority of the problems were external and needed the support of other departments, such as corrections for inadequate tooling, parts shortages, design changes to improve producibility, and the need for portable racks to store in-process materials. Gradually all these problems were given attention by every department that could contribute an improvement, and performance of the shop began to improve.

Producibility studies generally involved establishment of a task force with representatives from various departments, such as from the factory, industrial engineering, purchasing, and so on, where the difficulty crossed departmental boundaries and required coordination of activities carried on by different functions. These task forces would often include both workers and supervisors, and reports of these task forces were submitted to the director of manufacturing.

# "PRIDE IN EXCELLENCE" PROGRAM

As was stated, these various programs focused on giving adequate support to the first-line supervisor so that he or she could assist workers to do the assigned jobs. When all possible reasons for inadequate performance were eliminated, there remained the final ingredient for effective performance: namely, motivation of the workers. The program for assuring job satisfaction and motivation of employees to their full potential was designed as a personalized and formal method of recognizing employees for special contributions. These motivational programs were built around the slogan "Pride in Excellence," using the Greek letter pi, $\pi$, as its symbol.

A booklet for supervisors regarding the philosophy of the "Pride in Excellence" program stated:

> In this busy workaday world of ours, it is easy for the individual to feel lost or forgotten and to come to regard his special assignment as monotonous or insignificant. Pride in Excellence is the management approach that can assist your employees in gaining greater satisfaction from their efforts by working towards and achieving goals. It adds the dimension of interest to what may have become routine and tedious work.
>
> This attitude of pride in a job well done becomes its own reward; it gives the employee a sense of purpose — a feeling of worth — that is reflected in every task that comes his way.
>
> All of us have heard of, or been witness to, a "super human" performance by an individual or a team. We all recognize in these instances how much the "wanting to" has influenced the ability to overcome obstacles. This desire, this intangible and complex ingredient, this will to do something difficult, can be properly identified as motivation.
>
> Because this desire for achievement is so important to the success of any undertaking, it follows that it plays a critical role in each supervisor's life. Ability to motivate is what turns a manager into a leader.
>
> Motivation is not manipulation; it is the element of management that serves as a catalyst, the addition of which makes a man's work intrinsically worthwhile.

The program allowed awards and recognition to be extended to individual employees, groups of employees, supervisors, and suppliers. There were five formal steps in the program:

1. *Setting goals.* These must be realistic and obtainable but difficult enough to represent a challenge. Such goals might be an improvement in performance to meet a schedule, increase output, a reduction in cost, or a reduction in clerical or quality errors. The goals had to be personal so that each person knew what could be done to help reach the group's goals to feel a commitment to support it. The goals were to be specific so that each employee knew exactly what the goal was and that there was a way to measure progress toward the goal and a time limit on reaching it.

2. *Measuring progress.* Each group established its own scoring system for measuring progress, and as much as possible these were shown in graph form on uniform types of charts. The visibility of progress allowed for friendly competition among comparable groups.

3. *Recognizing achievements.* It was a fundamental belief of the program that a feeling of accomplishment, of success, or of pride in achievement and its recognition is one of the most powerful motivating forces in a work situation. The recognition must be genuine, however, and given only when goals have been achieved.

4. *Pride in Excellence recognition.* Recognition was achieved through various types of awards. A personal letter could be written to an individual employee signed by his or her immediate supervisor and possibly higher-level supervisors. Commendations could be presented in the form of formal parchment certificates that would be signed by several levels of supervisors. A higher-level award could be a pin or plaque — there were also other more elaborate awards.

5. *The award ceremony.* There were several ways in which the award could be made. Most awards were made in the work area of the recipient as soon as possible after the achievement had been recognized in a simple and sincere manner to show the appreciation of the company. At other times awards were made at a banquet or other special occasions.

In each shop unit there was an award for the "shop employee of the month." Usually 10 to 12 employees were nominated each month by the first-line supervisor and/or by peer groups in each work unit. The winner was picked by the general supervisor after conferring with the first-line supervisor. The "shop employee of the month" winner received a "Pride in Excellence" certificate presented by the general superintendent in a formal ceremony in his shop area. The winner was given a special 30-day pass to park at a special location near the shop. The parking stall was marked "Reserved for $\pi$." The employee was also given a personal gift such as a belt buckle, a clutch purse, or a fountain pen. These gifts were stamped with the name of the company, the Pride in Excellence program, and the name of the award winner. The picture of the winning employee was displayed prominently on the bulletin board in the work unit. Each winner could not again be nominated for a year.

The 16 persons receiving "shop employee of the month" award also competed for a monthly award at the factory level; that is, there was one factory award for each of the two factory areas. Each "factory employee of the month" then received a paperweight, marked with his or her name, presented by the factory manager at a luncheon for the employee in the executive dining room.

In addition, there were "divisional employee of the month" awards in which 11 nominees competed, one from each of the functional departments in the division. Six workers were chosen as winners, plus one supervisor.

Each one received a bronze plaque signed by the vice president and general manager and also received a special gift such as a gold pen. In addition, winners with their spouses were invited to a dinner at the most exclusive restaurant in the city attended by top-level executives. Corsages were provided for all women attending the dinner. In addition, each winner received limousine service for one day. The winner was called for in the morning at home by a uniformed chauffeur in a large limousine. In addition, all employees who normally rode in a car pool with the winner were also picked up by the limousine. When they arrived at the factory they were greeted by top-level supervisors and photographs were taken. At the end of the day the limousine service returned them to their homes. Typically this event was a gala occasion for the award winner's family and neighbors.

At the end of the year divisional award winners competed for the "employee of the year." Also a "supervisor of the year" was chosen. An executive council made up of representatives from each of the 11 major functional departments selected one employee and one supervisor as winners. These two winners, with their spouses, were given an extra two-week holiday with pay and an all-expense-paid trip (with all income taxes also paid for the value of the trip). In the past such trips were made to Australia, Bermuda, Holland, and Spain. Before, during, and after the trip, photos were taken of the winning couples and presented to them in an album. After the trip, winners received a special parking pass for a full year and were presented with a special plaque.

Pictures of winners of the year were permanently mounted in a large conference room used both by supervisors and workers for various types of meetings. In this room were other awards received by the company for outstanding performance. For example, an award recently posted was received from the governor of the state for the outstanding safety performance achieved by the factory.

There was also an award for the outstanding "crew of the quarter." Each member of the crew received a certificate and a personal gift such as a sweater with the company name, recognition pin, key rings, or beer mugs on which their names were engraved. Members of the "crew of the quarter" were invited to a luncheon in the executive dining room attended by senior executives.

A "crew of the year" was also selected, and winning members received a watch and a dinner for themselves and their spouses. They also received a special license plate for their automobiles that identified the award and other personal items.

In addition, there was a "shop of the month" award. This award was made on the basis of a point system given for work hours control, adherence to schedule, minimum overtime, effective quality and safety control, and cost improvement. A formal presentation was made with all shop employees in attendance, and an award plaque was displayed in the department during the month of the award. The picture of the supervisor of the shop was posted in the conference control room and remained publicly displayed for a 12-month period.

There was a special attendance award presented for perfect attendance during a one-year period. Recognition was given with a special certificate and pin indicating the number of continuous years of perfect attendance. One mechanic received a 30-year pin — the longest ever awarded. Each year about 350 to 400 attendance awards were presented. A single day's absence required a person's record to start over. A special paperweight was also awarded to the 11th year winners. Awards were presented at a special dinner for the winners.

There were several special safety programs. In each shop a worker was designated as a safety monitor. In each of the two factories, constructive evaluation of accidents in each unit resulted in awards to a "safety monitor of the quarter," and these winners competed for a "safety monitor of the year" award.

There were two individual safety programs. One emphasized the importance of wearing safety eyeglasses. Workers were made members of the "Wise Owl Club" if, while wearing safety glasses, they had an accident that broke the lens but prevented a possible serious eye injury. There was also a "Golden Shoe Club" for workers who had avoided a serious foot injury by wearing safety shoes when an accident caused a heavy article to fall on their feet. Members of each club received special pins and certificates that were presented at a special safety council dinner.

## ADMINISTRATION OF THE PROGRAM

The Pride in Excellence program was under the direction of Karl Haley who functioned with a single assistant. It was his job to set up the awards procedure; prepare the budget for the program; do the necessary paperwork; coordinate wording for the certificates; arrange recognition luncheons, dinners, banquets, and annual trips; purchase and distribute the various gifts and prizes; represent the program to the executive council where final awards were determined; and maintain contact with the shops to make certain that awards were granted on a consistent basis in all areas. In each shop unit he had a designated coordinator for the Pride in Excellence program. When an idea proved to be worthwhile, it was Haley who then conveyed the idea to other supervisors.

Haley also had to face resistance on the part of some supervisors who felt the Pride in Excellence program was a "Mickey Mouse game." He patiently explained to such supervisors the power of appreciation and recognition that helped people to feel good and provided the motivation to strive for good performance. A few supervisors were reluctant to accept invitations to attend the many recognition luncheons and dinners, but most supervisors and top-level executives welcomed and enjoyed such invitations, and many participated as speakers on such occasions. He also had occasion to contact individual workers to interpret the program to them. In almost every case where the program was understood it was accepted with enthusiasm.

To avoid having the program become stale, Haley was continually faced with the need to create new ideas for awards and methods for recognition. Gifts that were given to winners were changed as workers lost interest in old items and became excited about new items. For example, at one time key rings with individual names were very much desired, but after many workers received such awards there was a diminution of interest in them. At that point Haley arranged for a new type of award.

## Figure 1

Production Program Shortages

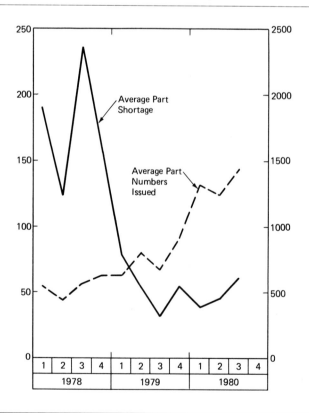

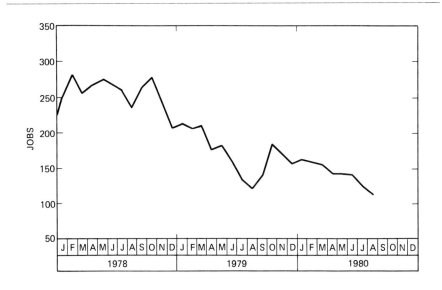

Figure 2

Jobs Behind Schedule

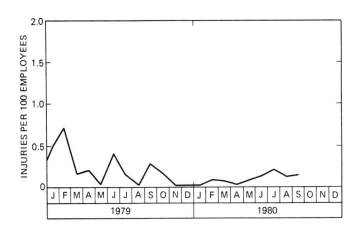

Figure 3

Safety Performance

The annual budget for the Pride in Excellence program was about $100,000. Of this amount about $65,000 was for awards and displays. The balance was for the salaries of Haley and other persons assigned to the program on a full-time basis. Cash awards and administration of the suggestion system were in a separate budget.

Cadin felt that the results of these programs had greatly improved the morale of the workers, had improved the effectiveness of supervisors, and had produced outstanding performance results as indicated in Figures 1, 2, and 3. However, Cadin was now faced with a rapidly expanding schedule that could require a doubling of employment, or more, in his organization during the next year. This would mean going from 6,000 employees to over 12,000 employees. He wondered whether the strength of his organization would permit him to undertake such an expansion program. He also pondered on what aspects of the expansion needed special attention and planning.

## DISCUSSION QUESTIONS

1. Do you believe in theory X or theory Y?
2. Cadin believed that only 15 percent of total job performance was under the control of the individual employee. Does such a small percentage justify the elaborate motivational program described in the case?
3. Donald Cadin felt that the first-line supervisors were the most important managerial level in the entire organization. Do you agree with this assumption? Why?
4. What was the purpose of the visual displays of the individual, crew, and unit performance and progress? Are there any risks in such displays?
5. What do you make of the stand-up meetings? Should they be sit-down meetings in a conference room?
6. What factors could diminish or eliminate the effectiveness of the Pride in Excellence program? How can the program be maintained to avoid becoming stale and ineffective? Is this program really worth its cost? Is it possible to establish a cost–benefit measure?
7. Will the expected employment of new employees to expand the work force change attitudes and the way in which workers respond to these programs? How can new employees be indoctrinated effectively to fit into the company's existing programs and environment?
8. What will be the possible effect on Cadin's programs if there is a severe downturn in operational levels requiring substantial layoffs?
9. What role, if any, does a labor union have in this program?
10. What demands does this program make on the various supervisory levels? What does this mean regarding the selection and training of supervisors?

# Bristol Sound Shipbuilding

For Bristol Sound Shipbuilding the problem of waste disposal had become increasingly difficult in recent years. Not only were costs of disposal rising rapidly, but companies such as Bristol Sound had become subject to regulation of their waste handling and disposal practices by the federal government. To study the waste management problem in Bristol Sound, Christine Anderson, vice president for operations, had appointed a three-person task force headed by Tom Watkins, a supervisor in the industrial engineering department.

## PRESENT SOLID WASTE DISPOSAL METHOD

One of the first efforts of the task force was to collect information on Bristol Sound's present solid waste disposal practices, as solid waste constituted the largest element of waste generated by the company. It was found that most solid waste material was picked up by Riverside Disposal Company. Bristol Sound rented containers from Riverside and paid Riverside to pick up any wastes placed in these containers. Table 1 shows the schedule of charges used as the basis for billings by Riverside during the preceding year. Monthly statistics on the number of containers dumped and tonnage picked up are given in Table 2. The average number of containers of each size rented at any one time were 5 yard, 30 containers; 10 yard, 6 containers; 20 yard, 14 containers; 25 yard, 3 containers; and 30 yard, 1 container. Five-yard containers were lifted by a hoist on the back of a Riverside truck, emptied into the truck, and placed back on the ground. Ten- to 30-yard containers were pulled onto the bed of a Riverside truck, taken to the dump site, weighed, dumped, and returned to the Bristol Sound yard.

### TABLE 1

Schedule of Riverside Disposal Charges, Previous Year

| Container Size[1] (yards) | Monthly Rental (per container) | Dumping Fee (per container) | Weight Charge (per ton) |
|---|---|---|---|
| 5 | $12.00 | $14.50 | None |
| 10 | 21.25 | 31.00 | $12.45 |
| 20 | 28.75 | 31.00 | 12.45 |
| 25 | 36.25 | 31.00 | 12.45 |
| 30 | 43.75 | 31.00 | 12.45 |
| 35 | 51.25 | 71.25 | 12.45 |

[1]Five- to 30-yard containers for loose waste; 35-yard containers primarily for compacted waste.

For the preceding year, total billings by Riverside had been just under $145,000, including the 5 percent state sales tax. However, a new schedule of fees as given in Table 3 had gone into effect on the first of January, and it was estimated that costs for the current year would be some $30,000 higher for an equivalent amount of waste. Conversations with Riverside's manager suggested that disposal fees would rise still higher in the future as Riverside was finding suitable dump sites to be increasingly scarce and more distant from its customers. Also, Riverside expected to incur substantial costs in complying with new federal regulations resulting from the Resource Conservation and Recovery Act.

Another project undertaken by the task force was to determine the impact of new federal regulations on Bristol Sound. This aspect of the solid waste problem was investigated by one of the task force members, George Blair, who summarized his findings in a memo to Tom Watkins. (A copy of the memo and attachments is shown in the appendix to this case.)

### TABLE 3

Revised Schedule of Riverside Disposal Charges

| Container Size[1] (yards) | Monthly Rental (per container) | Dumping Fee (per container) | Weight Charge (per ton) |
|---|---|---|---|
| 5 | $12.00 | $15.25 | None |
| 10 | 21.25 | 33.10 | $19.00 |
| 20 | 28.75 | 33.10 | 19.00 |
| 25 | 36.25 | 33.10 | 19.00 |
| 30 | 43.75 | 33.10 | 19.00 |
| 35 | 51.25 | 77.45 | 19.00 |

[1]Five- to 30-yard containers for loose waste; 35-yard containers primarily for compacted waste.

## TABLE 2

### Riverside Collections from Bristol Sound, Previous Year
### (Number of Dumps)

| Container size (yards) | Jan. | Feb. | Mar. | Apr. | May | June | July | Aug. | Sep. | Oct. | Nov. | Dec. | Total |
|---|---|---|---|---|---|---|---|---|---|---|---|---|---|
| 5 | 260 | 221 | 259 | 202 | 222 | 241 | 189 | 261 | 248 | 320 | 263 | 207 | 2,893 |
| 10 | 4 | 3 | 6 | 7 | 13 | 5 | 5 | 24 | 4 | 18 | 36 | 45 | 170 |
| 20 | 100 | 69 | 71 | 53 | 83 | 60 | 53 | 36 | 62 | 107 | 87 | 78 | 859 |
| 25 | 10 | 6 | 4 | 5 | 13 | 9 | 15 | 15 | — | 14 | 11 | 17 | 119 |
| 30 | 1 | 1 | 1 | — | — | 1 | 1 | 3 | — | 7 | 2 | 2 | 19 |
| Tons collected[1] | 419 | 241 | 214 | 179 | 327 | 193 | 208 | 264 | 227 | 558 | 426 | 506 | 3,762 |

[1]Does not include weight of waste in 5-yard containers.

Because it appeared that continuation of Bristol Sound's present method of solid waste disposal would lead to rapid escalation of costs in the future, the task force decided to seek alternatives that might help to hold costs down. After several weeks of investigation, the task force defined what it considered to be the feasible alternative disposal methods. These were compaction of waste before pickup, incineration, and incineration with energy recovery.

## COMPACTION ALTERNATIVE

The compaction alternative involved purchase of a compactor that would be used to reduce waste volume and, hence, the frequency of pickups by Riverside. A typical machine was the Bowles EC-300 stationary compactor, which could be purchased for $28,000. The compactor would be eligible for the 10 percent investment tax credit and was estimated to have a useful life of 15 years. These machines were quite sturdy so that, with reasonable care, maintenance costs were estimated to be only $100 per year for replacement of hydraulic hoses, seals, and so on. Costs of electricity for operation of the machine were estimated to be about $200 per year. The compactor would be mounted on a solid base and would feed compacted waste into a 35-yard container that would be dumped when full by Riverside Disposal.

It was estimated from observation in the yard and discussions with production supervisors that 50 percent of Bristol Sound's solid waste would be compactible. Wastes such as scrap metals, large pieces of wood, 55-gallon drums, and slag would have to be separated before compaction. Most sorting would be done before the material was brought to the compactor, preferably at the time that the material was placed in the waste containers. Compaction ratios might range from a conservative 3:1 to an optimistic 5:1, although only experience would determine actual performance.

Loading of the hopper on the compactor would be accomplished by dumping specially designed containers using a standard forklift. Bristol Sound owned a number of forklifts that could be used for this purpose, but it was estimated that 20 dumpable containers would have to be purchased at a cost of $1,000 each. It was thought that these would replace 20 of the 5-yard containers currently being rented from Riverside. One forklift operator working a single shift could probably handle all the collection and compaction in addition to a small amount of waste sorting and occasional maintenance on the compactor. Cost per hour of this operator, including fringe benefits, would be about $13.50.

## INCINERATION ALTERNATIVE

Data gathering for evaluation of the incineration options began with estimation of the amount and type of burnable wastes generated in the Bristol Sound yard. Since no data were available, the task force relied on observations made in the yard and estimates of yard supervisors. It was concluded that 40 percent by weight of the solid wastes generated by Bristol Sound might be burnable and that the composition by weight would be approximately 47.5 percent, Class 0; 47.5 percent, Class 1; and 5.0 percent, Class 2 waste. Standard descriptions of burnable wastes are given in Table 4.

The incineration process as conceptualized by the task force would begin with collection of burnable solid wastes in dumpable containers located strategically throughout the yard. These would be picked up by forklift, driven to the incinerator site, and dumped on a conveyor belt where obviously noncombustible material and potentially explosive items such as bottles and paint cans would be removed manually from the waste stream. From the conveyor, waste would fall into a hopper where a loading ram would compact it and automatically load it into the incinerator. In the incinerator chamber, waste would be ignited by the main burners. These burners required 15 gallons of #2 diesel fuel per hour of operation. Temperatures during combustion would reach as high as 1,800°F. Emissions from combustion would be drawn into a second burning chamber and reignited. The burner in the second chamber would use 6 gallons of #2 diesel per hour and ensure that emissions conformed to EPA standards.

Sterile ash would be the only solid material remaining after incineration. A ram would be used to force the ash out of the bottom of the incinerator and into a water bath. Finally, a conveyor would deposit the wet ash directly into a Riverside Disposal container. Total weight of the wet ash was estimated to be 15 percent of the original weight of the waste.

With a controlled flow feeder, it would also be possible to burn liquid wastes. Using the feeder, such liquids as paint thinners, solvents, and waste petroleum products could safely be introduced into the combustion chamber. In addition to assuring safe combustion of liquids, the feeder would permit control of the rate of material flow to assume that EPA emission requirements were met.

For analysis purposes the task force developed costs as shown in Table 5 for an incinerator with a capacity of 2,000 pounds per hour. The incinerator would be eligible for an investment tax credit of 10 percent; it was expected to have a useful life of 10 to 12 years. Operating costs of the incinerator would be the expense of a full-time operator at $18 per hour, a full-time forklift driver at $13.50 per hour, approximately $8,000 per year for maintenance and repair parts, plus the cost, at about $1.25 per gallon, of diesel fuel consumed.

Major savings from incineration would be obtained from the reduction in volume and weight of solid waste picked up by Riverside Disposal. Also, container rental fees paid to Riverside would be reduced, as it was expected that the dumpable containers purchased for use with the incinerator would replace 20 of the 5-yard containers rented from Riverside. Additionally, about $15,000 spent each year for disposal of combustible liquids and about

## TABLE 4

### Standard Classifications of Burnable Waste

| Classification of Wastes | | Principal Components | Approximate Composition (% by Weight) | Moisture Content (%) | Incombustible Solids (%) |
| --- | --- | --- | --- | --- | --- |
| Type | Description | | | | |
| Class 0 | Plastics | 100% combustible plastic, all types | Plastic, 100% | 0 | 0 |
| | Trash | Highly combustible waste. Paper, wood, cardboard cartons, and up to 10% treated papers, plastic, or rubber scraps; commercial and industrial sources | Trash, 100% | 10% | 5% |
| Class 1 | Rubbish | Combustible waste, paper, cartons, rags, wood scraps, combustible floor sweepings; domestic, commercial, and industrial sources | Rubbish, 80% Garbage, 20% | 25 | 10 |
| Class 2 | Refuse | Rubbish and garbage; residential sources | Rubbish, 50% Garbage, 50% | 50 | 7 |
| Class 3 | Garbage | Animal and vegetable wastes, restaurants, hotels, markets; institutional, commercial, and club sources | Garbage, 65% Rubbish, 35% | 70 | 5 |
| Class 4 | Animal solids and organics | Carcasses, organs, solid organic wastes; hospital, laboratory, abattoirs, animal pounds and similar sources | Animal and human tissue, 100% | 85 | 5 |
| Class 5 | Gaseous, liquids, or semiliquids | Industrial process wastes incinerated directly through a burner | Variable | Dependent on major components | Variable |
| Class 6 | Semisolids and solids | Combustibles requiring rotary retort equipment | Variable | Dependent on major components | Variable |

$5,000 spent annually for classified document destruction would be avoided.

## ENERGY RECOVERY

The task force investigated several forms that energy recovery might take if added to the basic incineration system. It was concluded that, for Bristol Sound, the most practical form of energy recovery would be generation of low-pressure steam. In addition to the cost of the basic incineration system, a boiler and associated equipment would have to be installed at a cost of $100,000 along with a chimney suitable for use with the boiler at an extra cost of $10,000. If the incinerator with energy recovery were operational within three years, the energy recovery system would qualify for a 10 percent energy recovery system tax credit in addition to the usual 10 percent investment tax credit. With the energy recovery system added to the basic incinerator, it was estimated that the cost of the full-time operator would rise to $20 per hour and annual maintenance and repair costs would rise to $12,000 per year.

Savings from incineration with energy recovery would be all of those obtained from incineration alone plus the value of the low-pressure steam obtained from the boiler. The facilities department had suggested numerous ways in which to use the steam, among them heating the paint shop, heating the pipe shop, running the pickling tanks, and sales to Ackoff Lumber Co. (located on property adjacent to the Bristol Sound Yard), which had expressed interest in purchasing excess steam. Value of the steam for any of these purposes was estimated to be about $220,000 per year. This was based on an assumed average energy content of 7,365 BTU per pound of burnable waste and system efficiency of 55 percent. It was also assumed that the steam would replace energy obtained from burning #2 diesel oil at a cost $1.25 with an effective energy yield of 105,000 BTU per gallon.

### TABLE 5

### Estimated Cost of Incinerator

| Component | Cost |
|---|---|
| Basic incinerator, 2,000-lb/hr capacity | $130,000 |
| Automatic loader with conveyor feed | 30,000 |
| Controlled-flow liquid feeder | 15,000 |
| Wet ash removal ram and conveyor | 30,000 |
| Installation | 50,000 |
| Training and cost overrun allowance | 20,000 |
| Forklift dumpable waste containers, 20 at $1,000 | 20,000 |
| Total | $295,000 |

# DISCUSSION QUESTIONS

1. Evaluate and rank from an economic standpoint the present solid waste disposal system and the three alternative systems investigated by the task force.

2. What impact would likely future changes in disposal cost, energy cost, and government regulations have on your evaluations?

3. Which of the waste disposal systems should be used by Bristol Sound? Provide justification for your selection.

# APPENDIX

TO:   Tom Watkins
FROM:  George Blair
DATE:  June 17, 1980
SUBJECT:  Federal Regulations Applicable to Bristol Sound Shipbuilding

Included in this memo is information on the Resource Conservation and Recovery Act, and the implications of the rulings promulgated on May 19, 1980 by the U.S. Environmental Protection Agency (EPA) in terms of Bristol Sound waste disposal practices and methods. The requirements set out in the following comments will all be effective November 19, 1980, unless otherwise specified.

Bristol Sound would presently fall in the category of a "Generator" of hazardous wastes. The regulations which apply to a company in this classification require the company to:

1) Determine which of the waste materials it generates are "hazardous" in terms of the Act. Basically, any waste which "ignitable, corrosive, reactive, or toxic" or is included in the comprehensive list of waste materials developed by EPA, is considered "hazardous".

2) Obtain an EPA identification number. Bristol Sound should receive a notification packet in the mail by July, 1980. The information requested by EPA in this packet and an application for an identification number should be sent to EPA's office for this region by August 15, 1980.

3) Obtain a facility permit if waste is accumulated on Bristol Sound property for more than 90 days. This may apply to Bristol Sound in regards to some chemical wastes which are stored in the yard under the direction of John Ball - Materials Control.

4) <u>Use appropriate containers and label them properly</u> for shipment. The regulations are not going to allow transporters of Bristol Sound waste to take the materials unless these requirements are satisfied. Proper labeling will also allow for better control and tracking of material. There is some confusion as to the condition or status of the materials in some containers.

5) <u>Prepare a manifest</u> for tracking hazardous waste from "cradle-to-grave".

6) <u>Submit</u> to the EPA an <u>annual summary</u> of hazardous waste activities.

Impacts of RCRA on Bristol Sound practices:

The significance of these regulations go beyond the mere additional activities required as outlined above. They will affect the company in other ways. Two things specified in the rulings suggest that incineration of waste material may be a good alternative disposal method in the future:

1) The controls placed on landfill operations may restrict to a greater degree, the disposal of materials in this manner. The restriction could reasonably be expected to cause the cost of landfill disposal to increase, and those increases will be passed on to the customer in the form of disposal rate increases. Thus Riverside Disposal, which has just raised its rates from $12.45/ton to $19.00/ton, could substantially increase the rates charged to Bristol Sound even more in the future.

2) The regulations discuss incineration as an alternative means of waste disposal very favorably. Included in the following pages is relevant information from the EPA on the RCRA rulings and requirements in general.

United States
Environmental Protection
Agency

Office of
Public Awareness (A-107)
Washington DC 20460

SW-737
3d edition
May 1980

# ♻EPA

# Hazardous Waste Information

## Hazardous Waste Facts *

Unavoidably generated in the production of many common materials (metals, paints, plastics, pesticides, clothing, fertilizers, medicines, etc.), hazardous waste emerged in the late 1970's as a national health and environmental concern. Agriculture, hospitals, laboratories, and governmental activities also generate hazardous wastes.

The news media have frequently reported on how the mismanagement of hazardous waste has damaged our land, water, and air. Just beginning to surface is an awareness of the financial burden the nation must bear for cleanup after those mistakes of the past. EPA studies indicate that total cleanup of potentially dangerous abandoned or uncontrolled disposal sites could cost as much as $44 billion. More important, but more difficult to quantify, are the personal costs to people exposed to these wastes, directly or indirectly.

Congress has provided an effective tool to help avoid repeating our past mistakes in managing hazardous waste—the Resource Conservation and Recovery Act of 1976 (RCRA), Public Law 94-580. Subtitle C of RCRA gives EPA authority to develop a nationwide program to regulate hazardous waste practices from "cradle to grave"—that is, from the time the waste is generated to its final disposal. Each State is encouraged to develop its own program, following EPA's guidelines. If the program meets RCRA's requirements, it receives EPA approval. EPA is directed to carry out a hazardous waste program in any State that has not received such approval or chooses not to develop and operate its own program.

The major provisions under RCRA for controlling hazardous waste are:

- definition of hazardous waste
- a manifest system to track hazardous waste from its generation to its final disposal
- standards for generators and transporters of hazardous waste
- permit requirements for facilities that treat, store, or dispose of hazardous waste
- requirements for State hazardous waste programs

Specific regulations for carrying out RCRA are set forth in the Code of Federal Regulations (40 CFR Parts 260 to 266 and 122 to 124). The program becomes effective 6 months following promulgation of the regulation identifying and listing hazardous wastes (Part 261). A waste is defined as hazardous in Part 261 if it is included in a list of waste sources, waste streams, and some specific wastes that are hazardous or if it is ignitable, corrosive, reactive, or toxic as determined by a specified extraction procedure (referred to in the regulation as "extraction procedure toxicity").

The control system starts when anyone engaged in hazardous waste activities notifies EPA, as required by section 3010 of RCRA. After receiving notification, EPA assigns an identification number to the notifier. Anyone who transports, treats, stores, or disposes of hazardous waste who does not notify EPA during the 90-day period following promulgation of the regulation identifying hazardous wastes may not begin or continue operation until an EPA identification number is assigned.

*Sources for the data in this fact sheet are EPA's 1975-78 industry studies and the 1979 draft *Environmental Impact Statement* and *Environmental Impact Analysis.*

## Quantities

EPA estimates that in 1980 U.S. industry will generate about 57 million metric tons (wet) of hazardous waste. About 34 million metric tons will come from the chemical and allied products industry.

| Industrial Hazardous Waste | |
|---|---|
| Generator | Percent |
| Chemicals and allied products | 60 |
| Machinery (except electrical) | 10 |
| Primary metals | 8 |
| Paper and allied products | 6 |
| Fabricated metal products | 4 |
| Stone, clay, and glass products | 3 |
| All others | 9 |

About 60 percent of hazardous waste is liquid or sludge.

Quantities of hazardous waste are expected to increase by about 3.5 percent annually. Much of this increase is attributed to sludge from equipment required for air and water pollution controls.

Ten States generate 60 percent of all the hazardous waste. They are (in order by volume): New Jersey, Illinois, Ohio, California, Pennsylvania, Texas, New York, Michigan, Tennessee, and Indiana.

EPA estimates that 90 percent of hazardous waste is currently managed by practices which will not meet new Federal standards.

EPA studies of industries that generate the major portion of hazardous waste in the United States indicated that about 80 percent of these wastes were disposed of on the generator's property, with generators using the following disposal methods:

- nonsecure pits, ponds, lagoons, or landfills                                            80%
- incinerated without proper controls                                                     10%
- managed acceptably as compared to proposed Federal standards—
  that is, by controlled incineration, treatment to render the waste
  nonhazardous or less hazardous, secure landfills, and recovery                          10%

**Environmental Damage and Cleanup**

Major routes for environmental damage are:
1. ground-water contamination via leachate
2. surface-water contamination via runoff or overflow
3. air pollution via open burning, evaporation, sublimation, and wind erosion
4. fire and explosion
5. poison via the food chain
6. human contact

### Extent of damage

A 1979 study by an EPA contractor indicated that 32,000 to 50,000 disposal sites may contain hazardous waste, and that from 1,200 to 2,000 of these sites could pose potential danger to health or the environment.

### Legal Authorities

Under section 7003 of RCRA, EPA can initiate legal action to require responsible parties to clean up a site that presents an "imminent and substantial" danger to health or the environment.

EPA is also using authorities under other acts it administers to respond to immediate hazardous waste problems. These include the Clean Water Act, the Safe Drinking Water Act, the Toxic Substances Control Act, and the Refuse Act.

**Federal Regulations**

EPA has prepared six regulations under Subtitle C of the Resource Conservation and Recovery Act:

| RCRA Section | Subject of Regulation | Final Regulation |
|---|---|---|
| 3001 | Definition of Hazardous Waste | Spring 1980 |
| 3002 | Standards for Generators of Hazardous Waste[1] | February 26, 1980 |
| 3003 | Standards for Transporters of Hazardous Waste[1] | February 26, 1980 |
| 3004 | Standards for Hazardous Waste Facilities (2 phases): | |
| | Preliminary facility standards | Spring 1980 |
| | Technical design standards | Fall 1980 |
| 3005 | Permits for Treatment, Storage, or Disposal Facilities[2] | Spring 1980 |
| 3006 | Guidelines for Development of State Hazardous Waste Programs[2] | Spring 1980 |

[1] The U.S. Department of Transportation also proposed amendments to its hazardous materials transportation regulations, which were published in the *Federal Register*, May 25, 1978

[2] The regulations covering permits for facilities and State hazardous waste programs are integrated with rules under the Clean Water Act, the Safe Drinking Water Act, and the Clean Air Act

Cradle-to-grave control of hazardous waste via manifests and reporting is the keystone of the Federal regulatory program; only facilities with permits may treat, store, or dispose of hazardous waste.

EPA anticipates receiving as many as 300,000 notifications between May and August 1980.

EPA and the States will issue an estimated 30,000 permits over the next 5 to 6 years to those who store, treat, or dispose of hazardous waste.

Other EPA Acts related to hazardous waste controls:

● Clean Air Act—sets standards for hazardous air pollutants.
● Clean Water Act—prohibits discharge of pollutants in significant amounts into navigable waters of the United States.
● Safe Drinking Water Act—authorizes EPA to set maximum contaminant levels for public drinking water systems.
● Federal Insecticide, Fungicide, and Rodenticide Act—authorizes EPA to regulate registration, treatment, disposal, and storage of all pesticides, including labeling requirements.
● Toxic Substances Control Act—authorizes EPA to obtain data on health effects of chemical substances and to regulate the manufacture, use, and disposal of a chemical substance or mixture where warranted.

## Technology

Environmentally adequate technology is available for treatment and disposal of hazardous waste. Costs vary widely among the different methods and also according to type and volume of waste handled (reducing comparably with larger quantities).

| Disposal Method | Cost/Metric Ton |
| --- | --- |
| Secure chemical landfill | $50-400 |
| Incineration (land based) | $75-2,000 |
| Land treatment | $2-25 |
| Chemical fixation | $5-500 |
| Surface impoundment | $14-180 |
| Physical, chemical, biological treatment | variable |

Administrative and technical requirements under the Federal hazardous waste regulations will lead to increased direct costs for controlling these wastes; however, these costs will balance favorably against the astronomical costs of cleaning up damage caused by mismanagement of hazardous waste.

A study of 23 industries made by EPA for an economic impact analysis indicates that costs for new controls will come to $686 million annually. This study covered 29,000 generators of 12.6 million metric tons of hazardous waste. The annual cost of proper hazardous waste management will be less than two-tenths of one percent of the sales of the industries studied, which amounts to $3 per American citizen.

Waste exchanges help to diminish disposal costs. At least 20 industrial waste exchanges are in operation in the United States. There are two types: the materials exchange, which handles, treats, and physically exchanges waste, and the information exchange, which serves only as a clearinghouse for generators and potential purchasers.

## State Hazardous Waste Programs

At the beginning of 1980, solid waste legislation in 40 States included at least partial authority to control hazardous waste; many of these States are upgrading their authority and are in the process of planning specific hazardous waste legislation.

EPA anticipates that many of the 40 States having authority will apply and may qualify for "interim authorization." With interim authorization, States can operate their own programs for 2 years after the effective date of the Federal regulations while upgrading their programs.

Within 2 years of promulgation of the final hazardous waste regulations, States with interim authorization must apply for and secure "full authorization." The three main criteria for "full authorization" are: (1) equivalence to Federal program, (2) consistency with other Federal and State programs, and (3) adequacy of enforcement.

Fiscal year 1980 grants specifically for hazardous waste program development total $18.6 million. The President's budget for FY 81 requests $30 million.

# Identification and Listing

## Rules for Identification and Listing of Hazardous Waste

The Resource Conservation and Recovery Act of 1976 (RCRA) requires the U.S. Environmental Protection Agency (EPA) to institute a national program to control hazardous waste. Specific regulations for carrying out RCRA are set forth in the Code of Federal Regulations (40 CFR Parts 260 to 266 and 122 to 124). The program becomes effective 6 months following promulgation of the regulation identifying and listing hazardous wastes (Part 261). This regulation includes a list of hazardous wastes as well as several characteristics for identifying hazardous waste.

The keystone of the program is control of hazardous waste from point of generation through treatment, storage, and ultimate disposal via transportation manifests, recordkeeping, and reporting. The control system starts when those who generate, transport, treat, store, or dispose of hazardous wastes notify EPA, as required by section 3010 of RCRA. After receiving notification, EPA assigns an identification number to the notifier. Anyone engaged in transporting, treating, storing, or disposing of hazardous waste who does not notify EPA during the 90-day period following promulgation of the regulation identifying hazardous wastes may not begin or continue operation after the effective date of the regulations without obtaining an EPA identification number.

The identification regulation promulgated under section 3001, Subtitle C, of RCRA (40 CFR Part 261) defines and lists solid wastes which are hazardous wastes and thus are subject to RCRA controls. In addition, the regulation establishes (1) criteria for identifying characteristics and for listing hazardous waste; (2) procedures for exempting wastes that are listed; and (3) procedures for petitioning EPA to modify the selected hazardous waste characteristics or the list. The regulation also delineates several wastes that are excluded from all or part of the RCRA regulatory control system.

The list and the characteristics are to be used by persons who generate, transport, treat, store, or dispose of solid waste to determine if the waste they handle is hazardous. EPA has determined that the listed wastes are hazardous. The responsibility for identifying a hazardous waste because of its characteristics rests primarily with the generator; however, other persons handling the waste also have an obligation to know if a waste they are managing is hazardous.

Once a solid waste is identified as hazardous, it is subject to all of the controls under Subtitle C--Hazardous Waste—of RCRA.

## Definition of Hazardous Waste

RCRA defines a hazardous waste in general as a solid waste that may cause substantial hazard to health or the environment when improperly managed. EPA was required to establish criteria for a more specific identification and for listing hazardous wastes. The criteria established under the Act were then used to develop characteristics and a list of hazardous wastes.

Characteristics of Hazardous Waste. Hazardous wastes are identified on the basis of measurable characteristics for which standardized tests are available. The identification regulation provides detailed technical specifications for four characteristics adopted by EPA:

- ignitability—posing a fire hazard during routine management
- corrosivity—ability to corrode standard containers, or to dissolve toxic components of other wastes
- reactivity—tendency to explode under normal management conditions, to react violently when mixed with water, or to generate toxic gases
- EP toxicity (as determined by a specific extraction procedure) —presence of certain toxic materials at levels greater than those specified in the regulation

List of Hazardous Wastes. The identification regulation contains a hazardous waste list of specific wastes, waste sources, and waste processes. Included in the list are wastes that possess any of the four hazardous waste characteristics as well as wastes meeting the criteria for general toxicity.

General toxicity is defined in the regulation as characteristic of waste which contain one or more constituents that have been found to have toxic effects on humans or other life forms. EPA can also consider other factors to determine if the waste may cause or potentially cause "substantial" hazard to human health or the environment. The other factors which EPA may consider are:

- the degree of toxicity of the toxic constituents of the waste
- the concentration of these constituents in the waste
- the potential for these constituents or their by-products to migrate from the waste into the environment
- the persistence and degradation potential of the constituents or their toxic by-products in the environment
- the potential for the constituents or their toxic by-products to bioaccumulate in ecosystems
- the plausible and possible types of improper management to which the waste may be subjected
- the quantities of the waste generated
- the record of human health and environmental damage that has resulted from past improper management of wastes containing the same toxic constituents

## Identifying a Hazardous Waste

The generator must determine if:

- the material is a solid waste; and
- the waste or any constituent is included in the hazardous waste list, or
- the waste meets any of the hazardous waste characteristics

## Exemption or Delisting

It is possible for the generator to get an exemption from regulation even if the waste is listed in the regulation. The regulation includes delisting procedures for generators to follow who believe their facility's individual waste is fundamentally different from the waste listed. The generator must demonstrate, or reference test data that demonstrate, that the specific waste does not meet the criteria which caused the Agency to list the waste. This provision reflects recognition that individual waste streams vary depending upon raw materials, industrial processes, and other factors.

## Small Generators

The regulation provides for the exemption of small generators from these initial hazardous waste controls. In general, facilities generating less than 1,000 kilograms of an identified hazardous waste are exempted; however, EPA has specified lower generation limits for certain wastes. Small generators should refer directly to the regulation to determine the applicability of the exemption to their wastes.

EPA intends to expand the coverage of small generators over a 2- to 5-year period. Generators will be notified of these changes as they develop.

## Excluded Wastes

Certain wastes are not subject to RCRA hazardous waste controls (but may be controlled under other laws). These include:

- domestic sewage
- industrial wastewater discharges
- nuclear wastes regulated under the Atomic Energy Act
- irrigation return flows
- garbage and refuse
- materials that are reused or recycled (Regulations to cover some of these uses or wastes will be promulgated by April 1981.)
- agricultural and silvicultural wastes returned to the soil as fertilizers or conditioners
- overburden from mining operations (except that derived from uranium and phosphate mining containing specified concentrations of radium)

# Notification Requirements

## Notification Requirements for Hazardous Waste Activities

The Resource Conservation and Recovery Act of 1976 (RCRA) requires the U.S. Environmental Protection Agency (EPA) to institute a national program to control hazardous waste. Specific regulations for carrying out RCRA are set forth in the Code of Federal Regulations (40 CFR Parts 260 to 265 and 122 to 124). The program becomes effective 6 months following promulgation of the regulation identifying and listing hazardous waste (Part 261). This regulation includes a list of waste sources, waste streams, and some specific wastes that are hazardous, as well as four characteristics of a hazardous waste: ignitability, corrosivity, reactivity, and toxicity as determined by a specified extraction procedure (referred to in the regulation as "extraction procedure toxicity").

The keystone of the program is control of hazardous waste from point of generation through treatment, storage, and ultimate disposal, via transportation manifests and reporting. The control system starts when those engaged in generating, transporting, treating, storing, or disposing of hazardous waste notify EPA as required by section 3010 of RCRA. After receiving notification, EPA assigns an identification number to the notifier. Anyone engaged in transporting, treating, storing, or disposing of hazardous waste who does not notify EPA during the 90-day period following the promulgation of the regulation identifying hazardous wastes may not begin or continue operation after the effective date of the regulation without obtaining an EPA identification number.

**Who Must Notify**

- anyone who generates or transports hazardous waste or owns or operates a facility that treats, stores, or disposes of hazardous waste must notify EPA. EPA will mail about 350,000 notification packages, which include a notification form, within 30 days of promulgation of the identification regulation. Those not receiving a package should contact their EPA regional office.

- a new generator or transporter must apply to EPA for an identification number before any hazardous waste can be transported. Application for an identification number must be made on the notification form.

- an owner/operator of a site that conducts more than one hazardous waste activity (for example, generation and disposal) may file a single form to cover all activities at that site.

- an owner/operator of more than one site must file a form for each site.

**When To Notify**

- EPA must be notified within 90 days of promulgation of the identification regulation.

**Where To Notify**

- The notification must be sent to the Regional Administrator of the EPA region in which the installation is located.

# Transporters

**Rules for Transporters of Hazardous Wastes**

The Resource Conservation and Recovery Act of 1976 (RCRA) requires the U.S. Environmental Protection Agency (EPA) to institute a national program to control hazardous waste. Specific regulations for carrying out RCRA are set forth in the Code of Federal Regulations (40 CFR Parts 260 to 265 and 122 to 124). The program becomes effective 6 months following promulgation of the regulation identifying and listing hazardous wastes (Part 261). This regulation includes a list of waste sources, waste streams, and some specific wastes that are hazardous, as well as four characteristics of a hazardous waste: ignitability, corrosivity, reactivity, and toxicity as determined by a specified extraction procedure (referred to in the regulation as "extraction procedure toxicity").

The keystone of the program is control of hazardous waste from point of generation through treatment, storage, and ultimate disposal, via transportation manifests and reporting. The control system starts when those engaged in generating, transporting, treating, storing, or disposing of hazardous waste notify EPA as required by section 3010 of RCRA. After receiving notification, EPA assigns an identification number to the notifier. Anyone engaged in transporting, treating, storing, or disposing of hazardous waste who does not notify EPA during the 90-day period following promulgation of the regulation identifying hazardous wastes may not begin or continue operation after the effective date of the regulations without obtaining an EPA identification number.

The regulation for transporters of hazardous waste (40 CFR Part 263) issued under the authority of section 3003 of RCRA was developed jointly by EPA and the U.S. Department of Transportation (DOT). The EPA regulation on transporters incorporates by reference pertinent parts of DOT's rules on labeling, marking, packaging, placarding, and other requirements for reporting hazardous discharges or spills during transportation. DOT, in turn, is amending its regulations on transportation of hazardous materials to include EPA's requirements. EPA believes that these joint efforts will make it easier for transporters to comply with all requirements and will eliminate overlapping administrative and enforcement activities. This coordination will also minimize additional costs for recordkeeping by transporters.

The regulation (Part 263) requires a transporter of hazardous waste to:

- obtain an EPA identification number
- comply with the manifest system for tracking hazardous waste
- deliver the entire quantity of hazardous waste to the facility designated by the generator on the manifest.
- retain a copy of the manifest for 3 years
- comply with DOT regulations pertaining to reporting of discharges or spills
- clean up any hazardous waste discharged during transportation

Notification
Requirement

Anyone who generates, transports, treats, stores, or disposes of hazardous waste is required to notify EPA within 90 days of promulgation of the identification regulation. Notification should be filed with the Regional Administrator of the EPA region in which the installation is located.

EPA
Identification System

A transporter who notifies EPA during the 90-day period following promulgation of the identification regulation receives an identification number. New transporters (those not handling hazardous waste during this 90-day period) may submit requests for an identification number to their EPA regional office. A generator of hazardous waste is prohibited from using the services of a transporter who does not have an EPA identification number.

Operation of the
Manifest System

The generator signs the certification on the original manifest and all copies, one for each person handling the waste. The transporter then signs and dates the manifest and returns one copy to the generator, who retains it until a copy is received from the designated permitted facility following delivery of the waste.

The transporter carries the manifest to the designated facility. When the shipment arrives, an agent for the facility signs and dates each copy and retains one. One copy is given to the transporter, who retains it for 3 years, and another copy is returned to the generator by the facility agent.

If more than one transporter is involved, the initial transporter must obtain the subsequent transporter's dated signature on the manifest. The remaining copies accompany the waste until it reaches the designated facility.

Rail Shipment
and
Bulk Shipment
by Water

For rail shipment or bulk shipment by water, the manifest need not accompany the waste. However, a shipping paper, which contains all the information on the manifest except EPA identification numbers, generator certification, and signatures, must accompany the waste. If transportation other than rail or water is used at any stage of the shipping process, then the manifest must accompany the waste at all times.

The waste may be transferred between two rail or bulk shipment water carriers without obtaining the subsequent carrier's signature. But the final rail or water transporter must obtain the dated signature of the agent for the designated facility on the shipping paper or the manifest.

All rail or water transporters are required to keep a copy of the shipping paper or the manifest for 3 years from the date of acceptance.

Hazardous Waste
Discharge

A discharge is defined as the accidental or intentional spilling, leaking, pumping, emitting, emptying, or dumping of hazardous waste onto or into the land or water.

All transporters are responsible for cleaning up any discharge of hazardous waste that occurs during transportation.

When authorities on the scene declare an emergency, they can temporarily suspend the requirement that waste can be handled only by those holding EPA identification numbers and complying with the manifest system. This suspension ceases when the emergency no longer exists.

In certain cases, DOT requires that the transporter telephone the National Response Center (800-424-8802) to supply information on a discharge. In the District of Columbia, the number is 202-426-2675.

A written report of each discharge must be submitted to DOT, which will forward a copy to EPA.

# Generators

Rules for
Generators of
Hazardous
Wastes

The Resource Conservation and Recovery Act of 1976 (RCRA) requires the U.S. Environmental Protection Agency (EPA) to institute a national program to control hazardous waste. Specific regulations for carrying out RCRA are set forth in the Code of Federal Regulations (40 CFR Parts 260 to 265 and 122 to 124). The program becomes effective 6 month following promulgation of the regulation identifying and listing hazardous waste (Part 261). This regulation includes a list of waste sources, waste streams, and some specific wastes that are hazardous, as well as four characteristics of a hazardous waste: ignitability, corrosivity, reactivity, and toxicity as determined by a specified extraction procedure (referred to in the regulation as "extraction procedure toxicity").

The keystone of the program is control of hazardous waste from point of generation through treatment, storage, and ultimate disposal via transportation manifests and reporting. The control system starts when those engaged in generating, transporting, treating, storing, or disposing of hazardous waste notify EPA as required by section 3010 of RCRA. After receiving notification, EPA assigns an identification number to the notifier Anyone engaged in transporting, treating, storing, or disposing of hazardou waste who does not notify EPA during the 90-day period following the promulgation of the regulation identifying hazardous wastes may not begin or continue operation after the effective date of the regulations without obtaining an EPA identification number.

The regulation (40 CFR Part 262) issued under section 3002 of RCRA requires a generator of hazardous waste to:

- determine if its waste is hazardous by consulting the list of hazardous wastes contained in the regulation or, if the waste is not listed, by determining if it possesses any one of four characteristics established in the regulation (ignitability, corrosivity, reactivity, or toxicity). Or, the generator may declare the waste to be hazardous based upon knowledge of the materials or processes used in producing the waste.

- obtain an EPA identification number

- obtain a facility permit if waste is accumulated on the generator's property more than 90 days

- use appropriate containers and label them properly for shipment

- prepare a manifest for tracking hazardous waste

- assure, through the manifest system, that the waste arrives at the designated facility

- submit an annual summary of activities

**Notification Requirement**

Anyone who generates, transports, treats, stores, or disposes of hazardous waste is required to notify EPA within 90 days of promulgation of the identification regulation. Notification should be filed with the Regional Administrator for the EPA region in which the installation is located.

**EPA Identification System**

A generator who notifies EPA during the 90-day period following promulgation of the identification regulation receives an identification number. New generators (those not generating hazardous waste during this 90-day period) must obtain an identification number within 90 days of beginning operation; requests for an identification number should be submitted to the appropriate EPA regional office.

**Waste Leaving the Generator's Property**

For waste leaving the site where it was generated, the generator must:

- use only transporters with identification numbers

- prepare a manifest—a shipping form—for all movements of hazardous waste sent to off-site treatment, storage, or disposal facilities

- keep records of these shipments

- report shipments that do not reach the facility designated on the manifest

**The Manifest**

A generator of hazardous waste is responsible for preparation of a manifest containing:

- name and address of the generator

- names of all transporters

- name and address of the permitted facility designated to receive the waste. (An alternate facility may be designated if an emergency prevents use of the first facility.)

- EPA identification numbers of all who handle the waste

- U.S. Department of Transportation (DOT) description of the waste

- quantity of waste and number of containers

- the generator's signature certifying that the waste has been properly labeled, marked, and packaged in accordance with DOT and EPA regulations

**Operation of the Manifest System**

The generator signs the certification on the manifest, including one copy for each person handling the waste. The transporter then signs and dates the manifest and returns one copy to the generator, who retains it until a copy is received from the designated facility following delivery of the waste.

**Waste Remaining on the Generator's Property**

Generators who accumulate waste on their property more than 90 days are considered to be "storing" waste, and are required to obtain a facility permit, under section 3005 of RCRA. The date accumulation began must be clearly marked on the container.

A generator who treats, stores, or disposes of waste on site will be subject to requirements under sections 3004 and 3005 of RCRA.

# CONTROLLED WASTE

## FEDERAL LAW PROHIBITS IMPROPER DISPOSAL

PROPER D.O.T.
SHIPPING NAME _____
(SHOW EPA'S CHARACTERISTICS BELOW (250.13-250.14))

EPA PROPERTIES _____

GENERATOR'S EPA                    MANIFEST
IDENTIFICATION NO. _____ DOCUMENT NO. _____

## CONTAINS HAZARDOUS OR TOXIC WASTES

# HANDLE WITH CARE!

IN THE EVENT OF A SPILL CONTACT
THE NATIONAL RESPONSE CENTER U.S. COAST GUARD,
800-424-8802 FOR EMERGENCY ASSISTANCE

© LABELMASTER, CHICAGO, IL 60626     STYLE WM-6

# Delaware Bay Ship and Fabrication Company

Preparation of the annual budget was always a difficult task for James Peters, production manager of the Delaware Bay Ship and Fabrication Company. Peters was responsible for all parts fabrication, the indoor assembly shop, all outdoor yard work, and the overhead departments that supported these activities. When Delaware Bay's business consisted largely of small boat and barge construction, it was relatively simple to estimate labor and dollar requirements based on the construction program forecast for the year. The company, however, had expanded into manufacture of heavy machinery and equipment some ten years previously, and it had become increasingly difficult to prepare budgets for the activities necessary to support the many different manufacturing programs under Peters's control.

## OVERHEAD BUDGET

In particular, preparation of the budget for overhead activities for next year was a source of more than usual concern. During the past several years the overhead rate had gradually risen to a point where Delaware Bay's prices were out of line with those of its competitors in the heavy machinery and equipment business. In small boat and barge construction, where most work was obtained through competitive bidding, Delaware Bay's high overhead rate had been a major factor in the loss of several contracts during the past six months — contracts that Delaware Bay needed badly to keep its facilities busy. As a result, the president of the company had directed Peters to reduce the portion of the company overhead under Peters's direct control by 15 percent for the coming year. Because the contribution to the company overhead rate per direct labor-hour by the activities reporting to Peters had been $5.44 in the previous year, this meant a reduction of these overhead charges by $0.82 per direct hour in the coming year.

Organizations included in the overhead charges of the production department were Peters's office and staff, the production control unit, the industrial engineering unit, the production engineering and services unit, and the general superintendent's office. Overall organization of the production department is shown in Figure 1. Internal organization and description of duties for each of the units and offices are illustrated in Figures 2 through 6.

FIGURE 1

Organization Chart, Production Department

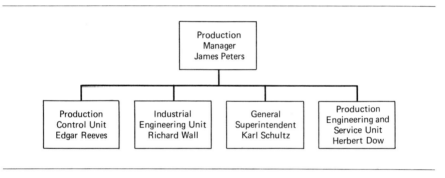

FIGURE 2

Organization Chart, Production Department Office

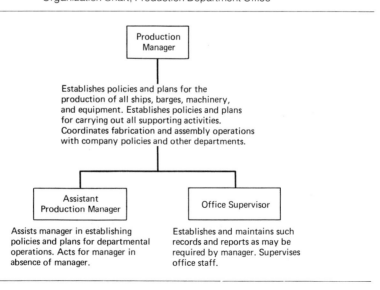

Actual overhead charges for the past year, together with actual direct labor-hours expended in the shops and yards are shown in Table 1. Actual overhead expenditures for the current year were 6.5 percent over the amount budgeted, whereas direct hours worked in the current year were only 92.4 percent of the anticipated number of hours.

Peters was faced with the task of reconciling the budget requests from his organization with the president's order that he reduce the overhead rate per direct labor-hour by 15 percent. As shown in Table 2, the forecast of direct labor-hours for next year showed a further decline of more than 9 percent from the total for the current year. However, budget requests for the various overhead activities (including Peters's estimate of the cost of operating his own office) totaled $16,779,000 (Table 3). If these budget requests were submitted to management without change, the overhead rate would rise to $5.52 per hour rather than be reduced to $4.62 per hour as directed by management.

Before making his decision as to where overhead budget requests should be cut, Peters decided to hold individual conferences with the heads of each of the overhead groups under his jurisdiction.

## FIGURE 3

Organization Chart, Production Control Unit

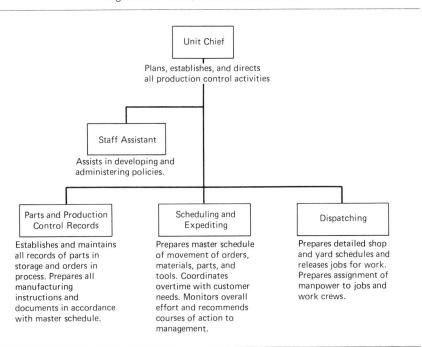

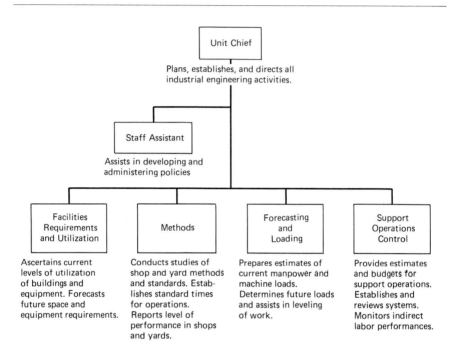

**FIGURE 4**

Organization Chart, Industrial Engineering Unit

Unit Chief

Plans, establishes, and directs all
industrial engineering activities.

Staff Assistant

Assists in developing and
administering policies

| Facilities Requirements and Utilization | Methods | Forecasting and Loading | Support Operations Control |
|---|---|---|---|
| Ascertains current levels of utilization of buildings and equipment. Forecasts future space and equipment requirements. | Conducts studies of shop and yard methods and standards. Establishes standard times for operations. Reports level of performance in shops and yards. | Prepares estimates of current manpower and machine loads. Determines future loads and assists in leveling of work. | Provides estimates and budgets for support operations. Establishes and reviews systems. Monitors indirect labor performances. |

## GENERAL SUPERINTENDENT'S OFFICE

The first conference was held with the general superintendent, Karl Schulz. Schulz began the discussion of his budget request by noting that in the current year the number of first-line supervisors had been reduced to the point where the ratio of supervisors to workers was 1 supervisor for every 16 employees. This reduction in the relative amount of supervision was made even though fabrication, assembly, and yard operations were spread out geographically and the work was becoming more specialized and required more supervision. As a result of the reduction in first-line supervisors, it was not uncommon for workers to be unsupervised when the supervisor was ill or attending meetings. Also, the lower work load had not reduced the number of shifts worked, and it was still necessary to assign supervisors to all three shifts.

Schulz explained that the reduction of over $600,000 in his budget request was accomplished by removing several more first-line supervisors and completely eliminating a level of supervision between the fabrication shop, assembly shop, and yard superintendents and the first-line supervisors in these areas. The effect of removing the level of supervision directly under the superintendents was to make it necessary for all first-line supervisors to report directly to the superintendent of the area. This meant that between 30 and 35 first-line supervisors would report to each superintendent in the future. Schulz stated that it would be impossible to reduce the amount of supervision further without seriously reducing shop efficiency. He also said that, if there were reductions in the budgets of production control, industrial engineering, and production engineering and services, it would be necessary for the shop and yard supervisors to perform some of the functions now performed by these organizations.

## FIGURE 5

Organization Chart, Production Engineering and Services Unit

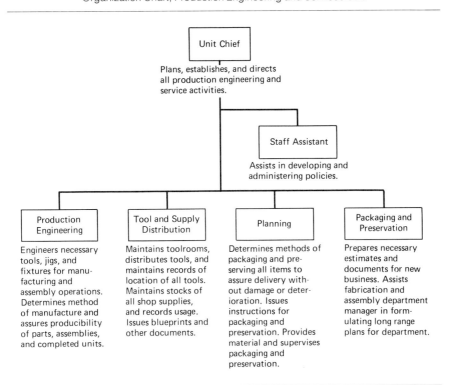

## FIGURE 6

Organization Chart, General Superintendent's Office

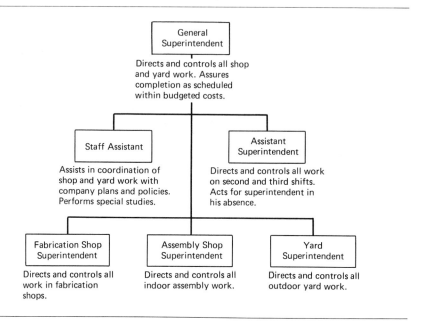

## INDUSTRIAL ENGINEERING UNIT

Peters met next with Richard Wall, industrial engineering unit chief. The industrial engineering unit's budget request was almost $195,000 lower than the actual amount spent in the current year, which Wall explained to be the result of a general reevaluation of the number of personnel required to support various industrial engineering programs. The nonlabor portion of the budget had been reduced very little from the current year's actual expenditure, as a large part of the $291,000 was for computer services necessary to operate the performance reporting system. Because of the nature of the system, it was not possible to reduce the cost of the system without giving it up entirely. Wall did not think that a manual system would be any less expensive than the computerized system, as an extensive study made several years previously of the cost of a manual system compared with a computerized system had indicated that the computerized system would be more effective and 45 percent less costly.

Wall stated that he believed that the budget request represented a fair estimate of the cost of maintaining the industrial engineering program at a minimum level. It would, of course, be possible to reduce the budget still further, but this would mean giving up some of the programs. The indus-

## TABLE 1
### Production Department Overhead Charges, Current Year[1]

| | January | February | March | April | May | June | July |
|---|---|---|---|---|---|---|---|
| Production manager's office | $ 15,819 | $ 14,343 | $ 17,811 | $ 14,343 | $ 13,275 | $ 17,022 | $ 14,343 |
| Production control unit | 237,567 | 214,662 | 266,331 | 214,665 | 204,327 | 259,848 | 214,662 |
| Industrial engineering unit | 148,170 | 134,124 | 167,019 | 134,124 | 128,790 | 160,866 | 134,130 |
| Production engineering and services unit | 980,343 | 885,018 | 1,082,859 | 808,494 | 1,047,345 | 1,033,926 | 650,340 |
| General superintendent's office | 327,645 | 299,196 | 374,070 | 299,199 | 284,412 | 368,946 | 299,196 |
| Total | $1,709,544 | $1,547,343 | $1,908,090 | $1,470,825 | $1,678,149 | $1,840,608 | $1,312,671 |
| Direct labor-hours, current year | 307,880 | 320,085 | 313,369 | 305,887 | 269,443 | 263,509 | 270,229 |

| | August | September | October | November | December | Total |
|---|---|---|---|---|---|---|
| Production manager's office | $ 14,379 | $ 18,138 | $ 17,490 | $ 19,194 | $ 25,680 | $ 201,837 |
| Production control unit | 214,671 | 231,900 | 178,290 | 177,486 | 208,533 | 2,622,942 |
| Industrial engineering unit | 134,127 | 151,101 | 119,262 | 113,715 | 142,038 | 1,667,466 |
| Production engineering and services unit | 668,721 | 810,030 | 750,027 | 691,983 | 618,198 | 10,027,284 |
| General superintendent's office | 299,196 | 360,174 | 248,139 | 270,333 | 312,015 | 3,742,521 |
| Total | $1,331,094 | $1,571,343 | $1,313,208 | $1,272,711 | $1,306,464 | $18,262,050 |
| Direct labor-hours, current year | 264,752 | 259,836 | 253,908 | 269,018 | 259,003 | 3,356,919 |

[1]Current year's figures were prepared in early December based on actual data for January through November and an estimate for December.

TABLE 2

Production Department Forecasted Direct Labor-Hours, Next Year

| Month | Labor-Hours |
|---|---|
| January | 258,000 |
| February | 264,000 |
| March | 265,000 |
| April | 263,000 |
| May | 255,000 |
| June | 254,000 |
| July | 252,000 |
| August | 252,000 |
| September | 250,000 |
| October | 244,000 |
| November | 243,000 |
| December | 242,000 |
| Total | 3,042,000 |

trial engineering department had already made severe curtailments of some of its programs such as forecasting shop loads and attempting to level them. This had caused difficulties with overloads in certain areas and had resulted in unanticipated overtime. Wall suggested that further reduction in the industrial engineering programs would have damaging effects immediately and perhaps some long-run harmful effects as well.

## PRODUCTION CONTROL UNIT

The third conference was held with Edgar Reeves, production control unit chief. Reeves had reduced his budget request by $285,000 from the actual amount expended in the current year. This reduction, according to Reeves, was accomplished largely by reducing expediters and the number of people conducting physical inventories of parts in storage. Both these functions could be reduced without affecting basic production control functions, although there would likely be an increase in parts shortages caused by lack of expediting and inaccurate parts records. Reeves said that it was impossible to tell what the cost of these additional parts shortages might be because effects were not felt immediately or directly. As far as the possibility of reducing the amount of labor in records, scheduling, and dispatching was concerned, Reeves said that the increasing complexity and variety of products were such that work load of these units was actually increasing, although total shop and yard work load was decreasing. He felt that maintaining staffs at their present levels in these areas was equivalent to a reduction in force. The $489,000 budget for nonlabor charges was only slightly reduced from

## TABLE 3

### Production Department Budget Requests, Next Year

|  | Labor | Nonlabor | Total |
|---|---|---|---|
| Production manager's office | $    183,000 | $     12,000 | $     195,000 |
| Production control unit | 1,848,000 | 489,000 | 2,337,000 |
| Industrial engineering unit | 1,182,000 | 291,000 | 1,473,000 |
| Production engineering and     services unit | 2,637,000 | 7,020,000[a] | 9,657,000 |
| General superintendent's office | 3,066,000 | 51,000 | 3,117,000 |
| Total | $8,916,000 | $7,863,000 | $16,779,000 |

[a]Perishable tools, shop and yard supplies, contracted services, and bottled gases.

actual charges during the current year. Almost $450,000 of this amount was for computer services used in maintaining parts and tool records and for scheduling, and there did not seem to be any way to reduce these costs without eliminating the scheduling system or ceasing to maintain parts and tool records.

## PRODUCTION ENGINEERING AND SERVICES

Dow, unit chief of production engineering and services, was the last to confer with Peters on the proposed budget. The budget for Dow's unit was quite large, principally because all perishable tools (items assumed to last for less than one year), shop and yard supplies, contracted services, and bottled gases (acetylene, oxygen, etc.) used in the shops and yard were charged to his budget. Dow said that he was not able in most cases to reduce the level of these nonlabor charges. Use of drill bits, cutters, degreasing compounds, acids, welding rods, acetylene, oxygen, and other supplies was essentially determined by the products being fabricated and processes being used. While Dow and the shop and yard supervision made every effort to impress upon workers the need for conservative use of these items, it was impossible to cut usage arbitrarily and still produce the product. Dow said that he had incorporated in his budget substantial cuts in the level of contracted services such as towels and overalls, but he did not feel that there was any more room for reduction in the nonlabor budget request.

Dow further indicated that he had made some personnel reductions in production engineering, tool and supply distribution, and packaging and preservation, which accounted for most of the reduction in the budget for next year below the current year's expenditures. He then explained the situation in each of the areas. Production engineering was cut somewhat, although the variety and complexity of items being manufactured had actually increased the work load. Further cuts seemed out of the question if the work was to be done. The number of personnel in tool and supply distribution had been cut to the point where some toolrooms and supply points were only open for a portion of each day. Workers needing tools or supplies either had to walk to a more distant point or wait until the attendant arrived. Packaging and preservation, normally a small operation, had been cut by two, one third of the work force.

The other area under Dow's supervision was the planning group, which prepared estimates and documentation for bids for new business. This group also assisted Peters in long-range planning for the department. Dow had made no cuts in this group as the declining work load in Delaware Bay's shops made it imperative that more effort be expended on bids for new business and long-range planning for the department.

Following the series of conferences, Peters looked once more through the budget requests and began the difficult task of cutting $2,725,000 from them.

## DISCUSSION QUESTIONS

1. Plot the month-by-month level of expenditures for the current year by each of the five organizations making up the production department.
2. Plot the month-by-month level of expenditures per direct labor-hour by each of the five organizations making up the production department.
3. Do you agree with the president's instructions to Peters directing him to reduce the overhead rate by 15 percent?
4. On what basis should Peters make the reduction — a straight percentage cut in all areas or on some other basis?
5. Assuming that Peters has to submit a budget that would result in an overhead rate of no more than $4.62 per direct labor-hour, what should that budget be?
6. Should overhead budgets be related to direct labor-hours, or should some other basis be used?

# Enterprise Fiberglass Company

Even before George Howard had finished his tour of duty as an officer in the Army Engineer Corps, he had decided to find employment as an engineer that matched his long-time interest — fiberglass hovercraft. Before being drafted in 1970, Howard had worked as an aircraft engineer, and it was through his experience in aerodynamics that he became seriously interested in the capabilities of hovercraft designs. The idea of designing and producing a commercially feasible hovercraft intrigued him. He was certain that fiberglass (also called fiber-reinforced plastics), as a construction material, could be a principal factor in making the hovercraft a versatile means of transportation, and even for recreational use, because of the material's high-strength and lightweight qualities.

After his discharge from the service, this deep interest in hovercraft continued, so that, when a position for an engineer became available in a firm producing prototype hovercraft, he quickly took the job. This work was short lived, however, because of the 1973 recession, and Howard found himself jobless like so many other engineers. While seeking other work Howard tried, on a commission basis, to sell small recreational hovercraft built by a California firm; he sold but one over a six-month period.

## PURCHASE OF THE BUSINESS

Partly out of the need for work, but mostly because he had always desired a business of his own, Howard purchased a business in the late fall of 1973 that had been incorporated earlier the same year. In return for his purchase of 4,000 outstanding shares at $1.00 par, he received the right to use the trade name, Enterprise Fiberglass Company. He also received approximately $2,000 worth of miscellaneous tools, equipment such as circular saws, countertops, and tables, and approximately $500 worth of fiberglass materials. The rest of the purchase price went for what Howard called "goodwill."

One factor that Howard had considered favorable in the purchase was the fact that the company was incorporated. With an incorporation expense of at least $800, including attorney fees, this had some value. Also, he believed, it would shield him from personal liability. Howard was also pleased that the lease of the building was being assigned at the same low rental rate — only $210 per month for nearly 700 square feet.

Howard had become interested in fiberglass while working with hobby kits to fashion furniture and other objects out of resin reinforced with glass fibers. The more he studied the physical properties of fiberglass, the more he recognized that the material, with its high strength-to-weight ratio and other qualities, was ideal not only for hovercraft bodies but for many other uses as well. He became skilled at the "hand lay-up" fiberglass process.

This process, relatively simple in comparison with construction procedures with other materials, formed the individual part by causing a liquid plastic and glass fiber mass to conform to the inside contours of a mold, also made of fiberglass, and shaped to that desired for the finished article. The mass was allowed to dry, and, after removal from the mold and sanding of the rough edges, the product was finished.

The fiberglass process was simple and yet used so extensively that Howard was certain that, until he could get production of his self-designed hovercraft under way, he could secure enough orders for fiberglass parts from industrial buyers to meet overhead and expand the present facilities.

Thus, of special importance to Howard in purchasing Enterprise was the promise he had received from a nearby snowmobile manufacturer that Enterprise could continue to produce fiberglass snowmobile bodies under an existing contract. Howard expected that this work would bring the company at least $10,000 in gross revenues within the next half year, at least enough business to get the company started.

## SEARCH FOR PRODUCT LINE

Toward the end of 1973 Enterprise seemed to be doing as well as could be expected of an infant company. Two young employees were hired to lay up the fiberglass snowmobile bodies from molds provided by the manufacturer. Meanwhile Howard continued to design and construct his first hovercraft. But, after several months, the snowmobile manufacturer suddenly ceased payments, citing the recession and lack of demand for snowmobiles. Enterprise was left without work — and over $5,000 in bad debts.

With no major contract to sustain Enterprise over the winter months, it looked bleak for the company. During these winter months, Howard kept himself busy on his hovercraft. An individual appeared at the shop one day and being quite wealthy — or so he claimed — advanced nearly $3,000 in cash to secure the first hovercraft produced for his personal recreational use. During the year that Howard worked on the craft, the customer lost interest and failed to produce additional cash. Howard continued to work on the hovercraft and invested an additional $5,000 before the hovercraft was completed. His efforts were rewarded to some degree when several articles about his hovercraft appeared in two major papers. One test run was televised by a major network on its local evening news program. Despite the excellent and free promotion, however, no offers were ever received for the hovercraft.

In early 1974 an acquaintance suggested that Enterprise start producing fiberglass motorcycle accessories because, with the fuel shortage, everyone was buying motorbikes and cycles. Soon Enterprise was producing motorcycle fairings and carry cases. Carry cases acted as saddle bags for storage, and fairings, mounted on the hand bars, served to shield the rider from wind and rain. Howard did not have records of how many such motorcycle accessories were sold in 1974, but he believed that gross sales amounted to at least $12,000, enough to get the company by its first year. After the oil embargo lifted, sales of motorcycle accessories dropped steadily.

Toward the end of the first full year of operation, Enterprise was finally able to enter a contract with a local company to manufacture small fiberglass switchcover boxes for fighter aircraft. This time the mold was not furnished to Enterprise but had to be constructed to the buyer's specifications. From this contract, Howard learned the exacting process of constructing the original piece, called a "plug," from which the mold is taken. This contract, lasting but a few months, was extremely profitable, grossing approximately $11,000 on an estimated total material and labor expenditure of between $3,000 and $4,000. After the contract ran out in early 1975, Howard was forced to lay off all but one senior employee.

Various products were tried that proved unsuccessful. One product, engineered by a creative brother-in-law, was a line of furniture lamps consisting of various-sized wood and glass frames into which were placed dyed and burned styrofoam shapes. The idea seemed novel and the lamps were aesthetically pleasing. After only ten lamps were sold in nearby retail stores, the product line was dropped. Other unsuccessful projects included construction of two 20-foot fiberglass pontoons and an attempt to produce dog dishes and flower pots out of an artificial mixture of marble and resin. The pontoons, each capable of holding 20 tons, were built in the hope that they could be sold to a builder of houseboats. Both projects were abandoned after it was found that there was no market for either of them, particularly the latter as plastic dishes and pots could be manufactured much more cheaply.

## TABLE 1

### Company Products, Gross Revenues for 1976

| Type | Price | Quantity Sold | Total Sales | % of Total |
|---|---|---|---|---|
| Boats | | | | |
|   Canoes | | | | |
|     17' | $250 | 30 | $ 7,500 | |
|     16' | 250 | 12 | 3,000 | |
|     12' | 150 | 17 | 2,550 | |
|   Dinghies | | | | |
|     6½ ' | 125 | 16 | 2,000 | |
|     10' | 250 | 2 | 500 | |
| | | | $15,500 | 21.4% |
| Motorcycle accessories | | | | |
|   Fairings | | | | |
|     Small | $ 50 | 35 | $ 1,750 | |
|     Medium | 70 | 6 | 420 | |
|     Full | 125 | 4 | 500 | |
|   Carry cases | 40 | 14 | 560 | |
|     Total sales | | | $ 3,230 | 4.5 |
| Retail sales of raw | | | | |
|   materials | | | $13,000 | 17.9 |
| Miscellaneous | | | | |
|   Camper tops | $325 | 3 | $ 975 | |
|   Baha kits | 125 | 1 | 125 | |
|     Total sales | | | $ 1,100 | 1.5 |
|       Total retail sales | | | $32,830 | 45.3% |
| Industrial | | | | |
|   Truck canopies | | | $25,554 | 35.3 |
|   Speaker horns | $ 14 | 48 | 672 | 0.9 |
|   Wing tips | 125 | 13 | 1,625 | 2.2 |
|   Cowlings | 250 | 18 | 5,000 | 6.9 |
|   Pipes | 32 | 55 | 1,748 | 2.4 |
|   Miscellaneous | | | 3,500 | 4.8 |
|     Total industrial sales | | | $38,099 | 52.6% |
| Other[1] | | | $ 1,500 | 2.1 |
| Total gross sales | | | $72,429 | 100.0% |

[1]Amount unaccounted for through Enterprise's records.

At one point business had become so slow in 1975 that Howard even began to build another hovercraft, much larger than the first one, despite the lack of potential buyers. However, during 1975 Enterprise did manage to secure several more industrial contracts similar to the one the year before. One such contract was the manufacture of fiberglass airplane cowlings and wing tips for a small airplane manufacturer. The company also began to produce a limited number of canoes and dinghies toward the end of the year. Unlike the fiberglass dune buggy bodies and camper tops, which were tried that year and dropped, canoes and dinghies remained a part of the product line.

In the first months of 1976, Enterprise entered its most important industrial contract when a local company, specializing in rebuilding and overhauling of heavy equipment, began ordering fiberglass truck canopies. The contract became demanding enough to warrant lease of a large building several miles from the shop, the hiring of four more employees, and the purchase of $5,000 of additional equipment.

After its long search for profitable products, Enterprise seemed to have found a steady product line. Yet, the product line remained varied and diverse. The products could be grouped according to the two large markets they generally served. The first market was the industrial market. Products in this market, besides airplane parts and truck canopies, consisted of miscellaneous engineering contracts, such as constructing original plugs. The second market was the retail market, most of which appeared to be recreation oriented: canoes, dinghies, motorcycle accessories, and shower stalls for private homes. Table 1 presents the 1976 product line by price, quantity sold, and the percentage of total gross revenues generated by each product.

## MARKETING AND DISTRIBUTION

Howard never liked the idea of using any method of distribution other than selling retail products directly out of the shop. He noted that the margin between the selling price and costs of material and labor was higher when the product was sold directly. He also argued that by selling directly, he could sell at lower prices than could his competitors, whereas if he used distributors he would have to charge at his own shop the same price as the retailer who purchased from distributors. Another reason Howard wanted to continue selling directly to the public was simple: he thoroughly enjoyed it. He has even said that, given a choice between being a retailer and a manufacturer, he would rather be a retailer. By both manufacturing and retailing he achieved a rough compromise, he felt, because he enjoyed the rewarding feeling of having sold to a retail customer a product that Enterprise made. He enjoyed this type of selling far more than attempting to find additional industrial contracts. He had said that seeking work from larger firms, having to meet with their purchasing managers, and trying to gain appointments with executives of potential industrial customers made him too nervous and uncomfortable.

Howard planned, in the first half of 1977, to find individuals who would enter into a franchise arrangement with Enterprise. The franchise holders would be required to pay Enterprise $3,000 and would also furnish necessary capital to purchase or lease manufacturing–retail facilities. In return for the initial fee, the franchise holder would receive molds from Enterprise for producing products in Enterprise's general product line. They would purchase needed materials through Enterprise, and Enterprise would train their employees in fiberglass production and fabrication. The franchise holders would retail the fiberglass products they produced from the molds acquired from Enterprise, and they would have the option of purchasing, at wholesale prices, additional products that Enterprise alone would produce. The franchise holders would also pay a percentage of their monthly gross receipts to Enterprise. This fee, to be negotiated between the parties, would be for the continued assistance from Enterprise in such matters as finding industrial contracts, introducing new products, and the right to use the Enterprise trade name.

Howard desired to maintain control over the franchise system by providing in the contract, that, should any franchise holder attempt to design its own molds or produce independently its own product line, the Enterprise molds would be withdrawn as well as all other support.

In marketing its boats, Enterprise offered a basically simple line, using but one design in its canoes. They varied only in length and color, three lengths and four colors being offered. Because all the canoes had keels and fairly shallow drafts, Howard presented them to customers as ideal for lakes. If asked, he did not recommended that they be used in fast-moving waters because they might ship water. He maintained, however, that Enterprise canoes were as strong as any other in the market and guaranteed them for one year. Howard did not emphasize comparative weights of the canoes but told customers who asked that they were about average in the market, approximately 70 to 75 pounds. He had determined these weights by occasionally weighing finished canoes to ensure that new employees were not using excess resin or glass reinforcement. All the canoes and dinghies had aluminum trim around the upper edges of the cockpit. The remaining construction was fiberglass, and there was no foam flotation.

Enterprise's pricing policy was to sell at lower prices than any of its competitors. Canoes were priced to cover direct labor and material costs but to remain at least $100 lower than any other seller of canoes. To determine prices for industrial contracts, Howard used the figure of $1.50 per pound, a price he heard was standard in the industry. Howard estimated the amount of materials used in each product by weighing the finished product and estimating the proportionate amount of glass reinforcement and resin that the finished part contained.

## INTERNAL OPERATIONS

Howard believed that the firm had lower fixed costs than did its competitors because of low rentals on its buildings and lack of inspections by regulatory agencies. However, when a state inspection finally occurred, the resultant fine was $150. Various discrepancies included inadequate machine guards, lighting, and ventilation and unsafe electrical wiring. Howard viewed this as a threat to his business since he feared that federal OSHA inspections would also begin.

Instead of designing its own molds, Enterprise sometimes used duplicate molds that were simply copies taken off of existing products. Fabrication of an original mold for a canoe, for example, could take up to as much as 1,000 hours of designing and forming. Howard did not feel that this was a necessary expense and believed that it would raise costs considerably, accordingly canoe molds were copies taken from competitive products.

Enterprise used two means to produce its fiberglass parts, the hand lay-up and the spray-up method. In the spray-up method a "chopper gun" costing approximately $2,000 was used and cut labor time by 30 to 40 percent. Labor time was saved because thin sheets of glass reinforcement did not have to be laid into the mold by hand, and the streams of resin were premixed with hardeners. In other respects, the two methods were similar.

Despite any labor savings, however, the spray-up method generally produced parts that were weaker than those produced by the hand laid-up process. Strength of a fiberglass part is a function of the glass-to-resin ratio — the higher the proportion of glass, the higher the strength. A higher resin content will be heavier and tend to be brittle. Hand lay-up produced an average ratio of 60 percent glass to 40 percent resin content. Spray-up averaged 30 percent glass to 70 percent resin content.

Canoes were produced at Enterprise by a combination of the two processes. Although the work looked rather simple, labor had to be skilled or defects in the fiberglass would occur. Howard estimated it took at least a year before a new employee was sufficiently skilled and good quality became consistent. Steps in the production process were as follows:

*Step 1: Preparing the Mold.* The smoother the inside of the mold, the easier it was to remove the canoe. The mold surface had to be clean and sanded to a fine finish to give a quality luster to the exterior finish. All such sanding was done by hand. At least three layers of wax were applied to the mold, each being buffed to a high gloss by hand as power tools melted the wax and damaged the mold. It was not uncommon for a new employee to ruin or damage at least one mold and canoe in trying to separate the two because the release wax had not been applied properly.

*Step 2: Applying the Gel Coat.* The gel coat provided the color to the part and its smooth finish. This was done by hand with a small spray can.

*Step 3: The Lay-up.* This step was the major part of the fiberglass construction. It is here that the basic components were joined into a solid lamination. For both hand and spray lay-ups, there were four basic substeps: (1) implacement of resin and reinforcement, (2) saturation of the reinforcement with resin, (3) removal of air pockets and wrinkles, and (4) removal of excess resin. All these steps were done by hand except the step saved by the chopper gun, but even here a layer of woven roving was laid into the hull by hand. The matlike layer of chopped glass and resin was still rolled out, as in the hand lay-up with steel rollers to remove air pockets. Excess resin was removed by flat rubber hand-held paddles.

Skill was needed in these steps to ensure proper impregnation of the glass with resin. Mixtures were important to achieve correct viscosity and proper thixotropy. The use of the chopper gun also required skill to attain a uniform spray — the tendency for new employees was to spray the layering too thick. Curing factors were watched carefully as humidity and temperature could affect the cure rates and abilities of materials to bond.

*Step 4: Removal of the Finished Part.* "Popping" the part from the mold had to be done carefully and without too much force. If all went well, the finished part would "pop" away from the mold without taking some of the mold with it or leaving a part of itself behind.

*Step 5: Edge Trim, Inside Gel Coat, and Final Assembly.* Upon removal, excess resin and glass around the edges were sanded off with an electric sander. A thin layer of gel coat was sprayed into the hull, usually of the same color as the exterior. Final assembly was done at the shop where seats and aluminum trim were mounted and riveted into place.

## PRODUCTION COSTS

Howard had not timed the exact amount of labor time incurred in each step. However, based on estimates from his employees, total direct labor time for the larger canoes was 14 hours, not counting curing times. The first four steps required 10 hours; final assembly required the remaining 4, including the hand lay-up of the seats.

Enterprise paid its employees between $3.00 and $3.50 per hour. One employee was paid $5.00 per hour because he was the most experienced and had worked with Enterprise since Howard purchased the company. Although labor costs were low, they were average in the industry, and labor was in ample supply. There was generally no unionization.

Labor turnover was high for two reasons. For those employees with experience it was not uncommon to move from one company to another, staying at one firm no more than a year or two. The major factor, however, was the unpleasantness of the work itself. Resins and glass fibers caused dermatitis, and catalyzed polyesters produced skin burns, as did the catalyst in pure form. Fiberglass dust presented respiratory hazards and required wearing a dust mask. A respiratory mask had to be worn as much as possible, as prolonged exposure to resin fumes could cause personality changes and even temporary impotence. Besides the possibility of skin burns, gloves were also worn because resin was sticky to work with and difficult to remove from the skin. The spray-up method presented a respiratory hazard because of air-suspended glass fibers caused by the chopper gun.

Because resins, once the catalyst is added, cure in a matter of hours, proper mixtures and timing were important. All equipment such as rollers had to be cleaned immediately after use because, once the resin hardened on the roller, the roller, which cost up to $20.00, had to be discarded. Of special importance was cleaning the chopper gun. If resin hardened inside the tubing or spray nozzle, the machine was ruined. The chopper gun also wasted material in normal usage because as much as 30 percent of the chopped glass and up to 10 percent of the resin were lost into the air during spray-up.

## TABLE 2

### Enterprise's Record of 1975 Operations

| | | |
|---|---|---|
| Sales | | $32,858.09 |
| Material costs | | 12,835.97 |
| Gross profit | | $20,022.12 |
| Expenses | | |
| Electric power | 167.90 | |
| Natural gas | 253.57 | |
| Water | 57.00 | |
| Telephone | 339.83 | |
| Payroll, employees | 5,942.00 | |
| Executive salary | 3,450.00 | |
| Taxes, Fed. Reserve Bank | 2,025.61 | |
| Taxes, I.R.S. | 121.69 | |
| Taxes, employment security | 220.54 | |
| Taxes, Dept. Labor, industry | 226.68 | |
| Taxes, state sales | 1,012.73 | |
| Taxes and fees, misc. | 151.63 | |
| Rent | 900.00 | |
| Advertising | 903.51 | |
| Accountant | 140.00 | |
| Tools, equipment, and main-<br>tenance | 2,391.91 | |
| Vehicle expense | 286.16 | |
| Contract labor | 60.00 | |
| Total expenses | | 18,650.76 |
| Net profit | | $ 1,371.36 |

Another kind of loss occurred at Enterprise but not from the production process itself. Howard discovered one of his employees laying up parts before the plant was opened to sell to his friends. Howard had no idea how long this had been going on or how much material was lost.

## FINANCIAL CONTROL

Howard used a cash-basis system for record keeping based on checkbook entries. Tables 2 and 3 show Mr. Howard's financial summary from which he determined the company's 1975 and 1976 net incomes. No records were kept as to the company's assets, and no depreciation schedules to depreciate equipment and amortize molds were used. Howard used an accountant only for figuring payroll deductions and annual corporate income taxes. The only data the accountant used were Enterprise's annual sales invoices and the checkbook entries.

## TABLE 3
### Enterprise's Record of 1976 Operations

| | | |
|---|---:|---:|
| Sales | | |
|     Wholesale | | $39,599 |
|     Retail | | 32,830 |
|     Total sales | | $72,429 |
| Material costs | | 28,200 |
|     Gross profit | | $44,229 |
| Expenses | | |
|     Electric power | 279 | |
|     Natural gas | 505 | |
|     Water | 60 | |
|     Telephone | 825 | |
|     Payroll, employees | 12,953 | |
|     Executive salary | 4,800 | |
|     Taxes, Fed. Reserve Bank | 4,061 | |
|     Taxes, I.R.S. | 28 | |
|     Taxes, Dept. Labor, industry | 914 | |
|     Taxes, state sales | 1,898 | |
|     Taxes and fees, misc. | 127 | |
|     Rent | 3,475 | |
|     Advertising | 2,059 | |
|     Accountant | 240 | |
|     Tools, equipment, and maintenance | 3,008 | |
|     Vehicle expense | 3,200 | |
|     Contract labor | 118 | |
|     Total expenses | | 38,550 |
| Net profit | | $ 5,679 |

Howard's chief goal for his company did not seem to center on a definite percentage figure for increased or sustained profits so much as it did around growth in the company's size and increased volume of sales. He said,

> I can't say that I want to become especially huge in this business — that would be a bit presumptuous at this early date. But I do definitely want to see my company continue to double sales each year. I want the company to grow to a good size so that I can start paying myself a decent salary soon.

To promote this growth in size and sales volume, Howard reinvested most of the net profits back into the company to be used for the purchase of additional assets and to generate larger volumes of manufactured products.

## DISCUSSION QUESTIONS

1. Determine likely market trends for Enterprise's major products.
2. Investigate any technical changes that have taken place in raw materials or fiberglass fabrication techniques and determine the impact of any changes on Enterprise's operations.
3. What will be the impact of state and federal safety and health regulations on Enterprise's production methods and facilities?
4. Analyze the adequacy of Mr. Howard's accounting, reporting, and control systems.
5. Develop a strategic plan for Enterprise for the next five years.

# Fibertex Plastic Corporation

The management of the Fibertex Plastic Corporation of Bellevue, Washington, a suburb of Seattle, faced the problem of planning for the proper location of the company. The existing lease on the building used as its factory was due to expire within the coming year. The management was considering five possible courses of action:

1. Remain in its present location.
2. Move to a new location within the Seattle metropolitan area.
3. Move to a new location within the Pacific Northwest.
4. Move into the Middle West.
5. Move to California.

## PRODUCT LINE

The Fibertex Corporation manufactured translucent building panels made from polyester resins reinforced with fiberglass mat. The paneling was made as flat or corrugated sheets varying in width from 24 to 42 inches and in length from 8 to 14 feet. There were 6 different corrugations such as sine wave form, shiplap form, hat section form, and so on. Up to 14 different colors could be used for each corrugation, although most items were limited to 4 or 5 colors. The intensity of the color could be varied from completely opaque to as much as 80 percent light transmission. Surface finish could also be varied to produce either a smooth finish or a crinkle finish. The panels were manufactured in light weight of 6 ounces per square foot or in heavy weight of 8 ounces per square foot.

The corporation had pioneered the development of a new method of manufacture. At the Bellevue plant the paneling was made in a continuous process in which the raw materials were inserted at one end of a 150 foot long machine and emerged from the other end completely processed. The method of manufacturing involved the impregnating of the fiberglass mat with the polyester resin between sheets of cellophane and passing the material through an oven containing platens that guided the material into the proper configuration. The heat in the oven caused the resin to cure into a hard, permanent material. Upon emerging from the oven, the panel was trimmed on the sides and cut to proper length ready for inspection and shipment. The continuous process machine had been designed and patented by the owners of the company.

Other companies generally manufactured paneling by the batch method, in which the mat was impregnated by hand and molded on plates that were piled one on top of another and rolled on a rack into an oven for curing. The continuous process machine at Bellevue produced a superior panel at lower cost than could be made by the batch method. The batch method, however, had the advantage of greater flexibility for small runs in that it permitted easier changeover between colors and configurations than did the continuous process machine.

Translucent plastic paneling was introduced to the market shortly after the end of World War II. Since that time it had received enthusiastic acceptance by the public. The paneling had the characteristics of light weight, great strength, corrosion resistance, transmission of light, and ease of handling. The material could be sawed, nailed, and handled in a rather rough manner without any damage. In contrast to glass, it was highly resilient to impact.

## MARKETING

The major home market for translucent plastic paneling was in patio roofs and enclosures, over breezeways, for skylights, for awnings, for greenhouses, and for carports. In addition, it was used for interior partitions and other decorative effects. In industry the material was used in roofs, windows, and partitions. There also appeared to be a potential market in such applications as truck bodies and fabricated parts, but this market had not yet been fully explored.

Although the price of the plastic paneling had been greatly reduced during the past several years, it was still considered a relatively expensive building material item. Lightweight paneling sold in the retail market at about 75 cents per square foot and the heavyweight material sold at about 95 cents per square foot.

The Fibertex Corporation distributed its translucent plastic paneling through the Panelette Distributing Company of Santa Monica, California. Panelette had succeeded in building up a national market for paneling under its trade name.

The management of Panelette had urged Fibertex to move its manufacturing plant to some location in the Middle West or in California. Panelette felt the potential market in California or in the Middle West was so much larger than that in the Pacific Northwest that it would be more economical to locate manufacturing facilities in the large market areas and ship to the small market areas. The management of Fibertex Plastic Corporation felt that the growing market in the Pacific Northwest justified a machine in this area although it recognized the desirability of production facilities close to the large market areas. The senior executives of Fibertex had lived in the Pacific Northwest for many years, and they and their families had a strong preference for remaining in the area.

## MANUFACTURING COSTS

The Bellevue plant was operated by a crew of five that consisted of an engineer who also managed production operations, three people who worked on the continuous machine, and an inspector who also handled shipping and receiving. These workers were paid the average going rate in the community. Mat was received by rail at an average cost of 69 cents per pound. Approximately 1¾ ounces of mat was used per square foot for the light paneling and 2½ ounces of mat was used per square foot for the heavy paneling. Practically all the balance of the paneling was resin, which was trucked from the Seattle warehouse of a national chemical manufacturer. Mat was purchased f.o.b. Huntington, Pennsylvania; resin was sold nationally by the chemical companies at a uniform delivered price of 32 cents per pound. Freight charges on mat shipped to the West Coast were $6.07 per hundredweight in carload quantities.

The resin was normally shipped in 475-pound barrels. Near the manufacturing plants of the resin companies it was possible to obtain bulk shipments of the resin at a savings of approximately 3 cents per pound. Fibertex bought resin from manufacturing plants located in Azusa, California and in Cleveland, Ohio. Other materials used in the manufacturing process averaged 3 cents per square foot. The value of the machine at Bellevue was upwards of $200,000 and was depreciated on a five-year basis on the assumption that it would be obsolete by that time. It had a capacity ranging from 2 to 15 lineal feet per minute, averaging about 6 feet per minute on most types of paneling.

The Fibertex Plastic Corporation had most of its funds tied up in equipment and working capital requirements for raw inventory, accounts receivable, and current cash needs. As a result management found it necessary to rent its building. An offer had been made by a local investor to provide the company with a building of its choosing anywhere within the Seattle metropolitan area that would be rented to the corporation on the basis of 2.25 percent per month of the cost of the building. The company anticipated that it needed for manufacturing operations 12,000 square feet at an average building cost of about $45 per square foot. At the present time the company was renting a building in Bellevue, 50 feet wide by approximately 160 feet long. Rail facilities were considered to be important although not absolutely necessary. One of the problems the company faced in building in the city of Seattle was the restrictions contained in the zoning code, the building code, and the regulations of the fire department. The company operated on a nonunion basis, although management had expressed willingness to work with any union that the employees desired to have as their representative. Four unions had already attempted to organize the workers, but the employees of the corporation had felt that the enlightened personnel policies of the company did not make the cost and obligation of union affiliation desirable.

## DISTRIBUTION COSTS

Dealers received a 25 percent markup on the paneling that they handled. Regional distributors had a 15 percent markup for their operation, and Panelette as the general distributor had a markup of 20 percent. Manufacturers' prices were quoted f.o.b. at shipping point. Approximately six major companies were attempting to sell the paneling on a national basis and had forced prices down to a point at which the margins were considered very thin. In addition, a large number of regional and local manufacturers were operating on very small volume using hand-batch methods in very simplified form. In the Seattle metropolitan area there were two such small local manufacturers.

Some manufacturers had made very lightweight panels down to 5 ounces and even 4 ounces per square foot to offer a very-low-priced product. These panels were sold for as little as 25 cents per square foot. Fibertex had refused to produce such panels because it felt the sacrifice in quality made very lightweight panels a poor buy for the customer even at very low prices.

Transportation charges for shipping the finished paneling between the Pacific Northwest and southern California were $9.94 per hundredweight for small quantities by truck down to $4.65 per hundredweight for full carload quantities by rail. Transportation charges from the West Coast to east of the Mississippi River were approximately double the rates between the Pacific Northwest and southern California.

While all the marketing problems at the present time were taken care of by the Panelette Distributing Company, management of Fibertex Corporation anticipated that it might have to handle its own marketing problems at some future date. This would require a capital investment in finished inventory as well as 8,000 square feet of additional space for warehousing. At the present time all finished paneling was shipped as rapidly as manufactured in lots of 10,000 to 15,000 pounds. Most shipments left the Bellevue plant by rail, although a small number were shipped by truck. Over 80 percent of the production of the Bellevue plant was sent to the southern California market. The balance was largely consumed in the Pacific Northwest with a small volume of drop shipments being made to the Middle West.

The expiration of the lease on the Bellevue property was still a year away, and management of Fibertex Plastic Corporation felt that it had plenty of time to work out a satisfactory solution to the problem. Hence, it was reviewed in a casual way from time to time.

## DISCUSSION QUESTIONS

1. Assume that you have been hired as a consultant to study the company's problem of plant location. Prepare a plan of how to organize and proceed with this study.
2. Compare Seattle, Los Angeles, and Chicago as locations for Fibertex by selecting appropriate business statistics from census data and other sources.
3. Select your home city or town or another city, and evaluate it as a potential location for Fibertex.

# Horizon Industries, Incorporated

Early in its corporate history Horizon Mining Enterprises had engaged in mining and smelting of nonferrous metals that it sold in pig form. Its activities were centered in the western United States with some smaller mining operations in Central America and the East Indies. While greatly expanding its mining operations over the years, the company also became involved in fabrication operations that were carried on in five plants, three in the South and two on the West Coast. Eventually Horizon, renamed Horizon Industries, Inc. in keeping with its diversified nature, had developed an annual sales volume of $1,200 million, of which less than 50 percent was derived from its original mining and smelting facilities.

As the company diversified, corporate management encouraged development of relatively autonomous divisions for each major product line. This arrangement worked well for a number of years. However, a mild recession coupled with increasing competition and falling profits caused the company's top executives to attempt to exercise increased control over activities of the various divisions. This control was exerted through newly established central corporate marketing, finance, accounting, personnel, manufacturing, and research staffs. While these staffs did not have direct-line authority over division activities, their investigatory and advisory activities resulted, in effect, in the return of a substantial degree of control to the corporate headquarters in Denver.

The corporate manufacturing staff was quite active in encouraging manufacturing departments of the various divisions to develop cost control and industrial engineering programs. Major attention was given to activities other than mining and smelting as it was believed that the fabricating plants could derive more benefit from this kind of assistance than could the mining and smelting operations. Also, in view of the fact that many of the people in top management positions had come up through the mining and smelting segment of the business, it was not considered good company politics to look too closely at practices that they may have had a hand in developing. However, the mining and smelting division had become so unprofitable that the central corporate staffs were directed to undertake a thorough review of these activities. As a part of this review program Ralph Norton, from the corporate manufacturing staff in Denver, was assigned to spend approximately six months investigating production operations in the mining and smelting division.

## LUMBER DEPARTMENT

Toward the end of his six-month assignment, Norton undertook an analysis of the lumber department, which was organizationally responsible to the production department of the mining and smelting division. Inclusion of the lumber department as a part of the mining and smelting division's production department was the result of development of certain mining properties in the western part of the United States more than 50 years previously. At the time the mines were being opened the availability of mine timbers, lagging, and framing materials by purchasing was not certain. To assure itself of an adequate and economical supply of timbers, the production department acquired timberland and constructed a sawmill to cut the necessary timbers. Although the lumber department was originally intended only to supply timber requirements for Horizon mines, the amount of timberland acquired over the years was considerably in excess of the limited needs for company operations. As a result the lumber department gradually shifted to producing commercial lumber, in both rough and finished condition for the open market. Although commercial products eventually increased to over 90 percent of its total output, the lumber department had remained under direct control of the production department of the mining and smelting division.

Since Norton, like many executives in Horizon's headquarters offices, was completely unfamiliar with the lumber department, he decided to visit its offices in Ashworth, Oregon. Wayne Logan, manager of the lumber department, met Norton at the Ashworth airport and, while driving to the offices, gave him a brief description of the lumber operations. The lumber department landholdings comprised about 300,000 acres of timberland in several counties. This land was adjoined by various private landholdings and also by land owned by the U.S. Forest Service. When originally acquired, the land was forested with virgin timber, of which a considerable amount remained uncut. The lumber department owned and operated a lumber mill at Ashworth that had started operation in 1917. In addition to timbers for the mining operations and commercial lumber, the lumber department also produced a full line of moldings and had recently begun to produce trusses, laminated beams, and prefabricated building components on a small scale.

At the lumber department offices in Ashworth, Norton met Nat Grinstead, Wayne Logan's assistant. Grinstead was an accountant who had been sent to the lumber department several years previously from the mining and smelting division's accounting department. Grinstead originally was brought in as Logan's assistant to help establish proper accounting procedures. After the accounting system was revamped, however, Logan believed that Grinstead was able to accept some additional assignments. Consequently, Logan and Grinstead had divided the managerial responsibilities in the following way: Logan retained the responsibility for mill operations, forest operations, and sales; Grinstead was placed in charge of accounting, purchasing, office management, inventory control, and traffic. In addition, Grinstead handled such miscellaneous matters as personnel, legal problems, and log sales. In talking with Grinstead, Norton concluded that Grinstead was probably a capable individual, although Norton observed that Grinstead tended to view most problems from an accountant's point of view.

## LUMBER MILL

Norton's first tour through the lumber mill on the day following his arrival in Ashworth was a revealing one. The mill superintendent showed Norton around the mill, in which he personally took a considerable amount of pride. The mill superintendent, who reported directly to Logan, was a veteran employee of the company, having started work in the mill 35 years earlier as a cutoff saw operator. He had worked at virtually every job in the mill and was obviously familiar with the duties of each of the 96 mill workers. According to Logan, the mill superintendent took a strong hand in supervising workers and stepped in frequently to solve production problems as they arose. Logan considered the mill superintendent to be one of his most capable supervisors since he ran the mill practically single handedly and rarely bothered Logan with any mill problems.

The mill itself was not a modern facility, although the buildings were well kept from outward appearances. The original mill building, built in 1917, had been expanded in 1933 and again 15 years ago. It now housed two headrigs, a gang saw, edgers, trimmers, and other equipment for sawing rough green lumber from logs.[1] From the sawmill the rough lumber was conveyed into a long shed on the green chain[2] from which operators pulled the various grades and dimensions of boards and placed them in temporary stacking pockets. After stacking, most of the green lumber was moved to an adjoining shed to await drying in the kilns. A small percentage was moved out into open storage in the yard either for sale as rough green lumber or to be air dried. The majority of lumber was kiln dried, cooled in cooling sheds, and then placed on the dry chain (similar to the green chain) from which workers pulled and sorted various grades and dimensions of boards and placed them in pockets. Although general sorting was done on the green chain, it was necessary to resort after drying due to change in grade of boards during the drying cycle. Some dry lumber moved directly to a separate building called the planing mill, which housed equipment necessary to produce surfaced lumber and moldings. However, most kiln-dried rough lumber was consolidated into loads that were placed in open storage in the yard to await processing in the planing mill when orders were received for specific sizes.

As Norton walked through these facilities, the mill superintendent explained that the saw mill, kilns, and planing mill had never really been designed as an integrated unit but were the result of continual additions and modifications through the years as the product mix of the mill changed and as new equipment was obtained. When asked about the age and condition of the equipment, the mill superintendent said that it varied from some pieces that were as old as the original mill to some that had been acquired as recently as last year. However, he believed that the exact age of various pieces of equipment was mainly of interest to the accounting department, which kept records of book value and depreciation for tax and financial statement purposes. From his standpoint, the mill superintendent stated that it was sufficient for him to know that the regular mill maintenance force of six persons, with some assistance from the operators themselves, was able to keep the equipment operating without too many breakdowns. Occasionally,

---

[1]Each headrig used a single, large circular saw to saw logs into smaller pieces or into boards. The gang saw consisted of several saws arranged side by side and used for simultaneously cutting smaller logs or pieces of logs into several boards. Edgers and trimmers were smaller saws used to cut the edges and ends of boards to their final rough dimensions.

[2]The green chain was a long conveyor carrying the lumber away from the edgers and trimmers. Workers were stationed at intervals along each side of the green chain. As the lumber moved past the workers, the workers pulled boards from the chain and stacked them in pockets, each pocket containing a single size and grade of lumber. "Green" refers to lumber freshly cut from logs and containing a high moisture content. "Dry" refers to lumber that has been dried by exposure to air for an extended period of time or has been kiln dried in a short period of time. Dry lumber has a low moisture content and is dimensionally more stable than green lumber and less subject to warping or cracking.

when a piece of equipment seemed to be getting too old and unreliable, he would request that Logan buy a new piece of equipment. There was, however, usually a long delay in getting anything new since authorization for release of funds for capital expenditures had to be made through the production department of the mining and smelting division. In numerous instances in the past, authorizations had been held up for a year or more because the mining and smelting division had stopped all capital expenditures due to poor sales in the primary metals market.

The mill superintendent felt that, in general, the mill was reasonably efficient. However, there were no cost centers and no detailed cost accounting as such was done. The mill superintendent had visited other mills in the local area and was convinced that the mill would compare favorably in the industry. He also noted that mill production had increased through the years while the labor force had stayed relatively stable. He attributed the reduction in labor force relative to output mainly to his own close attention to worker supervision and the fact that several pieces of automatic equipment, including conveyors, had been installed. The mill superintendent was not familiar with any of the industrial engineering programs that the corporate manufacturing staff had been encouraging at Horizon Industries' other plants, nor was he particularly sympathetic to the idea since the lumber industry in the local area had not, to his knowledge, ever made use of industrial engineers.

Adjacent to the main sawmill and planing mill was a smaller building in which trusses, laminated beams, and prefabricated building components were produced. This building was only five years old and was the most modern of those located at Ashworth. The mill superintendent introduced Norton to the supervisor of the manufacturing and fabrication operations who reported to the mill superintendent. In showing Norton around the building, the supervisor explained that the lumber department had begun manufacturing trusses on a very small scale about ten years previously and had expanded the operation five years ago when the new building was constructed. Trusses, beams, and prefabricated components were all made on special orders that came from two sources. One source was local construction and architectural firms that contacted Logan when they needed special components for industrial and commercial construction projects. The other source was building materials supply yards that the lumber department operated in Ashworth and two neighboring towns. These supply yards generally ordered components for residential construction for which they were supplying materials to local contractors. Although the total dollar volume of production was currently only $450,000 per year, the supervisor felt that sales could be much larger. The supervisor also noted that quite often it was possible to take poor-grade lumber and use it in manufacturing products that sold for three or four times the value of the original lumber.

# DEPARTMENT OPERATIONS

Following his tour through the plant facilities, Norton had a lengthy conference with Logan and Grinstead at which time they discussed in detail various aspects of the lumber department's operations. Logan began the discussion by explaining the lumber department's profit picture and place in the lumber market. Total sales of the lumber department in the previous year had been $12,192,000 and profits before taxes were $1,032,000, or 8.5 percent of sales. The breakdown of sales is shown in Table 1. This represented a return of 5.2 percent on a book value of $19,846,000 for the company's investment in timberland, plant, and equipment. The company's lumber sales constituted less than 0.1 percent of total softwood lumber sales in the United States.

When asked about the low profit rate on lumber sales, Logan explained that lumber market conditions in general were poor last year. During the year the industry average price, according to a trade publication, had been for pine, spruce, and fir and larch (the principal species marked by the lumber department), respectively, only $291.00, $210.00, and $223.50 per thousand board feet. Under these circumstances, Logan who dealt personally with the wholesale brokers through whom most of the lumber department's output was marketed, had been forced to accept lower prices than in the previous year. In the course of their discussion of the condition of the lumber market, Logan gave Norton copies of several analyses that had been prepared of lumber sales. These are shown in Tables 2, 3, and 4.

In addition to lumber sales, Logan also took personal responsibility for the sales of trusses, beams, and prefabricated components. Since the total sales volume of these items was small, they did not take much of Logan's time. Logan said that sales were generally handled on an informal basis. Local contractors and architects knew that the lumber department had a small facility for producing such items and either contacted Logan directly

## TABLE 1

### Lumber Department Sales

| Product | Sales | Profit | Profit/Sales (%) |
|---|---|---|---|
| Lumber | $ 6,990,000 | $ 126,000 | 1.8% |
| Chips | 723,000 | 237,000 | 32.8 |
| Land (including timber thereon) | 1,080,000 | 576,000 | 53.3 |
| Trusses, beams, and prefabricated components | 441,000 | (54,000) | (12.2) |
| Logs | 48,000 | 6,000 | 12.5 |
| Building materials supply yards | 2,910,000 | 140,000 | 4.8 |
| Total | $12,192,000 | $1,031,000 | 8.5 |

(in the case of unusual items or when relatively large quantities were involved) or ordered them from one of the lumber department's three building materials supply yards. On fairly standard items Logan had set prices based on the estimated cost of materials plus a rough estimate of the labor involved in producing them. For special items Logan made an estimate of the cost of materials and labor and checked these with the shop supervisor

### TABLE 2

#### Lumber Sales by Species

| Species | Board Feet (000) | Sales |
|---|---|---|
| Pine | 12,680 | $3,549,000 |
| Spruce | 640 | 125,000 |
| Fir and larch | 14,100 | 2,977,000 |
| Production department, mining and smelting division (breakdown by species not available) | 2,420 | 339,000 |
| Total | 29,840 | $6,990,000 |

### TABLE 3

#### Lumber Sales by Region

| Region | Sales Amount | % of Total |
|---|---|---|
| Oregon | $2,523,000 | 36.1 |
| Ten other western states | 1,664,000 | 23.8 |
| Rest of United States | 2,712,000 | 38.8 |
| Export | 91,000 | 1.3 |
| Total | $6,990,000 | 100.0 |

### TABLE 4

#### Lumber Sales by Product

| Product | Board Feet (000) | Sales |
|---|---|---|
| Surfaced dry | 25,810 | $5,353,000 |
| Surfaced green | 1,190 | 195,000 |
| Rough dry | 70 | 5,000 |
| Rough green | 20 | 2,000 |
| Moldings | 2,750 | 1,435,000 |
| Total | 29,840 | $6,990,000 |

before making a firm quotation. Logan indicated that the shop supervisor, because of his familiarity with operations and because of the small volume involved, was able to take care of most of the details of handling orders and supervising the shop. In fact the supervisor usually accepted purchase orders directly from the lumber department's building materials supply yards without consulting Logan, and he occasionally dealt directly with other customers.

The three building materials supply yards were run by managers who reported to Logan. The three managers had all worked in the yards for many years and were promoted to their positions largely on the basis of their practical experience with yard operations and seniority. Logan did not feel that it was necessary to take a strong hand in the operations of the yards as they had consistently shown a profit. A summary of yard operations prepared for Logan is shown in Table 5. Although Logan did not have an exact breakdown of the figures immediately available, he estimated that the sawmill supplied about 85 percent of the lumber sold in the yards and about 50 percent of the shingles, lath, and millwork. Trusses, beams, and prefabricated components were included in the millwork category.

Logan explained that the other major area for which he personally took responsibility was forest operations. The lumber department's landholdings consisted of 300,000 acres of timberlands lying mostly to the south and west of Ashworth, and it was from these forest lands that virtually all the logs for mill operations were obtained. Unlike many lumber producers, the lumber department bought logs from other sources only on very rare occasions. Some logs were sold to other local producers when the sawmill did not need them or when the location of the timber was such that it would be more economical to sell the logs than to haul them to the sawmill in Ashworth. For some years landholdings of the lumber department had been fairly static, with only minor changes when lands were sold or exchanged to consolidate the holdings. Because of the difficulty of building roads to gain access to

TABLE 5

Building Materials Supply Yard Operations

| Product | Total Sales | Gross Profit | | Net Profit (%) |
| | | Amount | As % of Sales | |
|---|---|---|---|---|
| Lumber | $ 696,000 | $ 156,000 | 22.4 | 1.9 |
| Shingles, lath, and millwork | 597,000 | 153,000 | 25.6 | 5.1 |
| Builders' supplies | 1,551,000 | 412,000 | 26.6 | 6.1 |
| Miscellaneous | 66,000 | 15,000 | 22.7 | 2.2 |
| Total | $2,910,000 | $ 736,000 | 25.3 | 4.8 |

timber when ownership in an area was mixed, efforts had been made whenever possible to work out exchanges of lands of equal value so that the lumber department gained ownership of continuous, large blocks of forest land. Accounting records showed a total of 3,055,600,000 board feet of timber on lands owned by the lumber department. This figure was based on the original timber cruises made when the land was acquired with adjustments for estimated harvesting and growth since that time.

Logan described present forest operations as an attempt to cut mature and overripe timber stands and to salvage infested, blown down, and burned timber. Current annual harvest was much less than could be cut on a sustained yield basis, although it was not certain exactly how much could be cut because of a lack of adequate information. In the past year the lumber department had embarked on a program of obtaining a complete, up-to-date timber inventory, but this was far from complete. Preliminary data obtained from this program indicated that the company lands might average about 16,800 board feet per acre. Unfortunately, much timber was inaccessible because of the lack of roads into many areas. Logan estimated that it would take about twice as many roads as now existed to gain access to most of the timber that could be logged at reasonable cost.

## INTERNAL CONTROL

Having described the operations for which he took responsibility, Logan suggested that Norton and Grinstead spend the rest of the afternoon going over areas for which Grinstead assumed primary responsibility. Grinstead's major interest, of course, was in the accounting system that he had developed when he first arrived at Ashworth. Grinstead described the system in considerable detail, and it was apparent that the system provided adequate information regarding the lumber department's financial condition. In place of the chaos that existed prior to Grinstead's arrival, particularly in the control of billings, accounts receivable, and inventories, the systems provided very up-to-date and accurate information through the use of systematic accounting practices and a small computer.

Besides his responsibility for the accounting system, Grinstead had assumed responsibility for purchasing, traffic, inventory control, and managing the lumber department office at Ashworth. Grinstead indicated that these functions were relatively minor in importance with the exception of inventory control. In the last year, control of inventories had become increasingly difficult, partly because of the depressed character of the lumber market. Because of lack of demand for lumber, yard inventories of rough kiln-dried lumber had increased to over a seven-month supply at current sales rates.

## ORDER PROCESSING

Grinstead also discussed problems that he had experienced with processing of customer orders. Because of his responsibilities for accounting, traffic, inventory control, and office management, Grinstead, in effect, managed the order processing system, although this was not considered as a separate function in the organization. Grinstead described the system as operating in the following way. Wayne Logan received most orders for lumber from the wholesale brokers. These he passed on to an order clerk who worked in the office under Grinstead's control. Usually Logan made delivery promises to the brokers based on his personal knowlege of the planing mill's work load, and the order clerk attempted to schedule orders to meet these deadlines. Some local brokers gave their orders directly to the order clerk, and all the lumber department's building materials supply yards orders were placed directly with the order clerk. The order clerk, in turn, wrote up planer tickets for each of the separate items on the order. These tickets served as directions to pick up rough lumber and deliver it to the planing mill and also as directions to the planer operators to produce the items.

Each day the order clerk released planer tickets for shipments scheduled during the day so that all items for an order could be run and loaded in trucks or rail cars in the same day. Planer tickets were released to the forklift operator in batches corresponding to one customer's order. Except on large orders involving several carloads of the same item, one planer operator worked on one customer's order and was supplied with rough lumber by a single forklift driver. Delays occurred when the forklift drivers were not prompt in getting raw material to the planers and also when the planers were shut down to change cutting knives or to reset the planers for another item. Depending upon the nature of a changeover, a new setup might take from half a minute to 10 or 15 minutes. Lost production as a result of resetting the planers might range from virtually nothing up to 1,000 board feet or more.

Aside from small overruns that inevitably occurred, no stocks of surfaced lumber or molding were carried as there was insufficient space for a surfaced lumber and molding inventory. Also, the wide variety of items produced, particularly moldings, made it impossible to carry all items in inventory.

As Grinstead described it, the difficulties that had recently appeared were in getting orders out on time and in keeping planer production volume up to a reasonable level. Despite efforts by the supervisors to exercise closer supervision over the planing mill workers, efficiency seemed to be decreasing gradually in the planing mill. As part of his efforts to pinpoint the nature of the difficulty, Grinstead had made several special analyses of one month's shipments. The results are shown in Tables 6 and 7.

## TABLE 6

### Shipments of Surfaced Dry Lumber, October

| October Shipments (1,000 bd. ft.) | Number of Products[1] |
|---|---|
| .0– 5.0 | 856 |
| 5.1–10.0 | 61 |
| 10.1–15.0 | 16 |
| 15.1–20.0 | 13 |
| 20.1–25.0 | 4 |
| 25.1–30.0 | 1 |
| 30.1–35.0 | 3 |
| 35.1–40.0 | 1 |

[1]A product is a specific dimension, grade, and species of lumber.

## TABLE 7

### Customer Order Size for Lumber and Moldings, October

| Customer Order Size (1,000 bd. ft.) | Number of Orders[1] |
|---|---|
| .0– 1.0 | 1,036 |
| 1.1– 2.0 | 215 |
| 2.1– 3.0 | 82 |
| 3.1– 4.0 | 31 |
| 4.1– 5.0 | 15 |
| 5.1– 6.0 | 18 |
| 6.1– 7.0 | 9 |
| 7.1– 8.0 | 7 |
| 8.1– 9.0 | 5 |
| 9.1–10.0 | 2 |
| 10.1–11.0 | 4 |
| 11.1–12.0 | 1 |
| 12.1–13.0 | 0 |
| 13.1–14.0 | 0 |
| 14.1–15.0 | 1 |
| 15.1–16.0 | 2 |
| 16.1–17.0 | 0 |
| 17.1–18.0 | 0 |
| 18.1–19.0 | 1 |
| 19.1–20.0 | 4 |
| 20.1–21.0 | 2 |
| . . . | . . . |
| 33.1–34.0 | 1 |

[1]An order is a customer request for a certain quantity of a lumber or molding product.

## DISCUSSION QUESTIONS

1. Based on the information that Ralph Norton had obtained so far at the lumber department, what would be your analysis of the strong and weak points of the lumber department operations? What tentative recommendations would you consider at this point?
2. How should Ralph Norton proceed with his investigation? What areas warrant further investigation? What information should be obtained? Where can Ralph Norton get the information?

# Icelandic Freezing Plants Corporation

At the end of a particularly hectic week, Olafur Gudmundsson relaxed for a moment in his easy chair and wondered what could be done to solve the problems he faced as traffic manager in the Reykjavik headquarters office of the cooperative known as the Icelandic Freezing Plants Corporation. In particular, he wondered whether a computer system could be designed and justified to replace the complicated hand clerical system he supervised for the control of production, inventory, and shipping at the 60 fish-processing plants that were members of the cooperative.

## ROLE OF THE COOPERATIVE

Mr. Gudmundsson was not only concerned with the complications of his operation, but he was also aware that the effectiveness of the control system could influence the sales program in a highly competitive market, the costs of processing, and the funds invested in inventory. His producers' sales association handled about 75 percent of the total export value of frozen fish from Iceland. Frozen fish exports were 30 percent of the total value of all exports.

Although Iceland had a population of only 200,000, its location adjacent to the rich fishing beds of the North Atlantic Ocean permitted it to achieve a place among the leading fishing nations in the world. Significant exporting of fresh and salted fish products from Iceland began about 1900 and expanded rapidly as technical progress took place in catching, processing, and shipping. Freezing of fish products began in the early 1930s and currently this was the leading export item of the country with approximately

100 quick-freezing plants in operation. It took a long time to develop a new market in a foreign country, and, for packaged products, great care had to be taken that the containers were printed in the proper language, showed the right weights and description, and conformed to local customs and legal requirements regarding labeling, size, and type of pack.

To improve the effectiveness of export marketing of frozen fish, the Icelandic Freezing Plants Corporation was formed in 1942 as a producers' sales association type of cooperative organization. Each of the 70 member plants was independently owned and operated and conducted its own fish processing, freezing, and packing. All marketing activities, however, were centralized under the cooperative. The plants operated their own fishing boats, and purchased some requirements from independent fishermen.

## ORGANIZATION STRUCTURE

Icelandic was a type of cooperative in which each member plant had one vote. Primary membership requirements were that each plant processed fish by freezing and engaged in export trade. At the annual meeting of the association, nine directors were elected. The directors in turn selected a chairperson and vice chairperson. The organization was then operated by an executive committee consisting of the chairperson and vice chairperson and three full-time professional staff members: the general manager, director of sales and marketing, and director of production. The executive committee met twice a week together to coordinate activities and to make policy decisions.

Reporting to the director of sales and marketing were the:

1. Manager for UK and Western Europe, located in Epsom, near London.
2. Manager for the United States, located in Scarsdale, near New York City.
3. Manager for Eastern Europe, located at the home office in Reykjavik.
4. Traffic manager, located at the home office in Reykjavik.

The director of production had a number of field inspectors reporting to him as well as the central purchasing agent who handled purchasing of supplies and warehousing. The director of production was responsible for preparing overall production budgets, engaging in research and development for improved production processes, designing new packaging, arranging that the proper supplies were delivered to each plant to meet their production schedule, and investigating new machinery that became available from suppliers throughout the world.

The general manager was responsible for the finances of the cooperative and in charge of the record-keeping procedures at the central office regarding production, inventory, and sales. He maintained close financial surveillance over subsidiary operations in the United Kingdom and United

States and also carefully watched over the financial conditions of each of the member plants. Because of the seasonal character of operations, it was necessary for almost all plants to borrow short-term funds from local banks or other financial institutions. These loans were supported by pledged warehouse receipts, for which Icelandic guaranteed direct payment when the pledged items were sold. In rare cases Icelandic made direct loans to member plants.

The cooperative organization maintained worldwide sales relationships, handled billing and shipping documents, and collected payment from their customers. Payments were in turn remitted to each plant for their shipments, less a charge of about 2 percent of sales for the cost of operating the cooperative. At the end of each year profits and losses of the cooperative were shared by the various member plants in proportion to the value of export sales from each plant. This required that the orders from customers be allocated to the member plants on an equitable and fair basis. It also required an elaborate record-keeping system.

## PROCESSING

Processing plants were widely dispersed around the 3,700-mile coast line of Iceland, although most were concentrated in the southwestern portion of the country near the capital, Reykjavik. Fishing boats delivered freshly caught fish to each of the freezing plants. The catch of approximately 30 different species of fish was highly seasonal, depending upon each species. At the freezing plants, fish were processed into more than 300 different products. Some plants specialized in as few as 50 items, several larger plants processed up to 150 items, but most plants handled 80–100 items. Although catching and processing of the fish products were highly seasonal, sales and shipments were fairly even throughout the year. Thus it was necessary for each freezing plant to maintain a large storage capacity for holding frozen fish and fish products. From January to May the main catch was cod, haddock, pollack and ocean catfish; May to September it was scampi (shrimp), herring, perch, plaice, lemonsole, and halibut; and October to December it was haddock, herring, and some cod.

Approximately 15 refrigerated ships periodically visited each freezing plant to take on a load and sail directly to the foreign market. Some of the ships were owned by a subsidiary of Icelandic; the others were chartered or booked for general trade. Each ship might stop at a number of freezing plants before it completed its load. The minimum pickup at any one freezing plant was about 1000 cases of fish products. Ships varied in carrying capacity from about 500 tons to about 3,000 tons of fish products and, when loaded, could have as many as 100 items for different customers picked up from as many as 30 different plants. On return trips company-owned ships handled miscellaneous cargos obtained through freight agents.

Most of the fish pack was distributed under the brand names of the company: "Icelandic," "Fresher," and "Sea Star." Some custom packing was also done under several private brand names for other marketing organizations. Products were classified into five major groups as follows:

1. Fillets in small consumer packs of about 1 pound and catering packs of about 5 pounds.
2. Fish blocks, weighing 10 to 18½ pounds, that were reprocessed by customers into fish stick products.
3. Shrimp, lobster, and scampi.
4. Herring products.
5. Animal products made from fish trimmings (for mink, pet foods, etc.).

The large product line was not only due to the various species of fish processed, type and size of pack, and various brand names, but also due to the following variables:

Boned or not
Skinned or not
Cellophane wrapped or not
Parchment wrapped or not
Individual wrap or block wrap
Type of parts — whole, heads, tails, fillets, backs, bellies
Arrangement of block — fish laid lengthwise or crosswise.
Minced fish

Package size for some items was as small as 5 ounces. These packages were packed in cases for shipment that weighed from 10 to 70 pounds.

## CONTROL SYSTEM

In addition to the high quality of its pack, an important competitive advantage was obtained by the ability to quickly respond to customer inquiries for orders requiring quick deliveries. This required an accurate and up-to-date centralized inventory control system. Operation of this system and the corresponding production orders and shipping orders were the responsibility of the traffic manager at the headquarters office, who reported to the manager of finance.

Periodically the manager of production of the cooperative worked with a committee representing different functions to prepare a plan of total production for the cooperative for the following months based on sales estimates for each product. Production orders for the next months for specific items were then issued to each plant, based on the estimated potential production of the plant. Actual production at each plant was, of course, dependent on the particular types of fish that were landed at the plant by the fishing fleet.

At the end of each fortnight (two weeks), each plant sent a telegram to the headquarters office reporting the quantity produced during the previous period by kind, type, weight, and brand. (This information was confirmed by mail from the headquarters to the plant.) At the central office production was posted manually to inventory cards. For each item there was a separate inventory card for each plant showing transaction date, identifying numbers, and three columns headed "In," "Out," and "Balance." As shipments were made from each plant, delivery tickets were posted to the same inventory card for the outgoing merchandise and the balance on hand entered in the last column.

Accumulated totals of production and deliveries were also recorded for each product at each plant and for all plants and were also summarized by all products at each plant and all plants. All this data was finally summarized in a report that showed, by product, total production, total deliveries, total orders, and balance on hand.

As sales orders were received, shipping schedules were prepared and shipping orders issued to each plant in proportion to its production of the items involved. In preparing the shipping schedules the traffic manager had to take into account the size of the refrigerator ship involved, ports that it would call on to deliver the product, size of the vessel compared with docking facilities at each plant (some of the smaller plants could not accommodate the larger ships), the sequence in which the ship had to be loaded (generally in the reverse order of unloading at the ports of destination), location of the inventory, minimum pickup of 25 tons at the plant, and the agreement for allocating sales orders among the plants.

The traffic manager also had to adjust for last-minute changes that might occur when loading the delivery ships. During the fish processing there was an inspection by government officials and company inspectors to assure proper adherence to health regulations. In addition, during the loading process the corporation had its own inspector make a final inspection to higher standards than the health inspectors to maintain the reputation of the company with its customers for top-quality merchandise. From time to time, these final inspectors would reject some merchandise, requiring the traffic manager to make rapid adjustment for the changes. Sometimes storms or sea conditions required changes after a ship was underway to drop off or add a plant to the scheduled trip. This was handled by radio. Also clerical errors that occurred in the records from time to time caused minor or major difficulties in the inventory control system.

Although marketing was a joint project of the various member plants through the organization of the cooperative, the primary risks continued to be borne by each individual plant. These risks included the timing, specifications, amount, and sales price of the pack that was sold. To give each plant equal and fair treatment with reference to the success of the marketing operation, there was an agreement on the manner by which sales orders received by the cooperative would be allocated to the member plants. This agreement provided that for each product item, on a calendar-year basis, cumulative shipments from a given plant as related to total cumulative sales of the item by the cooperative would be in the same ratio as cumulative production of the item at the given plant as related to total cumulative production of the item at all plants. There were, however, some special adjustments that were necessary from time to time. The example in the appendix to this case illustrates how the agreement was applied.

At the end of each calendar year, any carry-over inventory remaining was shipped first in the new year from each plant in proportion to the total production by item and by plant for the previous year. After the old pack was shipped, the new pack was allocated for shipment, in accordance with the agreement previously described.

After a shipping order was issued to a plant, actual shipment was confirmed by a delivery form in five copies issued by the plant in question and signed by the plant inspector and the supercargo. In addition, the master of the ship signed a "captain's receipt" for the cargo and for the documents he received for delivery to the consignee. During the time that a vessel was loading, the traffic manager had his representative, called the "supercargo," on board who collected all the documents involved and returned them to the central office when the ship sailed for its foreign destination. The central office then prepared or gathered together the shipping documents, consisting of the following:

*Bill of Lading*
Standard commercial form — multiple copies.

*Application for Export License*
Government form — describing items shipped, unit price in foreign currency and in Icelandic krónur; total value; when, where, and by whom produced; date of shipment; destination; buyer; commissions; and how shipped (c.i.f., f.o.b., etc.). Approval obtained from local government office.

*Certificate of Insurance*
Standard commercial form.

*Certificate of Origin*
Certifying source of items as Iceland and indicating ship, buyer, marks on boxes, and net and gross weight.

*Health Certificate*
Certifying shipment was of nonepidemic origin. Signed by the city health officer from location of origin.

*Shipper's Specification*
> Describing in detail each item and the number of cases for each item obtained from each plant.

*Certificate of Inspection*
> Listing of each item and the year the fish was caught. Based on the report of government inspectors at time of production and signed by a representative of the director of the Icelandic State Inspection of Fish located in the local government office.

*Temperature Report*
> Required only by certain customers indicating product temperature before loading, after loading, during transit, before unloading, and after unloading. Form prepared and supplied by the central office, but data supplied and the form signed and given or mailed directly by ship's officer to the customer.

These negotiable documents were delivered by the central office in Reykjavik to a local bank for payment from a letter of credit deposited by the customer or were mailed to the customer for payment. Almost all the documents were in English, but the currency was that of the buyer, except for the Soviet Union, which used £ sterling. Although the shipping documents were made up after the ship sailed, they were mailed by air to the destination and usually arrived before the ship was unloaded.

For each sales transaction, a sales report was prepared for each plant contributing to the shipment showing its share of the net value resulting from the transaction and listing all expenses for freight, insurance, commissions, exchange rates, export duty, import duty, and other sales expenses. The net amount in krónur was then sent to the bank of the plant by check or to a lending institution if the items involved had been pledged by warehouse receipts for a loan guaranteed by Icelandic. Finally, the traffic manager prepared a consolidated report for the customs officials and for the currency control officials of the Icelandic government on a standard form provided by the government.

The volume of paperwork amounted to approximately 5,000 shipping documents a year. On the average, a shipping document for a customer would contain three or four items obtained from three plants. In addition to the traffic managers, the control system was maintained by five full-time clerks plus two part-time workers used during periods of peak loads.

## NEED FOR SYSTEM IMPROVEMENT

The traffic manager received many complaints from the various plants who felt that they were not being fairly treated — particularly when their storage capacity was filled. Most of these complaints were made without any real knowledge by the plant managers who felt they had to constantly "needle" the traffic manager to keep him "honest" regarding a fair allocation of orders.

In thinking about a new system the traffic manager had the following objectives in mind:

1. Eliminate clerical detail and errors.
2. Eliminate decision making when allocation and routing rules could be automatically followed.
3. Avoid controversy with the plant managers.
4. Prepare the shipping schedules as rapidly as possible and as late as possible prior to the time each ship visited each plant for a load.
5. Make adjustments easily and rapidly in shipments for last-minute orders and for rejects while the ships were still loading at the processing plants.
6. Simplify the paperwork procedure.
7. Reduce the cost of processing the paperwork.
8. Tie together the inventory control system with the purchasing of supplies and packing materials.
9. Set up a system for maintaining sales and production statistics that could be used in preparing future production plans and marketing plans.

Additional statistical data were particularly desired. Sales managers in the various sales offices around the world wanted detailed marketing information regarding price movements and sales by items for their geographic area of responsibility as well as for other regions. It was also desirable to be able to analyze the difference in production costs for different markets. Some markets were more selective than others and require special processing to achieve a desired quality level. Cost data, however, were maintained on an individual plant basis and treated as confidential information by the plant owner. It was proposed, however, that the central organization could provide computer service for the individual plants to process their cost data, payroll, and other information and still maintain the security of confidential plant information. Some plants had already established effective cost control procedures; other plants operated with no cost information except for summary results that were available at the end of the year.

It was also desired to collect fishing statistics by the type and amount of fish caught in each area of the fishing beds at each season of the year so that long-term trends could be analyzed that might suggest improved fishing procedures.

At the end of the year the central office prepared an annual report by hand that typically consisted of about 65 pages, $8\frac{1}{2} \times 17$ inches, about half text and half tables that showed in detail and summary the operations of the organization. Preparation of the statistical tables for the report was a major project for the traffic manager and the traffic manager's staff.

One of the major computer companies maintained local offices in

Reykjavik for the sales or leasing of data processing equipment and also operated a service bureau. The traffic manager, however, was not certain that this company necessarily had the best equipment for his particular situation. He also faced the task of presenting a proposed capital budget to the board of directors of the corporation whose members were generally very conservative in responding to new ideas and changed procedures — particularly those that would involve additional expenditure of funds.

## DISCUSSION QUESTIONS

1. Prepare a summary list of all the documents involved in the control of production, inventory, and shipping, indicating source of each, to whom issued, general content, use, when issued, and time period covered.
2. What factors would you take into account in designing a control system for this situation?
3. Prepare a flow chart for a manual system of control.
4. Prepare a flow chart for a computer system of control.
5. For a computer system, design
   a. each output item
   b. each input item
   c. flow chart for a computer program
6. How would you evaluate a manual system as compared with a computer system?
7. Compare the problems described with the problems of an airline in making passenger reservations, with the problems of a banker in balancing loan requests with available funds, with the problems of a manufacturer of aircraft in controlling spare parts, and with the problems of a wholesaler in planning purchases.

## APPENDIX: ILLUSTRATION OF SALES ALLOCATION BY PLANT

Assume for a given item that 105,000 cases had been produced by four plants in the previous year with an inventory of 600 cases remaining on hand on January 1. In January 18,000 cases were produced and sales order 1 was received for 10,000 cases that was shipped in February. In February 19,000 cases were produced and sales order 2 was received for 4,000 cases to be shipped in March.

Columns A through F show the conditions prior to the allocation of order 1 for 10,000 cases. Six hundred cases were then allocated to use the inventory from the previous year, and the remaining 9,400 cases were assigned on the basis of 52.2 percent of the production at each plant. This was the ratio of total orders (9,400 cases) to total production (18,000). The allocation of order 1 and resulting conditions is shown in columns G through L, as of February 1.

| Column | A | B | C | D | E | F | G | H | I | J | K | L | M | N |
|---|---|---|---|---|---|---|---|---|---|---|---|---|---|---|
| Plant | Production in Previous Year | | Inventory on Hand January 1 | | Production in January | | Allocation of Order 1 | | | | Inventory Not Allocated February 1 | | Production in February | |
| | | | | | | | From Previous Year | From Production of Current Year | | | | | | |
| | Cases | % of Total | Cases | % of Total | Cases | % of Total | Cases | Cases | % of Prod. | % of Total | Cases | % of Total | Cases | % of Total |
| 1 | 30,000 | 28.5 | 200 | 33.3 | 8,000 | 44.4 | 200 | 4,200 | 52.2 | 44.6 | 3,800 | 44.1 | 1,000 | 5.3 |
| 2 | 40,000 | 38.1 | 300 | 50.0 | 3,000 | 16.7 | 300 | 1,560 | 52.2 | 16.6 | 1,440 | 16.8 | 3,000 | 15.8 |
| 3 | 20,000 | 19.1 | 100 | 16.7 | 1,000 | 5.6 | 100 | 502 | 52.2 | 5.5 | 480 | 5.6 | 8,000 | 42.1 |
| 4 | 15,000 | 14.3 | — | 0 | 6,000 | 33.3 | — | 3,120 | 52.2 | 33.3 | 2,880 | 33.3 | 7,000 | 36.8 |
| Total | 105,000 | 100.0 | 600 | 100.0 | 18,000 | 100.0 | 600 | 9,400 | 52.2 | 100.0 | 8,600 | 100.0 | 19,000 | 100.0 |

| Column | O | P | Q | R | S | T | U | V | W | X | Y | Z | AA | AB |
|---|---|---|---|---|---|---|---|---|---|---|---|---|---|---|
| Plant | Accumulated Production February 28 | | Inventory On Hand February 28 | | Distribution of Accumulated Orders (Including Order 2) | | | Preliminary Allocation of Order 2 (4,000 Cases) | | Accumulated Production of Shippers | | Adjustment A | Reallocation | |
| | Cases | % of Total | Cases | % of Total | Cases | % of Prod. | % of Total | Cases | % of Total | Cases | % of Total | Cases | % of Prod. | % of Total |
| 1 | 9,000 | 24.3 | 4,800 | 17.4 | 3,250 | 36.2 | 24.3 | −950 | −23.8 | — | — | 950 | — | — |
| 2 | 6,000 | 16.2 | 4,440 | 16.1 | 2,175 | 36.2 | 16.2 | 615 | 15.4 | 6,000 | 21.4 | −205 | −3.4 | 21.5 |
| 3 | 9,000 | 24.3 | 8,480 | 30.7 | 3,250 | 36.2 | 24.3 | 2,730 | 68.3 | 9,000 | 32.1 | −305 | −3.4 | 32.1 |
| 4 | 13,000 | 35.2 | 9,880 | 35.8 | 4,725 | 36.2 | 35.2 | 1,605 | 40.1 | 13,000 | 46.5 | −440 | −3.4 | 46.4 |
| Total | 37,000 | 100.0 | 27,600 | 100.0 | 13,400 | 36.2 | 100.0 | 4,950 / −950 | 100.0 | 28,000 | 100.0 | 950 / −950 | −3.4 | 100.0 |

| Column | AC | AD | AE | AF | AG | AH | AI | AJ | AK | AL | AM | AN | AO | AP |
|---|---|---|---|---|---|---|---|---|---|---|---|---|---|---|
| Plant | Accumulated Production of Shippers | | Adjustment B Reallocation | | | Adjusted Allocation or Order 2 | | | Accumulated Allocations | | | Inventory Not Allocated February 28 | | |
| | Cases | % of Total | Cases | % of Prod. | % of Total | Cases | % of Prod. | % of Total | Cases | % of Prod. | % of Total | Cases | % of Prod. | % of Total |
| 1 | – | – | – | – | – | 0 | 0 | 0 | 4,200 | 46.7 | 31.3 | 4,800 | 53.3 | 20.4 |
| 2 | 6,000 | 31.6 | 95 | 1.58 | 31.7 | 505 | 8.4 | 12.6 | 2,065 | 34.4 | 15.4 | 3,935 | 65.6 | 16.6 |
| 3 | – | – | –300 | – | – | 2,125 | 23.6 | 53.1 | 2,645 | 29.4 | 19.8 | 6,355 | 70.6 | 26.9 |
| 4 | 13,000 | 68.4 | 205 | 1.58 | 68.3 | 1,370 | 10.5 | 34.3 | 4,490 | 34.5 | 33.5 | 8,510 | 65.5 | 36.1 |
| Total | 19,000 | 100.0 | 300 / –300 | 1.58 | 100.0 | 4,000 | 10.8 | 100.0 | 13,400 | 36.2 | 100.0 | 23,600 | 63.8 | 100.0 |

February production resulted in conditions shown in columns M through R, at which point order 2 for 4,000 cases was to be allocated on the agreement basis of the ratio of accumulated sales to accumulated production. On February 28, this ratio was 36.2 percent (13,400 cases sold by orders 1 and 2, and 37,000 cases produced), and it was applied to the production of each plant to obtain the distribution in column S. By subtracting column H from column S, the preliminary allocation of order 2 was obtained in column V, which gave a negative value of 950 cases for plant 1 and overallocation of 950 cases to the other plants. This peculiar allocation resulted from plant 1 having high production in January and low production in February.

Because order 2 for 4,000 cases did not permit plants 2, 3, and 4 to overship by 950 cases, this amount had to be reduced from their allocation as shown by adjustment A. The reduction of 950 cases were 3.4 percent of their accumulated production of 28,000 cases (column X), and this ratio (column AA) was applied to the production of each plant (column X) to obtain the reallocation amount in column Z.

Another problem arose when it was discovered that plant 3 was short by 300 cases of the specific type of product (by brand label) that was required. This amount was then reallocated to plants 2 and 4 as shown by adjustment B in columns AC through AG.

By adding the amounts in columns V, Z, and AE, the adjusted allocation in AH was obtained, which then resulted in the conditions shown in columns AK through AP as of the end of February.

# John Stark

John Stark was one of 647 employees in the purchasing department of the Celerity Company located in the Philadelphia area. Celerity was a major manufacturer employing over 25,000 people and producing stoves, washing machines, oil burners, vacuum cleaners, refrigerators, and other electrical–mechanical appliances. John Stark had recently received a master's degree in business administration with honors from The Wharton School, and he had joined Celerity with great enthusiasm. This was his first major professional job, and he was anxious to succeed in his assignment as a buyer of small hardware. Three months later, however, John Stark's enthusiasm about his job had disappeared, and he felt frustrated and bitter. He became so disturbed about his situation that he actively began to seek other employment and only retained his job with Celerity to keep "beans in the oven" until he could locate another job. As an employee and a professional, he felt so distraught that he decided to write about his situation to his former professor at Wharton who had recommended the job to him. His letter follows:

Dear Professor Dobbins:

This letter pertains to my present position and the intense dissatisfaction that I am experiencing.

Upon your recommendation I joined the purchasing department at the Celerity Company approximately three months ago. After being keyed to peak performance during graduate school, I was anticipating being in a position where I could make a positive contribution. However, the actual situation is the exact antithesis of these anticipations. It is extremely frustrating and also depressing to be honed to a fine edge by advanced education and then be committed to a mundane, mechanical, and routine job.

The people in this organization think small. It is definitely the fault of a management that has become divorced from operations. Jobs have been so finely categorized, and responsibilities so minutely divided, that individual initiative has evaporated. Further, impositions in the form of extreme regimentation have reduced employees to a plodding, unthinking, uninspired lot.

Through the mechanisms of five-minute coffee breaks, forty-minute lunch periods, whistles, whistles, whistles, and the final insult of time clocks, capable and willing people are soon transformed into mechanical, disloyal beings. It is my firm conviction that, if more activities were left to individual initiative, a self-imposed honor system would produce a rapid and more efficient work flow through the Celerity Company complex.

Another source of irritation is the noise level in the office. It sometimes reaches such a level that it drowns out the all-important quitting time whistle. How management expects anyone to think under these conditions is beyond me. And of course the answer is self-evident because management does not expect anyone to think!

I realize that the expense of putting each person into a partitioned office would be prohibitive; however, the situation could be easily improved by sectionalizing buying groups through the use of movable partitions. Telephones are ringing constantly, and, to assure that each is heard, employees turn up the bell to full volume. You can imagine the overall effect of hundreds of telephones ringing at maximum volume.

Celerity is a technically oriented company with engineering talent accorded preferential treatment. Engineers are similar to commissioned officers in a military organization, with nontechnical people filling the ranks. This situation is logical in view of the company's competitive position depending on continued technological superiority. However, this preference is overemphasized, with resulting resentment among nontechnical personnel.

Engineers are not required to punch a time clock, do not have Pavlovian-type coffee breaks (where salivary gland reactions are triggered by whistles), are not restricted severely at lunch times (may even take enough time to go out to lunch), and in general are accorded respect with the assumption that they possess normal discretion and human intelligence. The result is much more job enthusiasm and dedication, which partially explains Celerity's continued technical excellence and marketing success. Some engineers are even known to work overtime, during the week, and on Saturdays, without overtime pay!

Salary levels further reflect this disparity in treatment of the two groups. The purchasing department is notorious for miserly salary levels and extended promotion periods. I am surrounded by personnel wearing five-year buttons who are still below the supervisor level. In fact, my hiring salary rate was higher than the present income of many unfortunates who have been here six or more years. My lead buyer has been with Celerity for over eleven years and is still not making enough to enable him or his family of five to take trips on his three-week vacation. Furthermore, he has not received a raise (not even a cost-of-living raise) in the past two years. He is not alone, because many senior employees have not received raises and are openly grumbling about it. Impressive titles are handed out in lieu of monetary rewards. These titles are apparently part of the Celerity Company fringe benefits, which incidentally are inferior in comparison with those of the more progressive companies. It is a fact that the best way to get a raise or transfer at Celerity is to terminate and get rehired into a new job classification.

The personnel in purchasing are intelligent and competent people who have been sincerely dedicated in the past but who are stymied in their advancement to a supervisor's position. The tragic part of this situation is that a supervisor's position only allows one to work overtime without pay! Many buyer supervisors are making considerably less than $20,000 per year and will remain at that pay level for years. In engineering the average hiring rate is $1,400 per month at present, and it keeps going up each year. The comparable rate for beginner purchasing department employees with equivalent education, skill, and responsibility is at least $200 per month less. Many people in purchasing are college graduates, but the salary levels are not commensurate with education.

Most new people hired in the department to do buying start at the lowest classification of buyer trainee and assist a buyer. Because of my education I got a break and started one rung higher on the ladder as a buyer. I am supposed to report to my lead buyer, a pleasant but unimaginative fellow who has been with Celerity for over eleven years. Actually, however, I am supervised by the buyer supervisor to whom my lead buyer reports.

My buyer supervisor is a really dedicated person and makes a sincere effort to do his job well. He had three years of college and is in his early thirties. He has been with Celerity for six years. As an administrator he gets along well with his staff, but he tends to be too easy with the vendors in an endeavor to be popular.

My buyer supervisor reports to the section supervisor, for whom I have great respect. He was trained as an engineer and is a very precise individual. His observations are keen, and his command of the situation is comprehensive. He believes in thorough consideration of a subject before commenting on it. His favorite expression to the people in our section is: "It's better to remain silent and be thought dumb than to speak and remove all doubt." He doesn't say much unless he knows what he is talking about.

There are no personal frictions or administrative problems in our group, but this is not true of other groups. Some of the supervisors tend to be somewhat crude, and they seem to be lacking in administrative ability. It looks to me as though several have been advanced to supervisory positions only by reason of their years of service and supposed knowledge of detail. In general, however, I sense no serious frictions or resentments against the supervisors since everyone recognizes that we are all hampered by the same restrictions of the system.

It is interesting to observe the current campaign going on to upgrade the purchasing department by hiring only college graduates who will advance faster because of their educational advantage, but, if they are advanced over the heads of the senior employees, then Celerity will lose its best trained and most experienced employees. If the college graduates are not moved up fast, they will leave and seek better positions. Senior employees have resigned themselves to a life of mediocrity and low salaries, but it is doubtful that the aggressive, ambitious college graduates will commit themselves to this future.

Incidental irritations are traffic to and from the plant, gravel parking lots, long walking distances, and insolent, suspicious gate guards. I realize that traffic is an enigma and that Celerity has done about all it can to alleviate the situation with staggered shifts. Parking lots are, of course, expensive due to land acquisition costs. Nevertheless, it adds insult to injury to put up with all those other things and then have to walk at least fifteen minutes to and from the car. The daily fight for a parking place, plus getting shoes and car covered with mud or dust (depending on the season), does not help matters.

Guards are instructed to be suspicious of everyone and several are naturally insolent (maybe because of their "power" position). This attitude on the part of the guards epitomizes the overall company atmosphere. Management can take an object lesson from "old biddy" schoolteachers and unsuccessful military officers who fail because of improper, suspecting attitudes. Celerity expects its personnel and suppliers to be positive-minded in relationships with the company. If management would only reciprocate, not only with its suppliers, but more importantly with its employees, then many of the problems outlined will cease to exist.

Please accept this letter as a sincere effort to relate some of the problems faced by Celerity and not just a collection of gripes. This "bottom of the barrel" approach may be somewhat emotionally charged, but it nevertheless contains some basic facts that may be useful for an objective analysis and corrective recommendations.

Thank you for your help in finding me this position. I hope you don't think of me as being ungrateful just because it hasn't worked out to my complete satisfaction as yet. I am only seeking a worthy challenge and hope to enjoy the fruits of my efforts as much in the business world as I did in your graduate seminars.

Cordially yours,
John Stark

# DISCUSSION QUESTIONS

1. How serious are the charges John Stark has made about his job situation? Can you classify the charges by ranking them from most important to unimportant?
2. Why do the difficulties exist?
3. What can be done about them?
4. Stark claims that the people in the organization "think small." Yet he says they are intelligent, competent, and sincerely dedicated. How can you reconcile the apparently contradictory statements?
5. In his letter John Stark gives his evaluation of various supervisors. How much reliability can you place on his observations?
6. He states that the company expects its personnel and suppliers to be "positive minded." What does this mean?
7. Stark complains about insufficient compensation but at the end of his letter says he is only seeking a "challenge." What do you think he really wants?
8. What does his letter say about John Stark himself?
9. Does his letter suggest that highly educated personnel need to be handled differently from those with less education? If so, what recommendations do you have for a supervisor who has to deal with this problem?

# Label-It, Incorporated

The Precision Moldings Company started out as a small but profitable privately held business corporation specializing in the custom injection molding of plastic parts. From its inception the company had been owned and operated by Bill Weber, a chemical engineer by training who had a good deal of experience in the plastics business. Over the years Weber had built up the business so that he was employing about 30 workers as a vendor of a variety of custom molded plastics parts for as many as 20 different customers at any one time. The majority of business consisted of limited production runs of a variety of parts ranging from plastic novelty items and gadgets to custom parts that were used in the products of companies who found it more economical to purchase such parts from an outside vendor rather than manufacture them in house. Label-It, Inc., a customer of Weber's for the past five years, was an account that fell into this category.

## PRODUCTS AND GROWTH

Label-It, Inc., a young, rapidly growing company, was founded by a product designer who had developed a small, hand-held tool that would emboss custom labels on strips of colored vinyl. The Label-It tool and labeling process was a unique product with a great deal of potential over a wide marketing range. However, Label-It had been marketing its product exclusively for industrial applications because it was relatively expensive to manufacture and only certain industrial applications could justify the high price tag. The product was expensive for several reasons. First, it was comprised almost entirely of cast metal and hand-machined parts. The only relatively inexpensive part of the product was a small subassembly composed of several plastic parts that Weber's company had been custom molding for Label-It. Second, Label-It did not manufacture any of the parts in its product. All parts were custom made and supplied by a number of outside vendors. Only final assembly and packaging were done by Label-It.

Jack Murray, the founder and president of Label-It, had always felt that the greatest growth and profit potential for his product lay in the vast consumer market, not only in the sales of labeling tools but more important in repeat sales of the consumable vinyl strips that were used to make the labels. Murray envisioned marketing hundreds of thousands of labeling tools and vinyl strip packages on an annual basis through various retail outlets such as department stores, discount drugstore chains, and the like, not only in the United States but in international markets as well. A marketing study that Murray had initiated reinforced his belief in the potential of a consumer-oriented product. As a result, Murray had started Label-It engineers on the design of a low-cost, inexpensive label tool that would sell for a price well within the reach of the average consumer. With the exception of a few metal springs and four metal fasteners, the new model was made entirely of injection-molded plastic parts. Since Murray intended to produce as many parts of the new model as possible in his own plant, Label-It contracted with a local tool and die company to make molds for the various parts. The cost of such custom molding was quite high, but the cost per part was not significant when amortized over projected sales of the new product.

In the years that Weber had been a vendor for Label-It, he had established a good business relationship with the Label-It staff and a close friendship with Murray. In fact, Weber and Murray had discussed a consumer-type label tool many times, and it was Weber who originally suggested the idea of a plastic design as a way of minimizing manufacturing costs. On several occasions in the past Murray had hinted to Weber about the possibility of Label-It, Inc.'s buying Weber's company. Murray saw two important advantages to such an acquisition: First, Label-It would get the expertise that it lacked in the area of plastics and plastic molding, and, second, it would get a manufacturing facility that was already in place and operating, with the capacity for manufacturing the new consumer model.

About three months prior to the scheduled start of production of Label-It's new model, Murray presented Weber with a formal offer for the purchase of Precision Molding Company. The offer included cash and stock options and the condition that Weber join the Label-It company with the title of vice president of manufacturing operations. Weber had been expecting Murray to make such an offer and was prepared to accept if the terms were favorable to him. Weber believed that Label-It's product would exceed expectations and that Label-It, Inc. would grow into a large, highly profitable corporation. With these and other considerations in mind, Weber accepted Murray's offer and was soon organizing and planning for production of the "Label-Riter," as the new model was called.

When the molds for the Label-Riter were completed, Weber made trial production runs of enough parts to assemble 50 labeling tools. Optimum injection machine settings and cycle times were used for these trial runs, and the molds proved satisfactory. The Label-Riters assembled from these parts operated as they were designed to do, and the few quality problems uncovered were considered to be minor. With the market introduction of the Label-Riter, production quotas increased rapidly, as the product was an immediate success. Within a few months actual sales of the Label-Riter were well ahead of what had been anticipated. Weber increased production of Label-Riter parts by shortening the injection molding cycle, which resulted in increased output. However, he suspected that the shorter cycle might result in dimensional problems because of the greater difficulty in controlling shrinkage of parts.

## QUALITY CONTROL PROBLEMS

When final assembly inspection began showing an increasing number of rejects, Weber ordered an analysis to determine the reason for rejection. Results indicated that 90 percent of the faulty Label-Riters were rejected either because of jamming of the vinyl label strips in the Label-Riter or the inability of the tool to print characters in a consistent pattern on the label. A consultation between Weber and the design engineer revealed that both problems were caused by failure to meet dimensional tolerances for the label guide, which was a small slotted part through which the vinyl label was fed into the embossing head of the tool. Width of the slot was specified as 0.2545 $\pm \frac{.0050}{.0000}$. Because of the width of the label strip that had to pass through the label guide slot, it was essential that the slot dimension be at least 0.2545 inches and desirable that it be as close as possible to this dimension.

Weber met with the shop supervisor of the injection molding operation. The supervisor was a long-time employee of Weber's who had been hired as a machine operator when Precision Moldings Company was first started. The supervisor had little formal education but was a conscientious worker and was well acquainted with the machinery. Eventually he had been promoted to his present supervisory position. When Weber explained the problem with the label guide slot, the supervisor noted that the operator of the machine on which the part was produced had informed him that he was having difficulty holding the slot dimension after the last shortening of the cycle time. To try to correct the problem, the supervisor had helped the operator in a trial-and-error procedure to find a combination of pressure and temperature settings that would compensate for the shorter cycle and keep the slot dimension within tolerance.

## FIGURE 1

### Supervisor's Control Chart

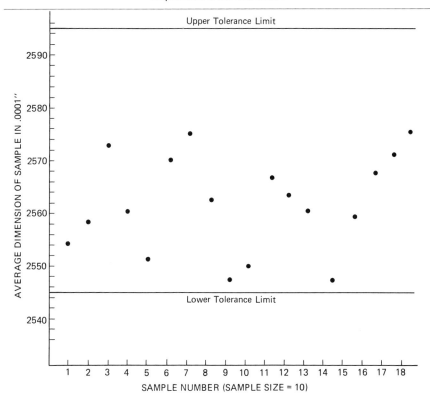

The supervisor also had made a control chart to aid the operator in holding the slot width within tolerance. He had directed the operator to use the chart whenever he was running the label guide part and had instructed him on how to use it. He then told Weber that the label guide part was being produced today and that, when he last checked the operator's control chart, it showed that the slot width was being held within tolerance. Weber asked to see the chart that the supervisor had designed. A copy of the chart is shown in Figure 1.

## STATISTICAL CONTROL CHARTS

After examining the supervisor's control chart, Weber suggested, instead, that $\overline{X}$ and $R$ charts be used to help diagnose the trouble in molding the label guide part and aid in controlling the process. Weber spent several hours instructing the supervisor on the construction and interpretation of $\overline{X}$ and $R$ charts. They discussed the formulas that the supervisor would use for his calculations and Weber made a list of the formulas for the supervisor.

**141**

FIGURE 2

Formulas and Factors used in Constructing Control Charts

Formulas to compute control limits for $\overline{X}$ and $R$:

$$UCL_{\overline{X}} = \overline{X} + A_2\overline{R} \qquad UCL_R = D_4\overline{R}$$

$$LCL_{\overline{X}} = \overline{X} - A_2\overline{R} \qquad LCL_R = D_3\overline{R}$$

Formula used to estimate process standard deviation for a controlled process:

$$\sigma' = \frac{\overline{R}}{d_2}$$

Formulas to compute control limits using $\sigma'$ and an aimed at value $\overline{X}'$:

$$UCL_{\overline{X}} = \overline{X}' + A\sigma' \qquad UCL_R = D_2\sigma'$$

$$LCL_{\overline{X}} = \overline{X}' - A\sigma' \qquad LCL_R = D_1\sigma'$$

$$\text{Center line}_R = d_2\sigma'$$

Factors required to use formulas:

| Sample Size | A | $A_2$ | $D_1$ | Factors $D_2$ | $D_3$ | $D_4$ | $d_2$ |
|:---:|:---:|:---:|:---:|:---:|:---:|:---:|:---:|
| 4 | 1.50 | 0.73 | 0 | 4.70 | 0 | 2.28 | 2.059 |
| 5 | 1.34 | 0.58 | 0 | 4.92 | 0 | 2.11 | 2.326 |
| 6 | 1.22 | 0.48 | 0 | 5.08 | 0 | 2.00 | 2.534 |

He also gave the supervisor a list, for several different sample sizes, of the $A$, $D$, and $d$ factors required in the formulas. The information for this list was taken from a comprehensive set of tables contained in a quality control manual that Weber kept in his office. These formulas and factors are shown in Figure 2.

Weber directed the supervisor to institute the new control procedure at the start of production the next morning. It was agreed that measurements would be made at the point of production by the machine operator and that the operator would measure five parts from each half-hour's production throughout the course of the workday. The supervisor would oversee the activity, calculate control limits, and plot points on the control charts.

On the day that the new charting procedure was begun and as the operator was taking his measurements for subgroup 11, the supervisor noticed an inconsistency in the way in which the operator was making the measurements. At that time the operator also informed the supervisor that he had been making his adjustments to the machine to aim at or slightly above the 0.2545 dimension. When the supervisor measured some parts made earlier, he found that the action taken by the operator had resulted in many parts with slots that were too narrow. He instructed the operator again on how to make the measurements and also directed him to aim the process at a higher dimension of 0.2570. The operator instituted these changes starting with subgroup 12. Measurements for the subgroups for the first two days' production are given in Table 1; subgroups 1–16 are for the first day, 17–32 are for the second day.

TABLE 1

Measurements for the First Two Days' Production

| Subgroup Number | Measurement for Each of the Five Items in the Subgroup | | | | |
|---|---|---|---|---|---|
| | 1 | 2 | 3 | 4 | 5 |
| 1 | .2551 | .2580 | .2529 | .2535 | .2531 |
| 2 | .2566 | .2600 | .2572 | .2516 | .2572 |
| 3 | .2516 | .2540 | .2552 | .2568 | .2554 |
| 4 | .2521 | .2598 | .2554 | .2538 | .2541 |
| 5 | .2547 | .2562 | .2541 | .2562 | .2553 |
| 6 | .2588 | .2551 | .2576 | .2602 | .2557 |
| 7 | .2547 | .2569 | .2540 | .2574 | .2571 |
| 8 | .2559 | .2526 | .2540 | .2529 | .2521 |
| 9 | .2502 | .2509 | .2525 | .2522 | .2504 |
| 10 | .2529 | .2546 | .2526 | .2510 | .2548 |
| 11 | .2536 | .2542 | .2541 | .2542 | .2550 |
| 12 | .2582 | .2557 | .2581 | .2562 | .2545 |
| 13 | .2566 | .2580 | .2558 | .2544 | .2572 |
| 14 | .2581 | .2563 | .2565 | .2588 | .2564 |
| 15 | .2562 | .2565 | .2561 | .2579 | .2568 |
| 16 | .2554 | .2565 | .2565 | .2566 | .2565 |
| 17 | .2560 | .2552 | .2568 | .2577 | .2565 |
| 18 | .2552 | .2559 | .2565 | .2556 | .2580 |
| 19 | .2558 | .2578 | .2545 | .2560 | .2562 |
| 20 | .2577 | .2580 | .2584 | .2586 | .2581 |
| 21 | .2552 | .2549 | .2551 | .2566 | .2545 |
| 22 | .2550 | .2559 | .2565 | .2560 | .2560 |
| 23 | .2557 | .2555 | .2560 | .2571 | .2565 |
| 24 | .2565 | .2545 | .2550 | .2555 | .2561 |
| 25 | .2545 | .2585 | .2547 | .2551 | .2549 |
| 26 | .2556 | .2563 | .2580 | .2575 | .2577 |
| 27 | .2544 | .2549 | .2574 | .2565 | .2573 |
| 28 | .2576 | .2563 | .2558 | .2577 | .2570 |
| 29 | .2546 | .2577 | .2549 | .2547 | .2558 |
| 30 | .2563 | .2565 | .2586 | .2562 | .2546 |
| 31 | .2548 | .2562 | .2565 | .2560 | .2556 |
| 32 | .2587 | .2556 | .2585 | .2560 | .2558 |

## DISCUSSION QUESTIONS

1. Based on the data in Figure 1, would you agree or disagree with the supervisor's statement that the slot width is being held within tolerance?
2. Prepare control charts for the first day's production as the supervisor would have done. How do you interpret these charts?
3. Compute the natural tolerance or spread for the process and compare it with the specified tolerance. What conclusions may be drawn from the comparison?
4. The supervisor suggested that the process be aimed at an average dimension midway between the upper and lower specification limits as a way of minimizing the number of reject parts produced. If reworking label guide slots that are too narrow to bring them within tolerance is less costly than scrapping the parts, would this be a good idea?
5. Prepare control charts for the second day's production. How would you interpret these charts?
6. At what dimension should the process be aimed?

# Maynard Farms

Tom Maynard and his two sons had been engaged in growing and packing fresh fruit in eastern Washington state for many years. One of the major crops grown on the farm was cherries. Tom expected that his company would handle approximately 1,350 tons of cherries during the coming season. A portion of this total represented output from his own farm, but in addition Maynard Farms contracted to pack and market fruit for other growers. For the services provided to other growers, Maynard Farms received 20 percent of the selling price of the crop.

Cherries are extremely perishable, and the price received at the marketplace is related directly to the condition of the fruit. Therefore, a processing plant that accommodates the cherries as they are picked is extremely important to the growers. On the other hand, an excess of plant, equipment, and labor can quickly change a profitable venture into a loss. Tom said, "We need the fruit from the other growers to provide sufficient volume to make this plant successful; the problem, however, is that all the growers want this fruit processed as soon as it is ripe and immediately after it is picked."

The location of the Maynard Farms processing plant in relation to the nearest highway is shown in Figure 1; the layout of the plant itself is shown in Figure 2. The Maynard Farms packing plant was 200 feet long (not including the cement loading and unloading dock) and 100 feet wide. In addition three smaller buildings were appended to the main structure: a 50-foot by 60-foot cold storage room, a 40-foot by 90-foot bulk cooling room, and a smaller room that served as a corridor from the main room to the cooling room and space for the compressor and humidifier.

FIGURE 1

Site Plan (not to scale)

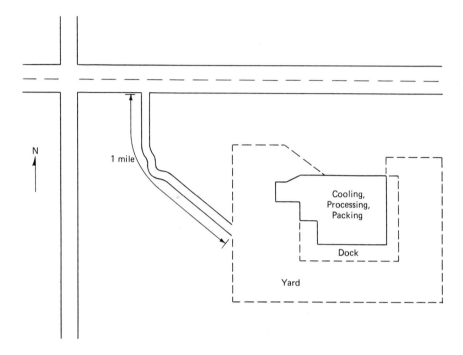

## GROWER OPERATIONS

A list of growers utilizing the plant, their locations in miles from the plant, round-trip travel times between each orchard and the plant, volume of cherries and time of picking for the most recent season, and total trips necessary to collect the fruit are given in Table 1. As shown in the table, not all fruit ripened at once. Variation occurred because of the degree of maturity of the trees, the extent to which the trees were fertilized and watered, and the respective altitude of each orchard. Trees at the lowest levels or closest to the Yakima Valley were the first to ripen. Locations of the orchards in relation to the packing plant are shown in Figure 3.

Growers hired their own pickers who worked from daylight until about noon, when the temperature in the orchards generally became too warm. After the fruit was picked it was placed in large bins stationed throughout the orchards, which were then picked up by Maynard trucks. The bins weighed over 1,000 pounds when filled and were collected and loaded on the trucks for transport to the packing plant. A truck could handle ten steel bins at one time, for a maximum capacity of approximately 5.5 tons of cher-

# FIGURE 2

## Plant Layout

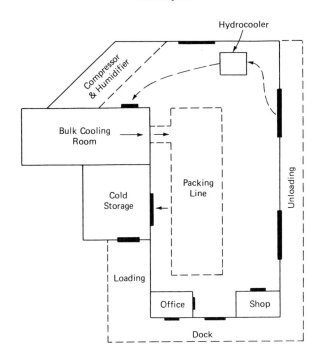

# FIGURE 3

## Location of Orchards

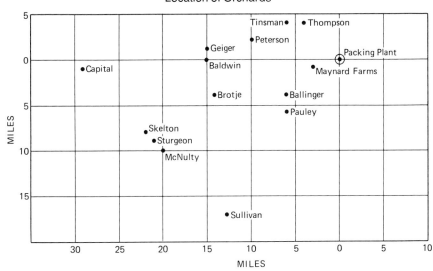

# TABLE 1

## Growers Using Maynard Packing Plant

The day columns span **June 8–30** and **July 1–5**.

| Grower | Round Trip Travel Time | Miles One-Way | Expected Total Volume | 8 | 9 | 10 | 11 | 12 | 13 | 14 | 15 | 16 | 17 | 18 | 19 | 20 | 21 | 22 | 23 | 24 | 25 | 26 | 27 | 28 | 29 | 30 | 1 | 2 | 3 | 4 | 5 |
|---|---|---|---|---|---|---|---|---|---|---|---|---|---|---|---|---|---|---|---|---|---|---|---|---|---|---|---|---|---|---|---|
| | | | | | | | | | | | | | | | | | | | | | | | | | | | July | July | July | July | July |
| Maynard | 20 | 3 | 342 | 27 | 36 | 36 | 36 | 36 | 36 | 36 | 36 | 36 | 27 | | | | | | | | | | | | | | | | | | |
| Tinsman | 60 | 10 | 22.5 | 4.5 | 4.5 | 4.5 | 9 | | | | | | | | | | | | | | | | | | | | | | | | |
| Thompson | 50 | 8 | 108 | | | | | 9 | 9 | 9 | 13.5 | 13.5 | 13.5 | 13.5 | 13.5 | 13.5 | | | | | | | | | | | | | | | |
| Peterson | 70 | 12 | 18 | | | | | 4.5 | 4.5 | 9 | | | | | | | | | | | | | | | | | | | | | |
| Sullivan | 130 | 30 | 90 | | | | | 4.5 | 4.5 | 9 | 18 | 18 | 18 | 18 | | | | | | | | | | | | | | | | | |
| Baldwin | 80 | 15 | 36 | | | | | | | 4.5 | 4.5 | 4.5 | 4.5 | 4.5 | 4.5 | 4.5 | 4.5 | | | | | | | | | | | | | | |
| Geiger | 90 | 16 | 40.5 | | | | | | | | | 4.5 | 4.5 | 4.5 | 4.5 | 9 | 9 | 4.5 | | | | | | | | | | | | | |
| McNulty | 130 | 30 | 5.4 | | | | | | | 2.7 | 2.7 | | | | | | | | | | | | | | | | | | | | |
| Sturgeon | 130 | 30 | 4.5 | | | | | | | 1.8 | 2.7 | | | | | | | | | | | | | | | | | | | | |
| Skelton | 130 | 30 | 9 | | | | | | | 1.8 | 1.8 | 1.8 | 1.8 | 1.8 | | | | | | | | | | | | | | | | | |
| Ballinger | 30 | 6 | 7.2 | | | | | 1.8 | 1.8 | 1.8 | 1.8 | | | | | | | | | | | | | | | | | | | | |
| Brotje | 90 | 18 | 180 | | | | | | | | | | | 18 | 18 | 18 | 18 | 18 | 18 | 18 | 18 | 18 | 18 | | | | | | | | |
| Capital | 110 | 30 | 247.5 | | | | | | | | | | | 9 | 9 | 9 | 18 | 22.5 | 22.5 | 22.5 | 22.5 | 22.5 | | 22.5 | 22.5 | 22.5 | 4.5 | 4.5 | 4.5 | 4.5 | 4.5 |
| Pauley | 40 | 8 | 72 | | | | | | | | | | | | | | | | | | | | 4.5 | 9 | 9 | 9 | 9 | 9 | 9 | 9 | 4.5 |
| Total/day | | | 1182.6 | 31.5 | 40.5 | 40.5 | 45 | 55.8 | 55.8 | 75.6 | 81.0 | 78.3 | 69.3 | 69.3 | 49.5 | 54 | 49.5 | 45 | 40.5 | 40.5 | 40.5 | 40.5 | 22.5 | 31.5 | 31.5 | 31.5 | 13.5 | 13.5 | 13.5 | 13.5 | 9 |
| Truck trips | | | | 6 | 8 | 8 | 9 | 12 | 12 | 15 | 17 | 17 | 15 | 16 | 11 | 12 | 11 | 9 | 8 | 8 | 8 | 8 | 9 | 6 | 6 | 4 | 3 | 3 | 3 | 3 | 2 |

ries per load. Maynard Farms owned three trucks and employed three drivers during the season.

Loading of the bins on the trucks in the orchard was usually accomplished using a forklift. Maynard Farms had five forklifts that were stationed in the orchards during the picking season. Forklifts were moved on an empty truck from orchard to orchard and to and from the packing plant, where they were stored when not in use. Typically, a forklift was taken to an orchard when picking began at that location and remained there until picking was completed. Standard procedure was for the truck driver to use the forklift stationed in the orchard to move each bin and place it on the truck. If the orchard did not have a forklift, the driver had to use a hydraulic hoist mounted on the truck to load each bin. Average loading time per bin was about five minutes when a forklift was used; use of the truck-mounted hoist added about 9 minutes per bin to the process because of the extra time needed to drive the truck through the orchard, position the truck properly for the pickup, and use the hoist. (These times included the unloading of any empty bins being returned to the orchard.) Pickup of bins in the orchards started about 7:00 A.M. when the first full bins would be ready for collection.

## CHERRY PROCESSING

When a truck arrived at the packing plant, the first step in processing was to weigh the truck and its load, remove the bins from the truck, and reweigh the empty truck. Empty bins were also loaded back on the truck for return to the orchards. One clerk ran the scales and kept the records. Average time for weighing, unloading full bins, and reloading any empty bins was ten minutes per truck.

Two forklifts and drivers were available for moving fruit in the packing plant. Forklifts were used to unload the full bins and reload empty bins on the trucks. The forklifts were also used to move full bins from the unloading dock to the hydrocooler, where the bins were emptied, and return the empty bins to the dock. It took a forklift about one minute to move a bin from the unloading dock to the hydrocooler, dump it, and return the empty bin to the dock.

The purpose of the hydrocooler was to reduce the temperature of the cherries quickly to 50° Fahrenheit as well as to wash away field dust and debris. Capacity of the hydrocooler was about 6 tons of cherries, which were cooled to the proper temperature in about 30 minutes. Once the hydrocooler was loaded with cherries and the fruit began cooling, additional cherries could not be added without lengthening the cooling cycle. That is, all cherries had to spend 30 minutes in the hydrocooler to ensure that the proper temperature was reached. After initial cooling, cherries were removed from the hydrocooler and placed in bins once again for transport to the bulk cooling room. A bin of cherries weighing about 1,000 pounds could be filled and moved to the bulk cooling room by a forklift in about two minutes. One worker was in charge of the hydrocooler, spending his time monitoring cycle times and temperature and assisting with dumping fruit into the cooler and emptying the cooled and washed cherries into the bins.

The bulk cooling room could accommodate about 100 bins full of fruit at any one time while still allowing room for moving bins in and out without a great deal of restacking. Bins were usually handled on a first-in, first-out basis in the cooling room. Minimum time that a bin stayed in the bulk cooling room was 12 hours, as the temperature of the cherries had to be lowered to 32° Fahrenheit to maintain freshness during transport to markets.

If the cherries were exceptionally clean and the hydrocooler was overloaded, it was possible to skip the hydrocooling process and place bins of fruit directly into the bulk cooling room. In this case, however, the fruit had to stay in the bulk cooler for 24 hours to reduce the temperature sufficiently. Also fruit that was not washed in the hydrocooler slowed the packing process considerably because of the need to remove dirt and debris normally removed during washing.

Containers of fruit were removed from the bulk cooling room by the forklifts and dumped onto a conveyor that took them to the packing line. About one minute was required to move a bin from the cooler and dump it on the conveyor. The packing line had a maximum capacity of approximately 5 tons per hour and was manned when operating at full capacity by 12 operators who sorted, graded, inspected, and packed the cherries into 12- or 20-pound boxes.

From the packing line, boxed cherries moved by conveyor to the cold storage room where they were stacked to await shipment. The cold storage room, which was kept at 32° Fahrenheit, had a capacity of 55 tons of packed fruit. Due to the perishability of cherries, the packed fruit was shipped as quickly as possible. The distributor through which most of the crop was marketed was notified by Maynard Farms when a truckload was expected to be ready. Generally, the distributor picked up the fruit a few hours after notification. Truckload weights ranged from 20,000 to 30,000 pounds, although early and late in the season smaller loads might be picked up. At the peak of the season, four workers were assigned to stacking boxes in the cold storage room and loading outgoing trucks. Prices paid by the distributor (per pound) during the most recent season were:

| | | |
|---|---|---|
| June | 1–8 | $ 0.50 |
| June | 9–12 | 0.40 |
| June | 13–18 | 0.32 |
| June | 19–season end | 0.28 |

The plant was not unionized, so management had great flexibility in making job assignments and varying working hours. Workers were hired by the hour with no guarantee of more than four hours of work a day. Truck drivers and forklift drivers were paid $11 per hour; the hydrocooler operator and scale clerk received $7 per hour; packing line workers and cold-storage workers received $6 per hour. Taxes and fringe benefits amounted to 35 percent of the hourly payroll. Time and one half was required for work in excess of eight hours per day.

## DISCUSSION QUESTIONS

1. Analyze the capacity of the Maynard Farms packing operation relative to the requirements of the growers (including Maynard Farms) using these facilities.
2. Develop a schedule of workers' hours for the season.
3. Make recommendations for changes in capacity and layout or operating procedures.

# Midcentral Foods, Incorporated

Midcentral Foods, Inc. produced and marketed a broad line of grocery products including cake mixes, dried soups, coffee, refrigerated bakery goods, and some specialty canned goods. Midcentral, which maintained its home offices in Cleveland, operated 13 plants, most of them east of the Mississippi, and distributed its products from 22 warehouses scattered across the United States. For many years, Midcentral had exported a limited quantity of its products to the larger Canadian markets in Ontario and Quebec. With the growth of these markets, Midcentral built a plant and warehouse in London, Ontario to serve the Canadian market. The Canadian operation was established as a separate corporation, Midcentral Foods of Canada Ltd., in which Midcentral held a controlling interest and the balance of which was owned by Canadian investors. Because of this controlling interest, the London plant was treated similarly to the U.S. plants rather than as a separate company. Considerable control over the plant's operation was exerted by the line and staff departments at Midcentral's head offices, although these departments had no formal organizational responsibility for the Canadian plant.

## CANADIAN PLANT OPERATIONS

The company's plan at the time the London plant was constructed was to build a facility that would be used initially for manufacturing one product with a gradual expansion into the full line of Midcentral products. The building also contained space for warehousing other Midcentral products imported from the United States. The first product selected for manufacture in the London plant was cake mix.

152

In the United States, Midcentral produced a full line of cake mixes of various types in several package sizes. Because of the limited size of the market, the London plant produced only five basic flavors: dark chocolate, chocolate malt, white, yellow, and spice. White and yellow mixes were also available with a package of marbling mix for making white marble and yellow marble cakes. The mixes were produced on a mixing and packaging line similar to the ones in Midcentral's U.S. plants; in fact, some of the equipment was surplus and outdated equipment from the U.S. plants.

In the three years that the cake mix line had been in production, most of the initial difficulties with equipment breakdown had been eliminated. Although the condition of the equipment prevented the line from reaching the 1,000-cases-per-shift production rate of similar lines in the United States, the maximum production rate of 500 to 600 cases per shift was more than sufficient to produce enough cake mix to fill the requirements of the Canadian market. Because of the continuous nature of some of the processing, the line was operated on a three-shift basis five days a week unless it was shut down for changeover or because of mechanical difficulties. On this basis the average production rate of the line, even allowing for shutdowns, was almost double the average sales rate. When the line was shut down for changeovers, for repairs, or because there was no requirement for additional production, workers who were not needed on the line were used for cleanup and maintenance work and in the warehouse. While this kept them busy, the underutilization of labor resulted in labor costs averaging about 30 percent higher in the London plant than in Midcentral's U.S. plants. As a result, some of the anticipated lower costs of producing cake mixes in Canada rather than importing them from the United States had failed to materialize.

When the London facility was built, two people who had previously managed distribution of Midcentral's products in Canada were chosen to manage the new plant. The former sales manager, an American who had lived in Canada for nine years, was designated as general manager of Midcentral Foods of Canada Ltd. Despite his new title, however, in effect he continued to spend most of his time performing the duties of sales manager, as the title of general manager did not convey with it a great deal of authority over the Canadian operations. Line and staff departments at Midcentral's main offices controlled much of the London operation through frequent visits to the London plant and by insisting on close adherence by the Canadian operation to policies and procedures followed in the United States. The assistant general manager in Canada was the former accountant and office manager of the old distribution organization in Canada. He also continued to perform largely the same duties as previously. One other person who had an important role in the operation of the London plant was the production manager, Norman Goodfield, an American who had been transferred from a U.S. plant when the London plant was built. The production manager controlled all operations in the plant and warehouse, although this in actuality involved much less responsibility than he had formerly had in the United States because of the small size of the plant.

## SCHEDULING AND INVENTORY CONTROL

One problem that had been rather serious since the start of production in the London plant was that of controlling the amount of inventories of both the cake mixes that were produced at London and the other Midcentral products that were imported from the United States for distribution in Canada. Prior to construction of the London plant and warehouse, inventories had been maintained in public warehouses and controlled from the main office in Cleveland. However, after the London facility was completed, use of public warehouses was discontinued, and these inventories became the responsibility of the assistant general manager. Difficulties stemmed from both improper ordering of products from the United States and improper scheduling of production on the London cake mix line. After a year of confusion, during which time it became obvious that the assistant general manager did not have time or the necessary training to develop an adequate control system, a production and inventory control clerk was hired to work under the assistant general manager.

The production and inventory control clerk, Stan Penkovich, had emigrated to Canada five years before being hired by Midcentral. He was trained informally by having visited several U.S. plants and the head office in Cleveland where he observed the operation of the production and inventory control systems. After several weeks of indoctrination, Stan took over complete responsibility for ordering products from the U.S. plants and issuing production schedules for the cake mix line. Some serious errors were made in the first few months after Stan took charge, but the situation gradually improved, particularly with regard to inventories of products made in the United States. Although ratios of inventories to sales of these products were higher than were comparable ratios in the United States, and although shortages occurred more frequently than they were experienced in the United States, they seemed to be controlled as well as might be expected in view of the small and erratic character of Canadian sales. However, scheduling of the cake mix line was not generally regarded as satisfactory and became an increasing point of contention between the production and inventory control clerk and the production manager. In particular, Norman Goodfield blamed the incompetence of the production and inventory clerk in scheduling the cake mix line for the fact that labor costs were always relatively higher than in the U.S. plants.

Ordering of products from the U.S. plants presented much less difficulty than did that of scheduling the cake mix line. Products from the U.S.

plants were ordered individually from warehouse stocks, but scheduling of the cake mix line presented problems in determination of the proper sequence for producing different flavors, length of a total production cycle through all flavors, length of run for each flavor, and amount of safety stock of each flavor.

In the U.S. plants, scheduling of lines similar to the cake mix line at London was accomplished through the use of a complex system developed by Midcentral's operations research group. This system involved the use of exponential smoothing with adjustments for trend and seasonal factors to determine expected usage during the production cycle, determination of the optimum length of a complete cycle through all flavors, and determination of optimum run lengths for individual flavors. During his visit to the U.S. plants, Stan Penkovich was introduced to the basic ideas underlying this system, and the suggestion was made that he try to use some of the concepts in simplified form. However, Stan did not gain enough understanding from the brief introduction to the system to enable him to implement any of it, and the operations research group did not feel that the size of the London plant justified a full study of the problem in view of its commitments to potentially more profitable studies in the United States. As a result, Stan developed his own system in which he issued a schedule each Thursday for the following week.

Flavors to be run the following week were scheduled on the basis of warehouse stocks on hand each Thursday and the sales rate. When a flavor was run, Stan tried to schedule about a four-week supply. This was the maximum amount that could be made in a single run because of very strict limits set by quality control on the maximum number of days that the product could remain in the warehouse before being shipped. In scheduling the maximum amount whenever possible, Stan felt that he was helping to reduce the number of costly changeovers in the plant. Also, the minimum amount of any flavor that was scheduled under any circumstances was 1,000 cases, as Stan understood that this was the smallest amount of any flavor that could be economically run.

Whenever possible, dark flavors were scheduled to follow light flavors. A full cleanout was not necessary when going from light to dark, whereas it was necessary to clean the line thoroughly when going from dark to light. In practice, however, it was often not possible to schedule a four-week supply of a flavor or follow the light-to-dark sequence. Warehouse stocks of more than one flavor might run low at the same time or they might run low in such a fashion as to force changeovers from dark to light.

Although the method of scheduling seemed to be reasonable to the production and inventory control clerk, there was substantial dissatisfaction with cake mix inventory levels. The production manager was generally critical of schedules that caused too frequent changeovers and changeovers from dark to light flavors, and the general manager had on several occasions planned seasonal cake mix deals and promotions requiring special packaging that could not be carried out because production of specially packaged mixes would have resulted in overstock of standard packages. Over a period of two years, poor scheduling was increasingly blamed for high labor costs, excess stocks of cake mix, inability to carry out promotions of cake mixes, difficulties in controlling stocks of raw materials and packaging, and loss of substantial quantities of mix that became overaged.

The situation finally reached crisis proportions when a planned promotion of cake mixes for the Christmas holiday season resulted in advertising appearing several weeks before the special cake mix packages were available on grocer's shelves. The plant also found it necessary to repackage about half the specially packaged mix when it was found that the mixes would not be sold before the holiday season was over.

## PROBLEMS AT LONDON PLANT

Following the cake mix promotion failure, the corporate sales manager, manufacturing manager, and production and inventory control manager from Midcentral's main office in Cleveland all made separate trips to London, as they had frequently done in the past, to ascertain what had happened and to offer their advice on what should be done to remedy the situation. The amount of money that was lost on the promotion was small when compared with the scale of similar promotions in the United States. However, the London plant was supposed to have potential for tremendous growth and was intended to serve as a pilot operation for future expansion in other foreign countries. Failure of the London plant to develop into a profitable, volume operation was causing serious misgivings about building plants in other countries farther removed from the United States and with markets less similar to that of the United States than the Canadian market. The London plant operated at a loss in its first two years of operations, and preliminary figures indicated that the third year would show only a small profit amounting to about 2 percent on Midcentral's investment. In contrast to this, Midcentral earned 20 percent (before corporate income taxes) on its U.S. operations.

Although personnel at the London plant were accustomed to frequent visits by executives from the head office, the visits of three executives from Cleveland, all in a period of less than a month, had such a disturbing effect that the general manager of the plant requested Midcentral's vice president of foreign operations to do something about the situation. (Midcentral's vice president of foreign operations held the nominal title of president of Midcentral of Canada and was the only formal direct organizational link between the U.S. and Canadian companies.) The result of this request was a meeting between the vice president of foreign operations and the three executives who had just visited London. When the discussion had gone on for some time without any decisions being reached, the production and inventory control manager suggested that perhaps the operations research group should be requested to study the situation, as the operations research group had developed the production control system used in the U.S. plants on the cake mix lines. This suggestion was agreeable to all, and a memo was written to the corporate operations research group requesting a study of the problem at the earliest possible date.

The person assigned to the study, John Brooks, had been involved previously in the installation of the production control system for cake mix lines in the United States. After discussing the situation individually with the three executives and the vice president for foreign operations, John scheduled a trip to London to talk personally to the plant personnel and gather data that would be used in analyzing the problem. Brooks's first reaction to the assignment was that it would be a simple matter to install a system similar to the ones used in the U.S. plants.

In his initial discussion of the problem with the general manager of the London plant, Brooks received a long lecture about the difficulties of selling in the Canadian market generally and the particular difficulties of selling cake mix when the plant seemed to be unable to deliver the merchandise in spite of the fact that it had too much capacity. The general manager supplied sales figures shown in Tables 1 and 2. Only aggregate figures for all cake mix sales were relevant for 1978, 1979, and part of 1980 because of the frequent changes that had been made to determine Canadian preferences for various flavors. A period of adjustment ensued when elimination of some flavors resulted in unanticipated changes in sales of other flavors.

## TABLE 1

### Total Cake Mix Sales
### (thousands of cases)

|           | 1978 | 1979 | 1980 | 1981 |
|-----------|------|------|------|------|
| January   |      | 19.6 | 18.0 | 21.9 |
| February  |      | 15.8 | 17.6 |      |
| March     | 14.2 | 13.1 | 16.7 |      |
| April     | 12.5 | 12.6 | 15.3 |      |
| May       | 8.9  | 10.3 | 10.9 |      |
| June      | 9.1  | 7.9  | 10.6 |      |
| July      | 8.8  | 6.5  | 8.5  |      |
| August    | 7.4  | 4.5  | 6.8  |      |
| September | 9.7  | 10.5 | 12.1 |      |
| October   | 17.1 | 15.7 | 14.5 |      |
| November  | 21.0 | 20.9 | 18.9 |      |
| December  | 19.4 | 23.0 | 23.5 |      |

## TABLE 2
### Cake Mix Sales by Flavor
### (thousands of cases)

| | Dark Chocolate | Chocolate Malt | White | Yellow | Spice | White Marble | Yellow Marble | Total |
|---|---|---|---|---|---|---|---|---|
| **1980** | | | | | | | | |
| April | 4.1 | .9 | 3.8 | 3.2 | 1.2 | 1.2 | .9 | 15.3 |
| May | 2.8 | .7 | 2.7 | 2.3 | .9 | .8 | .7 | 10.9 |
| June | 2.3 | .3 | 3.4 | 2.8 | .8 | .6 | .4 | 10.6 |
| July | 2.0 | .4 | 2.5 | 2.2 | .5 | .4 | .5 | 8.5 |
| August | 1.6 | .3 | 2.2 | 1.6 | .5 | .5 | .1 | 6.8 |
| September | 3.5 | .7 | 3.0 | 2.5 | .9 | .8 | .7 | 12.1 |
| October | 4.8 | .7 | 3.2 | 2.8 | 1.2 | 1.0 | .8 | 14.5 |
| November | 5.7 | 1.2 | 4.4 | 3.7 | 1.5 | 1.3 | 1.1 | 18.9 |
| December | 6.8 | 1.7 | 5.4 | 4.4 | 2.0 | 1.6 | 1.6 | 23.5 |
| **1980** | | | | | | | | |
| January | 6.9 | 1.5 | 5.0 | 4.1 | 1.7 | 1.4 | 1.3 | 21.9 |
| Total | 40.5 | 8.4 | 35.6 | 29.6 | 11.2 | 9.6 | 8.1 | 143.0 |

## TABLE 3

### Total Cost Per Case for Manufacturing
### Cake Mix, January 1981

|  | Cost Per Case |
|---|---|
| Dark chocolate | $6.83 |
| Chocolate malt | 6.67 |
| White | 5.53 |
| Yellow | 5.88 |
| Spice | 5.98 |
| White marble | 5.90 |
| Yellow marble | 6.25 |

The general manager also supplied the most recent figures, shown in Table 3, for the cost of manufacturing the various flavors of cake mix. He explained that the differences in cost between flavors were due to ingredient cost differences except in the case of marble mixes where some additional labor costs were incurred in making and inserting the marbling mix packets. In giving the figures to Brooks, the general manager commented that it was difficult for him to see how costs could be very accurate in view of the fact that there was so much moving of workers from the cake mix line and to other work in the warehouse. It was not easy, in his opinion, to determine the labor that should be charged to cake mixes and the labor that should be charged to the other products in the warehouse. Warehousing costs were allocated to each product line on the basis of number of cases handled.

Following his interview with the general manager, John Brooks talked at some length with Stan Penkovich. Stan was obviously pleased to talk to John since continuing friction between Stan and Norman Goodfield had led to a virtual ostracism of Stan by the plant personnel. Stan described the simple scheduling system that he used and emphasized that he was trying to do as well as he could within the limitations as he understood them. In particular, Stan felt that the lower limit of 1,000 cases in a run of a flavor and the upper limit of a four-week supply severely restricted flexibility in scheduling. Also, erratic sales and the fact that promotions were planned long before he was ever informed of them added to his problems in scheduling.

Another chronic problem that he faced was the enthusiasm of the general manager regarding future sales. On frequent occasions plans were made for sales far exceeding anything that ever materialized, and Stan was pressured into scheduling quantities of special packages that he knew were far in excess of requirements. It was clear that Stan felt that everyone in the plant expected him to do things that he either couldn't do or were against his better judgment and that he would have quit long before had it not been for the encouragement that the production and inventory control manager from the main office had given on his visits to the London plant.

## TABLE 4

### Estimated Cleanout Times on Cake Mix Line
(five-worker crew; all times in elapsed hours)

<table>
<thead>
<tr><th rowspan="2"></th><th></th><th colspan="7">Change to</th></tr>
<tr><th></th><th>White</th><th>White Marble</th><th>Yellow</th><th>Yellow Marble</th><th>Spice</th><th>Chocolate Malt</th><th>Dark Chocolate</th></tr>
</thead>
<tbody>
<tr><td rowspan="7">Change from</td><td>White</td><td>[a]</td><td>[a]</td><td>2</td><td>2</td><td>2</td><td>2</td><td>2</td></tr>
<tr><td>White marble</td><td>3</td><td></td><td>2</td><td>2</td><td>2</td><td>2</td><td>2</td></tr>
<tr><td>Yellow</td><td>3</td><td>3</td><td></td><td>[a]</td><td>2</td><td>2</td><td>2</td></tr>
<tr><td>Yellow marble</td><td>6</td><td>3</td><td>[a]</td><td></td><td>2</td><td>2</td><td>2</td></tr>
<tr><td>Spice</td><td>6</td><td>6</td><td>6</td><td>6</td><td></td><td>2</td><td>2</td></tr>
<tr><td>Chocolate malt</td><td>6</td><td>6</td><td>6</td><td>6</td><td>6</td><td></td><td>2</td></tr>
<tr><td>Dark chocolate</td><td>6</td><td>6</td><td>6</td><td>6</td><td>6</td><td>3</td><td></td></tr>
</tbody>
</table>

[a] Cleanout time negligible as mix does not change. Changeover requires only loading of different packages into packaging line.

The last person to whom Brooks talked was Norman Goodfield. Norman made it very explicit that he did not feel that any fancy system of scheduling was required. In his judgment, the crux of the scheduling problem was "that ignorant foreigner in the front office who does the scheduling." Norman said that he had long ago given up trying to teach Stan anything about the problems of running a cake mix line, as his early efforts to help him had not improved the scheduling at all.

After his initial caustic comments about the production and inventory control clerk, Norman Goodfield explained some of the characteristics of the cake mix line at London. The experience of the London plant was that its line operated best at a rate of about 500 to 600 cases per shift before allowance for changeover time. This was slower than in the U.S. plants but necessary because the equipment on the line could not operate reliably at higher speeds. Also, it was not economical to operate at a much slower rate because of difficulties in blending and mixing that arose when processing was done too slowly.

The major problem was, of course, short runs and costly changeovers. It was the plant's experience that about an hour's production was lost in shutting down the cake mix line and another hour was lost in starting it up. This was done routinely each weekend, but each unnecessary shutdown in midweek added to the labor cost. The entire mixing and packaging line was normally run by nine workers except when marble mixes were being packaged, in which case an additional worker was used to put the marble mix in the packages. When the line was shut down for a changeover to a new flavor, five workers were used for cleanout, and the extra workers were used in the warehouse, used on general cleanup work, or used to mix and package the packets of marble mix. Workers were used interchangeably at the various stations on the line. Average cost per labor-hour was estimated at $11.37 including all fringe benefits. When changeovers occurred, the best sequence was from light to dark, as this avoided the costly complete cleanout necessary to avoid contaminating the light color. In general, cost of a changeover was the labor cost alone; the amount of cake mix lost was negligible. The production manager estimated the amount of time necessary to make changeovers using a five-worker crew as shown in Table 4. This time was in addition to shutdown and start-up time.

When asked about the cost of storing cake mix in the warehouse, Goodfield showed Brooks a cost study prepared several months previously that indicated a cost of 28 cents per case per month, much higher than the cost of public warehousing used before the plant was built. The high cost was explained by Goodfield as being due to underutilization of workers from the cake mix line when the line was not operating and also to the fact that the warehouse was filled to less than half its capacity even when inventories were at their highest level in late fall.

## DISCUSSION QUESTIONS

1. If you were Brooks, what would be your recommendations regarding the use of exponential smoothing to forecast sales?
2. If you were Brooks, what would be your recommendation regarding the use of optimum cycle length, flavor sequence, and flavor run lengths for scheduling cake mix production?
3. What would be your immediate, short-term recommendation for resolving the apparent crisis in scheduling cake mix?
4. What are the underlying problems at the London plant and how can they be solved?

# Northumberland Machinery Works Ltd.

It had been a very bad morning for Colin Madison. Very bad, indeed! Madison had recently been promoted to be the manager of the experimental department of the Northumberland Machinery Works Ltd. located in Newcastle upon Tyne, England. The experimental department employed approximately 1,000 workers and was a major unit of the company. Half the workers were skilled tradespeople employed as machine operators making parts or as fitters doing assembly work; the other half were the supporting staff of clerks, checkers, storekeepers, material movers, and supervisors. Northumberland was one of the largest companies in its industry, manufacturing aero gas turbine engines ("jet engines") used primarily in aircraft. These engines were also used in ships, electric power generation, gas pumping, and other applications. The company manufactured a wide line of engines, from the smallest to the largest size. The shops under Madison's jurisdiction were primarily concerned with large jet engines.

Although the experimental department was under the jurisdiction of the director of manufacturing, it was essentially a "captive" shop for the engineering department. Its purpose was to manufacture parts, assemble and test new engines, and quickly test new ideas as they were developed in the engineering department. These new ideas might be minor improvements that could be immediately applied to existing engines, or they might be very advanced concepts that could take many years of experimentation before they could be applied practically to commercial jet engines.

Northumberland was constantly challenged by competitors. Each company in the industry was under great pressure to maintain its position by technological advancement, attractive pricing made possible by effective cost control, and the ability to maintain promised deliveries of engines and spare parts. Although these objectives placed a strain on all departments of the company, pressure on the experimental department was particularly severe. This led Colin Madison to wonder whether his recent promotion to manager of the experimental department was worth the stress and anxiety he continually faced. Now that he was in the position, however, his primary concern was to get control of his "mess" and then to keep control of his responsibilities and problems.

## INVENTORY PROBLEMS

Earlier in the day Madison had been confronted by John Flagg, the safety officer, who was making one of his routine checks on the shop. Flagg greeted Madison with "How come you have so much rubbish spilling over into the aisles? You know the aisle space between the yellow lines has to be kept clear."

"That's not rubbish, those are parts needed by the fitters."

"If they're needed, why don't they use them and get them out of the way?"

"They're not needed now!"

"If they're not needed then why the devil were they made?"

"They really are needed now, but we're short of a few parts, and the assembly that will use them can't get started. As soon as these shortages are corrected, the assembly work will move forward and we will get the aisles clear."

"Well, you'd better do something about the aisles right away."

Shortly after his conversation with the safety officer, Madison received a telephone call from one of the project managers in the engineering department asking why a build (final assembly) on an experimental engine was not under way when the DIB (development instruction to build) had been issued by the engineering department four months earlier. Madison agreed to check up on the delay and later in the morning found the build operation was held up for some missing parts. An examination of the five bond store (finished parts stores) added to the confusion. A physical check of the storage bins for the missing items revealed that the bins were empty. However, the computer printout showing inventory status, which was used only by the accountants, indicated that the parts were supposed to be available. The stores office also maintained a hand-processed ledger card for each part. When shortages accumulated, the appropriate cards were to have an entry that identified which DIB was awaiting completion of parts so that they could be delivered immediately upon receipt from manufacture. In this instance one part card did not specifically show an existing shortage for the DIB that Madison was expediting.

Upon further checking Madison discovered that the unmarked shortage on the part card was brought about because there had been a change in design and part number, and somehow the records had become mixed up. Madison called the project manager in engineering and told him; "If you wouldn't keep changing your mind I might have some sort of success in getting the parts issued."

The project manager responded, "Well, we keep changing our minds because the things we originally specified you can't deliver on time. We had to change our minds to provide a part that you could make more easily in order to meet our test date."

A further check of the computer printout revealed that there were many discrepancies between the actual physical inventory on the five bond stores shelves and the record that was maintained by the computer system. Somehow receipts and issues that were entered into the computer system did not always correspond to exactly what had taken place. Over a period of time there had been an increasing number of discrepancies between the computer records and the actual shelf stock. The computer records used by the accountants had not been available to the build shop personnel, and it appeared, therefore, that there was little incentive to ensure that the inputs to the computer for parts movements were correct.

Colin Madison, prior to his promotion to manager, was under the impression that the control system in the experimental department had worked reasonably well. At least the system had been in effect for a very long time. The accountants' computer printout, which Madison checked, reported only three items of data for each part: the quantity booked into five bond stores, quantity booked out, and stock that was supposed to be in inventory.

There was no raw material stock record, but there was a "batch costing system" that purported to report the work-in-progress in terms of part number and quantities. The batch costing system had been introduced as an accounting aid to account for work hours and cost per batch and to assign these to the correct job number for a development or research program. A previous check had indicated that twice as many job numbers were reported by the computer system to be active in work-in-progress as were actually in the shops. This was because many of the completed job numbers had not been closed properly and because of inadequate discipline in error correction. The report was updated on Friday and results issued the following Wednesday, but were largely ignored by operating personnel.

## ORDER RELEASE SYSTEM

Action in the experimental department was initiated when the engineering department released a DIM (development instruction to manufacture) authorizing manufacture of a specific part number. The engineering department kept track of what the parts were expected to be used for, and frequently a DIM would specify a quantity sufficient to cover several different projects that engineers had underway or anticipated would be required in the future. The second control document was the DIB that the engineering department issued authorizing the subassembly and/or final assembly for a test. The DIB was essentially a long parts list authorizing the storekeeper to withdraw the items from the five bond stores and issue them to the shops for action. Thus the DIM authorized the manufacture of a part and the DIB authorized the use of the part in an assembly or engine.

If a part was short, the storekeeper would make a blue entry ("blueing up") on the part card in the office ledger indicating the DIB awaiting the part. As soon as the short part arrived it was booked into the ledger and then booked out for issue against the DIB, and the shortage ("blue up") entry on the part card in the ledger was crossed out. Parts on the DIB that were short were copied onto a shortage list that was given to an expediter to trace through the shop and try to speed up completion.

Madison learned from the chief storekeeper that every available item for a DIB was pulled from the shelves as soon as the release was received from engineering. This was done even though many items were short, because, if the items were not pulled from the shelves, they might be subsequently taken for another engine DIB, and this would only increase the number of shortages on the original DIB. This practice resulted in a large number of "subinventories" that had been issued to the fitting bay (area for doing subassembly or final assembly work) and were lying about in an inactive state awaiting arrival of short parts. The theory was that the DIB would not be issued by the engineering department until all the DIMs had been issued and completed. Unfortunately, this theory would only work in a perfect world, according to the storekeeper. There seemed to be innumerable reasons why the system did not work and shortages arose to cause difficulties.

The storekeeper, Harry Phillips, explained his problems:

"The more out of step we are in terms of parts not being in stores on the date they're to be delivered, the worse job it is when the DIB hits us, because then we've got an instruction to issue stuff and it's not there. We have to mark up all of the part ledger cards for shortages, and then we have to progress those shortages down on the shop floor. We've got no other alternative but to put the available parts over into the fitting bay. They can't do anything with those until the shortages are ready. So there's work mounting up, and the fitting bay gets crammed with bits allocated to engines. At some future date the engineers may change their minds and say 'Well, we really don't want the engine to look like that any more — we want to change that part number for this part number.' We then find that the original part was issued, and we've got to bring it back, put it on the shelf, and reenter on the card, then run around and chase the new part. You can hardly imagine the sort of chaos that those piles of parts in the fitting bay get themselves into.

"When this problem became severe the engineering department, to protect themselves, started to issue the DIBs earlier, because they know that when a DIB hit the system, the expedite system identified the shortages. Instead of issuing the DIB with two months' lead time for an engine build, they began shoving it onto us four months ahead of the build schedule to give them an extra two months of visibility on the assumption that we would immediately prepare the shortage lists and have more time to get the parts in. This only exacerbated the whole process, because now the stores tries to operate four months ahead, and the piles of parts in the fitting bays get bigger, and the shortage lists get larger and —, oh dear!

"It seems to me that with the amount of money we have tied up in dead inventory in the fitting bay awaiting correction of shortages, we have more value on the floor than there is money in the vaults of the Bank of England. On top of that, the system requires enormous amounts of clerical time, expediting time, and control time, with everyone trying desperately to keep the system producing something at the end of the line. I don't know what it costs, but there are an awful lot of people trying to hold the system together with chewing gum and string."

After his conversation with Harry Phillips, Colin Madison went to lunch and mulled over the events of the morning. He concluded that there was no way he could stay out of trouble if he were to continue to depend on the present control system. Although the experimental department primarily served the engineering department, he also recognized that more than half his shopload came from orders received from the production department that used excess capacity or special machinery located in the experimental department. He would have to find a better way to keep both these customers satisfied. Although there was a single point of release of orders that he received from the production department, there were multiple order points from different projects in the engineering department. Each project had its own manager who vied for the attention and effort of the experimental department. As a result it was very difficult for Madison to establish appropriate priorities, and it seemed impossible to balance his work load with his capacity.

## COMPUTER SYSTEMS AND SIMULATION

Madison decided to discuss his problem with Robert Howe, a friend of long standing, who was a systems analyst with the company, designing computer systems for various activities. Howe had been very actively involved in developing new control systems for the production shops, but he had not been involved with the experimental department shops where there were a limited number of computer applications used primarily by accountants.

Howe immediately sensed the problem. He said, "All shop control problems are basically the same. It's the task of integrating a large number of variables and objectives. Unfortunately, there is no human brain that is capable of holding and organizing all of the variables and objectives and come out with an optimum solution. The problems are just too complicated. Sometimes it's easy to determine what the work load is, based on standard times for the various jobs ahead. This can give us the theoretical head count of the workers that we may need. Unfortunately, it doesn't always give us answers as to the required lead time, because there will be bottlenecks around limited machine capacity or difficulties that arise from shortages of raw materials, changes in design, new schedules and many other problems."

Howe also emphasized the need to divide problems into two broad categories: "There is the short-term control plan that indicates what work is to be done on what machines during the next shift or the next few days or even weeks. There also is the long-term strategic plan that anticipates the work coming along for months and years ahead to identify possible bottlenecks and difficulties arising from inadequate capacity, shortage of special machines, inadequate or excess employees, material requirements, and other variables that needed to be integrated. The tendency is to give primary attention to the short-term plan and respond to immediate pressures resulting in expediting and 'bit chasing.' Successful expediting can result in improving output by 1 percent, 2 percent, or perhaps 3 percent. Effective strategic long-term planning, however, can improve output by 50 percent or 100 percent or even 200 percent by anticipating problems and bottlenecks so that expediting can be greatly reduced and only required in unusual situations, rather than being the normal method of operation."

Madison's response was, "This all sounded very good, but how do you achieve it?"

Howe's response was, "By simulation."

Madison immediately asked the obvious question, "What's simulation?"

"Simulation," said Howe, "is to create a computer programme that reflects the variables that are involved in a shop — the various machines and their capacities, work to be done in terms of individual jobs, priority of each job, setup time and run time for each batch, and all the other variables that need to be taken into account. For a given plan of loading of work on to the shop, the computer programme will identify the consequences. It will indicate where and when the bottlenecks will occur; it will indicate the overloaded or underloaded sections of the shop and can indicate when work will be completed, given the constraints of the shop. If the first plan tested by the computer programme does not work, then we try a second plan, or a third plan, or as many plans as are required until a satisfactory solution is obtained. The results can be very impressive."

Madison wanted to know what was involved in developing a computer program that would simulate the experimental department situation. Howe was reluctant to estimate what such a program would cost or how long the development would take. Instead, he suggested that the two of them visit the production gear shop (a unit of the product centre) where a computer program had been developed and was working to simulate the activities in the shop.

## CONTROL IN THE PRODUCTION GEAR SHOP

The following day Madison and Howe visited Jim Strand, the PIPC manager of the production gear shop. The PIPC manager had responsibility for purchasing, make or buy decisions, inventory, and production control problems. Strand reported to the gear shop manager, along with the production engineer (responsible for methods and standard time allowances), the works manager (he had direct-line authority over the supervisors and operators), and the quality control manager.

There were approximately 140 pieces of equipment in the shop. These machine tools were divided among six machine departments, each containing similar or related equipment. The six departments were divided, in turn, into 33 machine groups. For example, department 2 had 9 machine groups, one for each type of grinding equipment: internal, external, angular, universal, hone, surface, thread, ring, and cone grinding. There were also three process departments divided into 11 process groups, including heat treating, carburizing, copper plating, and final inspection.

The 170 operators in the shop were classified into seven worker groups, such as turning, grinding, gear cutting, and so on. Operators in each group specialized in the equipment of one or several machine groups or process groups. The shop operated on a three-shift basis of 40, 37, and 35 hours per week. On each shift there was some flexibility in the starting and ending time for each operator. Overtime was also a frequent necessity to match the work load with available machines and operators. Overtime could occur on the sixth and seventh days of the week, or it could be an extension of a given shift's overlapping another shift. This overlap was possible due to the fact that there were more machines than workers on each shift.

Raw material used by the shop consisted of forgings, castings, and bar stock. Almost all metals were of a special grade suited to the design of the very-high-quality parts produced in the shop. Dimensions, tolerances, and form were very precise. Operations were on a "job shop" basis in which parts were produced in batches. Each batch represented a single part number, with unit quantities ranging from one to several hundred, but mostly less than 100 units per batch.

Where possible, the size of each batch was based on an economical batch quantity (EBQ). This involved a calculation taking into account setup time (or setting), machine time (or running) for each part, and carrying costs for interest charges on the value of the inventory. Although setting and machine times were based on "standard times" (called "rate fixed" times), some skilled workers could produce at a faster rate than the standard, and new workers or those with less skill might produce at a slower rate. As a result the shop created an "operator performance" factor used to establish the available standard time. This in turn established the scheduled or elapsed time that each batch would be on each machine. Attendance hours were converted to standard hours by allowance for "diversions" covering setting, waiting for work, tooling, inspection, breakdowns, and other types of delays.

The large number of variables interacting with each other made control of shop operations extremely difficult. Prior to introduction of the computer, the control system was a hand clerical operation. It was extraordinarily difficult to anticipate work loads, to optimize the scheduling, and to balance employment levels with work requirements. After struggling with the old system for some time without improvement, the PIPC manager, Jim Strand (who previous to his current position had considerable experience in designing and using computer systems), called upon the company's operations research group to analyze the situation in the gear shop and to suggest a new and better system of control.

Strand explained, "The operations research group over the last three years has developed a simulation of the gear shop's method of operation. The system is now beginning to really work, and I believe we use it quite well. We are not yet pushing it to its full advantage, because one of the hardest things is to get confidence in using a computerized model. The problem is trying to encourage people to *use* and *accept* computer output, and this requires that we continually demonstrate that the model produces accurate instructions. Frankly, there is need to overcome a strong anticomputer bias on the part of supervisors who formerly did their own clerical work for scheduling batches, machines, and personnel.

"One of the biggest battles we had in here was related to the way in which the gear shop was traditionally operated. In the past control was based on the part number and its various operations. Each time an operation was completed a progress person would go and move a ticket to show the batch status. Every day they had what they called a "bingo" session where the shop manager, the supervisor, and the shop control people got together and thrashed out the day's loading sequences. All this resulted in a great deal of arguing, pressure, and politicking as to which jobs would be expedited and moved forward and which jobs might be delayed.

"Since we have the computer system, all this has disappeared. What we have now, to put it quite simply, is a control board in each supervisor's office. The control board identifies each machine under his jurisdiction. Under each machine are three names — the operators on each of the three shifts. Below the three names are the batches assigned to the machine, identified by part numbers, arranged in the sequence that work is to be completed. All this information — the machine identification, the operator names, and the batch numbers — are on little tickets filed in pockets so that we can quickly and easily switch each ticket around as operators change on each machine and as the work load moves through the shop. Actual scheduling on the control board of each batch for each operator on each machine comes from a batch loading plan that is prepared by the computer. The computer does the calculating to optimize the schedule, based on a set of rules that have been written into the computer programme.

"Pockets on the control board are lined up on 30 columns, each of which has 50 pockets in a vertical line. There is a special section of the control board that has a ticket for each worker who is absent on authorized basis — for requested days off, for a training session, or on holiday; another section for unplanned absences; and other special sections that identify problem batches and batches that need to be highlighted. In this way everyone responsible for some part of the operations can be kept informed as to the current status of each batch.

## SLOPE PROGRAMME

"The computer programme is called 'SLOPE' standing for Shop LOad and Plan Evaluator. The basic purpose of the computer programme is to give us continuous information and assistance on the following management tasks:

1. *Planning*
   To evaluate in a realistic way the constraints of the available capacity and to develop production plans that are acceptable within these constraints.
2. *Controlling*
   To produce detailed control information to achieve the plan by providing
   a. batch sequence lists
   b. department and machine group standard hour targets
3. *Monitoring*
   By means of continuously monitoring the actual performance against the plan, the system ensures that current control information is available so that appropriate action can be taken when needed.

"I believe I can explain the basic SLOPE structure with a simple sketch showing the inputs and the outputs of the computer system (Figure 1). The computer provides us with a series of reports that give us control (Figure 2). We get these reports updated every week, and this seems to work quite well.

"We can also use the computer programme to test out alternate plans. For example, here is a chart (Figure 3) illustrating three plans that were

## FIGURE 1

### SLOPE — Structure

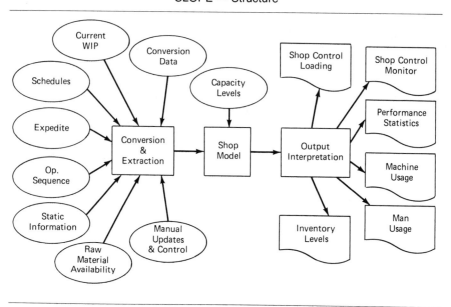

being checked for work-in-process inventory measured in terms of average days of work in queue. As you can see plan 1 ran the inventory up quite high, plan 2 dropped it quite low, and plan 3 kept it at a level rate. We can play with the programme to give us other consequences, and this improves our forward planning. For example, if we need to request additional machinery, we can quite clearly demonstrate the need by use of the SLOPE programme."

Strand showed Madison and Howe a general manual of about 125 pages that explained how the computer system was operated and used in the shop. This manual was intended for shop supervisors; it did not contain the technical details of the computer program itself. The three men then took a walk around the shop and visited the office of one of the supervisors who demonstrated the use of the shop control board based on the schedules produced by the computer printout. To test the system, Madison selected at random a specific part number. He found that the raw material had arrived in the shop last Friday on schedule. During the last three days the part was supposed to have been worked on a specific machine. The three men went out to the machine and found that the part, in fact, was on the machine in work and on schedule.

At the conclusion of his visit to the gear shop, Madison decided that he had some serious "homework" to do to devise a strategy for improving the control system in the experimental department.

### FIGURE 2

#### Computer-Produced Reports for Shop Control

---

(issued every two weeks)

---

Sample copies of the various reports are shown at the end of the listing.

| Report | Title and Explanation |
|---|---|
| 1 | Continuous Planning — Machines. |
| | Day = Day number (460) that is the first day of the first AP (accounting period) listed (7/1 = AP 7, week 1). Each calendar year is divided into 13 APs each of 4 weeks. |
| | Breakdown = percentage allowed for machine downtime. |
| | OP = Average operator performance factor for all operators in the M/C (machine) group. |
| | Diversions = Percentage of time allowed for setting, waiting for materials, and all other nonproductive time. The remaining time is assumed to be machine time related to the Sth (standard hours) for measuring expected work load. |
| | NO M/C = Number of machines assumed to be available. |
| | STH = Capacity available based on assumed number of machines, assumed number of operators, and assumed work load in priority sequence. |
| | MEN USED = Operators required, based on total Sth divided by average Sth per operator after allowances for overtime. |
| | M/C UTIL = Machine utilization factor (percentage) based on scheduled shifts. |
| | QUEUE (STH) = Sth in the batches the simulation program established to be in the shop at the beginning of the date indicated waiting to be worked upon. |
| | TASK (STH) = (Not shown) Work load based on master schedule of engine deliveries, with each part scheduled on the basis of its theoretical lead time, after allowances for inventories to establish "net requirements," the specific operations for each part, the batch sizes, the standard unit times, with allowances for breakdown percentage, OP factors, diversion factors, and assuming no restrictions due to limited machines or operators. Derived from the PHASED WIPET computer program (PHASED = end schedule PHASED back for each activity and WIPET = Work-In-Progress Evaluation Tabulation). |
| 2 | Continuous Planning — Men. |
| | NOM NO MEN = Nominal number of operators on payroll. |
| | EXP NO MEN = Expected number of operators in attendance after allowances for absenteeism, holidays, and soon. |
| | MEN USED = Equivalent number of operators available after allowances for overtime. |
| | STH = Sum of the Sth on report 1 for machines for all departments in the man group. |

FIGURE 2 (continued)

QUEUE (STH) = Sum of the corresponding values on report for machines for all departments in the man group.

WTG FOR WORK = Waiting hours for work to arrive when machine/men are unable to proceed due to sequencing of previous operations.

OVERTIME = Expected overtime hours.

D.P. = Department performance factor:

$$\frac{Sth}{Attendance\ hours}$$

3    Continuous Planning — Departments.

Summary of corresponding values on reports 1 and 2 for all queues within each department. (Sample report not shown.)

4    Continuous Planning — Departments-Shop Summary.

Summary of report 3 for all departments for the product centre.

5    Product Centre Summary.

USER STORE = Output to finished parts stores.

ARRS = Arrears in value.

OUTPUT = Value of output.

CUM = Cumulative output.

COMP STORE = Components in WIP in temporary storage.

MISC STORE = Work in WIP for other shops.

CLOSING INV = Closing WIP in value.

STH INPUT TO WIP = Sth in work completed.

P.W.E. TASK (STH) = PHASED WIPET load.

OVERALL D.P. = Departmental performance.

WAITING FOR WORK (%) = Percentage of attendance time waiting for work.

QUEUE (DAYS) = Average waiting time in each queue.

6    Summary Shop Code 5 — Performance to Due Date — AP 07.

Predicts the delivery distribution of parts of FPS in terms of weeks early or late, for the duration of AP 07.

7    Same as report 6 except in value in £000 instead of number of parts. (Sample report not shown.)

8    Same as report 6 except in percentage of lead time based on number of parts. (Sample report not shown.)

9    Same as report 8 except in percentage of lead time based on value in £000. (Sample report not shown.)

10    Same as report 6 except for AP 08 instead of 07. Also produced for AP 09 and AP 10. (Sample report not shown.)

11    Current Work-in-Progress.

AP = Scheduled requirements for next 6 APs.

P = Priority.

B = (Not used.)

D/D = Due date.

F/D = Forecast date.

QTY = Quantity.

I/D = Issue day of raw materials launched into shop for operations.

OPS. SCHEDULE = Operations scheduled in sequence.

COMPLETION DATES = Predicted dates to complete each operation.

12    Batch Loading Plan.

A batch sequence list that shows the opening queue at each machine group and subsequent arrivals forecast by the computer program. It depicts the best order in which these batches should be loaded based on the latest priority.

13    Planned Work-in-Progress.

Batch progress for future planned work-in-progress batches, giving predictions for materials to be issued in the future. (Sample report not shown.)

## Continuous Planning — Machines

### CNC   (M/C GROUP 1)   DEPT 0485

BREAKDOWN = 00.3    OP = 1.04    DIVERSIONS = 18.8    (MAN GP 1)

| | AP 7/1 | 7/2 | 7/3 | 7/4 | AP 8 | AP 9 | AP10 | AP11 | AP12 | AP13 | AP 1 | AP 2 | AP 3 | AP 4 | AP 5 | AP 6 |
|---|---|---|---|---|---|---|---|---|---|---|---|---|---|---|---|---|
| NO M/C | 7 | 7 | 7 | 7 | 7 | 7 | 7 | 7 | 7 | 7 | 7 | 7 | 7 | 7 | 7 | 7.0 |
| S T H | 424 | 474 | 364 | 601 | 2180 | 2003 | 1797 | 2489 | 2448 | 1850 | 2313 | 2545 | 2361 | 2090 | 2758 | 26697 |
| MEN USED | 13.5 | 15.1 | 11.6 | 19.2 | 17.4 | 16.0 | 14.3 | 19.9 | 19.5 | 14.8 | 18.5 | 20.3 | 18.8 | 16.7 | 22.0 | 17.7 |
| M/C UTIL | .64 | .72 | .55 | .91 | .83 | .76 | .68 | .94 | .93 | .70 | .88 | .96 | .89 | .79 | 1.05 | .84 |
| QUEUE (STH) | 1839 | 2053 | 2400 | 2468 | 3094 | 3045 | 2458 | 2304 | 2005 | 1591 | 1801 | 1715 | 1479 | 1203 | 890 | 1981 |
| TASK (STH) | | | | | | | | | | | | | | | | |

TARGET QUEUE    222STH

### F/LATHE   (M/C GROUP 2)   DEPT 0485

BREAKDOWN = 00.3    OP = 1.04    DIVERSIONS = 18.8    (MAN GP 1)

| | AP 7/1 | 7/2 | 7/3 | 7/4 | AP 8 | AP 9 | AP10 | AP11 | AP12 | AP13 | AP 1 | AP 2 | AP 3 | AP 4 | AP 5 | AP 6 |
|---|---|---|---|---|---|---|---|---|---|---|---|---|---|---|---|---|
| NO M/C | 3 | 3 | 3 | 3 | 3 | 3 | 3 | 3 | 3 | 3 | 3 | 3 | 3 | 3 | 3 | 3.0 |
| S T H | 285 | 295 | 313 | 313 | 852 | 1253 | 1169 | 1237 | 1237 | 940 | 1248 | 1252 | 1175 | 1142 | 1231 | 13942 |
| MEN USED | 9.1 | 9.4 | 10.0 | 10.0 | 6.8 | 10.0 | 9.3 | 9.9 | 9.9 | 7.5 | 9.9 | 10.0 | 9.4 | 9.1 | 9.8 | 9.2 |
| M/C UTIL | 1.01 | 1.04 | 1.11 | 1.11 | .75 | 1.11 | 1.03 | 1.10 | 1.10 | .83 | 1.10 | 1.11 | 1.04 | 1.01 | 1.09 | 1.02 |
| QUEUE (STH) | 355 | 468 | 933 | 889 | 1001 | 1213 | 1065 | 969 | 1084 | 1304 | 1304 | 1059 | 696 | 534 | 274 | 930 |
| TASK (STH) | | | | | | | | | | | | | | | | |

TARGET QUEUE    116STH

# REPORT 2

## Continuous Planning — Men

TURNING  (MAN GROUP 1)  DEPT 0485

INITIAL NO OF MEN  SHIFT1= 25  SHIFT2= 16  SHIFT3= 19  ABSENTEEISM= 2.2%  OVERTIME – WEEK= 0.0%  WEEKEND=11.9%

| | AP 7/1 | 7/2 | 7/3 | 7/4 | AP 8 | AP 9 | AP10 | AP11 | AP12 | AP13 | AP 1 | AP 2 | AP 3 | AP 4 | AP 5 | AP 6 |
|---|---|---|---|---|---|---|---|---|---|---|---|---|---|---|---|---|
| NOM NO MEN | 60 | 60 | 60 | 60 | 60 | 60 | 60 | 60 | 60 | 60 | 60 | 60 | 60 | 60 | 60 | 60.0 |
| EXP NO MEN | 52.8 | 52.8 | 52.8 | 52.8 | 45.1 | 47.7 | 48.9 | 56.3 | 57.5 | 39.8 | 50.1 | 57.5 | 56.0 | 47.2 | 54.2 | 51.0 |
| MEN USED | 59.5 | 59.4 | 59.4 | 59.7 | 50.7 | 53.8 | 55.2 | 63.5 | 64.9 | 44.9 | 56.5 | 65.0 | 63.2 | 53.3 | 59.9 | 57.5 |
| STH | 1874 | 1874 | 1874 | 1874 | 6412 | 6788 | 6955 | 7996 | 8162 | 5663 | 7120 | 8162 | 7954 | 6704 | 7554 | 86966 |
| QUEUE (STH) | 4007 | 4432 | 5249 | 5254 | 6246 | 6378 | 5125 | 4374 | 3992 | 3784 | 3869 | 3240 | 2855 | 2305 | 1348 | |
| TARGET QUEUE | | | 724STH | | | | | | | | | | | | | |
| WTG FOR WORK | 0 | 0 | 0 | 0 | 0 | 0 | 0 | 0 | 0 | 0 | 0 | 0 | 0 | 0 | 0 | 4020 |
| OVERTIME | 245 | 245 | 245 | 245 | 838 | 891 | 912 | 1050 | 1071 | 743 | 934 | 1071 | 1044 | 880 | 833 | 11247 |
| D.P. | .84 | .84 | .84 | .84 | .84 | .84 | .84 | .84 | .84 | .84 | .84 | .84 | .84 | .84 | .84 | .84 |

AP STH CAPACITY OF 1 MAN = 125.9

# REPORT 4

## Continuous Planning — Departments-Shop Summary

SHOP SUMMARY

| | AP 7/1 143 | 7/2 143 | 7/3 143 | 7/4 143 | AP 8 143 | AP 9 143 | AP10 143 | AP11 143 | AP12 143 | AP13 143 | AP 1 143 | AP 2 143 | AP 3 143 | AP 4 143 | AP 5 143 | AP 6 |
|---|---|---|---|---|---|---|---|---|---|---|---|---|---|---|---|---|
| NOM NO MEN | 143 | 143 | 143 | 143 | 143 | 143 | 143 | 143 | 143 | 143 | 143 | 143 | 143 | 143 | 143.0 | |
| EXP NO MEN | 123.9 | 123.9 | 123.9 | 123.9 | 105.8 | 111.9 | 114.7 | 132.2 | 134.9 | 93.3 | 117.4 | 134.9 | 131.4 | 110.6 | 127.1 | 119.8 |
| MEN USED | 139.3 | 139.1 | 138.7 | 139.7 | 118.9 | 122.7 | 127.1 | 147.0 | 145.1 | 99.9 | 127.8 | 150.0 | 138.6 | 117.6 | 129.4 | 130.2 |
| STH CAPACITY | 3968 | 3968 | 3968 | 3968 | 13554 | 14335 | 14694 | 16936 | 17282 | 11952 | 15040 | 17282 | 16833 | 14169 | 16282 | |
| P.W. TASK | | | | | | | | | | | | | | | | |
| STH | 4413 | 4438 | 4432 | 4451 | 15180 | 15662 | 16227 | 18796 | 18568 | 12799 | 16449 | 19178 | 17899 | 15105 | 16681 | 200278 |
| QUEUE (STH) | 6403 | 5752 | 6508 | 7103 | 8539 | 8190 | 6823 | 5900 | 5645 | 6464 | 6770 | 6124 | 5533 | 5833 | 5196 | 6454 |
| WTG FOR WORK | 0 | 0 | 0 | 0 | 0 | 285 | 9 | 0 | 365 | 375 | 179 | 0 | 1060 | 572 | 1324 | 4169 |
| OVERTIME | 549 | 547 | 531 | 549 | 1882 | 1813 | 1763 | 2132 | 1799 | 1309 | 1648 | 2139 | 2046 | 1552 | 1604 | 21863 |
| D.P. | .84 | .85 | .85 | .85 | .85 | .83 | .85 | .85 | .84 | .83 | .85 | .85 | .82 | .82 | .80 | .84 |
| NO M/C | 105 | 105 | 105 | 105 | 105 | 105 | 105 | 105 | 105 | 105 | 105 | 105 | 105 | 105 | 105 | 105.0 |
| 3SHFT MC UTL | .44 | .44 | .44 | .44 | .37 | .38 | .40 | .46 | .46 | .31 | .40 | .47 | .44 | .37 | .41 | .40 |

TARGET QUEUE 0 (7/1, 7/2) — 1668STH (7/3)

AP STH CAPACITY OF 1 MAN = 128.1

177

# REPORT 5

## Product Centre Summary

| | ACTUAL TO DATE | AP 7 | AP 8 | AP 9 | AP10 | AP11 | AP12 | AP13 | YR END PRED | YR END PLAN | AP 1 | AP 2 | AP 3 | AP 4 | AP 5 | AP 6 |
|---|---|---|---|---|---|---|---|---|---|---|---|---|---|---|---|---|
| USER STORE- ARRS £000 | | 565 | 602 | 614 | 641 | 599 | 701 | 805 | | | 838 | 874 | 689 | 799 | 862 | |
| - OUTPUT £000 | | 477 | 287 | 307 | 357 | 466 | 407 | 355 | | | 434 | 452 | 667 | 294 | 368 | |
| - CUM £000 | | | | | | | | | | | | | | | | |
| COMP STORE- ARRS £000 | | 151 | 160 | 143 | 99 | 116 | 106 | 104 | | | 102 | 125 | 139 | 127 | 109 | |
| - OUTPUT £000 | | 87 | 54 | 76 | 100 | 23 | 80 | 105 | | | 77 | 45 | 40 | 55 | 108 | |
| - CUM £000 | | | | | | | | | | | | | | | | |
| MISC STORE- ARRS £000 | | 58 | 89 | 26 | 26 | | | | | | | 47 | | | | |
| - OUTPUT £000 | | 82 | 18 | 81 | 13 | 43 | 54 | 15 | | | | | | | | |
| - CUM £000 | | | | | | | | | | | | | | | | |
| CLOSING INV £000 | 1484 | 1677 | 1818 | 1848 | 1885 | 1933 | 1939 | 1966 | | | 1983 | 1987 | 1865 | 1995 | 2078 | |
| STH INPUT TO WIP | | 17734 | 15180 | 15662 | 16227 | 18796 | 18568 | 12799 | | | 16449 | 19178 | 17899 | 15105 | 16681 | |
| P.W.E. TASK (STH) | | | | | | | | | | | | | | | | |
| OVERALL D.P. | | 0.85 | 0.85 | 0.83 | 0.85 | 0.85 | 0.84 | 0.83 | | | 0.85 | 0.85 | 0.82 | 0.82 | 0.80 | |
| WAITING FOR WORK (%) | | 0.0 | 0.0 | 1.5 | 0.0 | 0.0 | 1.6 | 2.4 | | | 0.9 | 0.0 | 4.8 | 3.1 | 6.3 | |
| QUEUE (DAYS) | | 7.7 | 10.2 | 9.8 | 8.1 | 7.0 | 6.7 | 7.7 | | | 8.1 | 7.3 | 6.6 | 6.9 | 6.2 | |

# REPORT 6

## Summary Shop Code 5 — Performance to Due Date — AP 07

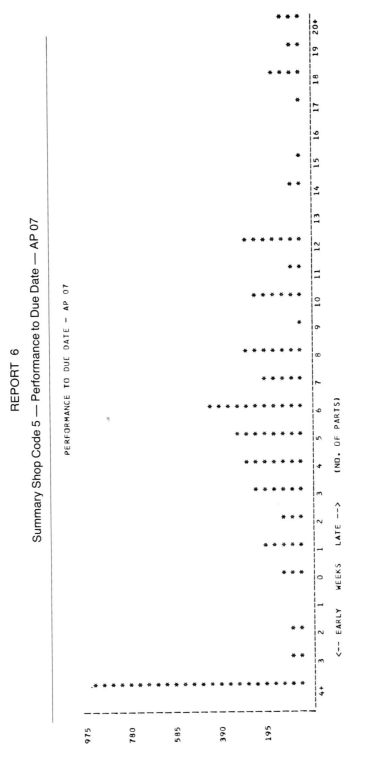

## REPORT 11

### Current Work-in-Progress at Day 503

```
PART NO. AP/09 /10 /11 P  B  D/D  QTY  CPS. SCHEDULE
             12  13  01      F/C  I/D  COMPLETION DATES   --------------------->
                                                          --------------------->

                      9 *  0 80/01  19  INSP RWT INSP MC/T FPS
                              505   479          504         505

                      9 *  0 80/01  21 C INSP RWT INSP MC/T FPS
                              505   479          504         505

                      *                (CNC INSP CARB LREL ANN S/B CNC RING HCB TRIM TEMP LREL)  WIP= 41.L/T CCVER REQD=  43

AX52378   11  8  6                4 * (INSP C/T FPS)                               QTY LESS THAN  15
CRITICAL   5  4  10       452

                                  1   (INSP RWT INSP C/T FPS)                      QTY LESS THAN  15

                                  2 * (STONE INSP RWT INSP C/T FPS)                QTY LESS THAN  15

                      1 *  0 79/09  42  UNIV EXT UNIV THC INT TFR EXT INT POL TRIM USON INSP CUR120 INSP STCNE INSP RWT
                              530   435      506 507  508 511 512 513 514 515 516  517  518   523    526  527   528    529

                                  3 * (UNIV EXT UNIV THD INT TFR EXT INT POL TRIM USON INSP)      QTY LESS THAN  15

                                  2 * (INSP C/T INSP TIN TUP DIF NIT LREL INSP RWT POL CONE INSP)QTY LESS THAN  15

                                  1 C (CNC F/L S/B EXT C/L TFR C/L TFR C/L CNC TFR C/L CONE INSP)QTY LESS THAN  15

                      1 *  0 80/01  47  C/L TFR C/L INSP RBORE INSP BORE CNC F/L S/B EXT C/L TFR F/L CNC TFR C/L
                              616   492      505 506 507  508     528 529  530 532 534 535 536 537 538 539 540 544 545 546 549

                      *                (C/L TFR C/L INSP RBORE INSP BCRE CNC F/L S/B EXT C/L TFR) WIP= 102.L/T CCVER REQD= 105

AX52530    0  10 18               1 * (INSP FPS)                                   QTY LESS THAN   9
CRITICAL  20  18 15       407

                                  1   (INSP C/T INSP PAINT INSP FPS)               QTY LESS THAN   9

                                  4 * (STCNE INSP C/T INSP PAINT INSP FPS)         QTY LESS THAN   9

                                  1 C (CRILL TAP RING EXI INT TFR TRIM INSP CUR120 INSP STCNE)   QTY LESS THAN   9

                      7 *  0 79/10  42  CNC HTA TFR HTA TRIM DRILL TAP RING EXI INT TFR TRIM INSP CUR120 INSP STONE INSP C/T
                              615   399      512 535 536 545 546  552 557 579 581 583 584  585  590   608  609   610    611
```

## REPORT 12

### Batch Loading Plan

DEPARTMENT 0485   MACHINE GROUP 1 (CNC   )   NO. OF MACHINES 7   LABOUR FROM MAN GROUP 1

**BATCHES LOADED**

| DAY | PART NO. | QTY | PTY | STH | CP. | RANGE | TO |
|---|---|---|---|---|---|---|---|
| 504 | *EU1C902 | 4C | 100 | 11.1 | 5 | 8 | 0487 |
| 504 | EU19855 | 38 | 10C | 6.3 | 26 | | C485 |
| 504 | AX55782 | 4C | 100 | 23.6 | 50 | | CUT |
| 504 | LK734C8 | 59 | 100 | 79.5 | 50 | | 0420 |
| 504 | LK57259 | 50 | 10C | 41.6 | 350 | 355 | C485 |
| 504 | LK56026 | 43 | 100 | 24.7 | 420 | 430 | C485 |
| 504 | LK42145 | 101 | 100 | 37.0 | 230 | 24C | C243 |
| 504 | JR12360 | 67 | 100 | 28.4 | 100 | | CUT |

**BATCHES ARRIVING**

| DAY | PART NO. | QTY | PTY | STH | CP. | RANGE | FRCM |
|---|---|---|---|---|---|---|---|
| 503 | JR12930 | 30 | 815 | 5.9 | 10 | | BOND |
| 503 | EU15314 | 48 | 815 | 18.1 | 6 | 7 | BCND |
| 503 | BR82856 | 30 | 817 | 13.5 | 10 | 30 | BCND |
| 503 | AX52953 | 75 | 817 | 23.2 | 110 | | BCND |
| 503 | AX52530 | 15 | 818 | 6.9 | 70 | | BCND |
| 503 | EU681C8 | 25 | 820 | 12.3 | 135 | 140 | C430 |
| 503 | EU15315 | 120 | 820 | 11.5 | 7 | | BCND |
| 503 | AX55782 | 43 | 820 | 25.4 | 50 | | BOND |
| 503 | RK37378 | 77 | 821 | 76.0 | 15 | 16 | 0430 |
| 503 | RK37378 | 51 | 821 | 50.3 | 15 | 16 | 043C |
| 503 | AX54839 | 125 | 923 | 20.0 | 50 | | BCND |
| 503 | AX52953 | 100 | 823 | 30.9 | 110 | | BOND |
| 503 | AX52530 | 25 | 823 | 11.6 | 70 | | BOND |
| 503 | EU53050 | 66 | 825 | 40.9 | 50 | 60 | BOND |
| 503 | EU10274 | 38 | 825 | 7.5 | 9 | | 0486 |
| 503 | EU18109 | 40 | 828 | 9.5 | 16C | | 0486 |
| 503 | NCW4687 | 12 | 829 | 5.8 | 220 | 240 | BOND |
| 503 | LK58762 | 32 | 831 | 13.3 | 10 | 20 | BCND |
| 503 | AX52953 | 35 | 831 | 10.8 | 110 | | BCND |
| 503 | LK76746 | 63 | 846 | 45.6 | 70 | 80 | 0485 |
| 503 | EU60755 | 16 | 851 | 4.0 | 80 | | 0486 |
| 503 | RU46003 | 25 | 853 | 5.6 | 80 | | 0430 |
| 503 | EU18110 | 1C4 | 900 | 61.7 | 9 | 10 | C430 |
| 504 | *EU10902 | 40 | 100 | 11.1 | 5 | 8 | BOND |
| 504 | *EU11692 | 50 | 807 | 14.7 | 40 | 50 | BCND |
| 504 | *EU11692 | 50 | 807 | 14.7 | 40 | 50 | BCND |
| 504 | *LK48224 | 36 | 812 | 0.0 | 80 | 90 | BCND |
| 504 | *NPK2571 | 60 | 815 | 20.1 | 90 | 100 | BOND |
| 504 | *RK22759 | 40 | 923 | 10.4 | 6 | 7 | BCND |
| 504 | *EU36583 | 50 | 823 | 19.3 | 5 | 6 | BCND |
| 504 | *LK57259 | 50 | 825 | 37.2 | 65 | 70 | BONC |
| 504 | *LK48216 | 50 | 829 | 30.6 | 10 | 20 | BCND |
| 504 | *RK37138 | 20 | 829 | 8.8 | 6 | | BCNC |
| 504 | *LK57259 | 50 | 834 | 37.2 | 65 | 70 | BONC |
| 504 | *LK48216 | 50 | 834 | 30.6 | 10 | 20 | BCND |

## FIGURE 3

### Dept. 0485 — Turning Days of Work in Queue

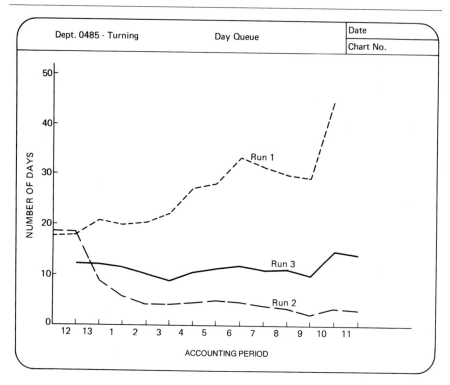

DISCUSSION QUESTIONS

1. How should Madison go about planning for improved control in the experimental department?
2. What similarities and what differences would you expect to find between the control system for the gear shop and a control system for the experimental department?
3. Would it appear that the computerized control system in the gear shop might work in the experimental department?
4. Jim Strand indicated that there was quite a bit of anticomputer feeling among the supervisors in the gear shop prior to the time that the SLOPE program was installed. He appears to be still having some trouble in gaining its full acceptance and confidence in its use. If a computer program were to be installed in the experimental department, how could these problems be avoided or overcome?

5. How long do you estimate it might take to develop a computerized control program for the experimental department? Approximately how much would you expect the cost to be? What kind of savings might result? What problems might be encountered?
6. If Madison is not familiar with computerized programs, how would he get started on developing such a new system of control?
7. Analyze each of the reports in Figure 2.
   a. What is the purpose of each report?
   b. Is the format satisfactory?
   c. What information does it provide the manager?
   d. What would you recommend for improvement in the data provided and the format?
   e. How much benefit does each report provide to the manager? Can he get along without the report? If so, what would he substitute for the information that the report provides?

# Ohio Equipment Company

The Ohio Equipment Company of Sandusky, Ohio had been in business for over three-quarters of a century. Founded in 1885 by a German immigrant, the company had established a reputation for manufacturing extremely durable, although not inexpensive, farm equipment and implements. Over the years, the company had grown from a small shop employing only a few people plus the owner to a medium-sized manufacturing company with several thousand employees and producing a full line of reapers, harvesters, combines, balers, cultivators, and other farm equipment. Although Ohio Equipment was only a fraction of the size of such industry leaders as the International Harvester Company and Deere and Company, the company's reputation for well-designed high-quality equipment was the envy of the industry. For many years, the general opinion among its competitors was that Ohio Equipment's major failing was a lack of aggressive promotion and selling, which resulted in its relatively small share of the total market.

For those persons familiar with the internal organization of the Ohio Equipment Company, the reason for the conservative approach to sales was apparent. Following the death of Ernst Mayer, the founder of the company, his three sons had taken over control of the company. Prior to Mayer's death, each of the sons had been in charge of the manufacture of one or more of the company's many products, In many ways the manufacturing operations were carried on as three separate projects housed in a single plant with limited central control. After Mayer's death, the three sons still continued to be interested principally in their own area of specialization. Although the eldest brother, who became president, took some steps to centralize control of the manufacturing operations, the three brothers never abandoned their long-established habits of personally supervising the design and production of their own products. Each brother believed that, if quality products were produced, sales would take care of themselves. In spite of this rather unconventional philosophy, the company grew at a modest, but steady rate, and the three brothers continued to operate the business without serious problems for more than 25 years.

## REORGANIZATION OF COMPANY

However, within a period of 6 years, each of the brothers retired from active management of the business, and each sold a substantial portion of his stock in the company upon retirement. Control of the company passed on to a new group of stockholders, unrelated to the Mayer family, who brought in a new president, Delbert Little. One of Little's first actions was to pull the very loosely knit organization together into a more conventional organizational structure. Where previously the company consisted of three separate empires run by each of the brothers, Little created the functional structure shown in Figure 1.

Along with the change in organization structure, a complete physical reorganization of the manufacturing and assembly facilities was undertaken. Instead of the three separate and relatively independent manufacturing and assembly operations, machinery and equipment were relocated and regrouped so that all similar operations were performed in the same area. A general plan of the factory after the reorganization is shown in Figure 2.

With the relocation of machinery, it was determined that a considerable amount of surplus equipment was available. In many cases duplicate equipment had been obtained for the separate activities run by each of the brothers, and the equipment was never utilized effectively. Centralization of the equipment permitted, in a number of instances, reduction of equipment requirements from three machines to a single machine. In other instances the need for six or seven similar machines was cut to three or four. When the reductions were made, the oldest and least efficient machines were declared surplus and sold. The equipment remaining was relatively modern and in good condition. The attention of the three brothers through the years to technical details and high quality had resulted in the development of a high degree of technical competence and the adoption of modern manufacturing methods. As a consequence, after the reorganization, Ohio Equipment possessed manufacturing facilities as modern and technically advanced as any in the industry.

Delbert Little advocated a more aggressive policy toward sales. The sales function was lodged in two departments, the equipment sales department and a new contract sales department (Figure 1). The equipment sales department concentrated on the sale of farm equipment through farm implement dealers. The contract sales department was established to solicit

FIGURE 1

Functional Organization Chart

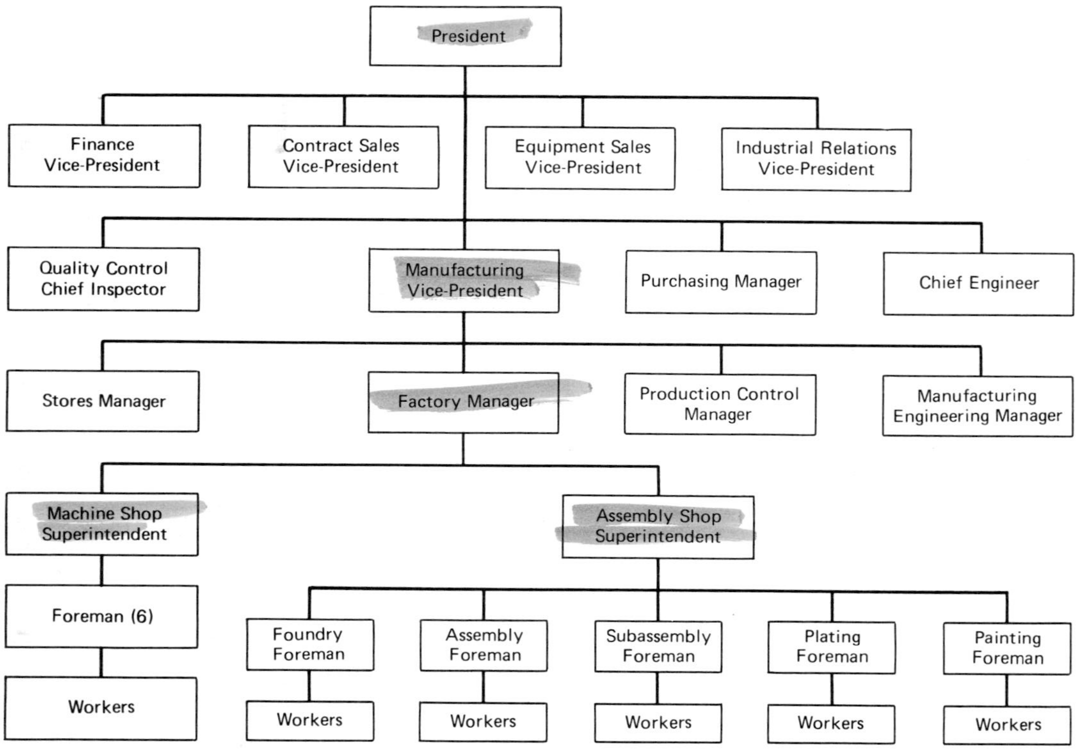

## FIGURE 2

### General Plant Layout

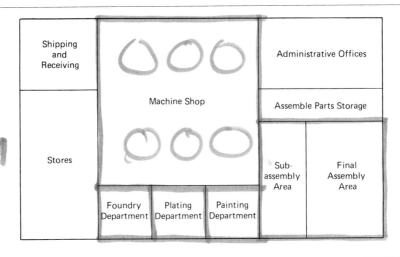

contracts for the production of machined parts, subassemblies, and assemblies for other manufacturers. It was Little's feeling that Ohio Equipment's relatively small size and modern production facilities made it ideally suited for producing small quantities of high-precision parts and assemblies.

With centralization of the manufacturing and assembly facilities, Ohio Equipment's plant began to operate much differently than it had in the past. Instead of specialization of workers and equipment for the production of a limited part of the farm equipment line, the production control department assigned work to shop areas based on a master schedule and relative loads in the various areas. As a consequence, neither workers nor supervisors were personally responsible for production of any particular piece of equipment as they had been in the past.

## FACTORY OPERATIONS

As shown in Figure 2 the factory was physically divided into the foundry, plating, and painting departments and the machine and assembly shops. The assembly shop was divided into subassembly and final assembly areas, and the machine shop was divided into six areas with machines of similar function grouped in each area. The foundry, plating, and painting departments were each run by a supervisor, whereas the machine and assembly shops were the responsibility of the machining and assembly superintendents. The six supervisors responsible for each of the six machine areas reported to the machine shop superintendent, whereas the subassembly and final assembly supervisors reported to the assembly superintendent. Although the foundry, plating, and painting supervisors nominally reported to the assembly superintendent, they operated their departments fairly independently.

Quality control, after the reorganization, was developed as a separate function headed by a chief inspector. Workers and supervisors were expected to perform a great deal of the inspection work themselves during processing and assembly, as they always had in the past. In addition, quality control inspectors performed certain inspections at key points in the factory. Generally, the quality control department's inspectors checked parts before they left the foundry, plating, and painting departments. In the machine shop the quality control department inspectors usually performed an end inspection after the completion of all machining operations on a part. On the average, in the foundry, plating, and painting departments and in the machine shop, there was one inspector on the floor for every 45 direct shop people. In addition, there was one quality control inspector for the subassembly area and one for the final assembly area.

Orders for parts, assemblies, or finished pieces of equipment were transmitted by either the equipment sales department or the contract sales department to the production control department. There orders were inserted in the master schedule, and shop orders and material requisitions were prepared. In the case of orders for items that had been manufactured previously, manufacturing engineering quickly reviewed the process planning and tooling after the shop orders and material requisitions were prepared. Only rarely were any changes required on orders or requisitions already prepared. Orders for new items were sent to manufacturing engineering for process planning and development of tooling after tentative master scheduling by production control, and the orders were then returned to production control for preparation of the shop orders and material requisitions.

Material requisitions prepared by production control were sent to the purchasing department. Shop orders for fabrication were released to the area in the factory performing the first operation four weeks in advance of the date that the processing was due to start. Along with release of the shop order, the production control department released instructions to the stores department to issue raw material to the shop. Shop orders were also released for the subassembly and final assembly areas four weeks in advance of the time that assembly was to begin. Fabricated or purchased parts to be used in the assembly areas were placed directly into the storage area in the assembly area immediately after completion or receipt from the vendor. Therefore, no instructions for release of such materials were necessary for shop orders for assembly.

Shop orders prepared and released by the production control department did not themselves contain any processing or assembly instructions. A shop order was a punched card showing the part number or assembly number, quantity required, date of start of first operation, location of first operation, completion date for the order, and reference number to the standing process or assembly orders. To signify completion of the order, there was a space on the card for initials of the shop or assembly worker involved in the last operation or assembly, and there was a space for the inspector's initials as to acceptance of the order. The inspector also wrote on the card the number of items accepted and their serial numbers, if any, that were subsequently keypunched into the card. The shop order card was then used as the source document for picking up the items in the finished goods inventory records.

The reference number to a standing process or assembly order on the shop order was used to select the proper processing or assembly instructions from files maintained in the shops and assembly areas. Processing and assembly instructions were prepared by manufacturing engineering for all new items as orders were received for them, and reproducible copies were placed in the shop files. When changes or corrections were made by manufacturing engineering, shop file copies were changed so that in theory the shop files always contained the latest processing and assembly instructions for any item that Ohio Equipment had manufactured since installation of the system.

When a shop order for fabrication of a part was received by the supervisor in the area in which the first operation was performed, the supervisor obtained a copy of the standing process order from the shop files and determined the day and machine on which the order would be placed in process. Usually it was not necessary for the supervisor to request issue of raw material by the stores department as the stores department physically moved material to the area in which the first operation was performed as soon as it received instructions to issue the material from the production control department. When the operator was ready to begin working on the job, usually several weeks later, material was then available in the immediate area. After completion of the first operation, the shop order and a copy of the standing process order were sent along with the lot through subsequent operations.

When an assembly order was received in the assembly shop, the shop superintendent assigned it to the subassembly area or final assembly area depending on the relative loads in the two areas and on the size of the items being assembled. The final assembly area was equipped to handle final assembly of farm equipment but could, if necessary, handle smaller assemblies and subassemblies. After an assembly order was assigned to one or the other of the assembly supervisors, it was the supervisor's responsibility to see that the order was completed on schedule. ? *Resp but no authority?*

Parts required for an assembly order were supposed to be in the parts storage area or delivered to it soon after the production control department released the assembly order to the assembly shops. However, because parts were not always in the parts storage area at the proper time, the supervisor who received an assembly order usually checked the parts storage area to see whether all necessary parts were on hand before determining exactly when the assembly work would be done. If some necessary parts were missing, the supervisor would ask production control to trace the missing parts and let the supervisor know when they would be available. In many cases, when parts were missing and schedules were tight, part of the assembly work was done and the partially assembled lot was held until it could be completed when the missing parts arrived. By close attention to follow-up on missing parts and by shifting the work force among various jobs that were in process at any one time, the assembly supervisors usually were able to meet schedule dates.

Because of the relatively small number of items on any assembly order, assembly work was generally done in lots. On occasion simple assembly lines were set up for orders involving larger quantities. Where small parts were involved, the usual procedure was for the worker to take the necessary parts from shelves in the parts storage area and carry them to the assembly bench. Larger parts that could not be moved by hand were moved by a forklift truck from the parts storage area to the assembly area, with the worker that required the parts making the arrangements for the movement.

Assembly workers were either sufficiently familiar with an assembly so that they needed no instructions or worked from written assembly instructions prepared by manufacturing engineering and exploded views prepared by the engineering department. If the assembly worker felt that the assembly instructions and exploded views were needed, the worker obtained copies from the files after he or she was assigned to work on an assembly order. When assembly instructions and exploded views were not available because of changes or delays in their preparation, some of the more experienced employees worked directly from engineering drawings.

In the final assembly area, several workers might work together on assembly of a single piece of farm equipment. In the subassembly area it was more typical for a single worker to work on a number of assemblies at once. Because of the necessity of shifting the work force to keep all jobs on schedule and the practice of partially completing an assembly when parts were missing, several workers might work on a single order at different times.

When work required by an assembly order was completed, the last employee to work on the order initialed the assembly order, and the quality control inspector was then asked to inspect the work. Inspection procedures that were specified by engineering varied considerably but usually consisted of a visual examination of completed items and a check that assemblies functioned properly. For instance, rotating gears or shafts were checked for any end play or stiffness by moving them by hand. Completed pieces of farm equipment were operated by the inspector to see that all controls functioned properly. After completion of inspection, the quality control inspector initialed the assembly order. Serial numbers were required on all complete pieces of farm equipment, all large assemblies such as gear boxes and transmissions, and all assemblies destined for the government. After completing inspection of these items, the inspector wrote the serial numbers on the assembly order.

# QUALITY COMPLAINTS

Shortly after the reorganization of the production facilities, both the equipment sales department and the contract sales department began receiving complaints from farm equipment distributors and other customers regarding various problems with quality. Problems involved parts with surface defects and dimensions out of tolerance, parts manufactured to old specifications rather than incorporating latest engineering changes, parts manufactured from incorrect materials, and, in a few cases, assemblies that had missing or incorrect parts. At first complaints were discussed with the manufacturing department and the quality control department as they occurred. However, when the frequency of complaints had risen to a point where Ohio Equipment's reputation as a high-quality manufacturer appeared to be threatened, a meeting was called of the equipment sales vice president, quality control chief inspector, and factory manager. As a result of this meeting, the factory manager held several meetings with the shop superintendents and supervisors at which time quality problems were discussed. At these meetings the necessity of closer control over quality was impressed upon those attending.

At the conclusion of the meetings with the shop superintendents and supervisors, the factory manager submitted a report to the vice president of manufacturing outlining the conferences that had been held and the continuing efforts that were being made by the shop supervisor to reinstill quality consciousness in the workers.

The quality control chief inspector also met with the inspectors and discussed the various complaints regarding poor quality. In an attempt to analyze possible sources of trouble, all rejection tags for the past year were analyzed by the chief inspector's office. These rejection tags, besides showing identification of items rejected and the reason for rejection, had a section in which it was mandatory for the inspector to check whether engineering, tooling, planning, purchasing, or a shop was responsible for rejection and to indicate specific action taken to solve the problem. In almost all cases tags indicated that a shop was responsible and contained the notation, "Operator has been warned." Findings of the summary of rejection tags were transmitted by the chief inspector to the manufacturing vice president who, in turn, "read the riot act" to the factory manager regarding quality consciousness at the operating level. Shortly afterward, the chief inspector wrote a memorandum to the vice president in charge of manufacturing in which the chief inspector reported that his inspectors had noticed a significant increase in quality in recent weeks.

Four months later the farm equipment sales department received the following telegram from one of Ohio Equipment's largest dealers.

Please be advised that main drive assembly, serial number 88-3694, on new combine, Model C-64A, froze after three hours of operation resulting in breakage of main drive shaft. Worker operating combine was seriously injured by broken shaft. Disassembly of main drive assembly revealed that missing idler bearing caused overheating and failure. We expect Ohio Equipment to acknowledge liability for repair of combine and any claims for compensation by injured worker.

Forsyth Equipt. Co.
Kansas City, Kansas

A quick check of the records of serialized assemblies revealed that the particular assembly that had failed was completed one month after the quality problem was thought to have been solved. Design of the combine included a long shaft that was attached to gears at its ends. The middle of the shaft was supported by an idler bearing assembly. It was this shaft that apparently failed. Before further investigation could take place, the following telegram was received.

Please be advised that worker injured due to failure of drive assembly died this morning because of injuries. Urgent that your company attorney contact us immediately to discuss liability.

Forsyth Equipt. Co.
Kansas City, Kansas

## DISCUSSION QUESTIONS

1. Who was responsible for the decline in quality after the manufacturing facilities were reorganized?
2. Were the steps taken to solve the quality problem adequate? If not, what defects still existed in the quality control system?
3. What changes, if any, would you recommend in Ohio Equipment's procedures that would reduce the likelihood of such incidents as the breaking of the combine drive shaft?
4. How much liability does a manufacturer, such as Ohio Equipment Company, have when its product fails in use and causes damage and injury?

# O-Nut, Incorporated

United Nut Growers was in the final stages of negotiation for the purchase of the entire assets of the O-Nut Orchard Development Company, Inc. The assets consisted of 1,000 acres of planted land containing approximately 65,000 eight-year-old "O" nut trees; 2,000 acres of cleared unplanted land suitable for the growing of "O" nut trees; sufficient building and equipment to support the existing operation; and a substantial supply of office, maintenance, and operating supplies. The tentative price that had been negotiated was $16,000,000, payable in cash at the time of transfer of ownership. The O-Nut Orchard Development Company had just completed harvest of its second annual crop of "O" nuts. It obtained a yield of approximately 2½ million pounds of unshelled nuts and had contracted for the sale of the entire crop for $1,155,000.

## "O" NUT INDUSTRY

"O" nuts varied in size from a filbert to a medium-sized walnut and had a texture and taste distinctly different from any other commercially available nut. Some people thought its taste was similar to that of an almond or chestnut, whereas others claimed it tasted similar to a filbert or brazil nut. "O" nuts could be used for party, dinner, and cocktail treats; as an ingredient or topping for cakes, pies, cookies, ice cream, and numerous other desserts; as a garnish for meats, fish, and fowl; and as an addition to various salads. A paperback book of "O" nut recipes, endorsed by a world-famous chef in a major hotel in Jamaica, was available upon request for chefs, dieticians, home makers, and others who were interested in using "O" nuts.

The discovery of the "O" nut as an edible fruit was made by Dr. Jim Adams in the late 1800s. Until 1922, however, when the first sizable commercial plantings were made, the "O" nut tree was valued primarily for its ornamental qualities and the majority of the plantings were sold for such purposes. A small portion of the plantings was used for growing "O" nuts. These generally resulted from an over-optimistic estimate of nursery requirements for ornamental plants.

For many years primary markets for "O" nuts were local natives and inhabitants of nearby islands who ate the nuts in their natural uncooked state. It was not until a group of agricultural economists took an active interest in the commercial use of "O" nuts that their potential value as a delicacy became apparent. In 1942, when the O-Nut Orchard Development Company, Inc. was formed, there were only 1,200 acres of "O" nut trees under cultivation. Most of these trees were approaching a state of maturity, and the production of raw unshelled nuts approximated 150,000 pounds. Many of these trees were originally planted to be sold as seedlings and not for the production of nuts.

Few new plantings were made between 1942 and 1948 because of World War II and the numerous and more profitable opportunities available to investors during that period. In addition, the existing, rapidly maturing trees provided a supply of "O" nuts that was neither easily harvested nor disposed of profitably in view of existing labor, equipment, and transportation problems. Eventually, however, the O-Nut Orchard Development Company sensed a change in the demand for "O" nuts and purchased 3,000 acres of timberland suitable for growing "O" nut trees. Within a few years 1,000 acres of this land were cleared and planted with approximately 70,000 newly grafted "O" nut trees. This planting represented a potential increase of tenfold or more in the future supply of "O" nuts and temporarily discouraged newcomers from entering the field.

At the time that United Nut Growers was negotiating the purchase of the O-Nut Orchard Development Company, there were approximately 2,500 acres of "O" nut trees under cultivation. Excluding O-Nut, the largest of the growers owned 400 acres of three- to five-year-old trees in the non-bearing stage. These trees were of a variety similar to those being grown by O-Nut. The remaining 1,100 acres under cultivation were owned by 13 independent firms and consisted of 500 acres of seven- to nine-year-old currently bearing trees and 600 acres of mature and overmature low-yield trees. In addition to O-Nut's 2,000 acres of cleared land, other producers had available an additional 1,000 acres of land suitable for growing "O" nut trees. The 600 acres of low-yield trees could be converted to the latest varieties of high-yield trees by regrafting.

# "O" NUT CULTURE

Original plantings of "O" nut trees were made by grafting cuttings from prize growing stock to select two-year-old nursery-grown rootstock. These trees yielded their first fruits seven years after the grafting date. Regrafting of mature rootstock resulted in initial yields four years after the regraft. No appreciable difference in the overall yield pattern appeared to exist between new grafts and regrafts except for the three-year difference in time between grafting and initial yields. Due to the need for more careful grafting and extensive root pruning and culturing required by regrafts, the original cost of regrafting was approximately double that of purchasing and planting newly grafted trees, which currently average $30 per tree. Part of this difference was recovered by the reduced maintenance resulting from the shorter nonbearing period of regrafted trees. Once a regraft was attempted, whether successful or not, further regrafting was inadvisable. The survival rate for new grafts was approximately 90 to 95 percent, as compared with 70 or 80 percent for first regrafts. For second, third, or additional regrafts, the survival rate approached zero. Under ideal conditions a maximum success rate of less than 25 percent had been achieved on second regrafts. Tree removal costs were estimated to average $15 per tree when thinning or replanting previously planted areas.

"O" nut trees reached a maximum height of 45 feet and were planted approximately 25 feet apart. Somewhere between years 11 and 13 (years 9 and 11 for regrafts), the trees had to be thinned by 50 percent to provide 35 feet of space between trees. If adequate spacing of trees was not provided,

TABLE 1

Expected Yield Pattern For O-Nut, Incorporated Trees
(yield in pounds per tree)

| Age | Yield |
|-----|-------|
| 1–6 | 0 |
| 7 | 20 |
| 8 | 40 |
| 9 | 80 |
| 10 | 100 |
| 11 | 120 |
| 12 | 160 |
| 13 | 160 |
| 14 | 140 |
| 15 | 140 |
| 16 | 120[a] |

[a]Fifteen percent annual decrease for all subsequent years.

excess shading resulted and the nuts did not ripen properly. Experience indicated that as much as an 80 percent loss in a crop could occur from overshading. Table 1 gives the expected average yield pattern for "O" nut trees of the variety existing on O-Nut properties. Research with new varieties of "O" nut trees had developed trees with yields up to 25 percent greater than those currently existing in O-Nut orchards. Indications were that further research might develop even more bountiful varieties. No other significant differences in the overall yield pattern or maturity rate had appeared.

## NUT HARVESTING

Harvesting of "O" nuts was seasonal and occurred during the months of September, October, November, and December. The mature nuts fell to the ground before being harvested. Because the nuts could not safely be allowed to remain on the ground more than 60 days without significant deterioration, they were harvested twice during the season.

Harvesting was done by handpicking nuts that had fallen to the ground. The majority of pickers were women between the ages of 30 and 45 years. Harvesters were generally employed on a four-month basis and recruited through ads in the daily newspapers. The average cost of hiring, equipping, and terminating was approximately $90 per employee. The cost was relatively independent of whether the employee worked the full four months or some shorter time. Full-term employees generally wore their equipment quite ragged, whereas short-term employees often absconded with their equipment.

Harvesters were paid on an hourly basis and received a wage of approximately $3.40 per hour with no fringe benefits. The expected output was 1,100 pounds of nuts per picker per day. The labor market had been favorable for the employer but was becoming increasingly tight as the overall production of "O" nuts increased and demand for harvesters increased. The future labor market was expected to become less favorable to the employer unless mechanical harvesting was introduced.

To facilitate the use of a mechanical harvester, the ground surrounding each tree had to be leveled, graded, and surfaced with a 4-inch layer of pea gravel or volcanic ash. This required several tons of gravel per tree and was estimated to cost $1,200 per acre complete, including grading, leveling, gravel, and surfacing. This special preparation was required because of the rocky nature of the soil (3- to 6-inch diameter rocks). The mechanical harvester accomplished its task by scooping up a ¼- to ½-inch layer of gravel including any fallen nuts, separating the nuts from the gravel by a screening process, and redepositing the gravel. Once applied, the gravel surfacing was estimated to last a minimum of 20 years. When the surface became too thin, a 1- to 2-inch layer of gravel could be added to the top of the existing surface. The need for a 4-inch initial layer arose from the need to cover rocks in the orchards.

The price of a mechanical harvester was $140,000. It was designed to harvest 20 to 25 acres per day depending on the planting configuration. The harvester required three full-time operators. Considering the difficulty of retaining competent skilled help on a part-time basis, it was anticipated that these employees would be hired on a full-time basis and be used elsewhere during the nonharvesting season. It was estimated that employees capable of being trained to operate and service the proposed mechanical harvester could be found and retained at a cost of approximately $8.85 per hour. In view of the difficulty in retaining skilled help on anything but a day-shift basis and the added risk to the equipment and the operators resulting from nighttime operation, single-shift operation of the harvester was recommended. The equipment required daily maintenance and cleaning of approximately 4 labor-hours. Gasoline, oil, and other operating and maintenance expenses were estimated at $8,000 per year per 8-hour shift. This cost would increase proportionately for any usage beyond the estimated 40 hours per week. Current delivery time for the proposed piece of equipment was eight months from the order date.

## PROCESSING

Total single shift capacity of "O" nut processing plants was approximately 3,000,000 pounds of raw nuts per year. Approximately 80 percent of the existing processing facilities was owned or controlled by a single processor. "O" nut growers were responsible for delivering their harvest to a local pickup point where they were graded, weighed, and transferred to large tractor-trailer vehicles that delivered them to the processing plant.

"O" nuts arrived at the processing plant in a paperlike husk. The husks were removed by tumbling the nuts in a high-velocity wind chamber. After this the nuts were placed in large dehydrators where they remained for at least two weeks. Once dehydrated the nuts could be kept for 10 to 14 months, which allowed the remaining processing to be conducted throughout the year rather than being required immediately following the harvesting period. Between the husking and dehydrating operations, all nuts were inspected visually and any defective nuts were removed.

After dehydration the nuts were graded for size and weighed into 300-pound batches to enter the final processing. The nuts proceeded to one of seven cracking machines, each machine being set up to process a specific size range. Good nuts were separated from spoiled nuts, shells, and other foreign matter by a flotation process. The good nuts sank to the bottom of the tank, whereas shells and other foreign matter remained on top. Immediately after flotation the good nuts were partially dried in a large centrifuge and, after another visual inspection, each batch passed through a flash dehydrator where any remaining traces of water or excess moisture were removed. After this second dehydration each batch was laboratory tested for moisture content, taste, and other properties. The nuts were then ready for roasting, final inspection, salting, and packaging. After roasting, the nuts were no longer separated by size and were processed in a continuous- rather than a batch-type process. Final packaging consisted of vacuum packing the processed nuts in unlabeled glass jars. Labels were applied just prior to shipping the processed nuts to local and regional distribution points. The approximate retail selling price of processed "O" nuts was $5.25 per pound; processors received $3.00 per pound for packaged nuts.

Information obtained from the more successful of the two small independent processors indicated that the smallest economic unit of processing capacity was 400,000 pounds of raw nuts per shift per year. Larger plants essentially consisted of multiples of this basic unit of capacity. The current cost per basic unit of capacity (400,000 pounds of raw nuts per year) was $875,000, excluding building and installation costs. Processing costs, excluding the cost of raw nuts and capital charges, averaged $0.15 per pound of raw nuts. This was equivalent to approximately $0.30 per pound of packaged nuts, because the weight loss due to shelling, dehydration, roasting, and inferior-quality nuts averaged 50 percent of the initial gross weight of the raw nuts.

## MARKET

The only quantitative information immediately available for making a reasonable long-range estimate of potential "O" nut sales was current and past sales of other varieties of nuts and condiments. After examining a substantial amount of data the following conclusions were drawn:

1. From a purely objective standpoint (i.e., nutritional value, taste, stability, etc.), "O" nuts were comparable to other common nuts such as walnuts, filberts, pecans, and almonds.
2. From a marketing, promotional, and processing standpoint, the "O" nut industry was 10 to 15 years junior to any of the major nut industries.
3. With efficient promotion techniques and good fortune, the "O" nut industry could achieve the current status of the major nut industries within 10 to 15 years.
4. A reasonably attainable 3- to 5-year goal for "O" nut sales would be a sales rate equivalent to that of filbert sales (3,000,000 pounds of processed nuts per year).
5. An optimistic yet potentially attainable 10- to 15-year goal for "O" nut sales would be a sales rate equivalent to that of walnut sales (30,000,000 pounds of processed nuts per year).

# ORCHARD OPERATIONS AND COSTS

The O-Nut Orchard Development Company employed 35 full-time field employees at a cost of $7.05 per hour. During the nonharvesting season these employees performed such tasks as pruning, fertilizing, spraying, and maintaining the grounds and equipment. It appeared that they could continue to carry out this function as long as the number of trees under cultivation did not exceed 65,000. During the harvesting season these employees assisted in the harvest by acting as field supervisors and recorders, by operating local collecting stations, and by operating a shuttle service between the pickers and the local collecting stations and between the local collecting stations and the processor's pickup point.

It appeared that unless mechanical harvesting was adopted these tasks could not be performed by the 35 full-time employees after an annual yield of 5,000,000 pounds or more was achieved. The mechanical harvester would eliminate the need for field supervisors and recorders. Local collecting stations, nevertheless, would have to be retained unless a road system capable of supporting large trucks was installed throughout the orchard. However, the shuttling of nuts from the single mechanical picker to the collecting station would be considerably more efficient than from the many handpickers. An opinion had been expressed that if mechanical picking were adopted the current full-time nonharvest work crew could support the full potential harvest of the 65,000 trees currently under cultivation.

The only other major expense of operating the orchard was for administration, sales, and miscellaneous tools and supplies. This cost was currently about $400,000 per year. Although most of these costs were essentially fixed, it was anticipated that there would be some modest increases in costs if the number of field employees and size of orchard operations were to grow.

## DISCUSSION QUESTIONS

1. Prepare a plan of operations for the next ten years including schedules of:
   a. annual planting
   b. annual thinning
   c. annual surfacing
   d. annual regrafting
   e. equipment purchases
   f. annual harvest
2. Evaluate the economic implications of your plan of operations.
3. Evaluate the competitive risks associated with your plan of operations.
4. Evaluate the proposed acquisition of O-Nut from the standpoint of the shareholders of United Nut Growers.

# Osburn Manufacturing Company

The Osburn Manufacturing Company had an excellent record of making deliveries on schedule. At times, however, the cost of maintaining this on-schedule delivery had been high. The delivery record had been maintained by intensive expediting, adding shop personnel, overtime work, and a complex system of priorities that, when used, had required the rescheduling of most of the work a second time and often a third time.

## MAJOR PROJECTS

The Osburn Manufacturing Company manufactured electric generators, mostly for the commercial market, but the company also engaged in certain military work. The total work load was divided among three projects:

*Project A* was a commercial program contract of large volume. The schedule policy associated with this project was to meet all schedule delivery dates. Fabrication time schedule allowances were standard; however, they could be compressed by 50 percent whenever necessary to maintain delivery schedules.

*Project B* was a commercial program that had been in production for three years. The schedule allowances were standard, and reorder for the fabrication or purchase of parts was based on minimum bundle breakage (i.e., when existing quantities of available parts awaiting subassembly or assembly were reduced to predetermined levels, a reorder was initiated for fabrication or purchase as required). Schedule allowances could be compressed 50 percent in certain instances.

## FIGURE 1

### Organization Chart

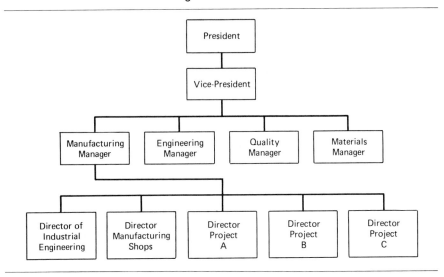

## FIGURE 2

### Sample Schedule Flow Chart

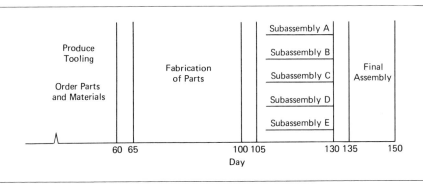

*Project C* was a new military contract of great importance. This project had top military priority as well as top priority within the Osburn Manufacturing Company. Engineering design had not been finalized, and many changes were being made in the design of the product.

Kevin Jostad, the manufacturing manager of the Osburn Manufacturing Company, was in charge of the entire manufacturing operation (Figure 1). Reporting to Jostad were the director of industrial engineering, the director of manufacturing shops, and the directors of projects A, B, and C.

The industrial engineering group was responsible for scheduling, shop loading, and work order releases. The manufacturing shops fabricated detailed parts, and subassembly and final assembly were accomplished in shops under the direction of one of the three project directors.

## SCHEDULING SYSTEM

The production schedule was prepared by the industrial engineering group. The procedure was to work back from a specified delivery date to determine when each operation should start. A simplified flow schedule is shown in Figure 2 to illustrate this procedure. The delivery date is shown as workday 150, the final assembly requires 15 days and is scheduled to begin on day 135, subassemblies are scheduled for completion on day 130 to allow time to deliver them to the final assembly area, and so on.

Certain of the flow times were accepted as standard. For example, five days were allowed as an average flow time to transport materials, parts, or subassemblies between departments. The time allowed to fabricate parts or complete assemblies was estimated in labor-hours and was based on the average time required to complete identical or similar jobs in the past.

The industrial engineering group knew the capacity of each shop in terms of labor-hours of output and would schedule the work into each shop accordingly. Work orders were numbered and sent to the shop in blocks. When an engineering change occurred, a new work order was issued to replace the one canceled by the change. The shops were instructed to work on orders according to their sequence number; however, it was understood that the shop supervisor could change the sequence to improve the effectiveness of work assignments in his or her shop.

Orders were regarded as behind schedule when the shops indicated that they could not complete an order and deliver it to the next assembly area according to the stated schedule. Flow time could be compressed, however, by working overtime on the order, by providing special delivery service to the in-process part, or by performing assembly work between the regular work stations.

Scheduling policies used by the Osburn Manufacturing Company were as follows:

1. Component schedules were to support delivery of the end item with adequate flow time allowance for each step involved in the transfer, inspection, paper flow, assembly, testing, and delivery of the end product.
2. The sales group had to consider standard manufacturing flow time requirements when negotiating contracts; however, sales should have sufficient latitude to be competitive on delivery schedules.
3. Other considerations in scheduling included the volume to be produced, fabrication shop loads, fabrication shop capacity, and availability of outside sources of supply.

4. All work was to be scheduled on the basis of standard flow times for the part concerned. All orders were to be worked in sequence, according to the manufacturing work order number.
5. The fabrication shops had to periodically report work orders as "ahead," "current," or "behind" schedule.
6. Whenever behind-schedule fabrication orders exceeded manufacturing capacity for the month ahead, an initial priority was issued for the more urgent work orders.
7. When orders with priority exceeded the manufacturing capacity for the month ahead, a second, higher priority was issued and assigned to the most urgent work orders. At this point the higher priority took precedence over the previous priority. If the backlog of work orders continued to grow, then additional higher levels of priorities would be issued in turn, each subsequent priority class being effective until the capacity was saturated with its work orders. At that point another level of priorities was necessary. For example, if the manufacturing capacity of a shop was 100 units a month, and there were more than 100 units scheduled for the shop, a priority would be established. If the work orders with the priority exceeded 100 units, they were reclassified into two levels of priorities, for example, A and AA.

## ADDITION OF PROJECT C TO SCHEDULE

Although the amount of work involved in each order varied, the shops had processed between 280 and 320 orders per month during the previous year. Project C was integrated into the production schedule of the Osburn Manufacturing Company about July 1. The work order releases during the following 12 months are summarized in Table 1. Shortly after the start of project C, the number of work orders behind schedule increased. This is summarized in Table 2.

Jostad attributed the increase in the work orders behind schedule to (1) the additional work load imposed on the fabrication shops, (2) the large number of releases that did not include a sufficient flow time, (3) the large number of changes in design (whenever the design was changed a new work order was released), and (4) the added shop work required when the orders were grouped by priorities and not according to the most efficient manner of production.

In November, priority A was assigned to those orders behind schedule and a higher priority, AA, to the orders in project C that were behind schedule. Both priorities authorized overtime work in the shops. Shortly after priority AA was established, the directors of the other two projects complained that their projects were suffering because manufacture of the detailed parts for their projects was delayed due to the preference given parts being manufactured for project C. They asked Jostad for a special priority for selected orders relating to their projects.

## TABLE 1

### Work Order Releases

| Month | Project A | Project B | Project C | Total |
|-------|-----------|-----------|-----------|-------|
| July | 120 | 60 | 120 | 300 |
| August | 80 | 80 | 140 | 300 |
| September | 70 | 90 | 160 | 320 |
| October | 40 | 170 | 200 | 410 |
| November | 70 | 60 | 300 | 430 |
| December | 30 | 80 | 280 | 390 |
| January | 40 | 90 | 200 | 330 |
| February | 60 | 80 | 180 | 320 |
| March | 80 | 110 | 160 | 350 |
| April | 60 | 60 | 240 | 360 |
| May | 40 | 80 | 260 | 380 |
| June | 60 | 70 | 210 | 340 |
| Total | | | | 4,230 |

Jostad decided to review the entire system of priorities and its impact on the present situation. He found that 84 percent of all orders processed during May had been assigned a priority and that most of the orders for detailed parts had been produced in quantities of less than one-half the originally specified lot size. Reducing quantities had been necessary to satisfy the immediate demands of the assembly lines for the three projects. The use of direct and indirect labor-hours associated with the production planning, control, and operation of the fabrication shops is summarized in Table 3.

## TABLE 2

### Work Orders Behind Schedule

| Month | Project A | Project B | Project C | Total |
|-------|-----------|-----------|-----------|-------|
| July | 4 | 2 | 0 | 6 |
| August | 4 | 3 | 0 | 7 |
| September | 6 | 2 | 12 | 20 |
| October | 7 | 4 | 140 | 151 |
| November | 14 | 40 | 260 | 314 |
| December | 70 | 60 | 220 | 350 |
| January | 71 | 80 | 260 | 411 |
| February | 80 | 90 | 250 | 420 |
| March | 90 | 110 | 260 | 460 |
| April | 100 | 120 | 290 | 510 |
| May | 100 | 130 | 340 | 570 |
| June | 110 | 130 | 370 | 610 |

## TABLE 3

### Direct and Indirect Labor-Hours, Fabrication Shops

| Month | Labor-Hours (000) | |
| | Direct | Indirect |
|---|---|---|
| July | 81 | 60 |
| August | 80 | 62 |
| September | 82 | 64 |
| October | 83 | 64 |
| November | 106 | 64 |
| December | 110 | 72 |
| January | 105 | 84 |
| February | 112 | 96 |
| March | 114 | 98 |
| April | 108 | 98 |
| May | 120 | 102 |
| June | 130 | 106 |

S. G Patten, the director of Project A, was very upset about the entire system of priorities. He believed that the entire future of the company depended on whether or not Jostad took some action to correct the situation. To make this point and vent his feelings he sent a letter to Jostad as follows.

TO: Kevin Jostad
FROM: S. G. Patten
SUBJECT: Scheduling

Lest you feel that the parable I am going to write and the comparison I am going to make is facetious, let me assure you that it is with only a sincere desire to see a ghastly condition corrected that I illustrate it in this manner.

At one time there were two cities — Johnstown and Smithtown — located fifty miles apart. There were four intermittent towns between these cities and in a direct line with each other, spaced ten miles apart.

A railroad was organized and single rails with periodic sidings were laid to join the two cities and pass through each of the interspaced towns. Trains were made up and scheduled to run regularly from one city to the other. Things went smoothly at first and the trains maintained their schedules.

Certain commitments were made by the railroad to deliver merchandise from one end of the line to the other end of the line. Soon, however, it was discovered that sometimes the promised time of arrival for some merchandise had arrived or had passed and the merchandise had not even been loaded in a car. This necessitated forced concentration on loading a car with the late merchandise and dispatching an engine under a special flag and with cleared track to rush the car through to the consignee.

This resulted in the other cars and trains along the railroad line going into sidings at each of the towns to let the Special through. This affected their schedule and made them late, causing in some cases an angry consignee to remind the railroad that his delivery date was not being met. The railroad, to meet this new urgent obligation, would dispatch this particular car or cars with special engine and flag to rush it through.

Daily more trains would start behind schedule and some of these would leave the yards with a "highball" special flag to clear the tracks. Those cars and trains that did start on scheduled time soon were forced on sidings so many times that they too fell behind schedule and were "specialed" to rush them through.

The train crews became more and more confused, trying to get all Specials through together on a single track.

Finally the railroad management concluded that the single flag would indicate just the Special, but two flags, one above the other, on the engine would give preference over just ordinary Specials.

With a sigh of relief, they sat back and congratulated each other on this simple solution.

Soon, however, they discovered most of the engines were pulling a Super-Special car with two flags.

Ah, now here was a problem! A conference was hastily called and it was decided that to get the trains through that were really important, they would fly a flag from the engine bearing a picture of the railroad president.

Now the really "hot" trains would surely get through; Specials and Super-Specials could and would go on sidings.

Soon it became impossible to assure any consignee that his car would arrive on time even though he might have it on a Special or a Super-Special train. If he couldn't promote a "picture of the president" flag on the engine, he would just have to wait.

In the early days of the railroad, Sunday was designated as a day to check, maintain, and repair equipment to keep it in proper running order. But the press of Specials, Super-Specials, and Picture Flag Specials became so great that, although the same number of trains were running, they had to highball each car out of the yard as soon as it was loaded and the door shut. Seven days of each week were now required to get the trains through and there was little or no time for maintenance.

It became positively hazardous to try to cross the track because of Specials, Super-Specials, and Picture Flag Specials whizzing by at all hours.

The consignees finally became so disgusted with the service that they transferred their business to competing truck lines servicing the cities. The railroad promptly became bankrupt and went into receivership.

A new company was formed and a complete investigation was made to determine how conditions could be corrected to restore the confidence of the shippers in schedule commitments made by railroad.

They discovered that, if cars were loaded promptly and dispatched from the yards on the promised starting date, they nearly always arrived on time. The need for Specials was rare, but when required they did receive prompt attention because the train crews now felt that a Special must really be important.

Are we, too, following the example of the first railroad organization? Will we meet the same fate? To illustrate just how serious this condition is, please observe our current situation closely.

## DISCUSSION QUESTIONS

1. How serious is the situation at the Osburn Manufacturing Company?
2. Evaluate the organizational arrangement of the management.
3. How can Jostad revise the priority system?
4. Should the Osburn Manufacturing Company slide the delivery schedule? Why?
5. How can work from different sections of the company be integrated and scheduled fairly?

# Othello Products, Incorporated

Othello Products, Incorporated consisted of a plant and office area of 60,000 square feet and employed 150 hourly and 32 salaried employees. Othello had been primarily a job shop operation producing various-sized lots of medium- to high-quality precision parts for a large number of local consumer goods manufacturers. For many years the volume of work in the shop had fluctuated widely from period to period. Consequently, Othello employees were either operating under "make work" or "get it out at any cost" conditions. This constant alternation between feast and famine caused numerous supervisory and managerial problems. To combat high costs and excessive employee turnover, the management of Othello initiated two new major programs. The first of these was a work standards program; the second was a program directed toward finding kinds of work that would provide some long-term stability to Othello's volume of business.

The work standards program was designed to provide a method for placing valid production rates on every operation of every work order issued to Othello's manufacturing organization. As an initial step, stopwatch time studies of over 800 basic operations performed on Othello's facilities were made. After the task of collecting the time studies was completed, the individual operational elements from these studies were sorted, classified, and cross-referenced. The final step was to develop a set of predetermined standard times particularly applicable to Othello's operation. It was hoped that this information would provide a means for making economical and accurate cost estimates, for setting shop production standards, and for controlling overall manufacturing costs.

FIGURE 1

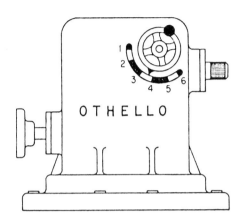

## VARIABLE SPEED GEAR REDUCER

The second program consisted of an all-out effort to find one or more long-term products or contracts. An ideal product was believed to be one that was compact, easy to store, labor intensive, and yet relatively simple to manufacture. It was felt that, if the product could be manufactured for inventory during slack periods, it could provide one means of leveling the overall production rate and labor force required by the firm. After approximately a year, one such product was identified. A sketch of this product is shown in Figure 1.

The product was a compact, variable-speed gear reducer used by a large manufacturer for whom Othello had previously made numerous experimental parts. The reducer appeared ideal in that the components required a considerable amount of medium-precision machining using equipment that Othello currently had available. Over 85 percent of the reducer's finished cost (excluding overhead and profit) consisted of direct labor. The manufacturer had issued an invitation for bids for the first production lot to a group of selected suppliers who were known to be competent in this kind of work.

Because Othello had made most of the parts for the experimental model, it had relatively complete information regarding the raw material cost and machining requirements of the component parts. Actual stopwatch

## TABLE 1

### Gear Reducer Assembly Requirements

| Activity Code | Activity | Quantity [1] | Unit Time [2] | Handling Time [3] | Cannot Precede | Tooling Cost [4] |
|---|---|---|---|---|---|---|
| a [5] | Start | | .00 | .00 | | $ 0 |
| b | Press main bearings | 2 | .59 | .21 | a | 3,500 |
| c | Press grease seals | 2 | .32 | .15 | a | 1,500 [6] |
| d | Insert welsh plugs | 4 | .13 | .08 | a | 375 |
| e | Mount on chain conveyor | 1 | .17 | | b,c,d | |
| f | Assemble main drive gear | 1 | 1.19 | .17 | e | 1,250 |
| g | Insert main drive gear assembly | 1 | .63 | .07 | f | |
| h | Position main drive gear bearing block | 1 | .30 | .07 | g | 75 |
| i | Insert and engage bolts | 4 | .04 | .02 [7] | h | |
| j | Tighten bolts with torque wrench | 4 | .06 | .04 [8] | i | 225 |
| k | Assemble reduction gear | 1 | .63 | .17 | e | (f) [9] |
| l | Insert reduction gear | 1 | .33 | .09 | k | |
| m | Position reduction gear bearing block | 1 | .16 | .07 | l | 25 |
| n | Insert and engage bolts | 4 | .04 | .02 [7] | m | |
| o | Shim for end play | 1 | .18 | .06 | m | 85 |
| p | Tighten bolts with torque wrench | 4 | .06 | .04 [8] | n,o | (j) [9] |
| q | Assemble idler shaft | 1 | .23 | .17 | e | (f) [9] |
| r | Insert idler shaft | 1 | .49 | | q | |
| s | Position idler shaft bearing block | 1 | .20 | .05 | r | 95 |
| t | Insert and engage bolts | 4 | .04 | .02 [7] | s | |
| u | Tighten bolts with torque wrench | 4 | .06 | .04 [8] | t | (j) [9] |
| v | Place gasket | 1 | .08 | .02 | e | |
| w | Place base plate | 1 | .29 | | j,p,u,v | |
| x | Insert and engage bolts | 12 | .04 | .02 [7] | w | |
| y | Tighten bolts with torque wrench | 12 | .05 | .04 | x | (j) [9] |
| z | Insert pressure and lubricant fittings | 4 | .15 | .04 | e | 35 |
| aa | Fill lubricant | 1 | .51 [10] | | y,z | 3,800 |
| ab | Plug lubricant holes | 2 | .10 | .05 | aa | (d) [9] |
| ac | Pressure test | 1 | 3.80 [11] | | ab | 1,800 |
| ad | Remove pressure fittings and plug holes | 2 | .29 | .04 | ac | 60 |
| ae | Dynamometer test | 1 | 1.87 [12] | | ab | 4,800 |
| af | Attach name and instruction plate | 1 | .30 | .08 | e | 900 |
| ag | Wipe clean | 1 | .26 | .03 | ae | |
| ah | Attach test results | 1 | .08 | | af,ag | |
| ai | Release from conveyor | 1 | .08 | | ah | |

[1] Number of cycles or repetitions of basic operation to complete the specified activity for each unit.

[2] Time in minutes to complete a single cycle of operation included in the specified activity.

[3] Time in minutes to pick up, position, lay aside tools, etc., if more than one activity is assigned to a specific work station. For example, if activities b and c are assigned to independent work stations the performance time is 1.18 and .64 minutes, respectively. If they are assigned to a single work station the performance time is 2.18 minutes (1.18 + .64 + .21 + .15 = 2.18).

[4] Cost of company-supplied tools and special equipment to perform specified activity. Must be included for every work station at which all or any part of the specified activity is performed.

[5] Dummy operation. Requires no time or labor. Assumes main castings are positioned on belt conveyor.

[6] Can use common tool if this operation is performed at the same work station as operation b.

210

time studies on many of the machine operations required had been made. It was believed that it would be easy to obtain accurate estimates of the remaining machining operations by applying the standard time data that were scheduled to be available well ahead of the final date for submitting the bid. The major unsolved problem was to determine the assembly costs.

## ASSEMBLY METHOD

To obtain accurate assembly costs, several workers and a process engineer were assigned the task of devising an appropriate assembly procedure. Data in Table 1 are the result of these efforts. To obtain these data each worker was allowed, uninstructed but under the surveillance of the process engineer, to assemble and disassemble a reducer. The experience gained was pooled and from the best method used by the various workers 34 basic assembly operations were defined. Each of these operations was then time studied using stopwatch techniques. The times shown in Table 1 represent the standard unit times.

The time study standards were based on 100 percent performance, this being the output that was expected from an average experienced worker having reasonable skill in the type of operation performed and working at a natural rate of speed. Because the time studies were made on employees who were considered to be relatively inexperienced in assembly work, an 85 percent skill rating was assigned to all operations. Because of the highly cooperative spirit of the employees, however, practically all operations were rated for effort at or above 115 percent. Thus, in almost all cases the stopwatch standards determined were met or exceeded in the actual assembly trials.

## DESIGN OF ASSEMBLY LINE

The only remaining task with regard to estimating the assembly cost was to lay out the assembly process in terms of specific work stations and determine the equipment and labor costs. It was company policy to maintain

---

[7]Activities i, n, t, and x can be combined without incurring handling time as they contain identical elements and require common tools.

[8]Activities j, p, and u can be combined without incurring handling time as they contain identical elements and require common tools.

[9]Requires identical tooling as activity shown in parentheses. Can use common set of tooling if operations are performed at the same work station.

[10]Activity completely automatic, no operator required.

[11]Activity completely automatic except for operator who must visually check for leaks. One operator can oversee the testing of up to four units simultaneously. Operator cannot perform any other function regardless of how many units he oversees.

[12]Activity completely automatic except for operator who connects hydraulic dynamometer coupling, records test results, and shuts down test equipment in case of an emergency. One operator can process up to two units simultaneously. Operator cannot perform any other function regardless of the number of units he or she oversees.

good working conditions, and thus it was felt that the design of work stations should provide each employee with a minimum of 5 linear feet of work space along the assembly line. This was considered possible since an area 85 feet in length and 25 feet in width was available for placement of the line and for in-process parts storage areas. It was felt that the entire line should be conveyorized as this would substantially reduce the problem of maintaining efficient performance. Estimates of conveyor costs indicated that the conveyor required for activities a through d of Table 1 would cost about $6,600, plus $300 per linear foot of conveyor. This was essentially a belt conveyor from which parts could be removed for processing and replaced for transporting to the next work station.

A chain conveyor was suggested for activities e through ai of Table 1 and was estimated to cost approximately $9,500 plus $525 per linear foot. This was a conveyor upon which the housing would be clamped and thus not removable at the work stations. This type of a conveyor would pace the line and allow completely automatic testing of the assembly as the unit would be accurately and positively located at each work station.

"Banking" facilities capable of holding up to ten parts at any given work station were available for the belt conveyor at an additional cost of $300 per station. No such facility was available for the chain conveyor. One of the conveyor firms that had been contracted quoted a price of $4,200 plus $175 per linear foot for small feeder conveyors that could serve as feeders to the main conveyor line for parts or subassemblies.

The contract upon which Othello was bidding was for 1,800 reducers a week for a period of six months. The invitation to bid provided that, if the winning bidder wished to absorb all equipment and tooling costs, that bidder would be free to build and sell the reducer in the open market under the bidder's own trade name. To Othello management this appeared to be an excellent opportunity for Othello to develop a new product line, and it was decided that, if the contract were received, an initial eight-hour single-shift five-day-week capacity would be installed that was 10 percent in excess of the contract demand. Since Othello was currently operating on a one-shift five-day-week basis, this plan would comply with current operations and allow for up to a 200 percent increase in production by going to two shifts of ten hours each on a six-day-week basis.

## DISCUSSION QUESTIONS

1. Sketch an assembly line designating specific work stations and the operations and activities performed at each work station. At what speed should the conveyor be designed to operate?
2. What are the approximate capital and labor costs per unit associated with the line you sketched? Assume that direct labor costs average $9.65 per hour.

# Petersen General Contractors

Petersen General Contractors was an established construction company doing work in several states in New England. Petersen generally handled small- to medium-sized commercial and industrial construction projects. Some recent projects that the company had completed were a 20,000-square-foot factory building, a four-story office building, and a water filtration plant.

## TELEVISION TOWER BID

The company was now in the process of preparing a bid for a television station for the erection of a 225 foot high television antenna tower and the construction of a building adjacent to the tower that would be used to house transmission and electrical equipment. Petersen was bidding only on the tower and its electrical equipment, the building, the connecting cable between tower and building, and site preparation. Transmission equipment and other equipment to be housed in the building were not to be included in the bid and would be obtained separately by the television station. The site for the tower was at the top of a hill to minimize the required height of the tower, with the building to be constructed at a slightly lower elevation than the base of the tower and near a main road. Between the tower and building was to be a crushed gravel service road and an underground cable. Adjacent to the building a fuel tank was to be installed above ground on a concrete slab. A sketch of the tower and building site is shown in Figure 1.

FIGURE 1

Television Tower and Building Site Plan

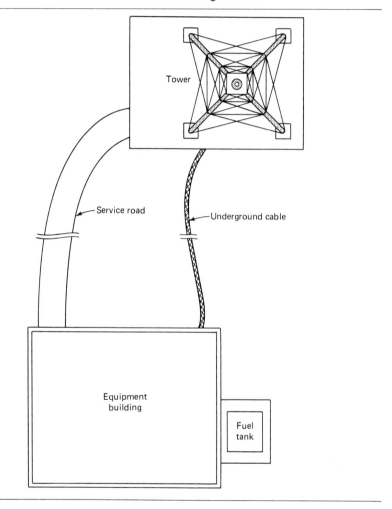

## PREPARATION OF COST ESTIMATES

Prior to preparing the detailed cost estimates, Petersen's estimator met with the company's general supervisor to go over the plans and blueprints for the job. In addition to preparing a cost estimate, the estimator was to prepare an estimate of the time it would take to complete the job. The television station management was very concerned about the time factor and it had requested that bids be prepared on the basis of the normal time and costs for completing the job and also for the fastest time for completing the

## TABLE 1

### Television Tower and Building Construction
### Time and Cost Estimate

| Activity Code | Activity | Normal Time Days[1] | Normal Time Cost[2] | Fastest Time Days[1] | Fastest Time Cost[2] |
|---|---|---|---|---|---|
| a | Sign contract and complete subcontractor negotiations | 5 | | 5 | |
| b | Survey site | 6 | $ 3,720 | 4 | $ 4,680 |
| c | Grade building site and excavate for basement | 8 | 3,900 | 6 | 5,490 |
| d | Grade tower site | 30 | 19,050 | 21 | 26,970 |
| e | Procure structural steel and guys for tower[3] | 85 | | 85 | |
| f | Procure electrical equipment for tower and connecting underground cable[3] | 120 | | 120 | |
| g | Pour concrete for tower footings and anchors | 42 | 24,930 | 25 | 35,010 |
| h | Erect tower and install electrical equipment | 38 | 34,050 | 25 | 46,860 |
| i | Install connecting cable in tower site | 8 | 5,220 | 4 | 5,850 |
| j | Install drain tile and storm drain in tower site | 35 | 10,800 | 18 | 15,300 |
| k | Backfill and grade tower site | 8 | 2,790 | 4 | 4,350 |
| l | Pour building footings | 29 | 9,090 | 21 | 12,300 |
| m | Pour basement slab and fuel tank slab | 14 | 3,150 | 11 | 4,620 |
| n | Pour outside basement walls | 34 | 7,650 | 30 | 8,430 |
| o | Pour walls for basement rooms | 9 | 2,400 | 7 | 2,880 |
| p | Pour concrete floor beams | 11 | 2,940 | 10 | 3,330 |
| q | Pour main floor slab and lay concrete block walls | 12 | 5,580 | 10 | 6,720 |
| r | Pour roof slab | 15 | 5,220 | 13 | 5,880 |
| s | Complete interior framing and utilities | 42 | 29,250 | 30 | 35,400 |
| t | Lay roofing | 3 | 810 | 2 | 1,020 |
| u | Paint building interior, install fixtures, and clean up | 19 | 2,760 | 13 | 4,050 |
| v | Install main cable between tower site and building | 35 | 13,080 | 25 | 13,620 |
| w | Install fuel tank | 3 | 540 | 2 | 660 |
| x | Install building septic tank | 12 | 1,890 | 8 | 2,250 |
| y | Install drain tile and storm drain in building site | 15 | 1,590 | 10 | 2,490 |
| z | Backfill around building, grade, and surface with crushed rock | 9 | 2,040 | 7 | 2,550 |
| aa | Lay base for connecting road between tower and building | 15 | 7,680 | 13 | 8,910 |
| bb | Complete grading and surface connecting road | 8 | 4,800 | 5 | 7,020 |

TABLE 1 (Continued)

| Activity Code | Activity | Normal Time | | Fastest Time | |
|---|---|---|---|---|---|
| | | Days[1] | Cost[2] | Days[1] | Cost[2] |
| cc | Clean up tower site | 5 | 720 | 3 | 1,500 |
| dd | Clean up building site | 3 | 630 | 2 | 1,200 |
| ee | Obtain job acceptance | 5 | | 5 | |
| | Total | | $206,280 | | $269,340 |

[1]Working days only
[2]For direct labor and rental of equipment only.
[3]Costs are included in Table 2.

job and the additional costs that this would entail. The result of the conference between the estimator and general supervisor was to determine that the activities shown in Table 1 would be necessary to complete the job. It was agreed that the estimator would prepare time and cost estimates for these activities.

In addition to determining the list of activities, the estimator and supervisor discussed in some detail how these activities could be sequenced as the list of activities in Table 1 did not necessarily indicate the order in which the work could be performed. In the course of the discussion, the estimator made the following notes.

Survey work and procurement of the structural steel and electrical equipment for the tower can start as soon as contract is signed.

Grading of tower and building sites can begin when survey is completed.

After tower site is graded, footings and anchors can be poured.

After building site is graded and basement excavated, building footings can be poured.

Septic tank can be installed when grading and excavating of building site is done.

Construction of connecting road can start as soon as survey is completed.

Exterior and interior basement walls can be poured as soon as footings are in.

Basement floor and fuel tank slab should go in after basement walls.

Floor beams can go in after the basement walls and basement floor.

Main floor slab and concrete block walls go in after floor beams.

Roof slab can go on after block walls are up.

Interior can be completed as soon as roof slab is on.

Put in fuel tank any time after slab is in.

Drain tile and storm drain for building go in after septic tank.

As soon as tower footings and anchors are in and tower steel and equipment are available, tower can be erected.

Connecting cable in tower site, drain tile, and storm drain can be put in as soon as tower is up.

Main cable between building and tower goes in after connecting cable at tower site is in and basement walls are up.

Tower site can be backfilled and graded as soon as storm drain, connecting cable, and main cable are in.

Clean up tower site after backfilling and grading is done.

Backfill around building and grade after main cable is in and after storm drain is in.

Clean up building site after backfilling and grading is done.

Following his meeting with the general supervisor, the estimator prepared cost estimates and time estimates for completing the various portions of the job. Estimates for both the normal time in which the work could be completed and the fastest possible time along with the corresponding costs were made as shown in Table 1. The cost figures in Table 1 are for the direct labor and equipment use costs only. Estimated costs of materials used in construction and purchased equipment to be installed in the tower are shown in Table 2. Company experience had shown that for this kind of job indirect labor and other overhead costs could be expected to amount to 65 percent of the direct labor and equipment use cost. The company also customarily added 15 percent to the total estimated cost for contingencies. Using this information, the estimator prepared analyses for the job: one for the cost of doing the work at normal rate and one for the cost of doing the job in the shortest possible period of time.

TABLE 2

Estimated Cost of Materials and Equipment

| Item | Cost |
|---|---|
| Structural steel and guys for tower | $ 70,800 |
| Tower electrical equipment and connecting cable | 21,780 |
| Sand, gravel, crushed rock, and cement | 15,330 |
| Lumber and millwork | 19,200 |
| Drain tile and sewer pipe | 10,800 |
| Septic tank, plumbing fixtures, fuel tank, and other hardware | 9,900 |
| Other miscellaneous materials | 9,960 |
| Total | $157,770 |

## DISCUSSION QUESTIONS

1. Working at a normal rate, in how many days can the job be completed? What should the bid be on this basis if Petersen attempted to obtain a profit of 10 percent before federal income taxes?
2. What is the shortest possible time in which the job can be completed? What should the bid be on this basis if Petersen attempted to obtain a profit of 10 percent before federal income taxes?
3. If the job is obtained and the work is to be completed working at a normal rate, what portions of the work should be supervised most carefully to ensure that the job is completed on time? What portions of the work should be supervised most carefully if the contract is let on the basis of completing the job in the shortest possible time?
4. If television station management felt that the estimated time for completing the job in the shortest possible period of time was still too long, what could be done?

# Quick-Lube

The Quick-Lube concept was developed by a group of investors to capitalize on the decline in full-service gasoline stations. The advent of mini-service stations had resulted in a dramatic shift in gasoline sales with the result that large numbers of stations offering lubrication services were going out of business or changing to self-service.

## THE LUBRICATION SERVICE

The promoters of Quick-Lube planned to provide a complete lubrication service: oil and filter change and greasing plus a check of other fluids — transmission, rear end, brake master cylinder, power steering, radiator, and battery. The objective was to provide fast, quality service at a fair price. Quality was to be achieved by hiring experts in lubrication and using top-quality lubricants and filters and by specialization in this particular type of service. Speed of service was to be achieved through a unique pit design that allowed one "pit" worker to work on two cars from below while one "top" person worked on those operations for the cars that could be done from above. The oil was metered into the car by a special power pump.

Each operation was systematized from the time the customer was directed to drive over the pit until the car was finished. The customer even served as a participant by filling out the work order and by starting the car after completion of service while the attendant made a last quality check. The originators of Quick-Lube intended to develop a chain of stations devoted exclusively to providing this service. The stations were to be of a standard design as much as possible and would incorporate two inside service lanes drawing cars from a single outdoor waiting line.

**219**

In a typical case, a customer would arrive at the end of the line of cars waiting for service. From inside the car, the customer could read the list of services and prices that were posted prominently near the entrance to the service lanes. Upon arriving at the head of the line, the customer would be directed to one or the other of the indoor service lanes. The customer would then fill out a work order and, if he or she wished, leave the car while it was being serviced. A lounge area with a view of the service lanes would permit the customer to relax while the service was performed. After completion, the customer would return to the car, pay the attendant, and drive out of the service area. It was intended that the entire service operation would take about ten minutes.

## SEQUENCE OF OPERATIONS

The developers of Quick-Lube had observed operations in existing service stations and had also done some experimentation with a test service lane built in an abandoned gasoline station. While these studies could not predict exactly how the system would work in practice, it was found that the service activities could be grouped into three major operations:

*Operation 1:* Guide car into service lane, take customer order, and open hood.
*Operation 2:* Place drain pan under car, remove drain plug, lubricate under-carriage, replace oil filter, check transmission (if standard) and differential, and replace drain plug.
*Operation 3:* Meter in replacement oil, check battery, radiator, brake master cylinder, and transmission (if automatic), shut hood, record ser-vicing, and receive customer payment.

It was expected that these operations might vary somewhat, depending on the make, model, and condition of the car.

Operations 1 and 3 would be done by the "top" worker; operation 2 would be done by the "pit" worker. Operations would be done in sequence with little or no overlap; that is, operation 2 would start after operation 1 was completed and operation 3 after operation 2 was done. Because the "pit" worker would be exposed to much dirt, grease, oil, and water (on rainy days), he or she would perform only operation 2. Conversely, the "top" worker would perform only operations 1 and 3. The "top" worker was also consid-ered to be the station manager. Stations were to be built so that the "pit" worker could cross from lane to lane while staying in the pit; the "top" worker could also work back and forth between lanes.

Approximate average times for the three operations were estimated to be two minutes for operation 1, five minutes for operation 2, and three min-utes for operation 3. However, experiments with the test lane suggested that

## TABLE 1

Probability Distributions of Completion Times for Service Operations

| Operation 1 | | Operation 2 | | Operation 3 | |
|---|---|---|---|---|---|
| Minutes | Cumulative Probability | Minutes | Cumulative Probability | Minutes | Cumulative Probability |
| 1.00 | .000 | 3.0 | .000 | 2.0 | .000 |
| 1.25 | .078 | 3.4 | .064 | 2.2 | .071 |
| 1.50 | .249 | 3.8 | .202 | 2.4 | .220 |
| 1.75 | .443 | 4.2 | .354 | 2.6 | .376 |
| 2.00 | .621 | 4.6 | .505 | 2.8 | .526 |
| 2.25 | .746 | 5.0 | .643 | 3.0 | .656 |
| 2.50 | .818 | 5.4 | .749 | 3.2 | .744 |
| 2.75 | .861 | 5.8 | .816 | 3.4 | .793 |
| 3.00 | .895 | 6.2 | .856 | 3.6 | .830 |
| 3.25 | .923 | 6.6 | .885 | 3.8 | .860 |
| 3.50 | .945 | 7.0 | .906 | 4.0 | .885 |
| 3.75 | .963 | 7.4 | .922 | 4.2 | .905 |
| 4.00 | .978 | 7.8 | .934 | 4.4 | .922 |
| 4.25 | .988 | 8.2 | .944 | 4.6 | .935 |
| 4.50 | .995 | 8.6 | .952 | 4.8 | .946 |
| 4.75 | .999 | 9.0 | .958 | 5.0 | .956 |
| 5.00 | 1.000 | 15.0 | 1.000 | 7.0 | 1.000 |

there would be considerable variation from car to car. It was not possible to develop operation times for all makes, models, and car conditions, but trials with over 200 cars serviced on the test lane suggested that the probability distributions of times for the operations might approximate those shown in Table 1.

## COSTS AND REVENUES

The promoters of Quick-Lube also prepared an analysis of the financial aspects of a Quick-Lube station for use in obtaining financial support and attracting persons interested in purchasing a Quick-Lube franchise. It was estimated that a typical station might involve an initial investment of approximately $50,000 as shown in Table 2. Once open, a Quick-Lube station was expected to operate 14 hours a day with two shifts and two employees per shift. Employees would work 8-hour shifts but would actually staff the station in 7-hour shifts, thereby permitting a half-hour in the morning for opening, a half-hour in the evening for closing and cleaning up, and a half-hour overlap between shifts to ensure a smooth transition between shifts without service delays. Estimated monthly fixed costs (assuming 25 days in a typical month) are given in Table 3. In the table, the supervisor-

## TABLE 2

### Initial Investment in Typical Quick-Lube Station

| | |
|---|---:|
| Working capital, $5,000.00 per month for 3 months | $15,000.00 |
| Building renovation, estimated | 15,000.00 |
| Initial promotion | 5,000.00 |
| Inventory | 1,720.00 |
| Tools and equipment | 2,680.00 |
| Professional fees, attorney and architect | 2,500.00 |
| Lease advance, $580.00 per month for 2 months | 1,160.00 |
| Utilities deposit and installation | 435.00 |
| Supplies and miscellaneous | 725.00 |
| Sign installation | 1,100.00 |
| Reserve for contingencies | 5,000.00 |
| Total | $50,320.00 |

managers are the "top" workers, and technicians are the "pit" workers. Variable costs for filters, grease, and so on were estimated to be $7.90 per car based on the sample of cars run through the test lane. The proposed schedule of charges for services and lubricants gave an average revenue of $12.90 per car — again based on the sample of over 200 cars run through the test lane.

The promoters of Quick-Lube calculated that, at 10 minutes per car for service, two attendants would be able to service 12 cars per hour, or a maximum of 168 cars per day. However, they felt that variations in the ar-

## TABLE 3

### Fixed Monthly Costs of Operation of Quick-Lube Station

| | | |
|---|---|---:|
| Wages (2 shifts, 2 employees on each shift) | | |
| 2 Supervisor-managers, | $6.00 per hour | $2,080.00 |
| 2 Technicians, | $4.00 per hour | 1,400.00 |
| Payroll taxes, 12% | | 418.00 |
| Lease (building) | | 580.00 |
| Lease (sign) | | 165.00 |
| Laundry and uniforms | | 164.00 |
| Repairs and maintenance | | 40.00 |
| Insurance | | 100.00 |
| Utilities | | 170.00 |
| Miscellaneous | | 100.00 |
| Promotion | | 500.00 |
| Interest expense[1] | | 625.00 |
| Total | | $6,342.00 |

[1]Based on $50,000 at 15%.

FIGURE 1

Quick-Lube Advertising Copy

# Lube & Oil plus Filter

*The sensible alternative to time consuming and costly service for your car.*

## Quality

- **Pennzoil products**
- **Fram oil filters**
- **Professional technicians**

## Comfort

- **Pleasant waiting area**
- **Coffee & magazines**

## Convenience

- **10 minute service**
- **No appointment needed**

*OPENING SOON AT THIS LOCATION*

rival rate of customers and delays caused by the longer operation times in Table 1 might reduce the actual service rate of a station to perhaps 90 cars per day. Based on this rate, a Quick-Lube station would generate gross revenues of $1,161 per day and monthly gross revenues of $29,025. Subtracting variable costs for 2,250 cars per month of $17,775 and the fixed monthly costs of $6,342, profit to the owner of a Quick-Lube station would be $4,908 per month or $58,896 per year. Even if costs were higher than expected and total customers lower than expected, the potential return on an initial investment of $50,320 in a Quick-Lube station appeared to be substantial. Proposed advertising copy for a Quick-Lube station is shown in Figure 1.

## DISCUSSION QUESTIONS

1. In what ways is Quick-Lube similar to a fast-food operation such as McDonald's hamburgers or Colonel Sanders' chicken?
2. In what ways does Quick-Lube differ from a fast-food operation?
3. Based on the data in the case, evaluate the feasibility of Quick-Lube station operations.
4. Identify critical problem areas that might significantly affect the operational and financial success of a Quick-Lube station.

# Regional Infant Care Centers

In the state of Washington, as in the United States as a whole, infant mortality rates had exhibited a long-term downward trend for many years. One component of the infant mortality rate was the neonatal mortality rate, defined as the death rate among infants from 0 to 28 days of age (excluding stillbirths). While the neonatal mortality rate in Washington declined to 11.1 deaths per 1,000 live births by 1974, it was thought that this rate could be reduced by the development of specialized facilities for care of newborn children with medical problems.

## REGIONAL CARE CONCEPT

Careful attention was given to this issue on the national level by a committee composed of representatives of interested professional medical societies. This committee prepared a statement urging development of regional systems of care for the newborn. As envisioned by the committee a regional system would provide three levels of care. Level I would be normal care offered by local hospitals to maternity patients and newborns; level I facilities would handle the majority of newborns with no medical problems or only minor difficulties. Level II centers would care for newborns with moderate medical problems that could not be handled by the level I hospitals; level II centers would be located in larger hospitals in the region and would receive most patients by referral from surrounding level I hospitals. Level III facilities would be capable of treating the most serious medical problems of the newborn, and only one or two such specialized facilities would exist in a region.

When the three-level concept was compared with existing facilities in the state of Washington, it was found that level I care was provided by some 80 hospitals throughout the state. Level III care was provided by facilities associated with the state university in Seattle and, to a certain extent, by facilities located in Spokane, in the eastern part of the state. Residents in the Vancouver area in the south could also obtain level III care at facilities in Portland, Oregon. Unlike level I and III facilities, which appeared to be reasonably well developed, level II facilities were almost entirely absent. Only one or two hospitals had undertaken efforts to develop capabilities that could be defined as level II care.

## ANALYSIS OF LEVEL II NEEDS

Because of the lack of level II facilities, several local, state, and federal agencies became interested in the possibility of developing a system of level II facilities in the state. However, it was recognized that the facilities should be planned in an organized fashion to provide good geographic coverage while at the same time avoiding creation of unnecessary capacity. In the past, hospitals had often developed services based on their own interests and desires with the result that there frequently was duplication and unnecessarily high cost. At the same time, needed services were sometimes not made available when the initiative was left entirely to the individual hospital. Because medical facilities are largely supported directly or indirectly by public funds, the development of additional facilities was a matter of public concern. Accordingly, a cooperative project, jointly funded by local, state, and federal agencies, was undertaken to improve the delivery of medical care to the newborn in the state of Washington. One element of this project was an assessment of the proper location and size of a system of level II centers for the state.

The level II facilities study team assembled a variety of information thought to be relevant to determination of the number, location, and size of the level II centers. Figure 1 shows location by county of 47,635 live births in Washington for 1973. Total live births, however, did not provide an estimate of the number of infants likely to require level II care. A search of the literature uncovered two different methods that had been used elsewhere to estimate demand for level II care. One previous study suggested that about 50 infants per 1,000 live births required level II care; another study estimated that the number would be about five times the neonatal mortality rate. In addition, physicians at the medical school in Seattle estimated that the number of low-birth-weight infants, defined as those weighing 2,500 grams or less at birth, might be a good guess as to the number of infants requiring level II care. This estimate was based on the fact that many low-birth-weight babies experienced medical complications and required special

FIGURE 1

Live Births by County of Residence
State of Washington

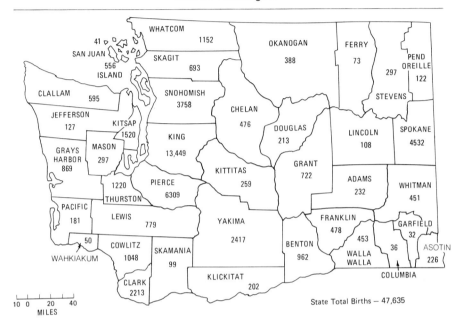

State Total Births — 47,635

care. It was recognized, of course, that some low-birth-weight infants would not experience difficulties, but the physicians felt that these healthy low-birth-weight babies would be about balanced by babies with higher birth weights that did experience complications. Table 1 shows total live births, low-birth-weight infants, and neonatal mortality by county for 1973.

Another piece of data thought to be essential in estimating the required size of the level II centers was the probable length of stay of infants in the facility. Field visits to hospitals around the state established that one hospital in Yakima was operating much as a level II center was expected to operate. A study of infants in this facility determined that the probability distribution of length of stay was approximately that shown in Table 2. The average length of stay was about 6 days, with the minimum 1 day and the maximum 35 days. The large number of infants with short lengths of stay, as shown in Table 2, was explained by a number of factors: Some recovered quickly and were released, some died, and about a third of all level II infants were likely to be transferred to a level III facility after a day or two in a level II center.

Because level II centers were to be scattered around the state, it was expected that transfer of infants from level I hospitals to the nearest level II

**227**

TABLE 1

Infant Statistical Data by County of Residence, 1973

| County | Live Births | Low Birth Weight[1] | Neonatal Mortality[2] |
|--------|------------|---------------------|------------------------|
| Adams | 232 | 14 | 5 |
| Asotin | 226 | 19 | 4 |
| Benton | 962 | 55 | 10 |
| Chelan | 476 | 24 | 10 |
| Clallam | 595 | 25 | 3 |
| Clark | 2,213 | 153 | 23 |
| Columbia | 36 | 5 | 1 |
| Cowlitz | 1,048 | 64 | 10 |
| Douglas | 213 | 14 | 5 |
| Ferry | 73 | 8 | 2 |
| Franklin | 478 | 37 | 9 |
| Garfield | 32 | 4 | 0 |
| Grant | 722 | 43 | 12 |
| Grays Harbor | 869 | 49 | 11 |
| Island | 556 | 43 | 10 |
| Jefferson | 127 | 6 | 1 |
| King | 13,449 | 816 | 143 |
| Kitsap | 1,520 | 71 | 20 |
| Kittitas | 259 | 13 | 2 |
| Klickitat | 202 | 14 | 2 |
| Lewis | 779 | 39 | 9 |
| Lincoln | 108 | 10 | 3 |
| Mason | 297 | 23 | 5 |
| Okanogan | 388 | 22 | 6 |
| Pacific | 181 | 17 | 1 |
| Pend Oreille | 122 | 8 | 2 |
| Pierce | 6,309 | 419 | 80 |
| San Juan | 41 | 0 | 0 |
| Skagit | 693 | 36 | 6 |
| Skamania | 99 | 4 | 1 |
| Snohomish | 3,758 | 192 | 44 |
| Spokane | 4,532 | 286 | 55 |
| Stevens | 297 | 17 | 2 |
| Thurston | 1,220 | 72 | 8 |
| Wahkiakum | 50 | 2 | 0 |
| Walla Walla | 453 | 26 | 3 |
| Whatcom | 1,152 | 52 | 11 |
| Whitman | 451 | 31 | 6 |
| Yakima | 2,417 | 141 | 16 |
| | 47,635 | 2,874 | 541 |

[1]Number of infants with birth weight of 2,500 grams or less.
[2]Number of infants dying 0 to 28 days after live birth.

center would usually be accomplished by surface transport. Most often transportation would be by an ambulance equipped to sustain the infant enroute and with space for a medical attendant. Infants requiring transfer

# TABLE 2

## Estimated Length of Stay in Level II Facility

| Days | Cumulative Probability |
|------|------------------------|
| 1 | .39 |
| 2 | .50 |
| 3 | .57 |
| 4 | .62 |
| 5 | .66 |
| 6 | .70 |
| 7 | .74 |
| 8 | .77 |
| 9 | .80 |
| 10 | .82 |
| 11 | .84 |
| 12 | .86 |
| 13 | .88 |
| 14 | .89 |
| 15 | .90 |
| 16 | .91 |
| 17 | .92 |
| 18 | .93 |
| 19 | .94 |
| 20 | .95 |
| 25 | .98 |
| 30 | .99 |
| 35 | 1.00 |

from the level II centers to level III facilities in Seattle, Spokane, or Portland would be moved by ambulance or, if necessary, by helicopter or aircraft.

## LEVEL II COSTS

Efforts by the study team to estimate costs of operation of level II facilities based upon analysis of historical cost data were not successful. Hospital accounting systems were found to be so varied that representative historical cost data could not be obtained with a reasonable expenditure of time and effort. Accordingly, cost estimates were based on a synthesis of significant cost elements. Included in the estimates were equipment, staff salaries, and indirect costs which would be incurred by hospitals, and education and training costs which might be borne by both hospitals and the state. Costs of drugs, supplies, laboratory procedures, physicians' services, and other fees related to the specific treatment of individual patients were not estimated.

A list of equipment required for a typical five bed intensive care unit is given in Table 3. Total equipment costs were found to be approximately $5,000 per bed for a five bed unit. Considering the likelihood of technical

## TABLE 3

### Estimated Equipment Needs and Costs for 5 Bed Intensive Care Unit

| Item | Unit Cost | 5 Bed Unit Needs | 5 Bed Total Cost |
|---|---|---|---|
| Isolette | $1,350 | 5 | $ 6,750 |
| Heated treatment table/ (radiant warmer) | 1,600 | 1 | 1,600 |
| Oxygen analyzer | 300 | 2 | 600 |
| Oxygen nebulizer, heater | 80 | 5 | 400 |
| Oxyhood | 60 | 2 | 120 |
| Oxygen blender | 500 | 1 | 500 |
| Resuscitation bags (Hope) | 60 | 5 | 300 |
| Heart rate monitor | 2,900 | 2 | 5,800 |
| Blood pressure monitor (Doppler) | 600 | 1 | 600 |
| Infusion pump | 350 | 2 | 700 |
| Suction apparatus | 250 | 2 | 500 |
| Phototherapy unit | 480 | 1 | 480 |
| Transport incubator | 1,200 | 1 | 1,200 |
| Trays: | | | |
| arterial catheterization | 85 | 2 | 170 |
| resuscitation/intubation | 150 | 2 | 300 |
| thoracentesis | 75 | 1 | 75 |
| lumbar puncture | 20 | 2 | 40 |
| emergency drugs | 25 | 1 | 25 |
| | | | $20,160 |
| Additional miscellaneous equipment | | | 4,840 |
| Total Cost | | | $25,000 |

advances and modifications in methods of patient care, it appeared that an amortization period of 5 years would be appropriate, resulting in an annual equipment cost of $1,000 per bed. After adding 20% for repair and maintenance, estimated annual equipment costs were $1,200 per bed.

Nursing costs per patient were difficult to estimate because of the influence of the number of babies in the unit at any one time and the possibility of utilizing nurses jointly between the neonatal unit and the newborn nursery for healthy infants. Experience suggested that one nurse would be required per four babies in the neonatal unit. With three shifts per day, weekly requirements were 21 shifts or 4.2 nurses per four babies. Taking into account vacations, holidays, and sick days, approximately 5 nurses were needed to provide care for 4 babies — approximately 1.25 nurses per baby. At a monthly cost of $1,200 per nurse, the monthly cost per baby was $1,500, or $50 per day in direct nursing cost. To this cost would be added the cost of any LPNs utilized in the unit, ward clerks, and inefficiencies arising from fluctuations in the daily census. Accordingly, total staff costs might well be $70 per day per baby, or $25,500 per year per baby.

Indirect hospital costs were perhaps the most difficult to estimate since many of these costs would not be appreciably affected by the decision to offer level II care. Included in these costs are administration and supervision, space charges, and costs of supplying support services such as inhalation therapy, 24-hour lab, and so on. As an approximation, it was estimated that these costs would be 50% of staff costs. Overhead costs on this assumption amounted to $35 per day per baby or $13,000 per year. An additional consideration in operating the system of level II facilities was the cost of continuing education and training necessary to improve and maintain nursing skills. It was estimated that 2 weeks of training would be required annually per nurse.

When the concept of level II centers was discussed in various meetings and preliminary working papers, quite different numbers of facilities were proposed. Guesses as to the proper number ranged from 5 to 15 or more level II centers for the state. An obvious problem with developing as many as 15 centers was the possibility that some of these centers would service rather small population concentrations. This led to the question of how small a patient load a level II center could have and still function effectively. With too few patients, a center would incur high capital costs on a per patient basis, and it would be difficult and costly to maintain skill levels of medical personnel. Some of the doctors queried on this point thought that an average census of one or two infants would be a lower limit on size; others thought that a level II center should have an average census of at least three or four infants.

## DISCUSSION QUESTIONS

1. Perform a preliminary analysis of the required number and location of level II centers for the state and the average number of occupants in each.
2. Analyze the dynamic characteristics of occupancy levels for the level II centers selected in Question 1. How large would each center have to be to provide 90 percent, 95 percent, 99 percent, and 100 percent protection against running out of space?
3. What additional information would you need and how would you go about performing a more accurate and detailed analysis?

# Southern Hydraulic Supplies Company

The Southern Hydraulic Supplies Company was a distributor of hydraulic supplies in the Gulf states area. Southern handled standard hydraulic fittings, tubing, and similar items. Generally Southern carried an entire line for each manufacturer whose products it handled and provided local stock for rapid delivery to customers. The items that Southern stocked were mainly used in the maintenance, modification, and manufacture of trucks, off-highway construction equipment, and machine tools.

Southern had grown from a small two-person operation to a $75-million-per-year business in a span of 25 years. The growth of its dollar volume was based on an excellent reputation for good service coupled with the general expansion of industry in the Gulf states. From its inception Southern had been a profitable business in sound financial condition.

Despite the continued growth of profits in absolute terms, however, Southern found that profits as a percentage of sales had declined from 11.3 percent of sales to 6.4 percent of sales. When management became aware of the seriousness of the problem, it was decided to undertake a thorough review of policies and procedures in the areas that could have significant influence on costs and profits — namely, product line, sales methods, stock handling and storage methods, billing and record keeping, and inventory replenishment. The last area was included as a major area for study because the company had been experiencing increasing difficulty with out-of-stock situations and unbalanced inventories.

## INVENTORY REPLENISHMENT PROCEDURES

Up until the time that the review of the inventory replenishment policies and procedures was begun, there had been no formal study of this phase of the company's operations. Since maintaining inventories was one of the company's major functions, Southern had always used experienced personnel to control the placing of orders and had relied on their judgment to make correct decisions. One thing that became immediately apparent as this phase of Southern's operations came under scrutiny was that the inventory replenishment problem had become vastly more complicated in recent years as the variety of items carried had tripled from what it had been five years previously to more than 15,000 separate stock items. Because no formal study had been made previously of the inventory replenishment operations, it was decided as a first step to get some general information about order placement costs and inventory carrying costs and also to analyze in detail several typical items of inventory.

Several years earlier Southern had installed a small computer for maintaining inventory records, writing purchase orders, and other record keeping functions. To use this equipment, efficiently, the master inventory records were updated only once weekly. Purchase orders were also prepared on a schedule of once each week. Purchase requisitions were turned in by the supervisors responsible for various types of stock, and these were accumulated until Friday when they were used to initiate purchase orders. In effect this meant that review of the inventory levels occurred once every five days as the supervisors turned in most of their purchase requisitions only once each week immediately before the scheduled machine run. In total, the cost of preparing and processing a requisition, preparing a purchase order, and making necessary record changes was estimated to be $12.50 per order.

Analysis of company records indicated that the following were reasonable estimates of the variable cost per year of carrying inventories (as a percentage of dollar value of average inventory):

| Cost Category | % of Total |
|---|---|
| Capital cost | 18 |
| Obsolescence | 5 |
| Insurance | 3 |
| Taxes | 2 |
| Storage and handling | 11 |
| Total | 39 |

One of the typical items of inventory analyzed in detail was a small hydraulic fitting. The fitting was purchased for $14.00 and sold for $19.50. The manufacturer from whom Southern procured the fitting did not offer any quantity discount on the fitting, but it would not fill orders for less than 50 fittings without adding a flat charge of $25.00 to the order. For this particular item, there were other distributors in Southern's immediate vicinity that could supply a comparable fitting made by another manufacturer. Because of this, orders that Southern could not fill immediately were lost.

The fitting was ordered from the manufacturer located about 1,500

## TABLE 1

### Analysis of Procurement Lead Times[1]
(working days between order issue and delivery of fittings)

| | |
|---|---|
| 8 | 11 |
| 12 | 14 |
| 6 | 9 |
| 5 | 8 |
| 7 | 9 |
| 8 | 7 |
| 8 | 6 |
| 9 | 8 |
| 13 | 13 |
| 9 | 10 |
| 10 | 7 |
| 8 | 7 |
| 11 | 12 |
| 7 | 10 |
| 8 | 9 |
| 5 | 10 |
| 7 | 7 |
| 6 | 8 |
| 9 | 14 |
| 7 | 6 |

[1]Average lead time = 8.7 days.

miles away and shipped to Southern by truck. An analysis of the time taken to receive the fittings from the day the purchase order was prepared until the fittings were received indicated that this varied between 5 and 14 working days. The historical record of the time between the preparation of the purchase order and receipt of the fittings is shown in Table 1. It was estimated that inspection of the shipments, preparation of receiving reports, and related activities cost Southern $12.25 per order.

Customer orders filled each day for one year (260 working days) were tabulated for this fitting and are shown in Table 2. No record was kept of customer orders that were cancelled because the fitting was out of stock. Further analysis of the records pertaining to this fitting revealed the fact that replenishment orders for the fitting were always for lots of 750 and that the amount of stock on hand averaged about 115 units on the days that purchase orders were issued for replenishment stock.

## DISCUSSION QUESTIONS

1. Analyze the cost of the system currently used for maintaining the inventory of this fitting.
2. What is the minimum cost of maintaining the inventory of the fitting if the once-a-week ordering system is used?

## TABLE 2

### Analysis of Orders for One Year[1]
(orders filled per day)

| | | | | | |
|---|---|---|---|---|---|
| 35 | 9 | 17 | 16 | 20 | 0 |
| 0 | 8 | 4 | 0 | 0 | 19 |
| 0 | 0 | 28 | 11 | 13 | 29 |
| 17 | 17 | 25 | 16 | 7 | 18 |
| 36 | 0 | 27 | 0 | 0 | 11 |
| 6 | 28 | 20 | 13 | 14 | 29 |
| 0 | 0 | 0 | 24 | 0 | 14 |
| 5 | 29 | 7 | 11 | 10 | 0 |
| 11 | 9 | 0 | 0 | 41 | 19 |
| 18 | 0 | 8 | 27 | 8 | 31 |
| 0 | 0 | 0 | 26 | 0 | 10 |
| 4 | 0 | 18 | 0 | 9 | 16 |
| 16 | 23 | 28 | 6 | 22 | 0 |
| 25 | 0 | 20 | 0 | 0 | 27 |
| 0 | 17 | 22 | 26 | 0 | 18 |
| 19 | 8 | 0 | 13 | 44 | 14 |
| 14 | 13 | 0 | 0 | 24 | 0 |
| 32 | 31 | 16 | 21 | 0 | 0 |
| 15 | 8 | 31 | 17 | 7 | 38 |
| 0 | 0 | 24 | 22 | 40 | 3 |
| 17 | 25 | 16 | 0 | 9 | 17 |
| 18 | 11 | 0 | 10 | 0 | 0 |
| 10 | 0 | 0 | 42 | 0 | 21 |
| 30 | 43 | 14 | 0 | 0 | 15 |
| 15 | 9 | 36 | 18 | 21 | 0 |
| 0 | 0 | 11 | 0 | 16 | 9 |
| 12 | 12 | 0 | 12 | 0 | 14 |
| 21 | 22 | 3 | 27 | 23 | 0 |
| 23 | 15 | 30 | 4 | 19 | 6 |
| 15 | 0 | 12 | 19 | 25 | 23 |
| 12 | 7 | 0 | 17 | 0 | 12 |
| 0 | 15 | 10 | 0 | 2 | 22 |
| 19 | 10 | 0 | 34 | 15 | 0 |
| 37 | 33 | 20 | 17 | 12 | 34 |
| 0 | 26 | 14 | 21 | 0 | 5 |
| 13 | 0 | 21 | 0 | 32 | |
| 0 | 6 | 0 | 18 | 8 | |
| 18 | 20 | 17 | 13 | 0 | |
| 20 | 13 | 37 | 24 | 5 | |
| 14 | 7 | 19 | 33 | 15 | |
| 19 | 0 | 0 | 26 | 20 | |
| 18 | 0 | 0 | 0 | 30 | |
| 0 | 39 | 35 | 18 | 23 | |
| 10 | 19 | 16 | 0 | 0 | |
| 15 | 16 | 13 | 16 | 11 | |

[1]Average orders filled per day = 13.1.

3. What would be the advantage, if any, of revising the computer procedures so that replenishment orders could be placed every day?
4. Based on the analyses in the preceding questions, what possibilities appear to be present for improving the management of inventories?

# Superior Steamship Company

Great Lakes dry bulk shipping operations are dominated by the transportation of iron ore pellets, which normally make up 50 to 60 percent of total bulk cargos. Together, iron ore, limestone, and coal comprise more than 90 percent of total tonnage. Because of the importance of the iron ore trade, shipping industry prospects are tied closely to pellet demand by domestic steel companies and supply from domestic iron ore mines.

## IRON ORE TRANSPORT ON GREAT LAKES

Two types of fleets are involved in moving iron ore: captive fleets and independent fleets. The so-called captive fleets are those owned by steel producers, such as U.S. Steel, Bethlehem, and Inland, which are utilized almost exclusively for floating their own iron ore requirements. The other steel producers rely primarily on independent fleets to meet their needs.

Most iron ore tonnage transported by the independent fleets is carried under long-term contractual relationships. Under these long-term contracts, the shipping company agrees to transport cargos up to the maximum tonnage, whereas the shipper agrees to use the services to the limit of their cargo "requirements." Thus, the shipping company, while prepared to handle full tonnage, is not guaranteed that full tonnage will be available. Much of this business is based on published freight rates. However, other negotiated arrangements also exist between fleet operators and steel producers. Table 1 shows the various published iron ore vessel rates in effect in 1980. All-rail rates from the iron ranges to Cleveland are also presented to illustrate the cost advantage of water transportation.

## TABLE 1

### Rail and Lake Freight Rates on Iron Ore Pellets Per Gross Ton

*Lake Freight Rates from upper lake ports
to lower lake ports*

| | |
|---|---|
| Head of lakes to lower lake ports | $6.15 |
| Marquette to lower lakes | 5.07 |
| Escanaba to Detroit and Lake Erie | 4.67 |
| Escanaba to Lake Michigan ports | 3.69 |

Note: These rates are free on and off with the loading and unloading charges being billed separately by the dock operators. An additional 40 cents per gross ton, payable to the vessel company, is charged on all iron ore cargos requiring an unloading time of over 24 hours. A charge of 40 cents per gross ton is made on delivery to docks not capable of handling vessels of more than 23-foot draft.

*All-Rail Freight Rates to consuming districts*

| | |
|---|---|
| Marquette to Sault Ste. Marie | $11.46 |
| Marquette range to Detroit | 18.63 |
| Marquette range to Hamilton and Welland | 23.61 |
| Marquette range to | |
|   Canton, Cleveland, Lorain, Massillon, Warren, Youngstown, and Sharon | 23.68 |
|   Pittsburgh district | 25.58 |
|   Weirton and Wheeling | 24.65 |
|   Johnstown | 26.29 |
| Mesabi range to | |
|   Canton, Massillon, and Youngstown | 29.78 |
|   Valleys district, Cleveland, Lorain, Pittsburgh and Wheeling districts | 31.07 |
|   Johnstown | 31.72 |

*Dock, handling, and storage charges on iron
ore at lower lake ports (per gross ton)*
*Ex self-unloading vessels*

| | |
|---|---|
| At Ashtabula and Cleveland, Ohio | |
|   Dockage | .18 |
|   From dock receiving area into cars or storage and into cars | 1.20 |
| At Conneaut, Ohio | |
|   Dockage of self-unloading vessels | .18 |
|   From receiving bin (via storage) into car (other than Conneaut apply rates for ex bulk vessels) | 1.17 |

## TABLE 1 (Continued)

### Rail and Lake Freight Rates on Iron Ore Pellets Per Gross Ton

*Ex bulk Vessels*

| | |
|---|---|
| At all ports | |
| From hold to rail of vessel | .72 |
| All ports (except Conneaut) | |
| From rail of vessel into car | .80 |
| From rail of vessel to storage yard | 1.71 |
| From storage into car | 1.09 |
| At Conneaut, Ohio | |
| From rail of vessel (via storage) into car | 1.17 |
| Crude iron ore only | |
| From hold to rail of vessel | .72 |
| From rail of vessel into car | .80 |

Source: *Skillings' Mining Review,* March 29, 1980, p. 25.

# FIGURE 1

## Major Bulk Cargo Ports

The domestic iron ore trade is protected from foreign competition under the Jones Act. The Jones Act restricts all commercial shipping between U.S. ports to U.S.-owned vessels that were built in the United States and are operated by U.S. crews. The Merchant Marine Act provides various subsidy programs for U.S. vessel operators to allow them to compete effectively in foreign commerce. Vessels competing in Jones Act commerce are not eligible for either construction or operating subsidies. However, a financing guarantee program under Title XI of the Merchant Marine Act is available to assist U.S. vessel owners in obtaining low-cost financing of domestically built ships, including those for the Great Lakes trades.

Domestic iron ore shipping is a one-way move. Vessels transport pellets down from the mines in northern Michigan and northern Minnesota to steel mills located around the lower lakes. Upbound, the vessels travel light — empty except for ballast. The shipping season on the Great Lakes is limited to about nine months due to winter ice. The normal season is from mid-April to mid-December, with some of the larger, ice-strengthened vessels able to operate into January.

Figure 1 identifies the more important bulk cargo ports on the Great Lakes. Iron ore pellets from the Mesabi Range in northeastern Minnesota are loaded at various ports along the northwestern shore of Lake Superior. Vessels cross Lake Superior and pass through the Soo Locks, near Sault Ste. Marie, Michigan. After reaching northern Lake Huron, the vessels take alternative routes depending upon their destinations. The Straits of Mackinac take some vessels into Lake Michigan and down to the steel-making centers near Chicago. Other vessels pass through Lake Huron to the St. Clair River and Detroit or continue on across Lake Erie to ports from Toledo to Buffalo. Considerable Lake Erie tonnage is transshipped by rail to steel centers in Ohio, Pennsylvania, and West Virginia.

Marquette Range iron ore is loaded either at Escanaba on northern Lake Michigan or at Marquette on the southern shore of Lake Superior. From Escanaba or Marquette, ore is transported to steel centers near Chicago, Detroit, or on Lake Erie. While Marquette shipments also move through the Soo Locks, most Escanaba shipments move directly down Lake Michigan to the Chicago area.

## CHANGES IN VESSEL DESIGN

Until recently, iron ore was moved on the Great Lakes in conventional bulk vessels that require that vessels be unloaded with shore-side machinery at each unloading dock. Although self-unloading vessels have operated on the Great Lakes since the early 1900s for the limestone, sand, and gravel trades, they were not generally employed in the iron ore trade until the late 1960s. In design characteristics, many self-unloading vessels resemble the conventional bulk freighters in hull configuration, power plant, and accommodations but differ in the cargo hold. Self-unloaders have sloped hoppers in the cargo holds leading to gates that, when opened, allow the pellets to drop onto a conveyor belt. The belt system carries the pellets out of the vessel to the end of a boom for discharge. The typical 250-foot boom provides flexibility in discharging pellets because of its ability to swing to different positions.

Additional investment in self-unloading equipment is justified primarily on the basis of faster unloading times. The larger the vessel, the more economical it becomes to unload cargo in this manner. Typically, a modern 1,000-foot self-unloader with 60,000 tons of capacity unloads at a rate of 10,000 tons per hour. This means that, after allowing for docking time, a 60,000-ton vessel can be unloaded in half the time it takes the conventional 30,000-ton bulker to unload. More rapid unloading permits additional cargo trips during the sailing season. In addition to the faster turnaround for the ship's owner, steel companies avoid the cost of shore-based unloading operations.

The average size of bulk vessels operated on the Great Lakes has been much smaller than vessels operated in similar trades on the oceans. There are several reasons for this: Depths in many Great Lakes ports and waterways are restricted and cargos must be limited to less than design capacity of many ships during portions of the shipping season. The Soo Locks near Sault Ste. Marie, Michigan are another constraint. The 110-foot width of the largest lock, finished in the late 1960s, is the reason for the 105-foot beam on the largest of the new generation 1,000-foot vessels. Still another reason for the relatively small average size of ships in the Great Lakes fleets is the fact that they operate in relatively cold fresh water. The ships do not encounter the severe corrosion damage to hulls and equipment and marine growth problems that occur in salt water. Consequently, maintenance costs have been low and useful lives very long. A number of ships built before World War I are still operating, and many of the ships in the U.S. flag Great Lakes fleets are more than 30 years old.

## ADDITIONAL CAPACITY REQUIREMENTS

Superior Steamship Company was one of five major independent fleet operators that carried iron ore pellets on the Great Lakes. Superior's iron ore trade had two basic patterns — Minnesota iron ore (head of the lakes) was transported to Lake Erie and Michigan iron ore (loaded at Escanaba) to the Chicago area. The Escanaba/Chicago trip was considerably shorter than the head of the lakes/Lake Erie run. Depending on the time it took to load and unload the vessel, the total trip time from Lake Superior to Lake Erie or Chicago and return was just under one week. The Escanaba to Chicago round trip could be accomplished in less than four days.

In the summer of 1980, George Kanestrom, executive vice president of Superior Steamship Company, was pondering the adequacy of capacity of the fleet to meet projected demand. He was concerned about both the fleet's ability to meet existing commitments to deliver iron ore and to accommodate new business. Superior's fleet capacity problem was accentuated by an opportunity to obtain, in 1982, a contract with a major new steel industry customer.

To accommodate its expanding business, Superior had, in 1979, authorized construction of a 1,000-foot, 60,000-ton-capacity, self-unloading vessel. This vessel was scheduled for completion at the beginning of the 1982 sailing season. It also was converting two smaller conventional bulk vessels to self-unloaders both to increase their effective seasonal capacity and to meet customer requirements for self-unloading capability. These actions would not bring fleet capacity to the level that customers might require after 1981 under existing contracts and also accommodate a major new customer. An analysis of Superior's fleet as projected for the 1982 sailing season, and

TABLE 2

Characteristics of Superior's Fleet

| Year Built | Dimensions (feet) | Average Trip Capacity[1] (gross tons) | Normal Service Season[2] (days) |
|---|---|---|---|
| Self-unloaders | | | |
| 1982 (under construction) | 1,004 × 105 | 58,000 | 280 |
| 1978 | 1,004 × 105 | 58,000 | 280 |
| 1959 (being converted) | 800 × 75 | 30,000 | 280 |
| 1958 (being converted) | 800 × 75 | 30,000 | 280 |
| 1959 | 690 × 75 | 23,000 | 280 |
| 1953 | 698 × 70 | 22,000 | 280 |
| Bulkers | | | |
| 1953 | 743 × 70 | 24,000 | 250 |
| 1952 | 647 × 70 | 21,000 | 250 |
| 1943 | 621 × 60 | 15,000 | 250 |
| 1927 | 631 × 65 | 15,000 | 250 |

[1]Actual average operating capacity is less than rated capacity due to seasonal waterway depth restrictions.

[2]Only vessels with hulls strengthened for ice conditions operate longer than the normal 250-day shipping season.

contractual commitments for the following few years indicated that, if existing customers required the full tonnages under contract and the new customer were added, capacity of the fleet would be inadequate. The deficiency appeared to be in the order of 1.5 million tons (head of the lakes/Lake Erie equivalent). Data on Superior's fleet are presented in Table 2.

If Superior were to be prepared to handle the 1982 existing contract and the new customer tonnage, it appeared that the alternatives would be either to acquire an additional 60,000-ton-capacity self-unloader vessel or to acquire a new 32,000-ton-capacity self-unloader. The annual capacity of the larger vessel (2.7 million tons) would be considerably in excess of forecast requirements, while the smaller vessel would bring capacity approximately in balance with contracted tonnage.

Capital costs and operating costs per ton of capacity were estimated to be greater for the smaller vessel. Cost data for vessels of each capacity are presented in Table 3. Income and cash flow projections for a 32,000-ton vessel operated at capacity and for a 60,000-ton vessel operated both at full capacity (assuming additional cargos are obtained) and at partial capacity are presented in Tables 4, 5, and 6.

TABLE 3

Capital and Operating Cost Data, 1980

| | 60,000-Ton Self-unloading Vessel | 32,000-Ton Self-unloading Vessel |
|---|---|---|
| Crew size, men | 31 | 31 |
| Average cost per man per day | 220 | 220 |
| Fuel cost per gallon | .75 | .75 |
| Fuel consumption, gallons per day | 11,500 | 7,000 |
| Food and supplies per day | 600 | 600 |
| Repair and maintenance per year | 600,000 | 450,000 |
| Insurance per year | 300,000 | 200,000 |
| Capital cost[1] | | |
| 1980 | 6,000,000 | 4,000,000 |
| 1981 | 33,000,000 | 21,000,000 |
| 1982 | 21,000,000 | 11,000,000 |
| | 60,000,000 | 36,000,000 |
| Depreciation | | |
| Book | 25 years, straight line | |
| Tax | 14½ years, double declining balance, straight line after 8 years, no residual values | |
| Investment tax credit | 10% on vessel construction in progress | |
| Federal income tax rate | 46% | |
| Financing[2] | Title XI debt, 87½% Equity, 12½% Term (level payment), 25 years Interest rate, 10% | |

[1]Including interest capitalized during the construction period.
[2]See tables 4, 5, and 6 showing debt service for each vessel.

Mr. Kanestrom realized that he would need to decide which alternative to recommend to James Hamilton, Superior's president, prior to the next executive committee meeting. He knew that Mr. Hamilton would be concerned about how either of the alternatives would fit into the overall financial objectives of the corporation. Financing for either size vessel would not be a problem because the Title XI program under the Merchant Marine Act provides for government guarantees on the debt associated with eligible vessels. Superior had used this method for financing previous vessels and had a commitment with respect to the vessel now under construction and the two self-loading conversions.

Uncertain about which alternative to recommend, Kanestrom decided to invite John Ward and Mike Myers, from sales and finance, respectively, to discuss the situation.

## TABLE 4
### 32,000-Gross-Ton-Capacity Self-unloading Vessel, Full Utilization

|  | 1980 | 1981 | 1982 | 1983 | 1984 | 1985 | 1986 | 1987 |
|---|---|---|---|---|---|---|---|---|
| Tons carried (000) | 0 | 0 | 1,472 | 1,472 | 1,472 | 1,472 | 1,472 | 1,472 |
| Projected income, (000) | 0 | 0 | $12,954 | $12,954 | $12,954 | $12,954 | $12,954 | $12,954 |
| Operating costs, 280 days |  |  |  |  |  |  |  |  |
| Wages |  |  | 1,910 | 1,910 | 1,910 | 1,910 | 1,910 | 1,910 |
| Fuel |  |  | 1,764 | 1,764 | 1,764 | 1,764 | 1,764 | 1,764 |
| Food and supplies |  |  | 168 | 168 | 168 | 168 | 168 | 168 |
| Repairs and Maintenance |  |  | 450 | 450 | 450 | 450 | 450 | 450 |
| Insurance |  |  | 180 | 180 | 180 | 180 | 180 | 180 |
| Season cost |  |  | $4,472 | $4,472 | $4,472 | $4,472 | $4,472 | $4,472 |
| Depreciation |  |  | 1,440 | 1,440 | 1,440 | 1,440 | 1,440 | 1,440 |
| Pretax income |  |  | $7,042 | $7,042 | $7,042 | $7,042 | $7,042 | $7,042 |
| Taxes |  |  |  |  |  |  |  |  |
| Current | (400) | (2,100) | 517 | 1,932 | 2,204 | 2,438 | 2,640 | 2,814 |
| Deferred | 0 | 0 | 1,622 | 1,307 | 1,035 | 801 | 599 | 425 |
| Net income | $ 400 | 2,100 | $4,903 | $3,803 | $3,803 | $3,803 | $3,803 | $3,803 |
| Projected cash flow |  |  |  |  |  |  |  |  |
| Net income | 400 | 2,100 | 4,903 | 3,803 | 3,803 | 3,803 | 3,803 | 3,803 |
| Depreciation |  |  | 1,440 | 1,440 | 1,440 | 1,440 | 1,440 | 1,440 |
| Deferred taxes |  |  | 1,622 | 1,307 | 1,035 | 801 | 599 | 425 |
| Capital cost | (4,000) | (21,000) | (11,000) |  |  |  |  |  |
| Net cash flow | $(3,600) | $(18,900) | $(3,035) | $6,550 | $6,278 | $6,044 | $5,842 | $5,668 |

|  | 1988 | 1989 | 1990–1995 | 1996 | 1997–2006 | 25-Year Total |
|---|---|---|---|---|---|---|
| Tons carried (000) | 1,472 | 1,472 | 1,472 | 1,472 | 1,472 | 36,800 |
| Projected income, (000) | $12,954 | $12,954 | $12,954 | $12,954 | $12,954 | $323,840 |
| Operating costs, 280 days |  |  |  |  |  |  |
| Wages | 1,910 | 1,910 | 1,910 | 1,910 | 1,910 | 47,750 |
| Fuel | 1,764 | 1,764 | 1,764 | 1,764 | 1,764 | 44,100 |
| Food and supplies | 168 | 168 | 168 | 168 | 168 | 4,200 |
| Repairs and Maintenance | 450 | 450 | 450 | 450 | 450 | 11,250 |
| Insurance | 180 | 180 | 180 | 180 | 180 | 4,500 |
| Season cost | $4,472 | $4,472 | $4,472 | $4,472 | $4,472 | $111,800 |
| Depreciation | 1,440 | 1,440 | 1,440 | 1,440 | 1,440 | 36,000 |
| Pretax income | $7,042 | $7,042 | $7,042 | $7,042 | $7,042 | $176,050 |
| Taxes |  |  |  |  |  |  |
| Current | 2,964 | 3,093 | 3,124 | 3,514 | 2,577 | 74,975 |
| Deferred | 275 | 146 | 115 | (275) | (662) | 0 |
| Net income | $3,803 | $3,803 | $3,803 | $3,803 | $3,803 | $101,075 |
| Projected cash flow |  |  |  |  |  |  |
| Net income | 3,803 | 3,803 | 3,803 | 3,803 | 3,803 | 101,075 |
| Depreciation | 1,440 | 1,440 | 1,440 | 1,440 | 1,440 | 36,000 |
| Deferred taxes | 275 | 146 | 115 | (275) | (662) | 0 |
| Capital cost |  |  |  |  |  | (36,000) |
| Net cash flow | $5,518 | $5,389 | $5,358 | $4,968 | $4,581 | $101,075 |

## TABLE 5
### 60,000 Gross-Ton-Capacity Self-unloading Vessel, Full Utilization

| | 1980 | 1981 | 1982 | 1983 | 1984 | 1985 | 1986 | 1987 |
|---|---|---|---|---|---|---|---|---|
| Tons (000) | 0 | 0 | 2,668 | 2,668 | 2,668 | 2,668 | 2,668 | 2,668 |
| Projected income (000) | | | $23,478 | $23,478 | $23,478 | $23,478 | $23,478 | $23,478 |
| Operating costs, 280 days | | | | | | | | |
| Wages | | | 1,910 | 1,910 | 1,910 | 1,910 | 1,910 | 1,910 |
| Fuel | | | 2,898 | 2,898 | 2,898 | 2,898 | 2,898 | 2,898 |
| Food and supplies | | | 168 | 168 | 168 | 168 | 168 | 168 |
| Repairs and Maintenance | | | 600 | 600 | 600 | 600 | 600 | 600 |
| Insurance | | | 300 | 300 | 300 | 300 | 300 | 300 |
| Season cost | | | $5,876 | $5,876 | $5,876 | $5,876 | $5,876 | $5,876 |
| Depreciation | | | 2,400 | 2,400 | 2,400 | 2,400 | 2,400 | 2,400 |
| Pretax income | | | $15,202 | $15,202 | $15,202 | $15,202 | $15,202 | $15,202 |
| Taxes | | | | | | | | |
| Current | (600) | (3,300) | 2,191 | 4,815 | 5,268 | 5,658 | 5,994 | 6,285 |
| Deferred | | | 2,702 | 2,178 | 1,725 | 1,335 | 999 | 708 |
| Net income | $600 | $3,300 | $10,309 | $8,209 | $8,209 | $8,209 | $8,209 | $8,209 |
| Projected cash flow | | | | | | | | |
| Net income | 600 | 3,300 | 10,309 | 8,209 | 8,209 | 8,209 | 8,209 | 8,209 |
| Depreciation | | | 2,400 | 2,400 | 2,400 | 2,400 | 2,400 | 2,400 |
| Deferred taxes | | | 2,702 | 2,178 | 1,725 | 1,335 | 999 | 708 |
| Capital cost | (6,000) | (33,000) | (21,000) | | | | | |
| Net cash flow | $(5,400) | $(29,700) | $(5,589) | $12,787 | $12,334 | $11,914 | $11,608 | $11,317 |

| | 1988 | 1989 | 1990–1995 | 1996 | 1997–2006 | 25-Year Total |
|---|---|---|---|---|---|---|
| Tons (000) | 2,668 | 2,668 | 2,668 | 2,668 | 2,668 | 66,700 |
| Projected income (000) | $23,478 | $23,478 | $23,478 | $23,478 | $23,478 | $586,960 |
| Operating costs, 280 days | | | | | | |
| Wages | 1,910 | 1,910 | 1,910 | 1,910 | 1,910 | 47,750 |
| Fuel | 2,898 | 2,898 | 2,898 | 2,898 | 2,898 | 72,450 |
| Food and supplies | 168 | 168 | 168 | 168 | 168 | 4,200 |
| Repairs and Mainte- nance | 600 | 600 | 600 | 600 | 600 | 15,000 |
| Insurance | 300 | 300 | 300 | 300 | 300 | 7,500 |
| Season cost | $5,876 | $5,876 | $5,876 | $5,876 | $5,876 | $146,900 |
| Depreciation | 2,400 | 2,400 | 2,400 | 2,400 | 2,400 | 60,000 |
| Pretax income | $15,202 | $15,202 | $15,202 | $15,202 | $15,202 | $380,050 |
| Taxes | | | | | | |
| Current | 6,534 | 6,750 | 6,802 | 7,450 | 8,097 | 168,825 |
| Deferred | 459 | 243 | 191 | (457) | (1,104) | 0 |
| Net income | $8,209 | $8,209 | $8,209 | $8,209 | $8,209 | $211,225 |
| Projected cash flow | | | | | | |
| Net income | 8,209 | 8,209 | 8,209 | 8,209 | 8,209 | 211,225 |
| Depreciation | 2,400 | 2,400 | 2,400 | 2,400 | 2,400 | 60,000 |
| Deferred taxes | 459 | 243 | 191 | (457) | (1,104) | 0 |
| Capital cost | | | | | | (60,000) |
| Net cash flow | $11,068 | $10,852 | $10,800 | $10,152 | $9,505 | $211,225 |

## TABLE 6
### 60,000-Gross-Ton-Capacity Self-unloading Vessel, Partial Utilization

| | 1980 | 1981 | 1982 | 1984 | 1985 | 1986 | 1987 |
|---|---|---|---|---|---|---|---|
| Tons (000) | 0 | 0 | 1,472 | 1,472 | 1,472 | 1,472 | 1,472 |
| Projected income (000) | | | $12,954 | $12,954 | $12,954 | $12,954 | $12,954 |
| Operating costs, 164 days | | | | | | | |
|   Wages | | | 1,118 | 1,118 | 1,118 | 1,118 | 1,118 |
|   Fuel | | | 1,697 | 1,697 | 1,697 | 1,697 | 1,697 |
|   Food and supplies | | | 98 | 98 | 98 | 98 | 98 |
|   Repairs and Maintenance | | | 500 | 500 | 500 | 500 | 500 |
|   Insurance | | | 240 | 240 | 240 | 240 | 240 |
|   Season cost | | | $3,653 | $3,653 | $3,653 | $3,653 | $3,653 |
|   Depreciation | | | 2,400 | 2,400 | 2,400 | 2,400 | 2,400 |
| Pretax income | | | $6,901 | $6,901 | $6,901 | $6,901 | $6,901 |
| Taxes | | | | | | | |
|   Current | (600) | (3,300) | (1,628) | 1,449 | 1,839 | 2,175 | 2,466 |
|   Deferred | | | 2,702 | 1,725 | 1,335 | 999 | 708 |
| Net income | $600 | $3,300 | $5,821 | $3,727 | $3,727 | $3,727 | $3,727 |
| Projected cash flow | | | | | | | |
|   Net income | 600 | 3,300 | 5,821 | 3,727 | 3,727 | 3,727 | 3,727 |
|   Depreciation | | | 2,400 | 2,400 | 2,400 | 2,400 | 2,400 |
|   Deferred taxes | | | 2,702 | 1,725 | 1,335 | 999 | 708 |
|   Capital cost | (6,000) | (33,000) | (21,000) | | | | |
| Net cash flow | $(5,400) | $(29,700) | $(10,077) | $7,852 | $7,462 | $7,126 | $6,835 |

| | 1988 | 1989 | 1990–1995 | 1996 | 1997–2006 | 25-Year Total |
|---|---|---|---|---|---|---|
| Tons (000) | 1,472 | 1,472 | 1,472 | 1,472 | 1,472 | 36,800 |
| Projected income (000) | $12,954 | $12,954 | $12,954 | $12,954 | $12,954 | $323,840 |
| Operating costs, 164 days | | | | | | |
| Wages | 1,118 | 1,118 | 1,118 | 1,118 | 1,118 | 27,950 |
| Fuel | 1,697 | 1,697 | 1,697 | 1,697 | 1,697 | 42,425 |
| Food and supplies | 98 | 98 | 98 | 98 | 98 | 2,450 |
| Repairs and Maintenance | 500 | 500 | 500 | 500 | 500 | 12,500 |
| Insurance | 240 | 240 | 240 | 240 | 240 | 6,000 |
| Season cost | $3,653 | $3,653 | $3,653 | $3,653 | $3,653 | $91,325 |
| Depreciation | 2,400 | 2,400 | 2,400 | 2,400 | 2,400 | 60,000 |
| Pretax income | $6,901 | $6,901 | $6,901 | $6,901 | $6,901 | $172,525 |
| Taxes | | | | | | |
| Current | 2,715 | 2,928 | 2,983 | 3,631 | 4,278 | 73,350 |
| Deferred | 459 | 243 | 191 | (457) | (1,104) | 0 |
| Net income | $3,727 | $3,727 | $3,727 | $3,727 | $3,727 | $99,175 |
| Projected cash flow | | | | | | |
| Net income | 3,727 | 3,727 | 3,727 | 3,727 | 3,727 | 99,175 |
| Depreciation | 2,400 | 2,400 | 2,400 | 2,400 | 2,400 | 60,000 |
| Deferred taxes | 459 | 243 | 191 | (457) | (1,104) | 0 |
| Capital cost | | | | | | (60,000) |
| Net cash flow | $6,586 | $6,370 | $6,318 | $5,670 | $5,023 | $99,175 |

*John Ward:* "I really think we need another 1,000 footer. The reason we have the opportunity for the new contract was our aggressiveness in expanding into 1,000-foot vessels. The only way we are ever going to get more business is by constructing a third 1,000-footer. They are the wave of the future."

*Mike Myers:* "But a 1,000-footer will give us excess capacity of 1.2 million tons per year. The annual capacity of the 1,000-footer is 2.7 million tons and our shortfall is only projected at 1.5 million tons (head of the lakes to Lake Erie equivalent) during 1982 and 1983."

*George Kanestrom:* "We always have the potential to idle some older capacity. We could lay up one or two of the smaller, older ships and fill the balance of the 1,000-footer capacity with those tons. We would save between $3,000,000 and $3,500,000 each in operating cost if we did not operate them for a season. They are mostly depreciated, completely paid for, and would cost relatively little to lay up. Of course, lay-ups of several ships might create crew morale problems which we'd rather avoid."

*John Ward:* "Furthermore, that shortfall is based upon contract business only. There is every reason to believe that our fleet will continue to be called upon by 'noncontracted' steel and ore companies for float help on a spot basis. This is an ongoing franchise, and we have been able to respond to these requests to our benefit because we had some extra capacity to work with. I believe that it is important to maintain that posture. Also, there is the potential for movement of Western coal. Detroit Edison will be needing more float as it expands in the mid-1980s, and we will probably have an opportunity to obtain some of this business."

*Mike Myers:* "But should we build to meet potential business or should we wait until we have the business and then build? I'm not so certain that the projected shortfall will materialize, and excess capacity can be costly. Furthermore, Superior already has a fairly high debt–equity ratio and this may not be the best use of our remaining borrowing capacity. Maybe the right answer is to do nothing and hope that we can carry our expanded contractual obligations with the existing fleet."

## DISCUSSION QUESTIONS

1. Identify the costs and risks to Superior associated with each of the alternatives.
2. Select and justify the preferred course of action.
3. What impact would a continuation of inflation in capital and operating costs, at rates prevailing in 1981, have upon the merits of your recommended alternative?
4. How do proposed changes (1981) in the Internal Revenue Code to liberalize depreciation influence the economics of these capital investment alternatives?

# Surfliner Boats

Surfliner's newly designed 35-foot diesel-powered cruiser was the company's first entry into the larger luxury powerboat market. Previously Surfliner had built smaller powerboats ranging from 18 feet to 24 feet in length. The smaller boats were designed for cruising in protectediwaters and slept from four to six persons. The new 35-foot Surfliner had accommodations for up to ten persons and was capable of cruising in more exposed coastal waters and much heavier weather conditions than were previous models. Features of the new cruiser included diesel power, complete navigation and radio equipment, master suite with separate bathroom, fully equipped galley, and lounge area with wet bar.

Surfliner was not a large manufacturer, but it had an excellent reputation among experienced boat owners in the region. During the 18 years that Surfliner had been building power cruisers, it had acquired expertise in all aspects of the construction of fiberglass hulled boats. In addition to its experience with pleasure boats, the company had, during the Vietnam era, built 23-foot patrol boats for the U.S. Navy. These were made principally for reconnaissance along rivers and coastal areas in Southeast Asia. Surfliner boats had a reputation for rugged and seaworthy construction and few maintenance problems.

## NEW CRUISER DESIGN

Development of the design and specifications for the new cruiser was handled by Surfliner's own engineering group. Once final approval to proceed with the project was given by management, it was planned to build full-sized mock-ups of the principal interior areas to facilitate arrangement of

## FIGURE 1

### Estimated Demand Curve for 35-foot Cruiser

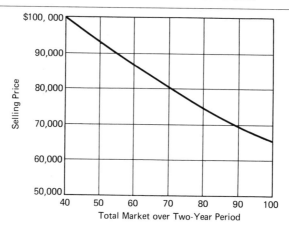

equipment and evaluate the attractiveness of alternative interior designs. Total cost for engineering and development work was estimated to be about $120,000, of which approximately $30,000 had already been expended on preliminary design and engineering.

Because sales were typically handled through independent dealers, Surfliner's sales and marketing staff was quite small and did not have the capability to undertake a thorough study of the market for the new model. Accordingly, a consultant was hired to analyze the market in the region for the proposed 35-foot model. The study examined only a two-year time horizon as management felt that the project would have to prove financially feasible and profitable within that time if it were to be undertaken at all.

The report prepared by the consultant analyzed the socioeconomic status of likely buyers, suggested possible sales approaches, and included an estimated demand curve for the cruiser as shown in Figure 1. The demand curve was based on the assumption that introduction of the new model through advertising and other promotional efforts would occur at about the same time as the start of construction of the first cruiser. Allowing for manufacturing lead time, the first unit would be delivered about two months later, after which time deliveries of succeeding units would continue on a regular basis until the end of the two-year period.

## PRODUCTION PLAN

Because Surfliner's plant was fully utilized in production of the line of smaller boats, it was planned to build the cruiser in a new building of about 12,000 square feet constructed adjacent to the existing plant. It was estimated that the building would cost about $15 per square foot, plus $15,000 for grading and paving around the building. The new facility as shown in Figure 2 was designed with five work stations through which the cruisers would move during manufacture. Lay-up of the fiberglass hull would take place at station 1. Succeeding operations would be performed in a fixed sequence at the following stations, with final finishing work accomplished at station 5. With this arrangement only one set of tools was required for each operation. However, it would be necessary to closely plan and monitor progress so that work at all stations would be completed at the same time and hulls could be moved simultaneously. Costs of molds, jigs, tools, and equipment for the production line in Figure 2 were estimated to total $165,000.

Surfliner management was first introduced to the concept of improvement curves as a method for estimating costs during contract negotiations for Navy patrol boats. Subsequent experience with Navy contracts had demonstrated the utility of improvement curves in planning schedules and labor levels as well. The improvement curve factor realized over the duration of the Navy contracts and on other commercial models for which data had been analyzed was about 90 percent. There appeared to be enough similarity be-

## FIGURE 2

### Layout of New Production Facility

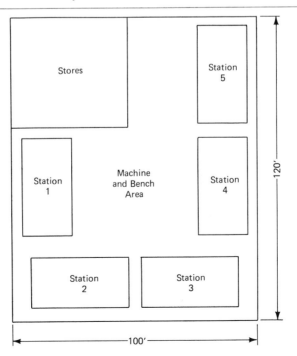

tween the new cruiser and previous models so that it was reasonable to assume that a 90 percent improvement rate could be achieved.

Estimates of first unit hours were made for operations performed at each of the five stations and also for machine and bench work performed away from the stations. Times for many of the operations, such as lay-up of fiberglass, were known with great certainty, as the company had considerable experience with this type of work. However, times for some operations, such as finishing the interior, were simply educated guesses. Taken together, estimated times for all operations for the first unit totaled 2,700 hours.

Production workers averaged 160 hours per month at a cost, including fringe benefits, of $16.00 per hour. Considering the layout of the production line, floor space available, and the mix of tools and equipment that was contemplated, it appeared that a maximum of about 35 production workers could be utilized at any one time. Direct costs of supervision for a one-shift operation in the new building were expected to be about $6,000 per month. Utilities, insurance, security, and other miscellaneous costs of operating the new production facility were estimated to be $8,000 per month. When the new cruiser came into production, the accounting department also expected to allocate to the project costs of $11,000 per month for such expenses as general management, sales, engineering support, purchasing, and so forth.

The purchasing department had made an extensive analysis of the costs of all construction materials, equipment, engines, and interior furnishings that would be required for the cruiser. Preliminary bids were obtained for major items such as engines, propellers, special marine fittings, tanks, galley units, bathroom fixtures, navigational equipment, and radios. For standard items such as fiberglass, resins, fasteners, tubing, wire, and common marine fittings, the purchasing department had adequate cost records. Total cost of all materials, equipment, and supplies used in the construction of the cruiser was estimated to be $33,000 per boat. Because of the rather small number of boats involved, it did not appear that there would be any significant opportunities to obtain quantity discounts.

## DISCUSSION QUESTIONS

1. Assuming single-shift operation, develop a two-year manufacturing plan and establish the price for the cruiser.
2. What plan and price should be adopted if second- and third-shift operations are permitted?
3. What are the strengths and weaknesses of a high-price–low-volume policy as opposed to a low-price–high-volume policy?
4. What impact does the limitation to a two-year planning horizon have on the answer to Questions 1 and 2?

# Teem Aircraft Corporation

Phil Wagenar was beginning to "cool off" as he sipped his coffee in the executive dining room of the Teem Aircraft Corporation. He and Dale Johnson were relaxing for a moment after their presentation to the selection board regarding their recommended placement of a major subcontract for the reaction control system for the X284 airplane. Phil Wagenar, senior design engineer, was still insisting that his point of view was right: "I tell you, Dale, your procurement evaluation system is no damn good — you can switch it around to get any answer you want. It's just a numbers game." With some resignation Dale Johnson, section manager in the purchasing department, reaffirmed his position: "What have you got that's better? When you have a large number of variables that must be evaluated and summed up, our system gives us the best compromise decision which can be justified."

The selection board had just adjourned to give its members time to study the facts presented by the analysis committee regarding the control system. A meeting had been scheduled for the following day at which time a final decision regarding this major procurement was to be made.

The Tucson division of Teem Aircraft was located in Tucson, Arizona and was engaged in a major effort to design and manufacture the X284 airplane. When the prime contract for the X284 had been placed with Teem by the Air Force, it had been agreed that the reaction control system would be subcontracted. The purpose of the reaction control system was to assist the aerodynamic surfaces at altitudes where aerodynamic surfaces lost their effectiveness. The subcontractor was to design the control system to performance specifications provided by Teem, with some of the general characteristics of the hardware indicated but with the detail design left to the supplier. Specifications provided such information as space limitations, weight limitations, response times, and other technical information that established the necessary constraints.

For major procurements, such as the reaction control system for the X284, a well-developed system of vendor selection had been established at Teem. The buyer assigned to the control system was Tom Osborne. He was to collect all the appropriate information regarding each of the vendors to be considered for the award. This information was to be submitted to an analysis committee that was responsible for making a selection recommendation to the selection board for final approval.

## POTENTIAL SUPPLIERS

Osborne set out to prepare a list of potential suppliers to whom invitations for bids (IFB) would be submitted. He carefully reviewed the requisition and related specifications and discussed the project with his supervisor, Dale Johnson, section manager in the purchsing department, and with the designers in the engineering department. To secure the best hardware for the program, the following items regarding potential subcontractors were considered:

1. Companies with known capabilities, including original research skills.
2. Companies that had made presentations previously to Teem indicating their capabilities in the field of this procurement.
3. Contacts and discussions that Osborne and other buyers had with people in the industry.
4. Recommendations that had been presented by other Teem divisions and other companies.
5. A thorough review of data — information and brochures — that were on file in the Teem procurement office.
6. Companies that had sent letters indicating interest, experience, and capability.
7. Review of trade magazines to identify the names of corporations with indicated interest in control systems. A study was also made of *Thomas' Register of American Manufacturers* for companies that were listed in this field.
8. Suggestions and recommendations made by Air Force personnel.

Based on these factors, Osborne was able to obtain names of 23 companies that could be considered as potential suppliers. He reviewed this list with Johnson, and they decided to compare the known characteristics of each company with the proposed work statement. This comparison reduced the list of potential bidders to 14. The remaining names were then reviewed with personnel in the engineering department, finance department, and other departments that were able to provide information of a preliminary nature regarding each supplier's past performance for on-time delivery, quality, financial responsibility, and security clearance status.

This resulted in a refined list of eight potential sources. The list of eight names was submitted to the chief purchasing agent for his approval, and he in turn submitted the list to the Air Force plant representative for final approval. Upon receipt of Air Force approval of the bid list, Osborne was ready to forward the invitations for bids requesting proposals and quotations to the eight suppliers as soon as the IFB was released by the analysis committee. The preparation of this list had taken approximately two weeks from the time that Osborne had first received the official requisition from the engineering department.

## BID EVALUATION PROCEDURE

During the time that the bid list was being prepared, an analysis committee had been organized consisting of Johnson from the purchasing department to chair the committee; Wagenar, the design supervisor to prepare the specifications for the control system; a supervisor from the quality control department to lend expertise in developmental and experimental work and working with subcontractors; and a supervisor from the manufacturing department who also had experience in evaluating subcontractors to supply general information regarding the primary types of manufacturing involved in the control system. The four members of the analysis committee were mature executives with broad backgrounds in the aircraft industry, and each had a reputation for exercising objective judgment.

The first task of the analysis committee was to set up a system of assigning points to each supplier that would form the basis of making the award to the winning company. They selected the major factors to be considered as follows:

1. Technical
2. Management
3. Financial
4. Manufacturing
5. Quality control

Each of the factors was then broken down into criteria that were of significance with reference to the specific program involved. The criteria for each factor were then weighted as shown in Table 1.

The criteria for each factor were broken down further into subcriteria; the management factor is shown in Table 2. Two basic principles were involved in the establishment of the detailed subcriteria. First, there was a recognition that vendor selection required judgment in making the final decision. It was difficult, if not impossible, to arrive at a single overall judgment decision directly. It was believed, therefore that the overall large and difficult problem could be broken down into a series of smaller problems.

## TABLE 1
### Criteria and Weights for Major Factors

| Technical | | Management | | Financial | | Manufacturing | | Quality Control | |
|---|---|---|---|---|---|---|---|---|---|
| Design approach | 40 | Plan | 20 | Cost proposal (price) | 30 | Departmental experience | 20 | Policy | 20 |
| Technical capability | 25 | Organization | 26 | Strength | 15 | Plan | 15 | Operational system | 25 |
| Development plan | 15 | Labor | 14 | Accounting system | 15 | Facilities | 13 | Technical capability | 15 |
| Reliability | 8 | Controls | 20 | Financial capability | 10 | Skills | 6 | Facilities | 10 |
| Specification conformity | 7 | Experience | 5 | Cost control | 20 | Tooling | 10 | Reliability | 15 |
| Release of proprietary rights | 5 | Reliability | 10 | Estimating technique | 10 | Controls | 16 | Record system | 15 |
| | | Labor relations | 5 | | | Quality assurance | 8 | | |
| | | | | | | Improvement plan | 7 | | |
| | | | | | | Training | 5 | | |
| Total | 100 | | 100 | | 100 | | 100 | | 100 |

## TABLE 2

### Management Subcriteria

| | | Points |
|---|---:|---:|
| Management plan | 20 | |
| Adequacy of plan — consistent with program requirements; depicts understanding of problems with logical solutions and actions | | 10 |
| Compliance with proposal instructions | | 3 |
| "Make or buy" plan (including procurement) | | 7 |
| Management organization | 26 | |
| Corporate structure | | 5 |
| Specific management organization, depth, lines of authority, experience | | 12 |
| Organizational stability | | 4 |
| Support organization | | 5 |
| Labor (total) | 14 | |
| Requirements and availability | | 7 |
| Labor acquisition plan | | 5 |
| Effect of current and future business on labor program | | 2 |
| Management controls | 20 | |
| Adequacy of management controls (time and dollars): type, frequency, effectiveness | | 12 |
| Top management participation | | 5 |
| Corrective action by management: what, how, effectiveness | | 3 |
| Management experience | 5 | |
| Similar projects or jobs successfully managed of a similar complexity and magnitude | | 5 |
| Reliability | 10 | |
| Management participation | | |
| Policy | | 3 |
| Procedures | | 3 |
| Organization | | 4 |
| Labor relations | 5 | |
| Total | 100 | |

Each of the smaller problems lent itself more readily to a solution that could be related to other solutions to obtain an overall judgment that could be substantiated and justified.

The second principle in setting up detailed criteria was to provide a basis for evaluating each supplier independently on an absolute basis rather than relating each supplier to the other suppliers and rating them on a relative judgment basis. It was expected that an absolute rating basis would involve less bias than a relative rating basis.

In evaluating each criterion, all suppliers first were given the full value of the points assigned on the preliminary assumption that each supplier met the requirements of the criterion. Points were then deducted from the maximum points allowed as deficiencies were observed.

The thought process in evaluating each subcriterion is illustrated in the following examples for Table 2. For the subcriterion "make or buy", the supplier was requested to identify how much it planned to make and how much it planned to buy. Particular attention was given to critical items of the design that the supplier was expected to make rather than buy to assure that the supplier had control of the manufacturing process for the critical items. A check also was made as to whether the supplier intended to make items that could be purchased at a lower cost or with better quality.

The subcriterion of Table 2 pertaining to corporate structure was investigated regarding centralization versus decentralization of control. Did the local functional executive report to the local plant manager or to the functional manager at the headquarters office? Was this a good or bad arrangement? What degree of control, effectiveness of communication, and lines of responsibility and authority existed between the functional executive at the local level and the functional executive at the headquarters level? To whom did the quality control executive report? Was the support to be received from the corporate headquarters real or imaginary? What was the role of the board of directors and the president as compared with the role of the manager at the divisional levels?

Subcriteria for management controls listed in Table 2 concerned the effectiveness of the specific controls used by the supplier for the program being procured. Elaborate controls were not necessarily required. The simplest controls that would adequately do the job were considered superior to elaborate controls that might involve greater costs without improving the effectiveness. Where coordination was necessary between the prime contractor and the subcontractor with reference to reports, the control systems were checked for compatibility. A check was made to determine if reports were prepared on a timely basis so that action could be taken promptly to correct an undesirable situation.

After preparation of the criteria list, the analysis committee reviewed the invitations for bids to be certain that suppliers were requested to submit sufficient information to evaluate technical and cost criteria. The invitations for bids were also checked to minimize unnecessary information that might be requested regarding other criteria. This policy had resulted from past situations when too much detail had been requested from suppliers. Excessive detail had caused high bidding costs for suppliers, and some members of management had charged that the analysis committees were "grading papers for the best science fiction writers" rather than evaluating companies. It was planned that technical cost data submitted would permit the number of suppliers to be reduced to three or four. Then a field survey of each of these companies would be made to provide the remaining detailed information required by the analysis committee to reach a final recommendation.

# EVALUATION OF BIDS

Upon release of the invitations for bids by the analysis committee, Osborne sent out the invitations to the eight suppliers remaining on the proposed bidders' list. Five weeks later six companies had responded. Two companies declined to submit proposals. The six proposals were given a preliminary evaluation by the analysis committee, and two companies were eliminated as unacceptable because their proposals failed to meet technical requirements of the specifications. The four companies remaining in the competition were:

> Bullard Scientific Company
> Military Division of the Eastern Corporation
> R. J. Matterson Company
> Amalgamated Manufacturers, Inc.

Amalgamated was a large company prominent in its field, but there was a question as to whether its proposal complied with the basic design requirements. The analysis committee decided to field survey all four companies and to verify whether there was compliance by Amalgamated with technical requirements of the procurement.

Osborne headed a team of functional specialists who visited each supplier for about two days and prepared documentation covering each of the criteria established by the analysis committee. These written statements by the functional specialists were submitted to the analysis committee along with other information collected by the buyer.

Each member of the analysis committee first evaluated his or her own area of specialization. Johnson from the purchasing department handled the management and financial factors with the assistance and advice of the other members of the committee. Then the evaluation of each factor was reviewed by the entire committee, which resulted in the scores assigned to each supplier as shown in Table 3. Having reached this step in the proce-

### TABLE 3

#### Factor Scores

|  | Technical | Management | Financial | Manufacturing | Quality Control |
|---|---|---|---|---|---|
| Bullard | 64.4 | 92.1 | 82.1 | 66.0 | 63.0 |
| Eastern | 50.0 | 86.8 | 82.1 | 71.0 | 80.0 |
| Matterson | 63.4 | 79.5 | 43.4 | 55.0 | 52.0 |
| Amalgamated | 51.6 | 83.5 | 100.0 | 69.0 | 66.0 |

dure, all that remained was to relate the values of each factor to one another and to compare the resulting points with the prices that were submitted.

Responsibility for weighting the factors relative to one another was assigned to the selection board. This information was withheld from the analysis committee until members of the analysis committee had evaluated the criteria for each factor. This was to prevent possible bias on the part of members of the analysis committee who might give too much attention to the heavily weighted factors and give inadequate attention to factors receiving little weight. For the control system the selection board assigned the following weights:

| Factors | % of Total |
|---|---|
| Technical | 50 |
| Management | 15 |
| Financial | 15 |
| Manufacturing | 10 |
| Quality control | 10 |
| Total | 100 |

Weights were applied to the score given each vendor for each factor, which resulted in the assignment of points shown in Table 4.

Prices proposed by the four bidders were as follows:

| Bullard | $23,138,248 |
|---|---|
| Eastern | 13,338,608 |
| Matterson | 19,055,880 |
| Amalgamated | 11,432,316 |

Because Amalgamated was the low bidder, its proposal was again carefully reviewed, particularly because of a technical question involved in its design. It was finally decided by the analysis committee to eliminate Amalgamated because of noncompliance with the design specifications.

The analysis committee now faced the necessity of a final recommendation. Johnson pointed out that Bullard had received 5.8 points more than

TABLE 4

Factor Points

| | Technical | Management | Financial | Manufacturing | Quality Control | Total |
|---|---|---|---|---|---|---|
| (Weights) | (50%) | (15%) | (15%) | (10%) | (10%) | (100%) |
| Bullard | 32.2 | 13.8 | 12.3 | 6.6 | 6.3 | 71.2 |
| Eastern | 25.0 | 13.0 | 12.3 | 7.1 | 8.0 | 65.4 |
| Matterson | 31.7 | 11.9 | 6.5 | 5.5 | 5.2 | 60.8 |
| Amalgamated | 25.8 | 12.5 | 15.0 | 6.9 | 6.6 | 66.8 |

Eastern but that Bullard's bid was higher by almost $10 million than the bid submitted by Eastern. He suggested, therefore, that the award be made to Eastern as designs submitted by both companies were acceptable. Wagenar, the engineer on the committee, violently objected to such a suggestion. He insisted that Bullard's design was significantly superior to that submitted by Eastern, and he felt that the superiority of the design justified the increase in cost.

Normally the analysis committee was expected to submit a unanimous recommendation to the selection board. After a great deal of discussion, however, Wagenar held out for Bullard while the other three members of the analysis committee insisted on Eastern. When it became apparent that agreement could not be achieved, it was decided to submit Eastern as the recommendation of the analysis committee, with the dissent of Wagenar noted, to the selection board.

## SELECTION BOARD

As a result of the nonunanimous recommendation, the selection board requested each point of view to be elaborated. Johnson pointed out that a change in the weighting of the various factors could change the total point relationship. He indicated that the range of weights assigned in previous competitions had varied as shown in Table 5. By assigning the weights shown in Table 6, Johnson was able to illustrate equal total points for Bullard and Eastern. Because this equalized the relative point advantage previously held by Bullard over Eastern, he felt that there should be no question about the award's being made to the lower bidder.

Wagenar presented a different point of view. He insisted that the original weighting of the selection board established the relative importance of each factor for this specific procurement and should not be changed. Further, he pointed out that the criteria used for evaluating the financial factor also included an allowance for price, as shown in Table 1. He believed that price should not be considered twice. If price were included in the point system, then actual prices should not be considered. On the other hand, if

### TABLE 5

### Range of Weights (%)

|  | Technical | Management | Financial | Manufacturing | Quality Control |
|---|---|---|---|---|---|
| High | 55 | 15 | 20 | 20 | 25 |
| Low | 35 | 5 | 10 | 10 | 10 |

## TABLE 6

### Factor Points Based on Revised Weights

|  | Technical | Management | Financial | Manufacturing | Quality Control | Total |
|---|---|---|---|---|---|---|
| (Weights) | (35%) | (5%) | (15%) | (20%) | (25%) | (100%) |
| Bullard | 22.5 | 4.6 | 12.3 | 13.2 | 15.7 | 68.3 |
| Eastern | 17.5 | 4.3 | 12.3 | 14.2 | 20.0 | 68.3 |

actual prices were to be considered separately, the price criterion should be removed from the point system. He had made such a recalculation and presented an adjusted point table as shown in Table 7. Here the difference between the two vendors had increased from 5.8 to 8.1 points, which he suggested substantiated his recommendation of making the award to Bullard.

Johnson countered this argument by pointing out that, although the point system included consideration of price, the dollar difference between the acceptable bidders was of such magnitude that it did not receive adequate consideration in the point system evaluation. Of the 15 points of total weight allocated to the financial factor, only 4.5 were allocated to price consideration. The lowest bidder received 4.5 points. Deductions for prices higher than the lowest bid from the 4.5 points were based on the following formula:

$$\text{Deduction for price for a given vendor} = \text{Weight} \times \left( 1 - \frac{\text{lowest bid}}{\text{vendor bid}} \right)$$

By this method of allocating points for price, there was only a 1.6-point difference in the total evaluation for the price criterion between Bullard and Eastern.

## TABLE 7

### Adjusted Factor Points
### (price criterion not included in financial factor)

|  | Technical | Management | Financial | Manufacturing | Quality Control | Total |
|---|---|---|---|---|---|---|
| (Weights) | (50%) | (15%) | (15%) | (10%) | (10%) | (100%) |
| Bullard | 32.2 | 13.8 | 14.4 | 6.6 | 6.3 | 73.3 |
| Eastern | 25.0 | 13.0 | 12.1 | 7.1 | 8.0 | 65.2 |
| Matterson | 31.7 | 11.9 | 5.4 | 5.5 | 5.2 | 59.7 |
| Amalgamated | 25.8 | 12.5 | 15.0 | 6.9 | 6.6 | 66.8 |

## TABLE 8

### Range of Scores, Adjusted Basis

|  | Technical | Management | Financial | Manufacturing | Quality Control | Total |
|---|---|---|---|---|---|---|
| High | 64.4 | 92.1 | 100.0 | 71.0 | 80.0 | |
| Low | 50.0 | 79.5 | 36.3 | 55.0 | 52.0 | |
| Range | 14.4 | 12.6 | 63.7 | 16.0 | 28.0 | 134.7 |
| (Adjusted weights) | (10.7%) | (9.3%) | (47.4%) | (11.9%) | (20.8%) | (100.0%) |

In the discussion that followed, it was claimed that the point system could not compensate for severe conditions. As an example, it was indicated that, if the point system were employed literally, a proposal would be penalized only 2.00 points for lack of an adequate design, 0.75 point if the company had no management experience on a similar job, 0.50 point if there were inadequate space in the plant to accomplish the manufacturing task, 1.00 point if the supplier did not possess proper inspection equipment, and 0.75 point if the supplier's financial stability was questionable. Under these circumstances a supplier could score 95 points but still, obviously, be incapable of meeting requirements of the procurement.

Wagenar retaliated by suggesting a further flaw in interpreting the points. He claimed that the weighting of each factor should not be applied to the total score within each factor but to range between the lowest and the highest score awarded for each factor. To illustrate this he presented Table 8, showing that the score range of 63.7 for the financial factor caused this item to receive undue importance as compared with the technical factor, which had a score range of only 14.4. He contended that this occurred even though the selection board had provided factor weights in which the technical factors were to be given primary consideration. Based on this argument he recalculated the raw scores as shown in Table 9 and reassigned the points

## TABLE 9

### Scores Above Minimum Score, Adjusted Basis
### (price criterion not included in financial factor)

|  | Technical | Management | Financial | Manufacturing | Quality Control |
|---|---|---|---|---|---|
| Bullard | 14.4 | 12.6 | 59.8 | 11.0 | 11.0 |
| Eastern | 0 | 7.3 | 44.3 | 16.0 | 28.0 |
| Matterson | 13.4 | 0 | 0 | 0 | 0 |
| Amalgamated | 1.6 | 4.0 | 63.7 | 14.0 | 14.0 |

## TABLE 10

### Factor Points Based on Table 9[1]

|  | Technical | Management | Financial | Manufacturing | Quality Control | Total |
|---|---|---|---|---|---|---|
| (Weights) | (50%) | (15%) | (15%) | (10%) | (10%) | (100%) |
| Bullard | 50.0 | 15.0 | 14.1 | 6.9 | 3.9 | 89.9 |
| Eastern | 0 | 8.7 | 10.4 | 10.0 | 10.0 | 39.1 |
| Matterson | 46.5 | 0 | 0 | 0 | 0 | 46.5 |
| Amalgamated | 5.6 | 4.8 | 15.0 | 8.7 | 5.0 | 39.1 |

[1] $\text{Points} = \text{Weight} \times \dfrac{\text{score above minimum}}{\text{range of scores}}$

as shown in Table 10. On the basis of this calculation he claimed that Bullard had an overwhelming advantage in the competition and should receive the award. After Wagenar's presentation, several members of the selection board indicated that they would like to study the new data in the tables before making a final decision. As a result, an adjournment was called after scheduling a meeting for the following day when the final decision was to be made.

## DISCUSSION QUESTIONS

1. What are the limitations and strengths of a point system evaluation?
2. Was the double consideration of cost justified?
3. Using a point system evaluation, how do you compensate for extremely good or extremely bad features that have been designated a small number of points?
4. Do you accept the proposed use of the range of scores rather than the total scores in calculating the factor points?
5. If you were a member of the selection board, how would you vote?
6. Design an alternative selection system.

# Torsion Tractor Company

In March 1980 the Torsion Tractor Company received an order for 300 tractor units of a new heavy-duty design. Major changes in the new design were a more powerful engine and an improved transmission and rear axle. The transmission was a heavier-duty design built to closer tolerances than previously. In addition, the new model had a two-speed rear axle with different gear ratios designed for heavier loads and built to closer tolerances than the standard axle.

After the intial order was received, Torsion Tractor found that several more customers were interested in the heavy-duty tractor design. The company obtained orders for 200 additional tractor units to be used in both on- and off-highway hauling in the western part of the country.

## PLANNING FOR NEW TRACTOR

The delivery schedule for the initial order for 300 units was 20 per month to begin in January 1981. Another order for 80 tractors was scheduled to be delivered at a rate of 10 per month beginning in April 1981. An order for 120 tractors from another customer was scheduled to be delivered at a rate of 10 per month beginning in August 1981. As soon as the contracts were received, the Torsion Tractor Company developed a master production schedule for the fabrication and assembly of the units. Delivery schedules were important because the market for tractors was highly competitive and customers viewed the ability of manufacturers to meet delivery dates as an important factor in placing orders. The heavy-duty tractor units designed by Torsion had also aroused considerable interest in the industry, with the result that several competitive manufacturers were bringing out tractor models with similar capabilities that would be available for delivery in late fall of 1981.

The Torsion Tractor Company was located in Pittsburgh where it owned one large plant at which the tractors were manufactured. The plant was equipped with a foundry, machine shops, and supporting facilities for the fabrication of parts. Tractors were assembled by moving them through successive positions in a line. Different tractor models were all assembled on this one line, with each position on the line performing the same type of work on each tractor as it moved down the line. A diagram of the tractor assembly line is shown in Figure 1.

Torsion Tractor produced many of the tractor parts in its own plant but purchased other parts as complete assemblies. Tractor frames, door panels, and floor panels were typical of the items fabricated in the Torsion shops. Wheels, axle assemblies, engines, transmissions, and radiators were typical of the items purchased as completed units from other manufacturers.

In the new heavy-duty tractor model the redesigned transmission and the two-speed axle assemblies were critical purchased parts. The new heavy-duty design of both required machining and finishing tolerances closer than

FIGURE 1

Schematic Diagram of Tractor Assembly Line
(not to scale)

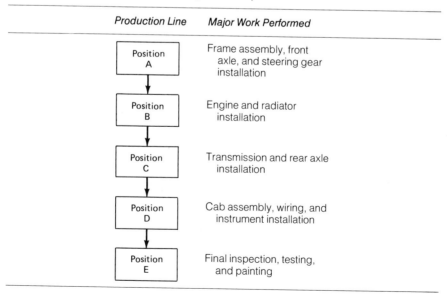

| Production Line | Major Work Performed |
| --- | --- |
| Position A | Frame assembly, front axle, and steering gear installation |
| Position B | Engine and radiator installation |
| Position C | Transmission and rear axle installation |
| Position D | Cab assembly, wiring, and instrument installation |
| Position E | Final inspection, testing, and painting |

those that had been used in previous models. For transmissions, the Milwaukee Machine Tool Company had been a reliable supplier in the past, and Torsion selected them as the supplier for the new transmissions for the heavy-duty tractor. Rear axle assemblies had previously been procured from three sources: Michael & Sons in Cleveland, West Coast Products in Oakland, California, and Milwaukee Machine Tool. Michael & Sons was a smaller company with limited production facilities; however, it had been a competent supplier of single-speed axles in the past. On occasion, the limited capacity of its production facilities had led to some slight delays in delivery, but this had never been a serious problem. West Coast Products owned a large, modern facility in Oakland equipped with a wide variety of up-to-date machine tools. It had been a very capable supplier of two-speed rear axles and was better regarded than Michael & Sons. In general, the two-speed axles were more complicated than the single-speed axles produced by Michael & Sons and required tolerances that would be difficult for Michael & Sons to attain with the equipment in its plant. Milwaukee Machine Tool had served as a subsidiary source of two-speed axles, supplying about one third of Torsion's requirements. Two other companies in the country supplied two-speed rear axles to competitors of Torsion, but Torsion had never used these firms as suppliers because of the satisfactory relationship it had with West Coast Products and Milwaukee Machine Tool. Also the quantity of two-speed axles purchased by Torsion was such that more than two sources of supply would lead to substantially higher costs because of short runs and the necessity for multiple sets of tools.

## AXLE PROCUREMENT

When the matter of procuring the new two-speed axle came under consideration by Torsion, Michael & Sons was quickly ruled out as a possible source both because of the lack of capacity and the fact that the new two-speed axle would require much closer tolerances than the single-speed axles with which Michael & Sons was experienced. Milwaukee Machine Tool had the capability to produce both the transmission and rear axle, but it was felt that it would not be a good policy to procure both the new transmission and rear axle from one manufacturer. This left West Coast Products, the other supplier of two-speed axles, as the logical choice, and a contract was negotiated with it for the production of the axles with delivery scheduled to support the master schedule for fabrication and assembly of the tractor units. The contract called for production of the axles according to designs supplied by Torsion Tractor. In total the contract with West Coast Products was for 500 axles plus an initial order of 25 spares. The total contract amount was $2,275,000, of which $1,845,000 was for the axles themselves and $430,000 was for design and procurement of tooling and special equipment necessary for production of the new two-speed axles. Under the contract, the tooling and special equipment was to be the property of Torsion but was to be located in the plant of West Coast Products. The quantity of tooling and special equipment was sufficient to support a production schedule of 35 axles per month on a two-shift five-day-week basis, which was West Coast's normal operating schedule. Because of the overlap in the contracts requiring a 40-unit-per-month production rate, West Coast anticipated operating on a partial third-shift basis and with some overtime to meet the schedule.

West Coast Products did not intend to produce all the parts for the new two-speed axles in its own plant. Standard nuts, bolts, and washers, some of the small fittings, a portion of the axle housing, and such things as gaskets and oil seals were procured from outside sources. About 40 percent of the total parts in the axle assembly was contracted for by West Coast from other suppliers. Delivery schedules for these purchased items, in turn, were developed to support the axle fabrication schedule in West Coast's plant.

Axles were shipped via rail from West Coast's plant in Oakland to Pittsburgh. Although transit time varied, it was assumed that the axles would arrive in Pittsburgh two weeks after shipment from Oakland as that was the longest time ordinarily experienced in transit. On one or two occasions, shipments had taken longer because of misrouting of cars, but these cases were exceptional. Torsion Tractor's purchasing department scheduled the rear axles to arrive 6 weeks or 30 working days prior to the scheduled shipment dates of finished tractor units. Normally 10 working days were required to receive the axles, uncrate and inspect them, and place them in the parts inventory. The axles remained in inventory another 15 working days before being moved to position C on the assembly line (Figure 1), where they were assembled into the tractor unit. The tractor units were ready for shipment 5 working days after moving into position C.

Through the early fall of 1980 all schedules for the design and production of parts for the new tractor were met by both Torsion Tractor and its suppliers. There were some difficulties with last-minute design and tooling changes; however, such things were anticipated and problems were corrected as they arose. Torsion Tractor had an excellent reputation for on-time deliveries and was willing to expend the necessary effort to expedite anything that might delay the schedule. By late fall, parts from various suppliers were arriving on regular schedules, and the Torsion Tractor plant was building up to the scheduled production rate on parts produced in the plant. Deliveries of the axle units from West Coast Products began in the middle of November 1980 at a rate of 20 per month. Starting in the middle of February 1981, this rate was increased to 30 per month. The first tractor unit was completed on December 29 and shipped as scheduled on January 3, 1981. Although minor production problems caused a good deal of overtime work in December and January, deliveries proceeded on schedule at the 20-per-month rate programmed for the first quarter of 1981.

By the end of March most of the early production problems had been solved so that overtime work was no longer necessary to meet delivery schedules. In fact, Torsion's manufacturing manager, Paul Burger, was pleased to find that a drop in labor-hours expended per unit was sufficiently large so that no overtime would be necessary to meet the accelerated delivery rate of 30 units per month scheduled to begin in April 1981.

## SUPPLIER STRIKE

On April 1 Burger was in his office reading several monthly reports when the purchasing agent, Chet Nelson, rushed in with a telegram he had just received from West Coast Products. The telegram notified Torsion Tractor that the shop employees of West Coast had gone on strike as of midnight, March 31, and that shipments of axles would cease immediately. The telegram had come as quite a surprise to Nelson since West Coast Products was well known for good relations with its employees. One reason why West Coast Products was considered to be such a reliable vendor was that its shop employees averaged 15 years' service with the company and there had never previously been a strike of any consequence.

In addition, the employees participated in a retirement program that involved placement of nonvoting stock of the company into a fund from which retirement benefits were paid. Because the level of benefits was determined by the value of stock in the fund, employees had an immediate interest in profitable operation of the company. In effect, the strike by employees against the company was a strike against themselves, particularly in view of the fact that the retirement fund held about 50 percent of total outstanding stock of the company.

Burger's first action was to call in Sid Bell, head of production planning for the Torsion plant, to notify him of the situation with regard to the axles for the new tractor model. In the ensuing discussion, Nelson pointed out that, although shipments had ceased on March 31, axles should continue to arrive until about the middle of April since two weeks' supply was always in transit. Referring to his shipment schedule, Bell estimated that there were enough axles on hand or in transit to support delivery schedules until June 1. The discussion ended with Nelson's volunteering to get more information about the strike and to check into other possible sources of supply. Although Bell could think of nothing that could be done by the people in Torsion's plant to remedy the situation, he volunteered to talk to the assembly superintendent about the problem. For the moment, the situation was not critical, but it would become critical in the near future.

Nelson called Oakland and was able to reach the assistant manufacturing manager at West Coast Products. The assistant manufacturing manager said that the strike had occurred as a result of a series of incidents involving disciplining of several shop employees for minor infractions of rules. While the strike did not involve any major issues, both management and the shop employees were adamant that the other side back down from its position, and it was difficult to say how long the strike would last. While discussing the situation with the assistant manufacturing manager, Nelson discovered that West Coast had an inventory of completed parts on hand that had not yet been assembled into completed axles, but the exact number of each part was not immediately available. Nelson inquired about the possibility for delivery of these parts to Torsion Tractor, but he could not get any commitment as the employees were picketing the plant.

Following his conversation with West Coast, Nelson spent the rest of the afternoon contacting Michael & Sons, Torsion's supplier for single-speed axles, and the two firms that supplied two-speed axles to Torsion's competitors to see whether they could supply the axles that West Coast could not supply. In these conversations, Nelson emphasized the exploratory nature of his inquiry and that he would like an estimate of the company's ability to supply the required axles. Michael & Sons was more than anxious to obtain the extra business, although it would strain its facilities to the utmost. Michael & Sons estimated that it could begin deliveries three months after an order was received if the tooling in West Coast's plant were moved to their plant. If new tooling had to be obtained, deliveries could commence in five months. One of the firms that supplied axles to Torsion's competitors did not feel that it had sufficient plant capacity to be able to supply the axles; the other firm was interested in the business and had adequate facilities to handle the order. This firm's estimate of delivery dates was about the same as Michael & Sons had given.

Dan Dailey, the tractor assembly superintendent, was quite concerned when Bell informed him of the strike at West Coast Products. Dailey had worked hard to smooth out various difficulties that had arisen in production of the first tractor units, and it was disappointing to him to see the delivery schedule upset at this point by something beyond control of the plant. He also pointed out several effects that an interruption in assembly of the tractor units would have on his department. While the new tractor units constituted only one third of total current work on the tractor assembly line, additional workers had just been hired and trained to increase the capacity of the line. These workers would have to be released or underutilized if production of the new tractors were halted. Either of these alternatives would be quite expensive. Also, the assembly superintendent pointed out that Torsion's machine shop and foundry and plants of Torsion's vendors were delivering other parts that would accumulate rapidly if production ceased. Slowing down or halting deliveries of these other parts would be expensive and might lead to further delays once production was resumed, as many of the parts were not standard and required special setups and tooling.

Early on the morning of April 4, Burger called a meeting in his office of Nelson, Bell, and Torsion's sales manager. The sales manager emphatically stated that something had to be done to maintain the delivery schedules; for competitive reasons deliveries had to be made on schedule at all costs, even if it meant losing money on the tractors. When Nelson mentioned that some finished parts were awaiting assembly at West Coast's plant, the sales manager suggested that every effort be made to move the parts out of the plant and ship them to Pittsburgh for assembly in Torsion Tractor's plant.

Nelson called West Coast Products immediately and persuaded West Coast to assign several administrative employees who were not on strike to the preparation for shipment of as many complete sets of parts as were on hand. Within two days, as many complete sets of parts as were available were moved out of the plant and shipped from Oakland via airfreight to Torsion Tractor's plant at Pittsburgh. There Torsion undertook assembly of the parts at its own expense. When the axles were assembled, this would add another 15 axles to the number already on hand, providing sufficient stock to meet deliveries as scheduled through June 15.

On Monday, April 11, one week after the crisis began, Burger invited Nelson, Bell, Dailey, the sales manager, and the foundry and machine shop superintendent to his office to again discuss the situation. A call to West Coast Products immediately before the meeting had revealed that there was no change in the strike situation, although management at West Coast doubted that the strike could conceivably last very long. Bell opened the meeting with a report of the status of the axle supply and its relation to tractor shipment schedules. With the axles on hand, those in transit, and the ones being assembled from parts, enough of the new two-speed axles were on hand to maintain shipments as scheduled through June 15.

## SOLUTIONS TO STRIKE PROBLEM

Nelson then reported on his conversations with Michael & Sons and the other firm that had indicated willingness to take over completion of the axle contract. Discussion of the possibility of changing suppliers resulted in the group's arriving at the conclusion that this was not an attractive alternative. If the tooling at West Coast's plant were moved out, deliveries could not commence before the early part of July. Also, if the strike ended while the tooling was being moved, West Coast could not get back into production. Procuring another set of tooling would not only be expensive but would also delay delivery for another two months, until the early part of September. And, if the strike ended while the second set of tooling was being procured, the cost of the second set of tooling would be a total loss. It also seemed unlikely that the strike would last long enough to require changing to another supplier. Of course, there was no guarantee that the strike would be short lived.

As the discussion progressed, Dailey, the assembly superintendent, announced that he had just thought of a partial solution to the problem. He suggested that Torsion Tractor build a dolly in its shops to take the place of the rear axle assembly. The dolly could be placed under the rear of the tractor at position C on the assembly line, which would permit movement of the tractor through positions D and E with the dolly in place rather than the rear axle. Tractors could then be stored outside the plant on dollies until such time as rear axles were available. Although this would not solve the delivery problem, production could proceed at a close to normal pace, with the tractors being completed to a point such that the only remaining work would be to install the axle assembly. Utilizing dollies in this fashion would prevent a shutdown of the assembly line and preceding operations. The sales manager did not feel that this was in any sense a solution to the problem of getting tractors completed; however, he did agree that dollies merited further investigation as a means of preventing a total shutdown of work on the tractors after the supply of axles was exhausted. Dailey agreed to take up the matter of the design and fabrication of the dollies with the engineering and manufacturing departments and report back to another meeting of the group on Wednesday, April 13.

On Wednesday morning, the same group that had attended the Monday meeting assembled once again in Burger's office. Dailey reported that the engineering department felt that it could easily draw up plans for a dolly that could be used in place of the rear axle assembly while the tractors were being worked on in the assembly department. The engineering department estimated that labor and materials for the dollies would cost $600 to $700 plus the cost of engineering drawings. One possibility was to build a dolly for each tractor unit, leasing the dolly with the tractor while it was stored outside the plant awaiting the axle assembly. A more economical system seemed to be to build five to ten dollies and use them only while the tractors were being worked on. Tractors could then be put on blocks while awaiting rear axles, and the dollies would be available for reuse.

However, an engineer in the engineering department had come up with still another idea that might be feasible, although considerably more expensive. The engineer suggested that it might be possible to redesign one part of the standard two-speed rear axle housing and several fittings so that standard two-speed rear axles might temporarily be used instead of the new heavy-duty axles. The engineer pointed out that installation of the standard two-speed axles would affect performance somewhat, because of the difference in gear ratios, but they would be serviceable until they could be replaced with the new heavy-duty axles when the supply of these units again became available.

The engineer estimated very roughly that the cost of modifying standard two-speed rear axles, installing them in the tractors, later removing them, and converting them back to the standard two-speed axle configuration would total about $1,500 to $1,600 per unit plus the cost of engineering work to determine what modifications would be necessary and to prepare drawings. At the production rate of 40 units per month, this solution would cost Torsion Tractor between $60,000 and $65,000 per month plus initial engineering costs.

After Dailey had completed his presentation of these two alternatives, Nelson pointed out that the second alternative, that of using the standard two-speed axles temporarily, would raise still another problem. Milwaukee Machine Tool, the firm that produced standard two-speed axles, was already working close to capacity on a single shift. Any additional two-speed axles would certainly have to be manufactured on second and third shifts for which Milwaukee would have to be paid a premium. As a first estimate, Nelson guessed that Milwaukee would be forced to charge an extra 15 percent because of the extra costs involved. At a 40-per-month delivery rate, this would add almost $20,000 more per month to the costs estimated for conversion of the axles alone.

## DISCUSSION QUESTIONS

1. At the time that the last meeting was held, what alternatives were available to Torsion Tractor? What risks and costs are associated with these alternatives? What course of action would you follow?
2. Did Torsion Tractor follow good procurement practice in obtaining its source of supply for the new axles?

# Transcontinental Aircraft Company

Gene Rock was an economic analyst in the facilities analysis unit of the missile and space division of the Transcontinental Aircraft Company. The evolution of the aircraft industry had led to the formation in most aircraft companies, Transcontinental among them, of separate divisions to handle the manufacture of missile and space vehicles apart from airframe manufacturing. At Transcontinental the missile division — later renamed the missile and space division — had been established as a division separate from the aircraft division approximately 20 years earlier.

Rock's job in the facilities analysis unit of the division was to prepare and evaluate data relating to requests for major equipment purchased by the manufacturing departments. The results of the analyses and investigations performed by Rock were included in the proposed capital budget — a total request for capital funds presented to the manufacturing department manager, the division capital expenditures committee, and the division manager. The division manager then recommended allocations of funds for capital expenditures on the basis of an evaluation of both the economic and intangible factors presented for each proposed purchase. His recommendations were passed on to the company's president and board of directors for approval.

## STRETCH PRESS REQUEST

For several years William Stensen, superintendent of the metal forming shop in which all stretch press forming was performed, had requested a new stretch press for his shop to replace two older stretch presses. A stretch press is a machine that places metal extrusions or sheets under tension.

While under tension, additional pressure is applied by means of dies or forms to obtain complex configurations. Each time the request was made, management had decided not to allocate funds for a new press.

Rock had again received a request from Stensen to include the new stretch press in this year's request for capital funds being prepared for consideration by the division manager. Although the economic and intangible factors associated with acquiring the press had been analyzed in previous years, it was necessary for Rock to reinvestigate the proposed purchase, as the condition of the existing machines and other factors changed from year to year.

Stensen's request was for a new 300-ton-capacity Simpson stretch press, model LO 300, estimated to cost $1,220,000. It would have a scrap value estimated at approximately 10 percent, or $120,000, at the end of its estimated economic life of 10 years. The new press would replace two older presses, an Eimer 300-ton press and a Simpson 90-ton press. Both presses had been installed by the company about 20 years previously. The presses had been moved several times as the manufacturing facilities were reorganized and were now in the division's metal forming shop.

As the first step in the analysis of the proposed purchase, Rock requested equipment condition reports on the machines to be replaced. These were prepared by an engineer from plant services and are shown in Figures 1 and 2. As shown in Figure 1, the Eimer press was acquired at a cost of

## FIGURE 1

### Equipment Condition Report, Eimer Press

EQUIPMENT CONDITION REPORT–EIMER

Equipment Condition Report

Property No. __4-FH-3547__          Serial No. ____235689____
Location: Plant __Missile__          Shop ____Metal forming____
Acquisition cost __$90,000__          Modifications __$10,000__
Manufacturer __Engineering Research Corporation__
Description and capacity __Hydraulic stretch press, Eimer--300-ton__
Condition code ___0-3___          Est. rebuild cost _____
Remarks __Machine is too slow.  Maintenance has been extremely high.  Overage__
__Machine has been modified with some parts deleted.  Five-year labor maintenance.__
__2,000 hours @$10.00 = $20,000__

Recommended disposition __Scrap.__

Survey made by __N. S. Wood__          Date ____9/26/80____

$90,000. Subsequently the press was modified, and $10,000 was spent on new jaws to hold material in the machine. Although it was not shown on the equipment condition report, Rock determined from other records and discussions with the plant services engineer that the machine was one of the first designed and built by that manufacturer. The condition code of O-3 on the equipment condition report indicated that in the opinion of the plant services engineer the machine was in poor condition and could probably be disposed of only as scrap. The Eimer press was used principally for the shaping of extrusions.

As shown in Figure 2, the Simpson press was acquired at a cost of $60,000. Although rated at 90 tons, the press had been "beefed up" to the point where it was approximately the equivalent of a 135-ton machine. The machine was used principally for sheet work but could also handle extrusions. The bed of the machine had been lengthened so that the original length limit of 22 feet for sheets had been increased to 32 feet. The Simpson press as shown on the equipment report was also in O-3 condition, although the plant services engineer estimated that at a cost of about $75,000 for parts and labor this press could be rebuilt to factory-new condition. As scrap the machines had a market value of about enough to cover the cost of removal.

To get more information regarding the request for the new stretch

FIGURE 2

Equipment Condition Report, Simpson Press

EQUIPMENT CONDITION REPORT–SIMPSON

Equipment Condition Report

Property No. __4-FH-6733__     Serial No. __345902__
Location: Plant __Missile__     Shop __Metal forming__
Acquisition cost __$60,000__     Modifications _____
Manufacturer __Simpson Corporation__
Description and capacity __Hydraulic stretch press, Simpson--90-ton__
Condition code __O-3__     Est. rebuild cost __$75,000__
Remarks __Maintenance has been high. Machine is too slow for present needs.__
__Overage. Five-year labor maintenance. 2,600 hours @ $10.00 = $26,000__

Recommended disposition __Scrap or rebuild completely.__

Survey made by __N. S. Wood__     Date __9/27/80__

press, Rock arranged to meet with the shop superintendent, Stensen. At the meeting Stensen recounted some of the history of the two presses. When acquired, the presses had operated rather poorly with considerable downtime — Stensen estimated it at about 50 percent. Eight years ago both machines had been extensively rebuilt. At that time particular attention was given to improving the hydraulic systems, which subsequently resulted in a considerable reduction in the downtime of the machines.

Stensen pointed out that, even though the machines were presently operating satisfactorily, they might fail completely at any time. Because of their ages and condition, their remaining life was unpredictable — they might last for five years or more or they might last only a week. He was convinced that, because of the heavy work load, sudden failure of these vital machines would be disastrous. When they failed, the company would have to replace them or subcontract all stretch press forming.

## REPLACEMENT PRESS

Stensen then recounted some of the operating difficulties with the present machines and the advantage of the new stretch press. One of the principal advantages of the new stretch press was that it would have curved jaws that conformed to the configuration of the part instead of the straight jaws on the present machines. The advantage of curved jaws was that aluminum sheets being stretched into curved shapes would stretch more evenly and with less loss of material because the transition from the straight jaw to the final curved shape would be reduced or eliminated. Substantial savings would result in lower material costs due to a reduction of the amount of metal trimmed away and in fewer losses from rejections because of uneven stretching. In addition, the jaws in the new machine would be movable and would be fully powered so that the forces that stretched the metal could be applied more evenly and in the correct direction.

From the standpoint of ease of setup, the new machine would result in substantial time savings. The jaws on the proposed machine were wedge action, which eliminated the necessity of inserting shims in the jaws to achieve even gripping of the material. Inserting shims on the old machines was a job that required a considerable amount of skill and, if improperly done, could result in a safety hazard. If the material was not gripped evenly, there was the possibility of the material's flying out of the jaws when pressure was applied.

The new press would also be equipped with newly designed more sensitive automatic controls and tension-sensing and recording devices. These would permit a much closer regulation of the stretching process and greater evenness of stretching in the material with resultant improvement in quality. The improved controls on the new press offered the possibility of extending the range of materials that could be formed by the stretching method. The

increasing use of materials such as steel and titanium that could not be handled on the old stretch presses was a major factor in reducing the usefulness
of the old presses in the missile and space field.

Upon further investigation of the uses and capabilities of the present
and proposed machines, Rock discovered that the stretch presses were used
mainly for forming aluminum parts. This method of forming had been
found to be very useful in the manufacture of aircraft parts because of the
stretch press's ability to obtain compound curves that could not be done by
any other process. As an example, stretch forming was used to produce aircraft skins in one piece that were formerly fabricated from several pieces.
This reduced assembly time and increased the structural strength of the
skin.

He also discovered that over 50 percent of the work done on the stretch
presses was support work for the aircraft division. Part of the reason for the
high proportion of support work was that the metal forming shop of the
missile and space division had production capability that the aircraft division
lacked. As a matter of fact, in addition to the work done in the missile and
space division shops, the aircraft division found it necessary also to contract
for some of its requirements for stretch-formed parts with other aircraft
manufacturers with stretch-forming capacity. Another reason for the high
proportion of support work for the aircraft division was the fact that aluminum parts of the sort that could be formed on the old stretch presses were
not required in as great quantities as formerly because of changes in the
design of missiles and space vehicles. The missile and space division stretch
presses consequently were not used to capacity by divisional work.

The proposed machine, however, was capable of handling either aluminum or light gauges of the harder metals, such as steel or titanium. Improved automatic controls were a prime reason for the added capability, as
precise control was required of the pressure and elongation forces between
the yield point (the point at which the stress causes a permanent set to take
place in the metal) and the ultimate fracture point, which differed by as little
as 10 percent.

At one time the possibility of obtaining an 800-ton dual-control press
rather than a 300-ton press was considered as this would permit the forming
of a wider variety of parts made from steel and titanium. The cost of over
$3 million, however, seemed to eliminate this alternative as a reasonable one
because future requirements for parts made of stronger metals were difficult to determine and because it was felt that explosion or other forming
technologies might one day be more suitable processes.

## COST DATA

Having familiarized himself with the circumstances surrounding the
request for the new press, Rock turned his attention to collecting actual and
estimated operating cost data on the present and proposed machines. This

information was used in preparing the basic comparisons of operating cost on which the economic justification of the new machine would be based. The major sources of data were cost accounting records containing operating information on the present machines and Stensen, the superintendent of the metal forming shop, who provided some estimates on costs of operation of the old machines as well as of the proposed press. To corroborate some of the estimates, Rock also consulted with the engineer from plant services who had prepared the condition reports shown in Figures 1 and 2. The engineer was sufficiently familiar with the equipment so that he could judge roughly the reasonableness of some of the estimates such as scrap loss and labor savings.

The cost accounting records indicated that about 12,000 hours of direct labor were charged to the Eimer and Simpson presses each year. The average labor rate for workers on these machines was $10 per hour. Stensen estimated that the improved automation controls and wedge action jaws on the new press would result in savings of about 4,000 hours per year in direct labor.

While it also might be possible to reduce the labor rate per hour on the new machine because of the lowered skill requirements in setting the jaws, Stensen felt that it would be difficult to prove that the workers now running the two old machines could really be replaced by lower-paid workers. In explaining this point Stensen also pointed out that, although the labor rate might stay about the same, it would certainly be easier to keep the new machine working at full capacity in spite of absences and turnover of employees. In the past, if the worker who was skilled in setting the jaws and operating the stretch controls was absent or left the company, there was a substantial temporary decrease in production.

Because of the curved jaws and automatic controls on the proposed press, there would be a substantial reduction in material requirements. The straight jaws on the old machines made it necessary to allow a large excess of material on either side of the curved section being formed so that the metal could make the transition from a curved to a straight surface between the die and the jaws without undue stressing or wrinkling. The amount of excess metal that had to be removed and scrapped after the forming process often amounted to 50 percent of the total amount of material used. The curved jaws of the new machine would reduce the transition and reduce the scrap loss by 75 percent or more in many cases. Also, the lack of precise control and even application of pressure on the old presses often resulted in additional material loss when the entire part was ruined in the stretching process and had to be scrapped. Much of this would be eliminated by the new press. Based on this, Stensen and Rock arrived at a joint estimate that at present operating rates the new press would reduce material costs from $300,000 per year on the old machines to $150,000 per year on the new press, a savings of $150,000 per year.

In contrast to the complete material loss when parts had to be scrapped, some of the parts were salvaged by reworking in various ways. Cost accounting records revealed an average of about $58,000 a year of rework cost attributable to the old Eimer and Simpson presses. Stensen said that these costs would be almost entirely eliminated by the new press.

Having determined the direct savings that would result from the acquisition of the new press, Rock turned his attention to the indirect savings that might occur. Stensen indicated that supervision of the operators of the new press would be simplified but that there would be no chance of reducing costs since none of the supervisors could be eliminated. Similarly, the time of other indirect labor, such as forklift drivers, would be reduced, but no employees would be directly eliminated by the installation of the proposed press.

The accounting department, however, charged some services such as janitorial services, time keeping, shop supplies, and so on, on the basis of direct labor-hours. Because the new press would require fewer labor-hours, there would be a saving by a reduction in this charge. The accounting department grouped all these items under the name "nonlabor maintenance" and charged these items at $7 per direct labor-hour. There was another indirect charge made by the accounting department that was also based on direct labor-hours: fringe benefits. The accounting department estimated that fringe benefits amounted to 14 percent of the direct labor rate.

The pro-rata nonlabor maintenance charge mentioned did not include the cost of maintenance above the normal amounts. The accounting department classified these additional maintenance costs as indirect costs but maintained separate records of the amounts expended for various machines. In the case of the Eimer and Simpson presses, which would be replaced, additional maintenance was averaging about $8,000 per year. Stensen guessed that there would be no such charges against the new press, and his judgment was confirmed by the plant services engineer. This information completed all the data that Rock required for his economic analysis.

Rock began his analysis by filling out the "Equipment Investment Comparison" sheet (Figure 3), on which he summarized all the pertinent cost information. The data sheet was divided into three parts. In the first part the investment in the existing equipment and in the proposed equipment was compared. In the second part the yearly utilization of the present and proposed equipment was recorded. In the third part annual operating cost estimates were computed and compared.

The final step in the economic analysis was the calculation of the rate of return and payoff period after income taxes. To do this it was necessary to fill out the "Investment Analysis" (Figure 4) and to determine the net cash flow after income taxes. On this form were recorded the cash flows, depreciation, and income taxes resulting from the proposed investment for each of the ten years of the life of the equipment.

The totals from the analysis in Figure 3 were recorded on lines 1 to 4 of

## FIGURE 3

### Capital Equipment Investment Analysis Data Sheet

DATE: _____

EQUIPMENT _____

USING ORGANIZATION _____ ANALYST _____

#### EQUIPMENT INVESTMENT COMPARISON

PRESENT EQUIPMENT | PROPOSED EQUIPMENT

1. Description _____    Description _____
   _____

2. Date acquired _____    Installation date _____
3. Original cost _____    Installed cost _____
4. Equipment life _____    Equipment life _____
5. Est. market value _____    Est. scrap value _____
6. Condition code _____
7. Est. rebuild cost _____

#### UTILIZATION COMPARISON

8. Total direct labor hours per year _____    Total direct labor hours per year _____
9. Labor rate/hour _____    Labor rate/hour _____

#### ANNUAL OPERATIONS COMPARISON

| Direct Costs: | Estimated | Estimated | Savings |
|---|---|---|---|
| 10. Labor | | | |
| 11. Materials | | | |
| 12. Scrap rework | | | |
| 13. Tooling | | | |
| 14. Inspection | | | |
| 15. Other | | | |
| 16. TOTAL DIRECT | | | |
| | | | |
| Indirect Costs: | | | |
| 17. Labor | | | |
| 18. Nonlabor maintenance | | | |
| 19. Material handling | | | |
| 20. Fringe costs | | | |
| 21. Power | | | |
| 22. Maintenance | | | |
| 23. Other | | | |
| 24. TOTAL INDIRECT | | | |
| 25. Other 1st yr. costs | | | |
| 26. TOTAL COST | | | |

Figure 4 and summarized on line 5. The payment (negative cash flow) for the initial investment in the proposed machine was assumed to occur at the beginning of year 1 (considered as time 0) and was entered on line 1 in

283

## FIGURE 4

### Investment Analysis

Equipment:  Stretch Press                                        Date:  10/21/80

| Savings Analysis | 0 | 1 | 2 | 3 | 4 | 5 | 6 | 7 | 8 | 9 | 10 | 10[a] |
|---|---|---|---|---|---|---|---|---|---|---|---|---|
| | | | | | | *End of Year* | | | | | | |
| 1. Asset cost | | | | | | | | | | | | |
| 2. Direct savings | | | | | | | | | | | | |
| 3. Indirect savings | | | | | | | | | | | | |
| 4. Gain on sale of asset | | | | | | | | | | | | |
| 5. Total cash flow before income tax | | | | | | | | | | | | |
| 6. Less depreciation | | | | | | | | | | | | |
| 7. Taxable income (5 minus 6) | | | | | | | | | | | | |
| 8. Federal income tax[b] | | | | | | | | | | | | |
| 9. Cash flow after income tax (5 minus 8) | | | | | | | | | | | | |
| 10. Cumulative cash flow after income tax | | | | | | | | | | | | |

[a]Salvage value.
[b]Based on current normal tax rate plus surtax rate.

FIGURE 5

---

## Depreciation Schedule

Item: _____

Original Cost: _____

Est. Salvage Value: _____

Amount Depreciated: _____

Asset Life: _____

| Year | Depreciation Fraction | Annual Depreciation |
|------|----------------------|---------------------|
| 1 | _____ | _____ |
| 2 | _____ | _____ |
| 3 | _____ | _____ |
| 4 | _____ | _____ |
| 5 | _____ | _____ |
| 6 | _____ | _____ |
| 7 | _____ | _____ |
| 8 | _____ | _____ |
| 9 | _____ | _____ |
| 10 | _____ | _____ |

---

column 0 as a negative figure. Cash savings for each of the ten years were recorded on lines 2 and 3. On line 4, the second column for the tenth year shows the positive cash flow that would result from the sale of the asset at the end of its economic life. It was recorded separately to distinguish it from the taxable cash flow resulting from the operating savings realized in the tenth year. Total cash flow before income tax was found by adding lines 1 to 4 and was shown on line 5.

The depreciation charges for each year were computed on a "Depreciation Schedule" (Figure 5) and recorded on line 6 of Figure 4. The company used the sum-of-years'-digits method for computing depreciation. The depreciation charges were then subtracted from the cash flow in line 5 to give taxable income on line 7. Federal corporate income tax was computed and the amount of the tax was indicated on line 8. Income tax was then subtracted from the cash flow in line 5 to give the cash flow after income taxes shown in line 9. Line 10 was the cumulative cash flow after income taxes and indicated the "crude" payoff period after taxes when the figures therein changed from minus to plus.

The cash flow after income tax was entered on the form "Calculations to Determine Prospective Rate of Return" (Figure 6). The form was used to find the rate of interest at which the present value of the net cash flow over the expected life of the asset equals zero. The rate of return found in Figure 6 was then recorded together with the crude payoff period from line 10 of

## FIGURE 6

Item:   Stretch Press

### Calculations to Determine Prospective Rate of Return

| Year | Cash Flow After Income Tax | Present Value | | | | | |
|---|---|---|---|---|---|---|---|
| | | PV Factor S.P. | P.V. | P.V Factor S.P. | P.V. | P.V. Factor S.P. | P.V. |
| 0 | | | | | | | |
| 1 | | | | | | | |
| 2 | | | | | | | |
| 3 | | | | | | | |
| 4 | | | | | | | |
| 5 | | | | | | | |
| 6 | | | | | | | |
| 7 | | | | | | | |
| 8 | | | | | | | |
| 9 | | | | | | | |
| 10 | | | | | | | |
| 10 | | | | | | | |
| Sum | | | | | | | |

FIGURE 7

Investment Analysis Summary

Item:   Stretch Press

| | |
|---|---|
| Asset cost | _____ |
| Total income (savings) after income tax | _____ |
| Net income after income tax | _____ |
| Crude payoff period after income tax | _____ |
| Rate of return after income tax | _____ |

Figure 4 on the "Investment Analysis Summary" (Figure 7). This last form also indicated the cost of the asset, the total savings (before allowing for investment costs), and the net income (after allowing for investment costs).

## CAPITAL BUDGET REQUEST

The economic comparison of the present and proposed presses and the investment analysis of the proposed press were contained in Rock's report to his supervisor, Boyd Cutter, facilities analysis unit manager. It was Cutter's job to supervise the assembly of all departmental requests for authorization for capital expenditures into a single capital budget request that was presented to the division manager. In addition to assembling the budget requests, the facilities analysis unit served as a first screening step in the submission of capital requests.

The system worked in general as follows. Individual departments initiated all requests for capital expenditures. The originating department identified the equipment or other capital improvement desired and made an estimate of the item or items that was submitted to the facilities analysis unit. Along with this information the originating department was expected to provide a justification for the request in the form of supporting data or arguments.

Besides processing the requests into a single document for presentation to the division manager, the facilities analysis unit had the authority to delete items from the budget request if there was insufficient justification or if the items were obviously of low priority as compared with other requests.

When the system was first initiated, many items were deleted; but with experience the requesting departments were able to anticipate which marginal items were likely to be deleted, and they refrained from submitting them. In cases where requests were deleted, the facilities analysis unit generally discussed the item with the requesting department and explained the reasons why the item was deleted. In most instances, the person initiating the request agreed to the deletion of the item as a result of this discussion.

The kind of analysis done by Rock on the stretch press was one method used to determine whether to include an item in the budget request. On smaller items, typically those items under $50,000, detailed analyses of the type developed for the stretch press were not made. Instead, the items were included in the budget request if, on the basis of a more general statement of need, they seemed to warrant inclusion in the budget. The type of analysis performed on the stretch press was not always applicable on all items over $50,000 that were requested to provide new capabilities. The type of analysis used for the stretch press was used only for equipment that was intended to replace existing equipment or methods and where comparisons could be made of the relative costs of operation of present and proposed equipment. On new program equipment, such comparisons were usually not possible, and, instead, the items were assigned priorities based on subjective estimates of the importance of the items. These estimates were made by the facilities analysis unit.

Another important function of the facilities analysis unit was to obtain an accurate cost estimate for any item requested. Usually this was obtained by actually contacting vendors and obtaining price quotations. Taxes, transportation charges, installation costs, peripheral equipment costs, and other extra costs were also added to the base equipment price — items that the requesting department often neglected to consider. As an example, in the case of the stretch press, the original departmental cost estimate was $1,000,000, in contrast to the final estimate of $1,220,000 for the press, which included allowances for installation charges and additional equipment. The facilities analysis unit was extremely careful in obtaining good cost estimates, as management was reluctant to make special authorizations for extra funds when cost estimates were too low.

After the cost estimates were obtained and the analyses of the requests were completed, the facilities analysis unit assembled the requests into a tentative manufacturing department capital assets budget for the next six months. Items lacking sufficient justification by the requesting department, items that were clearly not economically sound, and items that were not compatible with the long-range business plan for the division were not included in the tentative budget. The budget was divided into sections for the three major current programs in the manufacturing department. Figure 8 is a copy of the page of manufacturing department capital budget request summary on which the stretch press request appeared. For each item listed, a cost estimate, rate of return, date required, lead time, program classification (shown in column PRG), and cash outlay commitment by quarter were in-

FIGURE 8

Departmental Capital Budget Request

Division: *Missile and Space*
Department: *Manufacturing*      Budget Period: *First half*

| Item Number | Item | Capital Amount | Expense Amount | Total Amount | Rate of Return | PRG | Date Required | Lead Time | Commitments by Quarter (in thousands) | | | |
|---|---|---|---|---|---|---|---|---|---|---|---|---|
| | | | | | | | | | 1st | 2nd | 3rd | 4th |
| 18. | Hydraulic brake press | $61,000 | $12,000 | $73,000 | A | PI. | | | | | | |
| 19. | Induction furnace | 63,000 | 5,000 | 68,000 | 7 | S.S. | | | | | | |
| 20. | Stretch press | 1,220,000 | | 1,220,000 | * | S.S. | | | | | | |
| 21. | Profile mill | 250,000 | 5,000 | 255,000 | 27 | P.R. | | | | | | |
| 22. | 20-foot press brake | 175,000 | | 175,000 | D | PI. | | | | | | |
| 23. | Inert gas welding chamber | 390,000 | | 390,000 | A | P.R. | | | | | | |
| 24. | Precision grinders (2) | 160,000 | | 160,000 | 22 | S.S. | | | | | | |
| 25. | Electric discharge machine | 120,000 | 6,000 | 126,000 | C | PI. | | | | | | |
| 26. | Vertical boring mill | 500,000 | 195,000 | 695,000 | B | P.R. | | | | | | |
| 27. | 12-foot squaring shear | 75,000 | 12,000 | 87,000 | D | P.R. | | | | | | |
| 28. | Vertical profile mills (3) | 365,000 | 25,000 | 390,000 | 31 | S.S. | | | | | | |

*Rate was shown on original summary.

289

# FIGURE 9

## Capital Budget Item Justification

---

First half, 1982

Division: Missile and Space

Department: Manufacturing

Quantity: 1    Description: Modern stretch press, 300-ton capacity

Manufacturer: Simpson    Model or Type: LO 300    S.C.C. No.: _____

Alternative Mfg.: _____    Model or Type: _____    S.C.C. No.: _____

Justification (Airplane model(s) process spec. no., etc.):

    The extrusion and skin stretch-forming facilities available within the missile and space division are technologically and functionally obsolete. The existing machines considered for modernization and replacement were built 20 yrs. ago and deteriorated to the point where replacement is mandatory if in-plant capacity and capability are to be maintained.

    It is proposed that a Simpson model LO 300 with 32-foot length capacity, elongation and yield-sensing devices, and 80-inch-wide curved sheet holding jaws be procured to replace and modernize the existing stretch press facility. The proposed machine will have two tension cylinders capable of exerting 150 tons at any angle of pull. It will be capable of forming high-tensile steels and exotic materials at slow speeds and will be equipped for elevated temperature part forming.

    Out-plant stretch-forming capacity will continue to be utilized. The upgrading of existing in-plant facilities is not intended to change existing "make or buy" policies but will permit a more efficient operation and an extension of stretch-form capabilities to include the high-strength materials which will be used on advanced programs.

    Acquisition of a modern stretch press will result in operating economies. Less excess material is required using curved jaws, scrap will be reduced by proper elongation control, maintenance and repairs to the old machinery will be eliminated, and labor requirements reduced. The new machine will cost approximately $220,000. Savings will provide a  *  rate of return and a  *  year payoff period. The resale of the two existing machines will realize approximately enough to cover their removal cost. The existing machines have been recommended for retirement by the facility department. These machines will be scrapped upon activation of the requested machine.

    It is recognized that some programs included in the division business plan could require stretch-forming equipment in the 1,600-ton range (800 tons per tension cylinder). The replacement of the existing obsolete equipment with a machine of this size has been considered. However, configuration, size, and process definition for the advanced projects (spinning, stretching, explosive forming) are not considered firm enough for the investment required (approximately $3 million). It has been concluded that the requested 300-ton press would be adequate for the majority of future vehicle forming requirements and could most efficiently produce current and anticipated transport work loads.

    The deisgn of future aircraft and space vehicles utilizing such materials as René 41; B120VCA titanium; 7020T6, 2024T81, and T86 aluminum; stainless steel; magnesium; and beryllium places a greater demand on close control of forming parameters than do present-day aircraft materials. It is recognized that the technological as well as economic penalties for not having the proper capability will impose engineering design limitations and force utilization of inadequate machine tools. Reliance on outside capabilities usually presents intolerable time delays. The decision to maintain a modernized stretch-form and wrap capability favors the proposed request.

Requested by: _____

Approved by: _____

Approved by: _____
    Program Manager

| Item number | Capital amount | Expense amount | Total amount | Rate of return | PRG | Date required | Lead time | Commitments by quarter in thousands | | | |
|---|---|---|---|---|---|---|---|---|---|---|---|
| | | | | | | | | 1st | 2d | 3d | 4th |
| | $1,220,000 | | $1,220,000 | * | All | 15 mo. | 12 mo. | 1220 | | | |

*Data were shown on original summary.

cluded. Only those items costing over $50,000 were listed on this form in detail. Those items costing less than that were included in a lump-sum amount at the end of each budget section, and the only detailed information supplied was a simple listing of the names of the larger items making up about 65 percent of the lump sum. Items costing over $50,000 that were not analyzed for rate of return because they did not replace present equipment were given priorities of A, B, C, or D in the rate-or-return column. The exact meaning of the priorities was never spelled out in detail; however, everyone agreed that "A" items were absolutely necessary and that "D" items were not very critical. There was no formula or scale for converting a letter priority to a percentage rate of return for comparison purposes.

Each line item on the form in Figure 8 was also supplemented by a summary sheet with written discussions to justify the item. The page of the manufacturing department capital budget request that contains summary information regarding the stretch press is shown in Figure 9. The purpose of the supplementary sheets was to provide an opportunity to present a discussion of the intangible factors bearing on the purchase of the equipment.

After the tentative budget was prepared by the facilities analysis unit, there was a series of reviews, at any one of which an item might be deleted. The first review was by the manufacturing department manager and a committee of executives from the department. The second review was by the division capital expenditures committee. This committee analyzed the requests of the various departments in detail, made constructive criticisms on the presentations, and, in some cases, deleted an item or sent the request back to the originating department for further justification. The third step was review and approval by the division manager and his executive committee. Final review and approval of the companywide capital budget was by the president and board of directors of Transcontinental.

In the case of the stretch press, Rock's initial request was returned by Cutter, head of the facilities analysis unit, for a more detailed justification of the intangible benefits stated. Rock forwarded this request to Stensen, superintendent of the metal forming shop. The additional justification provided by Stensen did not convince Cutter that the proposed stretch press was completely compatible with the company's long-range business plan. However, it appeared that the issue was sufficiently critical to include the request in the tentative budget, which Cutter knew would receive further review at a higher level.

The manufacturing department manager and committee of executives from the department reviewed the budget and approved the stretch press as one item to be included in the budget request sent on to division level for review. At the division level, the capital expenditures committee reviewed the stretch press proposal along with other items in the budget and submitted the budget to the division manager.

During the deliberations of the division's capital expenditures committee, the stretch press proposal was discussed at some length, partly because of the substantial investment involved and partly because two committee members were convinced that this was a questionable investment for the division.

One committee member pointed out that the projected return on the investment was lower than the rate for other proposals and that the press capability did not seem compatible with the long-range business plan for the division. He said, "Since the division will be primarily concerned with making missiles out of steel, titanium, and the harder metals, a press to form aluminum and light-gauge metals may well be useless to us in the near future. There is a very likely possibility that we will not be making anything out of aluminum before long. Here we have an analysis based upon an economic life of ten years. Why, we can't even be sure what we'll be doing in five years, let alone ten years."

The other objector said, "Even if the present presses do fail, we can farm out the skin forming work to other aircraft manufacturers."

Another committee member pointed out, "Yes, but if we do we will have to pay for their overhead and profit as well as for transporting the formed sheets 1,000 or 2,000 miles. On this basis the investment in the proposed press is even more attractive."

Another member said, "That's very true. In addition, we would have no control over the production scheduling for our work. This could be disastrous to production schedules for the aircraft division. After all, we do a considerable amount of support work for them in our shops."

To this the first objector replied, "Well, if the aircraft division needs the press so bad, why don't they buy one themselves, instead of tying up over a million of our money?"

Another member countered, "But the fact remains that half the work done on the press is for the missile and space division. It seems to me that we are taking entirely too narrow a view of this matter. We should consider this kind of proposal not only from the division's standpoint, but also from the standpoint of doing what is best for the entire company."

Because opinion in the committee was rather sharply divided, it was decided that the proposal should be submitted to the division manager with the arguments on both sides of the question.

## DISCUSSION QUESTIONS

1. Make the necessary calculations to evaluate the proposed purchase of the new stretch press.
2. What additional factors should be taken into account beyond those discussed in the case?
3. How do you evaluate the procedures established in this company for making capital equipment decisions?
4. Assume that you are the division manager. What would your decision be?

# U.S. Fabrication Company

The U.S. Fabrication Company had received a production contract to manufacture 40 cabinets to house electrical equipment in Army tanks. This order was to be produced according to a prototype that had been designed and built by U.S. Fabrication under an earlier developmental contract. The design of the cabinet was rather complex to protect the equipment against physical damage and excessive moisture. Further, it was necessary to ventilate the cabinet. The following year, shortly after the cabinet was in production, the Army decided to purchase 2,800 more cabinets and entered into negotiations with U.S. Fabrication for a follow-on order.

On June 29, the cost estimating staff of U.S. Fabrication received authorization to prepare a technical and cost proposal for manufacture of the cabinets. The proposal was due no later than July 21. At the time the proposal study was undertaken, U.S. Fabrication was manufacturing the 40 cabinets on the production contract and had completed approximately 20 of these units. The request for quotations for the new production program involved 2,800 additional cabinets. Proposals were being solicited by the Army from several companies, and it was imperative that the proposal prepared by U.S. Fabrication be competitive. There were certain factors to be considered:

1. The contract would be awarded in September with production to start at once.
2. No request for new facilities would be allowed.
3. Tooling and/or testing equipment, if required, could be charged against the contract.

S. E. Paulsen, director of the planning department, was responsible for preparation of the cost estimate. In making the proposal, Paulsen called in people from finance, cost accounting, production, and purchasing. It was decided that bidding and cost procedures that had been used in the past would not be sufficient. For example, estimating the cost of purchased parts and material on the basis of past experience would not suffice. Paulsen intended to contact suppliers and get commitments from them in terms of the lowest prices they would quote. Quantities ordered, upon which quoted prices would be based, would be for the entire contract. Further, if any parts were standard and were used on other jobs, prices quoted were to reflect lower prices made possible by larger quantities resulting from companywide purchases.

## ESTIMATING COSTS

Costs of manufacture of these cabinets were forecast in great detail. First, performance on the 40-cabinet order was carefully analyzed. Table 1 shows projected costs (8.6 percent higher than the contract estimate) on the first production contract for 40 cabinets. These costs were based on actual costs for 20 cabinets completed, plus an estimate of costs likely to be incurred to complete the remaining work. Based on the completed 20 units, it appeared that the 40-cabinet contract would follow a 90 percent improvement curve. The improvement curve for previous work of the same general type, however, had ranged from a low of 77 percent to a high of 95 percent.

Paulsen held a meeting with the manufacturing group to develop ways to reduce cost on the follow-on contract. He prepared the following questions as a means of stimulating ideas for reducing costs:

1. Could raw material costs be reduced by purchasing metal to actual cutting size?
2. Could quality rejections of the final product be reduced by adding inspection at critical points in the manufacturing process?
3. Should a straight-line technique be used to assemble the cabinets? Could conveyors be used to facilitate assembly?
4. Although the tools used to manufacture the 40 cabinets could be used for this contract, should new tools be manufactured? (New production tooling would cost $120,000 and could reduce production labor costs by 6 percent.)
5. Could inventories be reduced by careful scheduling?

Paulsen felt quite confident about winning the contract. He knew that U.S. Fabrication was the only company that had experience in building cabinets of this type and that specifications in the proposal were those established by U.S. Fabrication in its original developmental contract. Furthermore, management had indicated its willingness to reduce profits to 5 percent, if necessary, to get the contract.

TABLE 1

Total Projected Manufacturing Costs for 40 Cabinets on
First Production Contract

| Costs | Cabinet Structure | Internal Brackets | Miscellaneous | Total |
|---|---|---|---|---|
| Tool labor | | | $ 5,820 | $ 5,820 |
| Tool material | | | 528 | 528 |
| Inspection labor | $ 558 | | 75 | 633 |
| Production labor | 17,175 | $ 948 | | 18,123 |
| Manufacturing over-head | 29,939 | 1,602 | 9,039 | 40,580 |
| Production material | 30,690 | 2,931 | 840 | 34,461 |
| Total | $78,362 | $5,481 | $16,302 | $100,145 |

| | | |
|---|---|---|
| Labor rates | | |
| Tooling, | | $10.26 per hour |
| Inspection, | | 9.66 per hour |
| Production, | | 9.30 per hour |
| Overhead rates | | |
| Manufacturing, | | $15.72 per hour of direct labor |
| Administrative, | | 17.5% of manufacturing costs |

## ALTERNATIVE PRICES

Paulsen decided that three different price estimates would be prepared:

1. Based on unit costs as incurred in the first contract (see Table 1) plus 10 percent profit.
2. Using a 90 percent improvement curve, material costs from the first contract and allowing an 8 percent profit.
3. Using an 85 percent curve, an 8 percent reduction in material costs, and a 5 percent profit margin.

Paulsen knew that, even if he prepared several estimates for study, he would eventually have to make a specific recommendation. There was some justification for using a better than 90 percent improvement curve, inasmuch as this program had been planned more carefully than had previous programs. On the other hand there was a great deal of risk involved in the estimates; for example, the prices quoted by suppliers were not necessarily firm contracts. Furthermore, unforeseen production problems could occur. Finally, there was a danger of bidding much lower than the competitive situation required to get the contract.

## DISCUSSION QUESTIONS

1. Is the $120,000 for new production tooling justified?
2. Prepare the three estimates Paulsen suggested. Are there any other estimates you believe should be made based on other assumptions?
3. What bid would you recommend?
4. To what degree should the bid be based on the company's expected cost or on the probable action of competitors?

# Vernon
# Medical Clinic

*To compensate for increased patient load.*

The Vernon Medical Clinic had recently expanded its staff from five to eight doctors. With this increase, the number of patients visiting the clinic grew to the point where it became necessary to plan either for an addition to the clinic building or for construction of an entirely new facility. Because of traffic conditions and the changing character of the neighborhood in the vicinity of the clinic, it was decided to sell the clinic building and construct a new clinic in a different location.

Land acquired for the new facility was located several miles distant. Because of the topography of the site, zoning regulation, and cost considerations, it was evident early in the planning process that the new building should be of single-story construction. It was estimated that the clinic required approximately 15,000 square feet of floor space to handle current patient loads plus expected growth in the next few years.

With these general guidelines, the architect selected for the project was instructed to develop several alternative building plans, concentrating largely on different floor plans and exterior treatments. At the same time, the clinic business manager began to assemble data on specific space requirements and patterns of movement in the clinic. It was expected that two months would be spent on these preliminary studies, after which a final building design and interior layout would be determined.

The business manager first established the fact the there were 14 major requirements for space in the clinic. These are described briefly in Table 1. Estimated space requirements are also given in the table. The waiting room, offices, examination rooms, laboratory, and other work and storage areas required about 11,600 square feet of floor space. An additional 3,400 square feet was needed for hallways and miscellaneous areas, giving a total require-

## TABLE 1

### Clinic Space Requirements

| Description of Area | Code[1] | Square Feet |
|---|---|---|
| Doctors' offices (10) | D | 1,300 |
| Nurses' work areas (10) | N | 600 |
| Examination rooms (12) | E | 2,000 |
| Laboratory and X-ray | L | 500 |
| Medical records | R | 600 |
| Height, weight, and history rooms (2) | H | 200 |
| Staff lounge | S | 600 |
| Business services and accounting office | B | 1,200 |
| Staff washrooms | F | 600 |
| Patient washrooms | P | 600 |
| Medical supplies storeroom | M | 200 |
| Reception and waiting room | W | 1,800 |
| Equipment cleanup and storeroom | Q | 600 |
| Utility and janitors' room | J | 800 |
| Hallways and miscellaneous | | 3,400 |
| Total clinic requirements | | 15,000 |

[1]Identifying code used in Tables 3, 4, and 5.

ment of approximately 15,000 square feet. It was anticipated that, within a year or two of completion of construction, the clinic facility would have to provide space for 35 medical staff and employees as shown in Table 2. Patient traffic was estimated to be a maximum of 300 per day when the clinic was operating at full capacity.

There were no historical records which would indicate how much traffic there might be between the various areas in the clinic. Accordingly, very rough estimates were made of the number of trips between areas based on a limited amount of direct observation and interviews with the staff. The

## TABLE 2

### Clinic Staff and Employees at Full Capacity

| Type of Personnel | Number |
|---|---|
| M.D.'s | 10 |
| Nurses | 10 |
| X-ray and lab technicians | 4 |
| Business manager and assistant | 2 |
| Clerk typists | 3 |
| Medical records clerks | 2 |
| Receptionists | 2 |
| Maintenance and janitors | 2 |
| Total clinic employment | 35 |

## TABLE 3

### Estimated Daily Trips Between Areas by Doctors

| | D | N | E | L | R | H | S | B | F | P | M | W | Q | J |
|---|---|---|---|---|---|---|---|---|---|---|---|---|---|---|
| D | — | 190 | 440 | 40 | 20 | 20 | 20 | 10 | 20 | — | 10 | 10 | — | — |
| N | — | — | 210 | 10 | 10 | 30 | 10 | 10 | 10 | — | 10 | 10 | — | — |
| E | — | — | — | — | — | — | — | — | — | — | 10 | — | 10 | — |
| L | — | — | — | — | — | — | — | — | — | — | — | — | — | — |
| R | — | — | — | — | — | — | — | — | — | — | 10 | — | — | — |
| H | — | — | — | — | — | — | — | — | — | — | — | — | — | — |
| S | — | — | — | — | — | — | — | 10 | 20 | — | — | — | — | — |
| B | — | — | — | — | — | — | — | — | — | — | — | 10 | — | — |
| F | — | — | — | — | — | — | — | — | — | — | — | — | — | — |
| P | — | — | — | — | — | — | — | — | — | — | — | — | — | — |
| M | — | — | — | — | — | — | — | — | — | — | — | — | 10 | — |
| W | — | — | — | — | — | — | — | — | — | — | — | — | — | — |
| Q | — | — | — | — | — | — | — | — | — | — | — | — | — | — |
| J | — | — | — | — | — | — | — | — | — | — | — | — | — | — |

## TAB_E 4

### Estimated Daily Trips Between Areas by Nurses

|   | D | N | E | L | R | H | S | B | F | P | M | W | Q | J |
|---|---|---|---|---|---|---|---|---|---|---|---|---|---|---|
| D | — | 130 | 60 | 10 | 70 | 10 | 10 | — | — | — | 10 | 60 | 10 | — |
| N | — | — | 210 | 10 | 160 | 20 | 40 | 30 | 10 | — | 40 | 150 | 70 | — |
| E | — | — | — | 30 | 40 | 80 | — | — | — | — | 50 | 60 | 110 | — |
| L | — | — | — | — | 10 | 30 | 10 | — | 10 | — | 10 | 40 | — | — |
| R | — | — | — | — | — | 10 | 10 | 30 | 10 | — | 10 | 290 | — | — |
| H | — | — | — | — | — | — | — | 20 | — | — | 20 | 80 | 10 | — |
| S | — | — | — | — | — | — | — | 10 | 20 | — | — | — | — | — |
| B | — | — | — | — | — | — | — | — | 10 | — | 10 | 20 | — | — |
| F | — | — | — | — | — | — | — | — | — | — | — | — | 10 | — |
| P | — | — | — | — | — | — | — | — | — | — | — | — | — | — |
| M | — | — | — | — | — | — | — | — | — | — | — | 10 | 10 | — |
| W | — | — | — | — | — | — | — | — | — | — | — | — | — | — |
| Q | — | — | — | — | — | — | — | — | — | — | — | — | — | — |
| J | — | — | — | — | — | — | — | — | — | — | — | — | — | — |

## TABLE 5

### Estimated Daily Trips Between Areas by Patients

|   | D | N | E | L | R | H | S | B | F | P | M | W | Q | J |
|---|---|---|---|---|---|---|---|---|---|---|---|---|---|---|
| D | — | 20 | 60 | 20 | — | 40 | — | 30 | — | 10 | — | 90 | — | — |
| N | — | — | 30 | 10 | — | 20 | — | 10 | — | 10 | — | 30 | — | — |
| E | — | — | — | 70 | — | 60 | — | 20 | — | 30 | — | 370 | — | — |
| L | — | — | — | — | — | 30 | — | 20 | — | 20 | — | 60 | — | — |
| R | — | — | — | — | — | — | — | — | — | — | — | — | — | — |
| H | — | — | — | — | — | — | — | — | — | 20 | — | 80 | — | — |
| S | — | — | — | — | — | — | — | — | — | — | — | — | — | — |
| B | — | — | — | — | — | — | — | — | — | 20 | — | 60 | — | — |
| F | — | — | — | — | — | — | — | — | — | — | — | — | — | — |
| P | — | — | — | — | — | — | — | — | — | — | — | 170 | — | — |
| M | — | — | — | — | — | — | — | — | — | — | — | — | — | — |
| W | — | — | — | — | — | — | — | — | — | — | — | — | — | — |
| Q | — | — | — | — | — | — | — | — | — | — | — | — | — | — |
| J | — | — | — | — | — | — | — | — | — | — | — | — | — | — |

FIGURE 1

Alternative Clinic Floor Plans

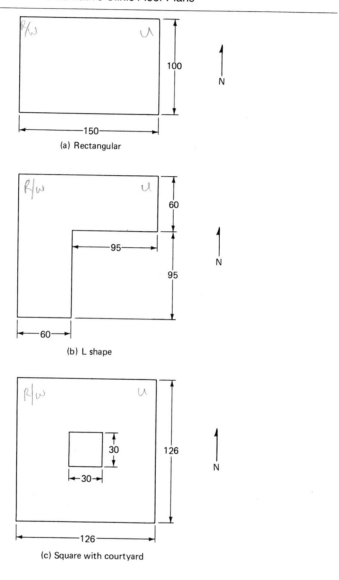

(a) Rectangular

(b) L shape

(c) Square with courtyard

most important components of traffic in the clinic were movements by the doctors, nurses, and patients. Aside from visits to the staff lounge and washrooms, other employees in the clinic tended to stay in their own work areas. In the case of the maintenance and janitorial workers, their duties required them to move about the building without any particular pattern except for the daily cleanup, when all areas were visited.

Estimates made of the number of daily trips between various areas for doctors, nurses, and patients are given in Tables 3, 4, and 5. The data in the tables are based on an assumed medical staff of ten doctors and ten nurses at full clinic capacity and a maximum daily load of 300 patients. Internal movement within areas is not shown in the tables. Also, there is no distinction for direction of movement, so that all trips between pairs of areas are summarized in one entry in the table. Because of the very approximate nature of the estimates, all data are given in multiples of ten trips.

While the traffic estimates were being prepared, the architect developed three alternative building floor plans, which are shown in Figure 1. In each case, the plan would provide about 15,000 square feet of floor space. Because of the location of access to the street and utility connections, it would be necessary to put the reception and waiting room in the northwest corner of the building and the utility room in the northeast corner. Other than these restrictions, other areas could be arranged as desired in the interior of the building.

## DISCUSSION QUESTIONS

1. Develop layouts for each of the alternative floor plans.
2. Select a floor plan and layout and justify the selection.
3. For the floor plan and layout selected, indicate how future expansion would be handled.

# York Container
# Company

The York Container Company was one of the large manufacturers in the container industry. The industry included large, medium, and small companies. Large companies had decentralized their production facilities throughout the country They engaged in active competition with each other by emphasizing customer service. Smaller manufacturers competed by offering price reductions ranging from 2 percent to 6 percent, coupled with less service.

## EMPLOYMENT FLUCTUATIONS

Myron Flint, production planning manager of the Midwest plant of York Container Company, faced a problem involving employment policy, inventory control, and production planning. Early in December the home office in New York City had dictated a new policy directing all branch plants to stabilize employment of production line workers to the extent that such a policy was possible without incurring unreasonable cost. During the past year employment of production line workers had fluctuated with seasonal requirements from a high of 150 to a low of 30.

The Midwest factory was one of the company's oldest plants and, although unionized, it enjoyed favorable relations with its employees. For years this plant had followed a policy of hiring and laying off employees as required by market demands. It drew largely upon transient workers and college students to fill labor needs during the busy summer and fall months. When college students left at the end of summer to go back to school, the factory had to hire and train a new group of employees for one or two months' work. Joe Asplund, the personnel director, estimated that it cost $640 to hire and train a new employee and $260 to terminate one. In contrast to the changes in employment levels of production line workers, the supervisory, maintenance, lithographing and enameling, and tinplate department employees were hired on a permanent basis; therefore, the number of people in these categories did not fluctuate with changes in seasonal demand.

## PLANT OPERATIONS

The Midwest plant had 12 standard can lines and 2 frozen-food container lines. Cans manufactured were of several types and sizes. Most cans were classified as open-top cans (i.e., the top was not sealed on the can until after the can had been filled). Some cans (e.g., beer cans) were manufactured differently from the typical fruit or vegetable can. These cans were sprayed with a protective coating on the inside of the can. Frozen-food containers came in a variety of materials and shapes. For example, the carton for frozen strawberries was made of paper with metal ends. The can lines produced cans at rates varying from 100 to 450 cans per minute, depending upon the size and complexity of the can. As a general rule, the larger the can, the slower the rate of production. The two frozen-food container lines produced at an average rate of 180 per minute. Standard can lines could only be used to produce beer cans and open-top cans, and frozen-food container lines could only be used to produce frozen-food containers. A list of can sizes produced at this plant, together with production rates, appears in Table 1.

A line changeover typically withdrew the line from production for two days and resulted in a cost of $1,100. This cost included wages of two maintenance workers who made the mechanical changeover, material scrap, and a charge for lost production capacity. Line operators and supervisors could be reassigned to other jobs during such changeovers. A line that had been idle, however, could be restarted again without any additional setup costs, provided that it was used to produce the same-sized can. Machine lines scheduled to be in operating condition on January 1 included two beer can lines, two frozen-food container lines, and three open-top can lines producing for can numbers 4, 5, and 9, respectively.

In past years the factory had operated two shifts during the peak season, running about ten can lines on the first shift and six on the second shift. In addition, two frozen-food container lines were operated on each shift. The average first-shift hourly pay rate for line operators and supervisors was $9.10 and $14.25, respectively. A 15 percent premium was paid to both lines operators and supervisors for second-shift operations. A 50 percent overtime premium was paid for all overtime work not exceeding 20 hours per week per crew (maximum of 4 hours per day).

TABLE 1

Cans Manufactured at Midwest Plant of York Container

| Can Number[1] | Approx. Size (diameter × height inches) | Production Rate | | Manufactur-ing Cost ($/carload) |
| --- | --- | --- | --- | --- |
| | | Cans per Line-Shift[2] | Carloads per Line-Month[3] | |
| 1 | 2¾ × 4¾ (beer) | 216,000 | 30 | 5,200 |
| 2 | 3¼ × 4¼ | 168 000 | 30 | 4,800 |
| 3 | 4 × 4¾ | 156,000 | 45 | 4,300 |
| 4 | 3 × 4¾ | 168,000 | 25 | 4,500 |
| 5 | 3½ × 2 | 168,000 | 15 | 7,000 |
| 6 | 3 × 4½ | 168,000 | 25 | 4,800 |
| 7 | 6¼ × 7 | 48,000 | 50 | 3,500 |
| 8 | 4 × 5½ | 139,000 | 50 | 4,100 |
| 9 | Miscellaneous | 144,000[4] | 25 | 4,600 |
| 10 | Frozen-food containers | 86,000 | 10 | 5,500 |

[1]Can number was a local plant code used for convenient identification. It was not related to the standard can size number used in the industry. Can numbers 9 and 10 were used to designate groups of special dimension cans or containers, most of which were infrequently produced and each of which required its own dimension identification.

[2]Line-shift is based on average output per line during eight hours of normal operation.

[3]Line-month is based on a single shift operating 21 days per month.

[4]Average production rate.

Storage space in the factory for finished cans amounted to 50,000 square feet and, when stacked to a height of 10 feet (the maximum), 500,000 cubic feet. The empty cans were stored in cardboard cartons that could be used to package the filled cans. A freight car contained approximately 3,200 cubic feet of shipping space.

There was no immediate alternative use for inside storage space; hence depreciation, building taxes, and so on were considered a fixed cost, and no specific charge was levied for the use of this space. A monthly charge, however, equal to 3 percent of the average monthly inventory value was applied to cover variable costs for capital investment in the inventory, deterioration of inventory, and other handling and maintenance costs associated with the use of both inside and outside storage space.

Adequate warehouse space was available nearby at a monthly rate of 14 cents per square foot (10 feet high). The rent was determined by the maximum number of square feet used in any single month. To load, transport, and unload a freight car lot of cans from the factory to an outside warehouse cost $450 per car. Shipments were made directly to the customers from the outside warehouses.

## PRODUCTION PLANNING

Deliveries fluctuated between 30 freight carloads per month to more than 300 cars per month. Table 2 shows the sales forecast that Flint intended to use in planning production for the next year. Flint expected to have 83

Table 2

Anticipated Inventory and Sales Forecast

| | Can Number | | | | | | | | | | Total |
| | 1 | 2 | 3 | 4 | 5 | 6 | 7 | 8 | 9 | 10 | (carloads) |
|---|---|---|---|---|---|---|---|---|---|---|---|
| Inventory on hand, Dec. 31 | 72 | | | 20 | 12 | | | | | | 104 |
| | | | | | | | | | | | |
| Sales | | | | | | | | | | | |
| January | 6 | | | 15 | 9 | | | | | | 30 |
| February | 12 | | | 25 | 12 | | | | 5 | | 54 |
| March | 21 | | | 55 | 39 | | | | 30 | | 145 |
| April | 39 | | | 55 | 57 | | | | 30 | 5 | 186 |
| May | 36 | 24 | | 50 | 42 | 40 | | | 25 | | 217 |
| June | 102 | 90 | | | | 40 | | 5 | 20 | 5 | 262 |
| July | 150 | 81 | 18 | | | 20 | | 20 | | 28 | 317 |
| August | 111 | 81 | 81 | | | 20 | 10 | | | 43 | 346 |
| September | 90 | 42 | 81 | | | | 40 | 25 | | 21 | 299 |
| October | 81 | 21 | 81 | | | | 10 | 25 | | 33 | 251 |
| November | 15 | | 54 | 15 | | | | | | 17 | 101 |
| December | 27 | | 36 | 15 | | | | | | 41 | 119 |
| Total | 690 | 339 | 351 | 230 | 159 | 120 | 60 | 75 | 110 | 193 | 2,327 |

## TABLE 3

### Workers Required to Operate Lines

| Job Title | Beer Can | Open-Top Can | Frozen-Food Container |
|---|---|---|---|
| Slitter operator | 1 | 1 | 1 |
| Tin and body blank feeder | 1 | 1 | 1 |
| Spray operator and line tender | 1 | 1 | 2 |
| Bottom end feeder | 1 | 1 | 1 |
| Inspector | 3 | 1 | 2 |
| Packer and sealer | 1 | 4 | 2 |
| Folder and stitcher | 2 | 0 | 1 |
| Checker | 1 | 1 | 1 |
| Car loaders | 2 | 1 | 1 |
| Total | 13 | 11 | 12 |

line operators and 7 supervisors on the payroll as of December 31. Finished goods inventories as of the same date were estimated to consist of 72 carloads of can number 1, 20 carloads of can number 4, and 12 carloads of can number 5.

Sales forecasts were typically optimistic, but not sufficiently so to justify reductions by the production planning group. Production plans were made so that the amount forecast for any given month was planned for production in the same month. Sufficient flexibility existed in delivery dates and production capacity that more specific planning could be delayed until the month prior to actual production. Hence, if the sales forecast called for 15 carloads of can number 4, it was sufficient to plan for the production of 15 carloads of can number 4 anytime during the month of January.

Each type of can line required a specific number of workers. Beer cans, open-top cans, and frozen-food containers required 13, 11, and 12 operators, respectively, plus a supervisor for each line. Detailed labor requirements for each of these lines are shown in Table 3.

## DISCUSSION QUESTIONS

1. What kinds of gains may accrue from stabilizing employment?
2. Outline the approach that you would take in solving York's labor stabilization problem.
3. Develop a production plan for the operation of the plant during the coming year. (Assume that inventory levels predicted by Flint for December 31 were normal for the end of the year and that there are 21 working days per month.)
4. What are some of the advantages and disadvantages of your solution?

# Appendix

## TABLE A

### Improvement Curves: Unit Values

| Unit | Improvement Ratios | | | | | | | |
|---|---|---|---|---|---|---|---|---|
| | 60% | 65% | 70% | 75% | 80% | 85% | 90% | 95% |
| 1 | 1.0000 | 1.0000 | 1.0000 | 1.0000 | 1.0000 | 1.0000 | 1.0000 | 1.0000 |
| 2 | .6000 | .6500 | .7000 | .7500 | .8000 | .8500 | .9000 | .9500 |
| 3 | .4450 | .5052 | .5682 | .6338 | .7021 | .7729 | .8462 | .9219 |
| 4 | .3600 | .4225 | .4900 | .5625 | .6400 | .7225 | .8100 | .9025 |
| 5 | .3054 | .3678 | .4368 | .5127 | .5956 | .6857 | .7830 | .8877 |
| 6 | .2670 | .3284 | .3977 | .4754 | .5617 | .6570 | .7616 | .8758 |
| 7 | .2383 | .2984 | .3674 | .4459 | .5345 | .6337 | .7439 | .8659 |
| 8 | .2160 | .2746 | .3430 | .4219 | .5120 | .6141 | .7290 | .8574 |
| 9 | .1980 | .2552 | .3228 | .4017 | .4930 | .5974 | .7161 | .8499 |
| 10 | .1832 | .2391 | .3058 | .3846 | .4765 | .5828 | .7047 | .8433 |
| 12 | .1602 | .2135 | .2784 | .3565 | .4493 | .5584 | .6854 | .8320 |
| 14 | .1430 | .1940 | .2572 | .3344 | .4276 | .5386 | .6696 | .8226 |
| 16 | .1296 | .1785 | .2401 | .3164 | .4096 | .5220 | .6561 | .8145 |
| 18 | .1188 | .1659 | .2260 | .3013 | .3944 | .5078 | .6445 | .8074 |
| 20 | .1099 | .1554 | .2141 | .2884 | .3812 | .4954 | .6342 | .8012 |
| 22 | .1025 | .1465 | .2038 | .2772 | .3697 | .4844 | .6251 | .7955 |
| 24 | .0961 | .1387 | .1949 | .2674 | .3595 | .4747 | .6169 | .7904 |
| 25 | .0933 | .1353 | .1908 | .2629 | .3548 | .4701 | .6131 | .7880 |
| 30 | .0815 | .1208 | .1737 | .2437 | .3346 | .4505 | .5963 | .7775 |
| 35 | .0728 | .1097 | .1605 | .2286 | .3184 | .4345 | .5825 | .7687 |
| 40 | .0660 | .1010 | .1498 | .2163 | .3050 | .4211 | .5708 | .7611 |
| 45 | .0605 | .0939 | .1410 | .2060 | .2936 | .4096 | .5607 | .7545 |

| | | | | | | | | |
|---|---|---|---|---|---|---|---|---|
| 50 | .7486 | .5518 | .3996 | .2838 | .1972 | .1336 | .0879 | .0560 |
| 60 | .7386 | .5367 | .3829 | .2676 | .1828 | .1216 | .0785 | .0489 |
| 70 | .7302 | .5243 | .3693 | .2547 | .1715 | .1123 | .0713 | .0437 |
| 80 | .7231 | .5137 | .3579 | .2440 | .1622 | .1049 | .0657 | .0396 |
| 90 | .7168 | .5046 | .3482 | .2349 | .1545 | .0987 | .0610 | .0363 |
| 100 | .7112 | .4966 | .3397 | .2271 | .1479 | .0935 | .0572 | .0336 |
| 120 | .7017 | .4830 | .3255 | .2141 | .1371 | .0851 | .0510 | .0294 |
| 140 | .6937 | .4718 | .3139 | .2038 | .1287 | .0786 | .0464 | .0262 |
| 160 | .6869 | .4623 | .3042 | .1952 | .1217 | .0734 | .0427 | .0237 |
| 180 | .6809 | .4541 | .2959 | .1879 | .1159 | .0691 | .0397 | .0218 |
| 200 | .6757 | .4469 | .2887 | .1816 | .1109 | .0655 | .0371 | .0201 |
| 250 | .6646 | .4320 | .2740 | .1691 | .1011 | .0584 | .0323 | .0171 |
| 300 | .6557 | .4202 | .2625 | .1594 | .0937 | .0531 | .0289 | .0149 |
| 350 | .6482 | .4105 | .2532 | .1517 | .0879 | .0491 | .0262 | .0133 |
| 400 | .6419 | .4022 | .2454 | .1453 | .0832 | .0458 | .0241 | .0121 |
| 450 | .6363 | .3951 | .2387 | .1399 | .0792 | .0431 | .0224 | .0111 |
| 500 | .6314 | .3888 | .2329 | .1352 | .0758 | .0408 | .0210 | .0103 |
| 600 | .6229 | .3782 | .2232 | .1275 | .0703 | .0372 | .0188 | .0090 |
| 700 | .6158 | .3694 | .2152 | .1214 | .0659 | .0344 | .0171 | .0080 |
| 800 | .6098 | .3620 | .2086 | .1163 | .0624 | .0321 | .0157 | .0073 |
| 900 | .6045 | .3556 | .2029 | .1119 | .0594 | .0302 | .0146 | .0067 |
| 1,000 | .5998 | .3499 | .1980 | .1082 | .0569 | .0286 | .0137 | .0062 |
| 1,200 | .5918 | .3404 | .1897 | .1020 | .0527 | .0260 | .0122 | .0054 |
| 1,400 | .5850 | .3325 | .1830 | .0971 | .0495 | .0240 | .0111 | .0048 |
| 1,600 | .5793 | .3258 | .1773 | .0930 | .0468 | .0225 | .0102 | .0044 |
| 1,800 | .5743 | .3200 | .1725 | .0895 | .0446 | .0211 | .0095 | .0040 |
| 2,000 | .5698 | .3149 | .1683 | .0866 | .0427 | .0200 | .0089 | .0037 |
| 2,500 | .5605 | .3044 | .1597 | .0806 | .0389 | .0178 | .0077 | .0031 |
| 3,000 | .5530 | .2961 | .1530 | .0760 | .0360 | .0162 | .0069 | .0027 |

## TABLE B
### Improvement Curves: Cumulative Values

| Units | Improvement Ratios | | | | | | | |
|---|---|---|---|---|---|---|---|---|
| | 60% | 65% | 70% | 75% | 80% | 85% | 90% | 95% |
| 1 | 1.000 | 1.000 | 1.000 | 1.000 | 1.000 | 1.000 | 1.000 | 1.000 |
| 2 | 1.600 | 1.650 | 1.700 | 1.750 | 1.800 | 1.850 | 1.900 | 1.950 |
| 3 | 2.045 | 2.155 | 2.268 | 2.384 | 2.502 | 2.623 | 2.746 | 2.872 |
| 4 | 2.405 | 2.578 | 2.758 | 2.946 | 3.142 | 3.345 | 3.556 | 3.774 |
| 5 | 2.710 | 2.946 | 3.195 | 3.459 | 3.738 | 4.031 | 4.339 | 4.662 |
| 6 | 2.997 | 3.274 | 3.593 | 3.934 | 4.299 | 4.688 | 5.101 | 5.538 |
| 7 | 3.216 | 3.572 | 3.960 | 4.380 | 4.834 | 5.322 | 5.845 | 6.404 |
| 8 | 3.432 | 3.847 | 4.303 | 4.802 | 5.346 | 5.936 | 6.574 | 7.261 |
| 9 | 3.630 | 4.102 | 4.626 | 5.204 | 5.839 | 6.533 | 7.290 | 8.111 |
| 10 | 3.813 | 4.341 | 4.931 | 5.589 | 6.315 | 7.116 | 7.994 | 8.955 |
| 12 | 4.144 | 4.780 | 5.501 | 6.315 | 7.277 | 8.244 | 9.374 | 10.62 |
| 14 | 4.438 | 5.177 | 6.026 | 6.994 | 8.092 | 9.331 | 10.72 | 12.27 |
| 16 | 4.704 | 5.541 | 6.514 | 7.635 | 8.920 | 10.38 | 12.04 | 13.91 |
| 18 | 4.946 | 5.879 | 6.972 | 8.245 | 9.716 | 11.41 | 13.33 | 15.52 |
| 20 | 5.171 | 6.195 | 7.407 | 8.828 | 10.48 | 12.40 | 14.61 | 17.13 |
| 22 | 5.379 | 6.492 | 7.819 | 9.388 | 11.23 | 13.38 | 15.86 | 18.72 |
| 24 | 5.574 | 6.773 | 8.213 | 9.928 | 11.95 | 14.33 | 17.10 | 20.31 |
| 25 | 5.668 | 6.909 | 8.404 | 10.19 | 12.31 | 14.80 | 17.71 | 21.10 |
| 30 | 6.097 | 7.540 | 9.305 | 11.45 | 14.02 | 17.09 | 20.73 | 25.00 |
| 35 | 6.478 | 8.109 | 10.13 | 12.72 | 15.64 | 19.29 | 23.67 | 28.86 |
| 40 | 6.821 | 8.631 | 10.90 | 13.72 | 17.19 | 21.43 | 26.54 | 32.68 |
| 45 | 7.134 | 9.114 | 11.62 | 14.77 | 18.68 | 23.50 | 29.37 | 36.47 |

| | | | | | | | | |
|---|---|---|---|---|---|---|---|---|
| 50 | 7.422 | 9.565 | 12.31 | 15.78 | 20.12 | 25.51 | 32.14 | 40.22 |
| 60 | 7.941 | 10.39 | 13.57 | 17.67 | 22.87 | 29.41 | 37.57 | 47.65 |
| 70 | 8.401 | 11.13 | 14.74 | 19.43 | 25.47 | 33.17 | 42.87 | 54.99 |
| 80 | 8.814 | 11.82 | 15.82 | 21.09 | 27.96 | 36.80 | 48.05 | 62.25 |
| 90 | 9.191 | 12.45 | 16.83 | 22.67 | 30.35 | 40.32 | 53.14 | 69.45 |
| 100 | 9.539 | 13.03 | 17.79 | 24.18 | 32.65 | 43.75 | 58.14 | 76.59 |
| 120 | 10.16 | 14.11 | 19.57 | 27.02 | 37.05 | 50.39 | 67.93 | 90.71 |
| 140 | 10.72 | 15.08 | 21.20 | 29.67 | 41.22 | 56.78 | 77.46 | 104.7 |
| 160 | 11.21 | 15.97 | 22.72 | 32.17 | 45.20 | 62.95 | 86.80 | 118.5 |
| 180 | 11.67 | 16.79 | 24.14 | 34.54 | 49.03 | 68.95 | 95.96 | 132.1 |
| 200 | 12.09 | 17.55 | 25.48 | 36.80 | 52.72 | 74.79 | 105.0 | 145.7 |
| 250 | 13.01 | 19.28 | 28.56 | 42.08 | 61.47 | 88.83 | 126.9 | 179.2 |
| 300 | 13.81 | 20.81 | 31.34 | 46.94 | 69.66 | 102.2 | 148.2 | 212.2 |
| 350 | 14.51 | 22.18 | 33.89 | 51.48 | 77.43 | 115.1 | 169.0 | 244.8 |
| 400 | 15.14 | 23.44 | 36.26 | 55.75 | 84.85 | 127.6 | 189.3 | 277.0 |
| 450 | 15.72 | 24.60 | 38.48 | 59.80 | 91.97 | 139.7 | 209.2 | 309.0 |
| 500 | 16.26 | 25.68 | 40.58 | 63.68 | 98.85 | 151.5 | 228.8 | 340.6 |
| 600 | 17.21 | 27.67 | 44.47 | 70.97 | 112.0 | 174.2 | 267.1 | 403.3 |
| 700 | 18.06 | 29.45 | 48.04 | 77.77 | 124.4 | 196.1 | 304.5 | 465.3 |
| 800 | 18.82 | 31.09 | 51.36 | 84.18 | 136.3 | 217.3 | 341.0 | 526.5 |
| 900 | 19.51 | 32.60 | 54.46 | 90.26 | 147.7 | 237.9 | 376.9 | 587.2 |
| 1,000 | 20.15 | 34.01 | 57.40 | 96.07 | 158.7 | 257.9 | 412.2 | 647.4 |
| 1,200 | 21.30 | 36.59 | 62.85 | 107.0 | 179.7 | 296.6 | 481.2 | 766.6 |
| 1,400 | 22.32 | 38.92 | 67.85 | 117.2 | 199.6 | 333.9 | 548.4 | 884.2 |
| 1,600 | 23.23 | 41.04 | 72.49 | 126.8 | 218.6 | 369.9 | 614.2 | 1001. |
| 1,800 | 24.06 | 43.00 | 76.85 | 135.9 | 236.8 | 404.9 | 678.8 | 1116. |
| 2,000 | 24.83 | 44.84 | 80.96 | 144.7 | 254.4 | 438.9 | 742.3 | 1230. |
| 2,500 | 26.53 | 48.97 | 90.39 | 165.0 | 296.1 | 520.8 | 897.0 | 1513. |
| 3,000 | 27.99 | 52.62 | 98.90 | 183.7 | 335.2 | 598.9 | 1047. | 1791. |

## TABLE C
### Present Value of a Single Payment

| Period | 5% | 6% | 7% | 8% | 9% | 10% | 12% | 15% | 20% |
|---|---|---|---|---|---|---|---|---|---|
| 1 | 0.952 | 0.943 | 0.935 | 0.926 | 0.917 | 0.909 | 0.893 | 0.870 | 0.833 |
| 2 | 0.907 | 0.890 | 0.873 | 0.857 | 0.842 | 0.826 | 0.797 | 0.756 | 0.694 |
| 3 | 0.864 | 0.840 | 0.816 | 0.794 | 0.772 | 0.751 | 0.712 | 0.658 | 0.579 |
| 4 | 0.823 | 0.792 | 0.763 | 0.735 | 0.708 | 0.683 | 0.636 | 0.572 | 0.482 |
| 5 | 0.784 | 0.747 | 0.713 | 0.681 | 0.650 | 0.621 | 0.567 | 0.497 | 0.402 |
| 6 | 0.746 | 0.705 | 0.666 | 0.630 | 0.596 | 0.564 | 0.507 | 0.432 | 0.335 |
| 7 | 0.711 | 0.665 | 0.623 | 0.583 | 0.547 | 0.513 | 0.452 | 0.376 | 0.279 |
| 8 | 0.677 | 0.627 | 0.582 | 0.540 | 0.502 | 0.467 | 0.404 | 0.327 | 0.233 |
| 9 | 0.645 | 0.592 | 0.544 | 0.500 | 0.460 | 0.424 | 0.361 | 0.284 | 0.194 |
| 10 | 0.614 | 0.558 | 0.508 | 0.463 | 0.422 | 0.386 | 0.322 | 0.247 | 0.162 |
| 11 | 0.585 | 0.527 | 0.475 | 0.429 | 0.388 | 0.350 | 0.287 | 0.215 | 0.135 |
| 12 | 0.557 | 0.497 | 0.444 | 0.397 | 0.356 | 0.319 | 0.257 | 0.187 | 0.112 |
| 13 | 0.530 | 0.469 | 0.415 | 0.368 | 0.326 | 0.290 | 0.229 | 0.163 | 0.093 |
| 14 | 0.505 | 0.442 | 0.388 | 0.340 | 0.299 | 0.263 | 0.205 | 0.141 | 0.078 |
| 15 | 0.481 | 0.417 | 0.362 | 0.315 | 0.275 | 0.239 | 0.183 | 0.123 | 0.065 |
| 16 | 0.458 | 0.394 | 0.339 | 0.292 | 0.252 | 0.218 | 0.163 | 0.107 | 0.054 |
| 17 | 0.436 | 0.371 | 0.317 | 0.270 | 0.231 | 0.198 | 0.146 | 0.093 | 0.045 |
| 18 | 0.416 | 0.350 | 0.296 | 0.250 | 0.212 | 0.180 | 0.130 | 0.081 | 0.038 |
| 19 | 0.396 | 0.331 | 0.277 | 0.232 | 0.194 | 0.164 | 0.116 | 0.070 | 0.031 |
| 20 | 0.377 | 0.312 | 0.258 | 0.215 | 0.178 | 0.149 | 0.104 | 0.061 | 0.026 |
| 21 | 0.359 | 0.294 | 0.242 | 0.199 | 0.164 | 0.135 | 0.093 | 0.053 | 0.022 |
| 22 | 0.342 | 0.278 | 0.226 | 0.184 | 0.150 | 0.123 | 0.083 | 0.046 | 0.018 |
| 23 | 0.326 | 0.262 | 0.211 | 0.170 | 0.138 | 0.112 | 0.074 | 0.040 | 0.015 |
| 24 | 0.310 | 0.247 | 0.197 | 0.158 | 0.126 | 0.102 | 0.066 | 0.035 | 0.013 |
| 25 | 0.295 | 0.233 | 0.184 | 0.146 | 0.116 | 0.092 | 0.059 | 0.030 | 0.010 |
| 30 | 0.231 | 0.174 | 0.131 | 0.099 | 0.075 | 0.057 | 0.033 | 0.015 | 0.004 |
| 35 | 0.181 | 0.130 | 0.094 | 0.068 | 0.049 | 0.036 | 0.019 | 0.008 | 0.002 |
| 40 | 0.142 | 0.097 | 0.067 | 0.046 | 0.032 | 0.022 | 0.011 | 0.004 | 0.001 |
| 45 | 0.111 | 0.073 | 0.048 | 0.031 | 0.021 | 0.014 | 0.006 | 0.002 | 0.000 |
| 50 | 0.087 | 0.054 | 0.034 | 0.021 | 0.013 | 0.009 | 0.003 | 0.001 | 0.000 |

## Interest Rate

| Period | 25% | 30% | 35% | 40% | 50% |
|--------|-------|-------|-------|-------|-------|
| 1 | 0.800 | 0.769 | 0.741 | 0.714 | 0.667 |
| 2 | 0.640 | 0.592 | 0.549 | 0.510 | 0.444 |
| 3 | 0.512 | 0.455 | 0.406 | 0.364 | 0.296 |
| 4 | 0.410 | 0.350 | 0.301 | 0.260 | 0.198 |
| 5 | 0.328 | 0.269 | 0.223 | 0.186 | 0.132 |
| 6 | 0.262 | 0.207 | 0.165 | 0.133 | 0.088 |
| 7 | 0.210 | 0.159 | 0.122 | 0.095 | 0.059 |
| 8 | 0.168 | 0.123 | 0.091 | 0.068 | 0.039 |
| 9 | 0.134 | 0.094 | 0.067 | 0.048 | 0.026 |
| 10 | 0.107 | 0.073 | 0.050 | 0.035 | 0.017 |
| 11 | 0.086 | 0.056 | 0.037 | 0.025 | 0.012 |
| 12 | 0.069 | 0.043 | 0.027 | 0.018 | 0.008 |
| 13 | 0.055 | 0.033 | 0.020 | 0.013 | 0.005 |
| 14 | 0.044 | 0.025 | 0.015 | 0.009 | 0.003 |
| 15 | 0.035 | 0.020 | 0.011 | 0.006 | 0.002 |
| 16 | 0.028 | 0.015 | 0.008 | 0.005 | 0.002 |
| 17 | 0.023 | 0.012 | 0.006 | 0.003 | 0.001 |
| 18 | 0.018 | 0.009 | 0.005 | 0.002 | 0.001 |
| 19 | 0.014 | 0.007 | 0.003 | 0.002 | 0.000 |
| 20 | 0.012 | 0.005 | 0.002 | 0.001 | 0.000 |
| 21 | 0.009 | 0.004 | 0.002 | 0.001 | 0.000 |
| 22 | 0.007 | 0.003 | 0.001 | 0.001 | 0.000 |
| 23 | 0.006 | 0.002 | 0.001 | 0.000 | 0.000 |
| 24 | 0.005 | 0.002 | 0.001 | 0.000 | 0.000 |
| 25 | 0.004 | 0.001 | 0.001 | 0.000 | 0.000 |
| 30 | 0.001 | 0.000 | 0.000 | 0.000 | 0.000 |
| 35 | 0.000 | 0.000 | 0.000 | 0.000 | 0.000 |
| 40 | 0.000 | 0.000 | 0.000 | 0.000 | 0.000 |
| 45 | 0.000 | 0.000 | 0.000 | 0.000 | 0.000 |
| 50 | 0.000 | 0.000 | 0.000 | 0.000 | 0.000 |

TABLE D

Present Value of an Annuity

| Period | Interest Rate | | | | | | | | |
|---|---|---|---|---|---|---|---|---|---|
| | 5% | 6% | 7% | 8% | 9% | 10% | 12% | 15% | 20% |
| 1 | 0.952 | 0.943 | 0.935 | 0.926 | 0.917 | 0.909 | 0.893 | 0.870 | 0.833 |
| 2 | 1.859 | 1.833 | 1.808 | 1.783 | 1.759 | 1.736 | 1.690 | 1.626 | 1.528 |
| 3 | 2.723 | 2.673 | 2.624 | 2.577 | 2.531 | 2.487 | 2.402 | 2.283 | 2.106 |
| 4 | 3.546 | 3.465 | 3.387 | 3.312 | 3.240 | 3.170 | 3.037 | 2.855 | 2.589 |
| 5 | 4.329 | 4.212 | 4.100 | 3.993 | 3.890 | 3.791 | 3.605 | 3.352 | 2.991 |
| 6 | 5.076 | 4.917 | 4.767 | 4.623 | 4.486 | 4.355 | 4.111 | 3.784 | 3.326 |
| 7 | 5.786 | 5.582 | 5.389 | 5.206 | 5.033 | 4.868 | 4.564 | 4.160 | 3.605 |
| 8 | 6.463 | 6.210 | 5.971 | 5.747 | 5.535 | 5.335 | 4.968 | 4.487 | 3.837 |
| 9 | 7.108 | 6.802 | 6.515 | 6.247 | 5.995 | 5.759 | 5.328 | 4.772 | 4.031 |
| 10 | 7.722 | 7.360 | 7.024 | 6.710 | 6.418 | 6.145 | 5.650 | 5.019 | 4.192 |
| 11 | 8.306 | 7.887 | 7.499 | 7.139 | 6.805 | 6.495 | 5.938 | 5.234 | 4.327 |
| 12 | 8.863 | 8.384 | 7.943 | 7.536 | 7.161 | 6.814 | 6.194 | 5.421 | 4.439 |
| 13 | 9.394 | 8.853 | 8.358 | 7.904 | 7.487 | 7.103 | 6.424 | 5.583 | 4.533 |
| 14 | 9.899 | 9.295 | 8.745 | 8.244 | 7.786 | 7.367 | 6.628 | 5.724 | 4.611 |
| 15 | 10.380 | 9.712 | 9.108 | 8.559 | 8.061 | 7.606 | 6.811 | 5.847 | 4.675 |
| 16 | 10.838 | 10.106 | 9.447 | 8.851 | 8.313 | 7.824 | 6.974 | 5.954 | 4.730 |
| 17 | 11.274 | 10.477 | 9.763 | 9.122 | 8.544 | 8.022 | 7.120 | 6.047 | 4.775 |
| 18 | 11.690 | 10.828 | 10.059 | 9.372 | 8.756 | 8.201 | 7.250 | 6.128 | 4.812 |
| 19 | 12.085 | 11.158 | 10.336 | 9.604 | 8.950 | 8.365 | 7.366 | 6.198 | 4.843 |
| 20 | 12.462 | 11.470 | 10.594 | 9.818 | 9.129 | 8.514 | 7.469 | 6.259 | 4.870 |
| 21 | 12.821 | 11.764 | 10.836 | 10.017 | 9.292 | 8.649 | 7.562 | 6.312 | 4.891 |
| 22 | 13.163 | 12.042 | 11.061 | 10.201 | 9.442 | 8.772 | 7.645 | 6.359 | 4.909 |
| 23 | 13.489 | 12.303 | 11.272 | 10.371 | 9.580 | 8.883 | 7.718 | 6.399 | 4.925 |
| 24 | 13.799 | 12.550 | 11.469 | 10.529 | 9.707 | 8.985 | 7.784 | 6.434 | 4.937 |
| 25 | 14.094 | 12.783 | 11.654 | 10.675 | 9.823 | 9.077 | 7.843 | 6.464 | 4.948 |
| 30 | 15.372 | 13.765 | 12.409 | 11.258 | 10.274 | 9.427 | 8.055 | 6.566 | 4.979 |
| 35 | 16.374 | 14.498 | 12.948 | 11.655 | 10.567 | 9.644 | 8.176 | 6.617 | 4.992 |
| 40 | 17.159 | 15.046 | 13.332 | 11.925 | 10.757 | 9.779 | 8.244 | 6.642 | 4.997 |
| 45 | 17.774 | 15.456 | 13.606 | 12.108 | 10.881 | 9.863 | 8.283 | 6.654 | 4.999 |
| 50 | 18.256 | 15.762 | 13.801 | 12.233 | 10.962 | 9.915 | 8.304 | 6.661 | 4.999 |

| Period | Interest Rate | | | | |
|---|---|---|---|---|---|
| | 25% | 30% | 35% | 40% | 50% |
| 1 | 0.800 | 0.769 | 0.741 | 0.714 | 0.667 |
| 2 | 1.440 | 1.361 | 1.289 | 1.224 | 1.111 |
| 3 | 1.952 | 1.816 | 1.696 | 1.589 | 1.407 |
| 4 | 2.362 | 2.166 | 1.997 | 1.849 | 1.605 |
| 5 | 2.689 | 2.436 | 2.220 | 2.035 | 1.737 |
| 6 | 2.951 | 2.643 | 2.385 | 2.168 | 1.824 |
| 7 | 3.161 | 2.802 | 2.508 | 2.263 | 1.883 |
| 8 | 3.329 | 2.925 | 2.598 | 2.331 | 1.922 |
| 9 | 3.463 | 3.019 | 2.665 | 2.379 | 1.948 |
| 10 | 3.571 | 3.092 | 2.715 | 2.414 | 1.965 |
| 11 | 3.656 | 3.147 | 2.752 | 2.438 | 1.977 |
| 12 | 3.725 | 3.190 | 2.779 | 2.456 | 1.985 |
| 13 | 3.780 | 3.223 | 2.799 | 2.469 | 1.990 |
| 14 | 3.824 | 3.249 | 2.814 | 2.478 | 1.993 |
| 15 | 3.859 | 3.268 | 2.825 | 2.484 | 1.995 |
| 16 | 3.887 | 3.283 | 2.834 | 2.489 | 1.997 |
| 17 | 3.910 | 3.295 | 2.840 | 2.492 | 1.998 |
| 18 | 3.928 | 3.304 | 2.844 | 2.494 | 1.999 |
| 19 | 3.942 | 3.311 | 2.848 | 2.496 | 1.999 |
| 20 | 3.954 | 3.316 | 2.850 | 2.497 | 1.999 |
| 21 | 3.963 | 3.320 | 2.852 | 2.498 | 2.000 |
| 22 | 3.970 | 3.323 | 2.853 | 2.498 | 2.000 |
| 23 | 3.976 | 3.325 | 2.854 | 2.499 | 2.000 |
| 24 | 3.981 | 3.327 | 2.855 | 2.499 | 2.000 |
| 25 | 3.985 | 3.329 | 2.856 | 2.499 | 2.000 |
| 30 | 3.995 | 3.332 | 2.857 | 2.500 | 2.000 |
| 35 | 3.998 | 3.333 | 2.857 | 2.500 | 2.000 |
| 40 | 3.999 | 3.333 | 2.857 | 2.500 | 2.000 |
| 45 | 4.000 | 3.333 | 2.857 | 2.500 | 2.000 |
| 50 | 4.000 | 3.333 | 2.857 | 2.500 | 2.000 |

## TABLE E
### Uniformly Distributed Random Numbers

| | | | | | | | | | |
|---|---|---|---|---|---|---|---|---|---|
| 53076 | 98356 | 71012 | 72913 | 57081 | 50378 | 24782 | 59604 | 68503 | 87115 |
| 67675 | 66328 | 31868 | 81477 | 44108 | 30976 | 97286 | 11185 | 85146 | 80501 |
| 11682 | 77634 | 35669 | 48952 | 11988 | 76536 | 47230 | 5101 | 56004 | 447 |
| 80779 | 52122 | 53345 | 65387 | 98605 | 43790 | 96415 | 48056 | 23627 | 15127 |
| 18002 | 40596 | 31530 | 47181 | 56785 | 91219 | 98542 | 55551 | 52010 | 42465 |
| 74217 | 49876 | 28094 | 41249 | 78516 | 83703 | 49785 | 37480 | 43103 | 15747 |
| 10332 | 39877 | 18937 | 66983 | 80203 | 5878 | 25213 | 86229 | 53043 | 65949 |
| 81641 | 6872 | 15397 | 58928 | 98026 | 56147 | 41803 | 27564 | 16801 | 49977 |
| 43916 | 21062 | 73384 | 28830 | 15617 | 27292 | 47003 | 80081 | 60913 | 65541 |
| 76522 | 33375 | 75162 | 85546 | 76477 | 51924 | 56899 | 87600 | 11637 | 32607 |
| 89274 | 71515 | 72226 | 76519 | 30405 | 13914 | 88805 | 6010 | 56571 | 62411 |
| 32280 | 90189 | 77336 | 40196 | 34756 | 49649 | 3071 | 44055 | 58885 | 55252 |
| 43878 | 83500 | 48961 | 20485 | 1404 | 55651 | 50495 | 41115 | 45496 | 87123 |
| 92040 | 11812 | 5970 | 16516 | 68018 | 38973 | 22272 | 71589 | 45584 | 73886 |
| 6359 | 2591 | 68104 | 91446 | 22993 | 21631 | 36380 | 53439 | 58588 | 61660 |
| 86313 | 36575 | 40153 | 37869 | 28847 | 5297 | 49395 | 51115 | 55731 | 29636 |
| 87662 | 73748 | 84288 | 29618 | 52395 | 70084 | 53295 | 15741 | 99974 | 74435 |
| 24285 | 66547 | 48913 | 73717 | 53551 | 65409 | 21248 | 56997 | 85000 | 35454 |
| 69098 | 76804 | 13315 | 96064 | 99615 | 35505 | 85816 | 44036 | 39764 | 6913 |
| 19215 | 42140 | 60830 | 83484 | 32894 | 51061 | 1645 | 31020 | 41339 | 67819 |
| 98487 | 1399 | 87220 | 35500 | 81485 | 9378 | 93859 | 14486 | 55827 | 24842 |
| 52206 | 36683 | 53151 | 73242 | 83242 | 19358 | 84254 | 96160 | 94802 | 49007 |
| 93275 | 36216 | 90302 | 89493 | 87642 | 66725 | 25401 | 72950 | 94381 | 32159 |
| 53993 | 07594 | 26512 | 74082 | 15915 | 70083 | 52465 | 93485 | 44128 | 31367 |
| 72734 | 80239 | 16993 | 40338 | 75399 | 85135 | 69427 | 2434 | 12818 | 03234 |
| 20823 | 36035 | 11101 | 01463 | 50068 | 5666 | 15313 | 75499 | 19621 | 44791 |
| 18203 | 39387 | 32534 | 41814 | 38175 | 88661 | 63836 | 62019 | 61531 | 77848 |
| 32030 | 42255 | 75125 | 48994 | 53716 | 47878 | 47411 | 84658 | 96763 | 92145 |
| 32626 | 32699 | 04949 | 05213 | 66642 | 15814 | 72257 | 07122 | 58807 | 78031 |
| 42589 | 05796 | 44046 | 50050 | 99642 | 28893 | 33291 | 92302 | 72065 | 16855 |
| 45818 | 6379 | 22194 | 95072 | 16463 | 4221 | 83866 | 11458 | 55554 | 54878 |
| 15188 | 51600 | 35924 | 01054 | 45465 | 84325 | 66904 | 02428 | 06880 | 18112 |
| 56103 | 99032 | 40717 | 51157 | 97265 | 49433 | 88443 | 47471 | 44185 | 87971 |

| | | | | | | | | | |
|---|---|---|---|---|---|---|---|---|---|
| 89959 | 49977 | 27971 | 19762 | 84439 | 79377 | 62707 | 42935 | 49401 | 56964 |
| 79082 | 70637 | 01453 | 40502 | 38065 | 52271 | 00787 | 80762 | 35583 | 63603 |
| 22815 | 10297 | 04490 | 50398 | 44966 | 31144 | 64458 | 78696 | 88324 | 29508 |
| 62014 | 56652 | 42726 | 41713 | 37607 | 42638 | 54659 | 67205 | 00259 | 57143 |
| 68594 | 76822 | 31362 | 80684 | 58100 | 28842 | 83207 | 58900 | 70070 | 40103 |
| 77866 | 66073 | 79150 | 37985 | 43637 | 42600 | 17149 | 95556 | 96339 | 72246 |
| 45063 | 57832 | 12466 | 54501 | 11314 | 96443 | 75026 | 50885 | 27642 | 93890 |
| 12734 | 19579 | 03176 | 47576 | 48602 | 45393 | 85097 | 31695 | 9856 | 67375 |
| 64837 | 54064 | 78104 | 01776 | 60400 | 68663 | 45096 | 90193 | 81828 | 92087 |
| 56683 | 73431 | 70175 | 43790 | 96677 | 58275 | 50851 | 93630 | 88019 | 27138 |
| 07263 | 98095 | 12841 | 26402 | 65134 | 94661 | 09645 | 58195 | 71850 | 04143 |
| 48058 | 25821 | 89441 | 36557 | 28807 | 06601 | 42032 | 54674 | 82623 | 80138 |
| 48051 | 19019 | 48678 | 40788 | 20914 | 17274 | 18822 | 53466 | 84952 | 87683 |
| 25867 | 34598 | 86636 | 57225 | 10061 | 94130 | 83161 | 13024 | 7262 | 97539 |
| 70560 | 25520 | 90985 | 66630 | 30384 | 61363 | 11016 | 17455 | 98874 | 84514 |
| 11130 | 30614 | 38973 | 22382 | 80797 | 53708 | 25215 | 88232 | 38211 | 67251 |
| 70042 | 12020 | 12248 | 37901 | 60797 | 46160 | 44691 | 89594 | 88327 | 32170 |